WHAT, HOW, FOR WHOM

The Decisions of Economic Organization

WHAT, HOW, FOR WHOM

The Decisions of
Economic Organization

HENRY N. SANBORN

Professor of Economics
Towson State College

Cotter-Barnard Company, *Publisher*
P.O. Box 8466
Baltimore, Maryland 21234

PREFACE

All too many people, upon receiving a passing grade in economics, sigh with relief because they honestly don't feel they understand the subject. And all too often they are right. One of the reasons for this is that the many facts, theories, definitions, and diagrams seem unrelated to one another and to the real world, though economists know better. In short, students fail to see the forest for the trees.

This introduction to economics hopes to remedy that in two ways: first by tieing a good bit of elementary economics around the basic decisions of economic organization—what, how, for whom, and by whom to produce, and present versus future consumption, emphasizing repeatedly the importance of prices in these decisions, whether under private enterprise or socialism. The second way is to omit much of the theoretical detail, especially the theory of the firm. The book is short enough to leave time for that in a normal semester. No theory is presented as an end in itself, but only to explain how the basic economic decisions are made.

The entire book should take no more than eight weeks. Even in a one-semester course, this leaves time for a book of readings and other supplements, particularly on macroeconomics, which is covered lightly in this book. Chapters 1 to 7, 10 and 12 are on microeconomics, while Chapters 8, 9, and 11 are usually covered in the macro portion of the course.

At the end of each chapter there are "Study Questions." These questions can be an important aid to both learning and teaching. They follow step by step the material covered in the chapters. The more complicated is the text material, the more detailed are the Study Questions. For those questions marked with asterisks, brief answers are appended, though more complete coverage is usually in the chapter itself. By going through these questions, checking in the chapter for the answers and then writing out the answers, a student should know what is expected of him and should be able to identify precisely any part which he cannot understand. At such stumbling blocks, which hopefully will be few, one should re-read the material carefully, then, if necessary, seek aid from the teacher or from fellow students.

One should go through the Study Questions shortly after reading a chapter, then a week or two later, and before exams. Concentrate on the more difficult questions until all can be answered without checking back. This done, the main points of the subject will be retained long after the course and bothersome exams are over. And that's the primary objective, isn't it?

For the teacher, the Study Questions can serve as lecture outlines. By following them in class, he can cover the text material, adding along the way other ideas which the questions bring to mind.

Occasionally, it helps to regain a broad picture of the subject, both to appreciate where a particular topic fits in and to anticipate what topics will be covered later. To this end there are two aids: (1) the Table of Contents, which includes the sub-headings of each chapter, and (2) the comprehensive chapter summaries which precede the Study Questions.

For centuries, there has been no period when economic principles were not applicable to current events. Some added relevance to the text may be derived by reading a newspaper which covers national economic news thoroughly. Two suggestions are *The Wall Street Journal* and *The New York Times,* each of which is in most college libraries and is available at reduced student rates.

More than most economics texts, this one takes up normative issues, such as the desirability of competition, farm price supports, labor unions, import quotas, government efforts to raise the growth rate, and others. The author's bias in favor of individual freedom is quite obvious. You can agree or disagree. Your understanding how an economic system works is the primary objective of the book. Persuading you to like what the author likes is incidental, and probably futile anyway.

Permission to quote is gratefully acknowledged from the following: The University of Chicago Press, The Institute of Economic Affairs, and *The New York Times,* © 1962, 1964, 1965, 1966, 1967, 1970 by the New York Times Company. Reprinted by permission. Also *The Wall Street Journal* and Cartoon Features Syndicate for the use of cartoons which appeared in the *Wall Street Journal.*

The expository breakdown of economic activity into several basic economic decisions is usually credited to Professor Frank H. Knight. Anyone familiar with the "Chicago" tradition in economics will perceive that this book owes much to Professor Knight and to his successors at the University of Chicago.

TABLE OF CONTENTS

political votes • Profits under socialism • What capital cost and profits represent • The consequences of excluding capital cost from price • Needs versus wants • Public needs • Losers' claims and profit equalization • Evaluation of "what to produce" under competitive private enterprise: efficiency, freedom, fairness • Compulsory profit equalization • Profit rates and nonmonetary goals • Summary

4 HOW TO PRODUCE   100

The meaning of this decision • Businessmen's objective: low costs to maximize profits • Society's interests: minimize real cost to maximize total output • Proof that in minimizing money cost the producer minimizes real cost • Evaluation of "how to produce" under competitive private enterprise: efficiency, freedom, fairness • The roles of prices and profits • Simultaneity of what and how decisions • Labor or machines? • Summary

5 DIMINISHING RETURNS   112

A hypothetical illustration • The marginal physical product: MPP • Statement of the principle • Why there are diminishing returns • Diminishing returns applies to nonhuman inputs too • How many laborers would you hire? • Operate in the region of diminishing returns • Assumptions of the principle • Effects of changes in the assumed conditions • The law of variable proportions • Population growth, Malthus, and diminishing returns • Summary

6 WHO GETS WHAT IS PRODUCED   127

Distribution to the highest bidders • Income depends on contribution to production • How to measure an input's effect on output • Two incorrect measures of MPP • MPP and VMP: VMP = MPP x product price • Proof that inputs are paid the value of their contributions to production • Motives of employers and workers • Can input proportions be varied so finely? • All incomes are value contributed • Are all expenses for inputs? • Do companies perform the relevant experiment? • Wage determination by demand and supply • The determinants of demand, of supply • Labor shortage and surplus • Unemployment • One competitive wage? • Evaluation of competitively determined distribution of income: efficiency of input utilization, fairness, the fairness of non-input payments, worker satisfaction and payment equal to value contributed, value contributed and a person's worth, the standard of living of income recipients, freedom • Freedom and efficiency: nonmonetary goals • Summary

7 WHO DOES WHAT JOBS   162

The meaning of this decision ● Worker preferences and labor allocation ●
Freedom of occupational choice ● Worker preference and wage
differentials ● The unpleasant jobs get done ● The lump of labor fallacy ●
Adjustments in labor allocation to changes in consumer tastes ● Short-run,
long-run adjustments ● Barriers to occupational freedom ● Occupational
licensure ● Collective bargaining and occupational choice ● Monopsony ●
Minimum wages ● Non-price job rationing: race discrimination ● Summary

8 SPECIALIZATION AND THE GAINS FROM TRADE   186

The meaning of specialization ● Self-sufficiency: the opposite of
specialization ● The correct degree of specialization ● Economic
interdependence ● Routine jobs ● Comparative advantage ● An illustrative
example ● Absolute cost differences are not relevant ● Cost ratios further
considered ● The invisible hand again ● Summary

9 MONEY, THE PRICE LEVEL, AND RELATIVE PRICES 197

The functions of money ● What is money? ● Why demand deposits are
counted as money ● Money and the output of society ● The equation of
exchange: $MV = PT$ ● An outline of the causes of and the effects of
changes in M, V, P, and T ● The price level and the value of money ●
What's wrong with inflation? ● Relative prices contrasted with the price
level ● Real economic forces contrasted with monetary forces ● An
important goal: a stable price level along with changing relative prices ●
How to achieve this ● The wage-price controls of 1971 ● Summary

10 INSTITUTIONAL FEATURES OF A PRIVATE
ENTERPRISE SYSTEM   220

Competition: conditions, absence, forms, and rivalry, government policy ●
Individual freedom: economic freedom; meaning of freedom to
consumers, workers, employers, and investors ● Knowledge of alternatives:
importance, sufficiency of overlapping knowledge, short and long run
adjustments, knowledge for consumers, workers, and investors, sources of
knowledge ● The difficulty of centralizing useful knowledge: the
importance of unique local circumstances ● Laws of contract: meaning,
importance for buyer-seller, employer-employee, entrepreneur-lender, and
interbusiness relationships ● Stable government by law: meaning,
government by men, private enterprise and government by law, examples
of government by men—New York rent controls, Peru vs. IPC, oil import
quotas ● Property rights: use, transfer, income ● Summary

1

The Economic Problem and Five Decisions

On a Monday morning about 7 to 9 A.M. when you're leaving for work or school and perhaps would rather stay home and sleep, did you ever contemplate how many millions of others are doing the same thing? And with the same enthusiasm? Did you ever contemplate a panoramic view of this massive coming and going that occurs twice every workday and on a lesser scale continues all the time night and day? And did you ever wonder whether all this uncoordinated and seemingly aimless and frenetic activity makes any sense?

One person who apparently doubts the usefulness of it all is Mr. Jean Tinguely, described by the *New York Times* as "the Franco-Swiss creator of philosophical machines." Before 300 participants of the Second World Congress of Communications in a Changing World, half of them educators, Mr. Tinguely put together a "towering contrivance" and "while he toiled with wheels and girders, he had a girl in a red and blue dress sing to the accompaniment of a trombonist a song that wandered on with lines like these:

Too many tellyphones
Too many cars
Too many cigars
Too many guns
Too much of everything. . . .

"Then Mr. Tinguely escorted an elderly Chinese man with a long white beard to the center of the stage on which he had erected the fearsome assemblage of steel. The ancient equipped with a dustpan and broom, soon had work to do as brown bottles emerged from behind a green screen hanging on a chain and went down to doom beneath a foot-high hammer.

"Beer cascaded and glass flew toward the front row of seats while the assistant cheerfully swept up what fell on the stage." The audience at the Loeb Student Center at New York University "stood up and applauded."

1

"Mr. Tinguely mounted the stage and said: 'Thank you for having the patience to let me tell my story.' " [1]

Unfortunately, we all do not have Mr. Tinguely's flair for the dramatic and poetic. Our story, therefore, will require even more patience. And our story will differ from Mr. Tinguely's in other respects. The hustle and bustle of economic activity, we shall see, does make sense. The main economic problem facing society is not too much, but too little. This book will explain how people, living in a private enterprise economy, cope with this fact that there is not enough to go around for everyone to have all he wants.

The Main Economic Problem: Scarcity

Unless you are exceptionally fortunate, you cannot buy everything you want. Neither can your relatives or your friends or your neighbors. In fact, virtually no one can. But you do have the capacity to acquire some of the things you want. However, that capacity—salary, inheritance, allowance, savings, labor power—is limited. So the more you acquire of one particular thing, the less of other things you can get. You must economize on the purchase of given items. If you buy the first thing that comes to mind (say a shiny new sports car), then you may be able to get so few other things, that your total satisfaction may be less than had you bought a second-hand sedan and more of the other things. Thus, to economize is to choose among alternatives to get the maximum benefit from a limited means of satisfying wants.

This illustrates the main economic problem of society: scarcity—*there is not enough to go around for everyone to have all he wants, including leisure.* On the one hand there are the many wants of people. On the other, there is productive capacity—labor, knowledge, natural resources, capital equipment—which can be employed to satisfy *some* of these wants. But the productive capacity is not great enough to produce all the things everyone wants.

For any *one* person it might seem that all he needs is more money to acquire more things. However, the more he acquires, the less someone else will get, because his having more money did not enable society to produce any more than before. And if everyone had more money, prices would rise, but output would not. Remember, printing money does not create productive capacity. And the output of society is limited by its productive capacity—its workers, capital equipment, technology, and natural resources.

---

[1] Quotations are from an article by Harry Gilroy headlined, "Tinguely's Smashing Machine Deals Blow to Overproduction," *New York Times*, Nov. 21, 1967.

Ubiquity of the economic problem. We can summarize this economic problem with the term "scarcity." Anything is "scarce" if people cannot have all of it they would want if it were free. Scarcity in this sense is a fact of life for nearly all individuals in both rich and poor countries, capitalist and socialist systems, past and present, and, from all evidence, for the foreseeable future. The average family income in America is about $10,000 and one-eighth of all families have incomes below $3600. If we were ten times as rich, we would still want more and better things. Ever since Adam and Eve found fault with Providence in the Garden of Eden, it has seemed human nature for people to want more than they can get and for new wants to replace those fulfilled. And, for about two-thirds of the world's population, whose family incomes are below $500 a year, even the most basic wants are meagerly met. So the main economic problem seems as pressing today as ever.

The Five Basic Decisions Of Economic Organization

Every society faced with the problem of scarcity has to organize economic activity. This organization entails five basic economic decisions:

1. What to produce.
2. How to produce.
3. For whom to produce.
4. By whom to produce.
5. Present versus future consumption.

Each of these involves *choices among alternatives.* What happens if no one elects to make these decisions? Nonsense. The decisions get made somehow, whether unconsciously by millions of uncoordinated individuals or explicitly by an economic czar or national planning board. The objective of this book is to explain how these economic decisions do get made in a private enterprise system where no person or group does consciously sit down and say, "How shall we determine for society what will be produced? " First, let us see what each decision means. Then, after a few general comments about why and how to study economics and some definitions of economic terms, we shall take up in detail each of these five decisions.

What to produce. Just as an individual can buy many different combinations of goods and services with a limited amount of money, so society can produce many different combinations of goods and services with a limited productive capacity. And just as the more an individual purchases of one good or service, the less he can purchase of others, so with society: the production of any given good or service is at the expense of other goods and services which could have been produced instead. Should we have more schools? Then let's cut back the defense program. You want more schools *and* more defense? Then we'll expand both by taking productive capacity out of housing and highways. Or, if society expands these as well as schools and defense, then something else must be cut back—cars, refrigerators, vacation resorts, air conditioners, clothes—something. We have a limited productive capacity—just so many laborers, so much capital equipment, technical knowledge, and natural resources. And, while these may increase over time, at any given time they are limited. Therefore, the economy's total output at any given time is limited. More of one thing produced means less of something else.

At a time of some unemployment, total output may be increased with an apparent sacrifice only of unwanted leisure. However, the amount of unemployed resources is limited. In prosperous times, only about 3% to 5% of all workers are unemployed and most of this is normal job shifting. Furthermore, anything produced from formerly unemployed resources is still produced at the expense of other goods and services which could have been produced with these resources.

Thus, the basic decision "what to produce" answers this question: of all the possible combinations of goods and services that could be produced with our limited productive capacity, which should or will this productive capacity be used to produce? In a free society, no one person provides the answer to this question. But the question is answered somehow, and in a way that reflects the varying shades of preference of many millions of individuals. How this question is answered we shall consider shortly. It can be done many ways. But it must be done. Any society where everyone cannot have all he wants will have the problem of deciding what to produce.

How. The second basic economic decision is how to produce. Nearly any given good or service can be produced with many different combinations of inputs (labor and nonhuman resources). A decision "how to produce" is a choice among alternative *methods of production.* Again, these choices must be made for every good or service whether the economy is private enterprise or socialist, democratic or authoritarian. And again, no one person decides "how to produce" in a free society, but somehow such decisions get made by the thousands of individuals who manage private and government businesses. How do they know which method is best for society? Or do they? See Chapter 4.

For whom. The third and perhaps most controversial basic economic decision is for whom to produce or who gets what is produced. Clearly, there are many different ways in which the output of society could be divided among the population. And, since there is not enough for everyone to have everything he wants, some dissatisfaction is likely to result, no matter how the output is distributed. As with the first two economic decisions, so with this—no one person determines the outcome, but the decision is unavoidable in any society with the basic economic problem of scarcity.

By whom. The fourth decision, who does what jobs, answers this question: to what specific tasks will the various inputs, human and nonhuman, be directed? How is it decided in which occupations, industries, and companies the various inputs will be employed? Of course, this decision is related to the first two: the allocation of inputs by occupation and industry depends upon what will be produced and how. And conversely, what and how depend on the allocation of inputs. However, the way one depends on the other may differ from one economic system to another, which is why this is listed as a separate decision.

Present versus future consumption. This is a choice between using our productive capacity on the one hand to produce goods and services *for current consumption*—radios, dishwashers, haircuts, nightclub entertainment—*or* on the other hand using this productive capacity *to produce more productive capacity*—more radio or dishwasher factories, more barbershops or barber schools, more nightclubs, or, more generally, more capital equipment, more research, and more education.

This decision between present and future consumption is only to a limited extent related to the conservation of depletable resources. For example, the issue is not whether an iron deposit should be used now or ten years from now, even though the latter might also increase future relative to present consumption. Rather, the fifth economic decision is more whether the iron deposit and other inputs including labor should be used now to produce cars and refrigerators or now to produce car and refrigerator factories, making possible a greater output of cars and refrigerators in the future.

At a given time and with a limited productive capacity, the more of society's productive capacity that is used for producing goods and services for current consumption, the less that can be used for producing more productive capacity, which use is called *investment.* Investment means the use of productive capacity to produce more productive capacity. Included in investment are the creation of capital equipment, research into new methods of production and new products, and education, both formal and on-the-job training, which raises the productive capacity of people. Conversely, the greater the investment in a given year, the lower will be the possible output of goods and services for current consumption in that year. But, as a result of investment in a given year, the possible consumption of a later time will be greater than if the investment had not occurred.

For example, consider two hypothetical possibilities. We are in 1975 and the economy's hypothetical output (net national product) is $1500-billion of goods and services. First possibility: $1300-billion dollar's worth of goods and services are consumed *in* 1975, and the other $200-billion is spent for factories and other new productive capacity. Because of the $200-billion investment, the economy can produce an output of $1520-billion in 1976 (if we arbitrarily assume a 10% return on the $200-billion investment).

Second possibility: The $1500-billion output of 1975 is divided differently—$1200-billion dollars' worth of consumer goods and services are produced and $300-billion of new productive capacity is created. Now in 1976 the economy can produce an output of $1530-billion, $10-billion more than under the first assumption.

More Investment In 1975 Means Higher Output In 1976				
Possibility	1975 Output	Consumption	Investment	1976 Output[a]
	(billions of dollars)			
First	$1500	$1300	$200	$1520
Second	1500	1200	300	1530

[a] assuming a 10% return on investment in 1975. Thus, 1976 output equals 1975 output, plus 10% of the addition to productive capacity created in 1975. Normal growth from sources other than capital investment is omitted.

What is the difference? In the second example, the economy consumed less and invested more of its $1500-billion output than in the first example. As a result, output in the second year, 1976, is $10-billion greater under the second possibility. More is available in 1976 for consumption *or* investment. This illustrates the point made above: for any given year, the less of its productive capacity society devotes to producing for current consumption and the more for future consumption, the higher will be the output and possible consumption later. And, stated differently, the greater is investment or the growth of productive capacity in any given year, the lower must be the consumption in that year of greater growth.[2]

Actually, this choice between investment and consumer production is

---

[2] This assumes that inputs devoted to investment would have been used to produce consumer goods; they would not have been unemployed.

simply a special case of "what to produce." It is listed separately because of the widespread interest in economic growth. How fast a nation's output and standard of living grow depends largely on the portion of its productive capacity allocated to investment instead of to consumption. Russia's output has grown faster than America's the past few decades primarily because a greater portion of Russia's productive capacity has been used for investment. Heavily populated underdeveloped countries like India have difficulty increasing their output, because their consumption level is so low they cannot divert much productive capacity from consumption to investment without causing starvation. This is why some investment or aid from outside is so essential for their development.

A Definition Of Economics

Economics is the study of the adjustments and arrangements society makes to meet the main economic problem of scarcity. It has been defined as the study of how society allocates scarce resources among alternative ends to maximize satisfaction. In short, it is how the five basic decisions are made, the problems that arise in making them, and what should be done about these problems. Since many problems arise and many solutions are proposed, economists have plenty to do.

Why Study Economics?

Informed voters. A person must have some understanding of economics if he is to make sensible decisions as a voter. It is the voters who decide what kind of economic system they will live in. It is the voters, through elected representatives, who determine government policy on prices, taxes, economic growth, labor unions, poverty, unemployment, inflation, monopoly, tariffs, balance of payments, money supply, and many others. These are important issues. How they are settled affects significantly the opportunities open to each individual and the extent to which each family can enjoy the comforts of life.

Rest assured, a skillful proponent of socialism can make his society sound just as appealing as can a skillful advocate of private enterprise. With free speech, there are clever people proposing all sorts of radical changes, some of which might be worth adopting, and any of which might sound sensible to an uninformed audience. To distinguish reasoning and facts from fallacy, demagoguery, and misrepresentation, an understanding of basic economic principles is necessary.

The role of government in the economy has expanded greatly in the past 40 years. Some feel the trend should continue, others that it has been a mistake. A voter should understand the reasons for and against such policies as minimum wages, encouragement of collective bargaining, social security, progressive taxation, public housing, deficit spending, price controls to avoid inflation, and so on. In part, one's views on these depend on personal values, but an understanding of basic economics is also relevant for each.

Special interests. Besides the broader questions about the relationship between the government and the economy, there are a host of smaller specific economic issues about which voters should be educated. Many times government considers proposals which have these characteristics: (1) the proposed action will greatly benefit a small segment of the population—supports on wheat prices, restricted entry into interstate trucking, quotas on oil imports, tariffs on Japanese cameras, subsidies to shipbuilders, building a particular dam, granting a contract in a particular locality; (2) the proposed action would adversely affect the rest of the population (a) by limiting the freedom of people to enter certain occupations or industries (barber licenses, trucking permits), (b) by requiring taxes on the general public who may not benefit from the action (a dam), and/or (c) by raising prices of a particular item (any tariff or import quota does this)—but these adverse effects are quite slight to any particular individual; (3) there is a plausible but often fallacious argument that the benefits to the special group will benefit the general public—for example: "prosperity in the economy as a whole requires

"If the election were held tomorrow, would you make
the same foolish mistakes you did last time?"

prosperous wheat and cotton farmers," "without farm subsidies, food production would decline to near starvation levels." Both are fallacious; both involve a failure to understand elementary economics. (This is not to say there may be no sound reasons for subsidizing farmers.)

Now suppose (1) voters are unable to distinguish sound from fallacious arguments; (2) voters are unaware of and/or unconcerned about the adverse effects of most programs; (3) the special interest groups are acutely aware of how government action in their behalf affects *them*. Then, in the competition to get elected, the winning candidates will be those who promise to support the local special interests and who ignore the general interest. Through "logrolling," each elected representative then supports the interests of other groups who support his. The result is inequities, limited freedom, and a total output which is less satisfying to society than that which could be produced. Some education in economics would improve the outcome greatly.

The government's inevitable powers to tax and pay out, to restrict entry into occupations and industries, to regulate prices and outputs—these powers provide a constant temptation for claims by those who want more than they receive through the competitive market. Since nearly all such claims serve a special group at the expense of the remainder of the population, the general population must be aware of its interests, if they are to be served.

An example: interstate trucking regulation. Would you like to transport goods for sale by truck across state lines? With some minor exceptions, you need a license from the Interstate Commerce Commission. Furthermore, the rates you charge must be approved by the ICC. Acquiring the license is not automatic by any means. You have to show there is a "public need" for your services. Existing companies, which don't welcome more competition, will argue before the ICC that they can handle all the business. The mere fact that you may have some customers lined up doesn't prove any such need, as was illustrated in the case of Mr. Joe Jones, Jr., a partially disabled Negro veteran and father of ten, whose life savings (plus a substantial loan from the government's Small Business Administration) were invested in his trucking company. Although he had two customers for regular deliveries, his request for permission to operate out of Atlanta was denied seven times by the ICC, which ruled that the area was adequately served by existing companies. To dramatize his predicament, Mr. Jones parked his tractor in front of the ICC building on Constitution Avenue in Washington with his motor running loudly. Thanks to attendant publicity from the Huntley-Brinkley newscast and newspapers and pressure by his Congressman, he finally did get his license. But most other rejected applicants are not so persistent or fortunate.[3]

---

[3] *The Washington Evening Star*, July 21, 1966.

Besides restricting entry, the ICC regulates rates charged. The ICC encourages the truckers operating between any given areas to get together in deciding the rates they will seek. Except for ICC sponsorship, such collusion in setting prices would directly violate the government's antitrust laws. Clearly, the result of this collusion will not be lower prices than if the collusion had not occurred. Assuredly, the prices will be higher than if determined competitively. And once its rates are approved, a firm may not reduce them to get business from competitors.

The ICC's zeal in keeping prices up was ludicrously illuminated in the famous yak fat case of 1965. Trucker Leroy Hilt submitted plans for shipping large quantities of yak fat from Omaha to Chicago at 45 cents per 100 pounds. Right away, most of the largest railroads of the midwest—including the Illinois Central, the Burlington, the Great Western, the Rock Island, the Chicago and Northwestern, and the Milwaukee—demanded that the ICC disallow the rates as too low. After hearing presentations from the railroads, the ICC's Board of Examiners obligingly informed Mr. Hilt that he would not be allowed to transport yak fat. In fact, Mr. Hilt never wanted to anyway, *and neither did the railroads.* (The yak is an ox common to Tibet. Outside of zoos, there is no use of yaks in America.) Mr. Hilt merely wanted to prove a point about the ICC—which decided it would be the better part of descretion not to prosecute Mr. Hilt for his hoax.[4] At least the ICC is evenhanded in suppressing competition—it has repeatedly prevented railroads from cutting their rates when truckers complained.

Now who benefits and who loses from the ICC's trucking regulations (which, of course, are ultimately the responsibility of Congress)? The gainers are the firms already in the industry who face less competition and can charge higher prices. Also benefitting are the truck drivers who work for the large prosperous firms, since their wages are higher. These interests are vocal and acutely aware of how Congress and the ICC act on trucking matters. The losers are the people like Joe Jones who are prevented from entering the occupation or business of their choice and the consuming public which pays higher prices for everything carried by interstate trucking. And the public loses further because the creation of these arrangements in one area of economic activity makes legislators more amenable to granting similar favors elsewhere, especially when such is winning political strategy. And it *is* winning strategy because the gainers are aware of their gains and the losers, who far outnumber the gainers, are unaware.

For the benefit of a few disturbed but economically uneducated voters, the government justifies these trucking regulations with vague assurances that they are necessary for the public interest, that they prevent destructive competition, that they keep a proper balance among rail, trucking, and other

---

[4] *The Washington Post,* August 15, 1965.

forms of transportation, that they merely assure "fair" competition, etc. The government also justifies regulation of prices and entry into the industry by pointing illogically to the benefits from other unrelated regulations of the trucking industry, such as safety standards and liability laws.

Unfortunately, there are many such instances where government policy benefits special interests at the expense of the general public. The time to study them in detail is after one understands elementary economics. Only then can one intelligently evaluate the plausible arguments used to justify such policies. Most important and of direct relevance to the trucking regulations, one needs to understand (1) the role of prices and profits in determining what to produce, (2) how prices and profits are themselves determined under competitive private enterprise, and (3) the significant differences between competitive and monopolistic prices and output. We turn to these points in the next chapter.

In summary, a voter needs to understand economics to choose among alternative economic systems and roles of government, to tell whether particular government policies contribute toward or hinder the achievement of his preferred system, to evaluate the many claims for special favor by particular groups, and to evaluate the economic programs advocated and supported by the candidates he votes for. Without such understanding, it is likely that the winning candidates will follow policies which the majority would oppose if they understood the policies.

Aside from voter intelligence and all that follows from it, there are other lesser reasons for studying economics, which we hope you will accept. First, there is the excitement and enjoyment of learning per se, of acquiring knowledge about a vast area of human activity and being able to converse and read further on it. Learning is fun, especially if the subject is interesting. As a commercial for the *New York Times* says, "You will be more interesting to others and to yourself." Economics may also help as background knowledge for selecting an occupation, operating a business or household, and investing one's savings. However, economics has little to say about how to conduct these activities and offers no formula for making a fortune in the stock market.[5]

Theory And Reality

Elementary economics seems abstract and theoretical. Some readers may impatiently say, "Let's get to the specific problems and forget the theory." We *shall* mention some current problems. But tomorrow's problems may be different from today's. So more important than studying current

---

[5] Neither does any other subject.

events is an understanding of general principles, the basic causal relationships of economics, which can be applied to economic problems today and tomorrow. To tackle specific problems (like the effects of the carpenter's union) without learning the underlying theory (how wages are determined), is like trying to study cancer, heart disease, and pneumonia without first learning anatomy and physiology.

It makes little sense to say, "that's good in theory, but it doesn't work in practice." The *only* quality that makes a theory good is that it *does* work in practice—it does provide an explanation of how things work and a basis for predicting. Theory is abstract and seems "unrealistic" because it is not a detailed description of particular events, but considers phenomena which are part of and common to many different events. For example, the mechanics of determining wages vary greatly among different companies; but wage theory is useful because nearly all companies consider the same variables in setting wages (product price, the availability and productivity of workers, and prices of other inputs) and they react in the same direction to changes in these variables.

A Suggested Attitude: Skeptical, Open-minded And Seeking The Truth

When a person studies physics, he probably doesn't start with any notion of the relationship between the energy of a condensed substance and its temperature. But often, people who study economics have already formed conclusions about economic relationships. Furthermore, they often have an emotional desire (not present in studying physics) that certain propositions be correct (that labor unions benefit the working man, or that private enterprise results in equitable wages, or doesn't). Frequently, these original ideas are incorrect and the attachment to them blocks the comprehension of correct principles.

Our suggested attitude is to *be more interested in finding out the truth than in ascertaining that the truth be one thing or another.* This requires one be open-minded, willing to learn, to have a skeptical and questioning attitude about his own views and those of books, teachers, and friends, to accept conclusions on the basis of evidence and reasoning, and to be willing to adopt new conclusions if the evidence points elsewhere.[6] One may still care what the outcome is, but don't let this care preclude intellectual integrity. Do not live the part of a trial lawyer or a debator who (perhaps rightly) is more concerned with winning an argument than with ascertaining the truth.

---

[6] Maybe Santa's most durable gift to children, after the truth about him is revealed, is a healthy inculcation of skepticism.

"If you're really Santa Claus, give me the names
of all your reindeer."

Definitions

An **input** is anything which creates or produces goods or services. Sometimes the word "input" refers to the input agent, the thing which does the producing, such as a laborer or a piece of machinery. Other times "input" refers to the input service, that is, to what the input agent does. For example, in terms of input agents, the delivery of a piano is done by a truck, driver, movers, and perhaps indirectly by some managerial and clerical agents in the office of the moving company. Or, in terms of input services, the piano is moved by some trucking services, driver services, etc.

Wages are payments for input services; so are the rentals for a computer or a building; so generally are the profits of a business. The purchase price of an input agent—the price of a machine or building, or the price of a slave—such prices are based on the expected value of the input services which will be rendered by the input agents.

Output is anything produced by inputs. Some outputs, like machines and buildings, become inputs which help create further outputs. Output may be a tangible commodity like an orange or a service like a football game or some legal advice.

Production is the use of inputs to create output. Production consists of one or more of these services: (1) transforming materials into more valuable form (as steel, glass, rubber, etc. are transformed into an auto); (2) transporting goods to where they are more valuable (from manufacturer to retailer); (3) rendering direct services as by doctors, teachers, barbers, airlines, baby sitters, and real estate agents; (4) carrying inventories of goods for consumer convenience. It is a mistake to view production solely as the creation of physical objects. The other aspects are just as important for satisfying consumer wants.

Productive capacity. Society's productive capacity is its ability to produce outputs: it is the total of society's input agents, including, as part of labor or as a separate input, the state of knowledge of productive techniques, or, for short, technology, also referred to as "the state of the arts."

Capital. This word has several distinct meanings in economics and business literature. Generally, the reader can tell from the context which is meant. In economics, capital usually means nonhuman productive capacity, though sometimes land is not included in the term. Sometimes, however, capital means money available for investment, or assets which can readily be turned into money.[7] Defined to mean nonhuman productive capacity, "capital" does not denote a hoard of cash or a bank account. Rather, capital is the value (in dollars) of some actual physical assets—buildings, equipment, machinery, inventories.

Production and consumption further distinguished. In the data which the government compiles and publishes, "consumption" is measured as total spending by consumers for goods and services currently produced, plus the rental value of private housing. But many of the things consumers buy in a given year last into later years—toasters, coats, watches, etc. Therefore, the sum of these things *purchased* by consumers in a given year does not exactly measure the *consumption* of these in that year.

A more correct view of consumption (and production) is given by these three propositions: (1) Nearly all production is the rendering of services. It is the *services* of capital and labor which turn steel, glass, rubber, etc. into a car. And it was prior labor and capital *services* which turned the basic raw materials into useable steel, glass, and rubber. Only a small fraction of the value or a car is attributable to "natural resources" in their original, undiscovered state. And the same is true of most manufactured goods. (2) Nearly all consumption is the consumption of services, even though physical goods are used. People consume the *services* of a car, clothes, dishes, etc. over a long period. True, some goods like food and fuel are physically extinguished

---

[7] In accounting, a company's "net worth"—assets less liabilities—is sometimes called "capital."

the instant they are consumed. (3) Durable consumer goods, while in use, are part of society's capital. They render consumer services when used. Admittedly, it is not feasible to calculate capital on this basis, although the national income accounts do treat private houses as capital and ascribe to consumption the rental value of houses in use.

Classification Of Input Agents

The economy's inputs, sometimes called factors of production or productive resources, are traditionally divided into three categories: land, labor, and capital. Here, "land" includes all "natural resources" like oil, minerals, waterpower. Otherwise, "land" and "natural resources" are listed as separate classes of inputs. Another input category sometimes listed separately is "entrepreneurship" (defined below).

This tripartite division of inputs stems from the three social classes in post-feudal Europe: landlords (the aristocracy), laborers (the masses), and the middle class (capitalists, mostly owners of small businesses). Their respective incomes were rents (to landlords), wages (to laborers), and, to the capitalists, profits and interest. The primary purpose of this classification has been to raise questions about the proper division of income among the classes, which questions in turn resulted from (and in) many incorrect notions of what determined these incomes.

Today, there is little point in this land-labor-capital division, if there ever was. The population is not divided into these distinct social classes. Small land-owning farmers are among the poorest prople, while workers in high-paying occupations are in the top ½% of the income bracket. Capitalists are also both rich and poor. Moreover, as we now recognize, all inputs are paid the value of their contributions to production, a point not realized by those who, prior to the late 19th Century, tried to explain the distribution of income.

From an economic standpoint, the significant difference between one input and another depends on how effectively one input can be substituted for another to produce the same range of outputs. But these differences are often greater among subdivisions within any of the three traditional input classes, land, labor, and capital, than among the three classes. That is, economically, there is more difference between an opera singer and a human ditch digger, both "labor," than between power shovels and human ditch diggers, both diggers, one capital and the other labor.

The distinction between land (including all natural resources) and capital is supposed to divide the nonhuman inputs into God-given and manmade. There is sometimes the feeling that the God-given part should be free. But most of the value of "natural" resources results from man's efforts at cultivation, irrigation, mineral exploration, extraction, and refinement; so the distinction is fuzzy at best. Anyway, payments for the use of land now amount to less than 3% of total incomes in America.

One useful distinction is between human and nonhuman inputs. Without slavery, there is no purchase and sale of human input agents as there is of nonhuman. Because of this, there are important differences in the way society decides how to invest in human and nonhuman inputs. As explained in Chapter 11, education expenditure is not as responsive to financial profitability as is capital investment. There are also differences in the arrangements by which human and nonhuman inputs are paid for their productive services—generally labor receives an agreed upon wage, while capital receives a residual left over after contractual expenses are paid. Finally, people care about the nonmonetary conditions of work (noise, interest, location), whereas nonhuman inputs are unconcerned about these (at least until temperamental robots are developed). Therefore, the most significant classification of inputs is into these two: human and nonhuman.

Basic Economic Roles

In the "game" of economic activity, five basic roles are played by various individuals and institutions: (1) consumers—those who acquire the outputs and use the services of the outputs, (2) producers (laborers and capitalists)—those who own inputs and offer for sale the services of these inputs, (3) saver-investors, (4) entrepreneurs, and (5) government. We shall elaborate briefly on the last three roles.

The saver-investors are those who produce more than they consume. The excess which they produce (if the economy is operating properly) is devoted to investment, which adds to society's productive capacity. The redirection of this "excess" is often quite indirect. Suppose Mr. A earns (after taxes) $9000, but consumes $8000 worth of goods and services and saves $1000. Then inputs elsewhere, which would have produced $1000 more of consumption goods for him had he not saved, will be bid into investment use by the investment of A's $1000 savings. Probably this $1000 went through a financial intermediary: deposited in a bank by A then lent to an investor, or from A to a life insurance company which purchased bonds issued by an electric utility which uses A's savings to buy capital equipment. Whatever the route, saving by someone is a necessary condition for investment.

An entrepreneur is an individual or group who purchases input services and decides what outputs these inputs shall produce. He is an organizer of inputs, an innovator, and a risk taker. Generally, the entrepreneur is a "residual income recipient," that is, one who receives whatever (if anything) is left from a company's income after selling the output and paying the contractual expenses. Countries with the highest standards of living are those in which social and political conditions have encouraged (or have not discouraged) venturesome people to become entrepreneurs. A leading economist, Professor Frank Knight, has said: "To find men capable of managing business efficiently and secure them to positions of responsible control is perhaps the most important single problem of economic organization on the efficiency side." [8]

Successful entrepreneurs—and many are not successful—have exceptional energy, and a strong desire to be their own boss; they work long hours, are good at developing new products or new processes, at organizing businesses, at evaluating managerial and technical talent, and are willing to risk their time and money on ventures which may be very profitable or may result in large losses. These prople, though relatively few in numbers, play an important role in determining what and how to produce—especially in the development of new products and methods. It is they who most avidly seek out and take advantage of opportunities for profits. And, as we shall see, this profit-seeking is a vital cog in the determination of what and how to produce.

The minimum role which government must play in a private enterprise economy is to define the rights of prople, especially of property ownership, to prevent fraud and private violence, enforce contracts, adjudicate disputes among individuals, regulate the money supply, and prevent abuses of monopoly. In general, we may say the government sets and enforces the "rules of the game." In addition to these functions, most governments directly determine, to some extent, what, how, and for whom to produce.

Of course, every individual is a consumer. And nearly every individual either is a producer or depends for his consumption on the income earned by a producer within his family. Most families are also saver-investors to some extent. But relatively few people are entrepreneurs.

Now where does a business or firm fit into this scheme? A business is a voluntary association of input sellers lead by an entrepreneur and operated to produce and sell outputs. Most firms are also consumers of the outputs of other firms. In most cases, the entrepreneurial functions (organizing, innovating, and risk-taking) are performed by owners of some nonhuman inputs used in the business.

Consider two arrangements for a furniture factory: (1) The owner of the business owns the factory, land, and equipment and works in the business without a specific salary. After expenses, his profit consists of (a) a payment for his labor services, (b) a payment for the services of capital he provided, and (c) a payment for entrepreneurship.

(2) Suppose the company, producing the same output with the same

---

[8] Frank Knight, *Risk, Uncertainty and Profit*, Houghton Mifflin, 1921, p. 283.

inputs, rents its plant and equipment and hires a plant manager. With the same sales revenue, but with expenses increased by the rents and manager's wages, its profits will be lower and consist solely of (c) payment for entrepreneurship. In this second arrangement, the owner of the company does no work in the company and owns none of the property used by the company. What is he paid for? If he receives anything, it is for organizing the company, for anticipating before others a consumer desire, and for taking the chance of losing should the company not be able to sell its output at a price sufficient to pay its inputs.

The Big Picture About Economic Organization

One should appreciate the immensity and complexity of organizing economic activity. Everyday, millions of goods flow into wholesale and retail stores throughout the nation. Everyday, millions of goods are manufactured and millions others are bought by consumers. What makes the flow of things being produced correspond to the desires of consumers? How is it that goods are nearly always available to consumers, and yet are not piling up on the shelves? What assures that anyone will provide the milk, vegetables, electricity, hotel space, school facilities, books, clothes, pens, pliers, beds, legal services, barber services, and so on that the Jones family is able and willing to buy and the Smith family and so on among families of varying desires and incomes all over the nation? What gets people working to make these things in sensible proportions and what assures that anyone will create the nonhuman inputs and organize inputs to produce any particular item? No central group controls or directs all this economic activity. How come then that all this coming and going to work, producing and transporting, results in an overall production that is sensible and satisfying, rather than chaotic and ridiculous? Or does it? It is this economic organization that is broken down into and described by the five basic economic decisions, though, of course, all five decisions are made simultaneously and remade continuously.

We look at the economy as a whole, in the abstract. When you consider "what to produce" or "how to produce" do not think of how you as an individual consumer or businessman would make the decision. Rather, think of a general explanation of these decisions which applies to all individuals in the economy, a description which tells a man from outer space or from Russia how the decisions are determined under private enterprise.

This is what we turn to next. And the central themes of our story are the roles played by prices (including wages) and by the pursuit of self interest.

Summary

The main economic problem, which exists in all societies, is that there are not enough goods and services to go around for everyone to have all he wants. This exists because of a limited productive capacity, not from a limited supply of money.

The decisions of economic organization, which must be made because of the economic problem, are: (1) what to produce, (2) how to produce, (3) who gets what is produced, (4) who does what jobs, and (5) producing for current consumption or for future consumption, by producing more productive capacity.

Economics is the study of how these decisions are made.

A knowledge of economics enables one to evaluate the economic system and to understand various economic problems and proposals. When this knowledge is weak, elected officials often adopt policies that informed voters would oppose and that unjustly favor a small, knowledgeable group at the expense of others.

To understand means to discover truth and this requires a skeptical, questioning attitude toward any given proposition.

Definitions of input, output, production, consumption, and productive capacity are given.

Inputs may be classified into three categories—land, labor, and capital, or into two groups—human and nonhuman.

Economic activity requires performance by consumers, producers, saver-investors, entrepreneurs, and government. A business is an intermediary between sellers of inputs (mostly workers) and buyers of output (mostly consumers) and is led by an entrepreneur.

Study Questions for Chapter 1

1. What is the main economic problem of society?

2. Explain why providing prople with more money does not solve society's main economic problem.

3. Why is the main economic problem not peculiar to private enterprise?

4. What basic economic decisions must be made because of the main economic problem.

5. Explain what each decision involves—the meaning of what, how, for whom, by whom, and present versus future consumption.

6. What three activities bring about per capita economic growth?

7. What happens to current consumption if economic growth is increased (a) in the year of the rise in growth, and (b) later? Explain.

8. Define economics.

9. Why study economics?

10. Explain the characteristics of special interest claims and why these claims often prevail even when contrary to the general welfare.

11. What is the essential quality of economic theory as opposed to current economic events?

12. Why should theory be studied before current economic problems?

13. What attitude is suggested in studying economics (or any other subject)?

14. Why is this attitude—skepticism—recommended? What is the presumed objective of studying any subject?

15. Define: input, output, production, consumption, capital.

16. Explain the sense in which "production" is the rendering of services and "consumption" is the utilization of services.

17. What are the three standard categories of inputs?

18. What is an alternative two-fold division? Why is it recommended over the other?

19. Explain the five basic economic roles played by individuals and institutions: consumers, producers, saver-investors, entrepreneurs, and government. What does each do?

20. How does a business firm fit into this scheme?

2
What To Produce

Does It Matter What Is Produced?

Clearly it does. While man may not live by bread alone, some bread helps. And so do thousands of other goods and services. Getting the maximum satisfaction from our limited productive capacity depends critically on which and how much goods and services are produced. If we employed half our productive capacity erecting pyramids to glorify our political leaders, then, however fully employed we might be, our level of satisfaction would be far below its present state. There is an infinite number of possible combinations of goods and services which we could produce. How is the actual outcome determined? Does this outcome serve society as well as some of the possible alternatives which could be adopted instead?

Our main purpose in this chapter is to describe how "what to produce" is determined under private enterprise. We shall also consider how good a job private enterprise does and whether a socialist system would do the job differently or better. The most basic conclusion is that, whatever the economic system, *prices* of goods and services play an indispensable role in any sensible determination of what to produce.

Who Determines What To Produce?

In a private enterprise system, the owners of businesses may produce whatever they please, providing they can hire someone to do the work and excepting certain things which are illegal, like counterfeit money, or are impossible, like perpetual motion machines. Thus, it would seem that the owners of businesses who give the orders "make this," or "do that" are the ones who decide "what to produce."

However, this is a superficial, misleading, and, therefore, essentially incorrect conclusion. The primary objective of businessmen, whether they manufacture Beethoven records, artificial mustaches, or tiddlywinks, is to make profits. And profits, with adequate competition, are made by producing what consumers prefer. The businessman may be quite indifferent or even disdainful of what he produces. His production choices are based on what is profitable and this in turn depends on consumer choice.

To understand who determines what to produce, think of the three main economic groups—input owners (mainly laborers), input organizers (businessmen), and output buyers (consumers)—ranged from left to right in that order. Businessmen are in the middle, an intermediary between people who have productive services to sell and those who want to purchase outputs. The only one of these three groups which really cares what is produced is consumers. Input sellers seek the highest prices for their input services. The janitor or accountant or switchboard operator is mainly concerned with his salary and other work conditions, not with what his employer is producing, even though his job is to help produce a particular good or service. Similarly, the owner of nonhuman inputs—buildings, land, steel, electric power—wants the highest price and is generally unconcerned with what the purchaser does with the input after it is sold. The businessman is mainly concerned with making profits and will produce whatever best serves that end. But consumers do care what is produced. To get their patronage, businessmen cater to consumers, since this is the way to make profits. At least this is the way it works when there is competition among producers and where consumers are knowledgeable about alternative products available, including prices and quality. Thus, from the motivations of people as input owners, business organizers, and consumers, we see that "what to produce" is determined ultimately by consumers. Whether this should be the case is another question. To concentrate on the way private enterprise works, we are neglecting government efforts to promote some production (like wheat) beyond the quantity consumers would bring about or to discourage other production (like whiskey) by high taxes or outright prohibition.

Some readers may feel the role of consumer choice relative to businessmen's decisions has been exaggerated. Are not consumer choices strongly influenced by advertising, and if so, is not the businessman more decisive in determining what to produce? If businessmen were really so indifferent about what they produced, why would they spend so much on advertising to convince consumers to purchase particular goods and services?

Certainly, advertising influences consumers, but so do other factors— friends, books, experiences with particular products, family size, age, sex, psychological pressures for status, security, prestige, comfort, enjoyment, and so on. The existence of such influences, including advertising, does not mean the consumer does not make his own choice.[1]

---

[1] We cannot pursue here the metaphysical question whether free will exists at all. For our purposes, free choice exists as long as the individual is

Moreover, how do businessmen decide which products to advertise in the first place? Basically, by their guesses about what will appeal to consumers. A businessman may produce and advertise product X and may still be largely indifferent about X in that he would as soon produce and advertise Y or Z if he felt they would be as profitable. Advertising reflects estimated consumer choices and it constitutes persuasion, not coercion, so that it is still free consumer choice that determines which of competing producers and advertisers will be successful. (This is not to say that fraudulent and misleading advertising does not occur and should not be prevented.)

Once a producer has created and organized productive capacity to produce a particular product, then he does care whether consumers buy that product. If consumers don't buy, he loses. If they buy heavily (at high prices and/or quantities), he gains. However, much of society's nonhuman productive capacity wears out in five or ten years. Therefore, investors are continually faced with decisions whether to replace depreciating capacity to produce product A or to use the same funds to produce something else. That is, they are continually in the position of "starting from scratch" with investible funds, a position from which they will produce and advertise whatever they think consumers will buy, not something they are committed to produce because their productive capacity is not good for anything else.

The Roles Of Prices And Profits In Determining What To Produce

So far we have asserted that consumer choice determines what to produce. But businessmen make the immediate production decisions. The next question is this: how do businessmen know the preferences of consumers? Actually, no one individual or group "knows" these preferences. Our question may then be restated: how is it production is geared to consumer preferences when production decisions are made by millions of individual businessmen, none of whom has a total picture of what consumers prefer? And what gets production shifted from one product to another as consumer preferences change? This is where prices and profits come in. (Note that any role of profits is also a role of prices, since profits are a difference between output prices and input prices, per unit of output.)

Prices and profits act as signals which register the preferences of consumers. Imagine what would happen if the production of some good in demand were suddenly halted. Suppose by some unhappy coincidence one morning all the producers of diapers decided to close business and dismantle their shops. There would surely continue to be a howling demand for this

---

not physically coerced by other people to buy particular products, nor forcibly prevented by others from buying what sellers are willing to sell him.

product. Some enterprising producers of other textile products would enter the diaper business, but necessarily on a small scale at first. Prices would be bid up and encourage further expansion, up to the point, but no further, where profits in the diaper industry equalled those in alternative areas of investment. What would a rise in the birthrate do to diaper production? Since businessmen are watching these statistics carefully, output might expand simultaneously with demand and no increases in profits would occur, nor a rise in prices, unless input prices had to be bid up to attract more inputs into the industry. But if the simultaneous expansion of output with demand had not occurred, prices and profits would have risen. We could inquire similarly into the relative profitability of various styles and fashions within the diaper industry with the same conclusion that relative profits, registering consumer preferences, will determine the outcome.

The roles of prices and profits in determining what to produce may be illustrated by the following sequence. Suppose we start at "equilibrium" with profit rates the same in all industries and suppose the industry in question is small enough relative to the economy so that it does not have to bid up input prices to expand production.

1. There is a rise in the demand for product A. (With a given level consumer incomes, a decline in demand will occur for some other good(s), but we shall concentrate on A.)
2. The price of A rises as consumers bid for its limited quantity.
3. This price rise, which did not cause the costs of production to rise, results in increased profits for the producers of A.
4. The increased profits induce an expansion in the production of A (and a decline in other fields where demand went down, and from which inputs shift into A).[2]
5. To sell this increased output, producers must lower prices from the higher level of (2).
6. The lower prices, with constant production costs, cause profits to decline from the high level of (3), but not below the original level.
7. The decline in profits is a signal for businessmen in A to stop attracting inputs from non-A to A.

---

[2] The net shift of inputs from, say, industry B where demand went down to A where demand rose may be indirect. Some workers may go from B to C and D, while those from C and D go to E and F, and some in E and F shift to A (even though there was no change in consumer demand for the products of C, D, E, or F). Or, the reduced employment in B may occur mainly from a failure to replace workers who would have quit jobs there anyhow, while new entrants to the labor force go to A. Many combinations could be evisioned to give the net effect of a shift in total employment from B to A.

When step (7) is completed, the profitability of producing A is the same as before step (1) and the same as the profitability of producing other goods and services. If the change in tastes is permanent, industry A will continue producing at the expanded annual rate of production.

Suppose we let directional arrows have the following meanings: ↑ means increase, ↓ means decrease, and → means leads to. Then we may summarize these steps like this:

↑ consumer demand for A → ↑ product price → ↑ profits →
↑ production of A → ↓ product price → ↓ profits, until the profitability in A is the same as elsewhere.

The changes in prices and profits acted as signals to redirect production as a result of the rise in demand.

"It's just as we suspected—the whole hippie movement
was started by a bead manufacturing company!"

Two of the important social benefits of this process are: (1) it gets produced what people, through dollar votes, show they want, and (2) the redirection of inputs and production occurs automatically and to the appropriate extent, without any central authority telling prople what to produce or where to work or what prices to charge. As an exercise, you might trace through steps analogous to (1) to (7) which would follow from a decline in consumer demand or from the introduction of a technological change.

These steps apply primarily to a rather sudden and unanticipated rise in consumer demand for a product. Sometimes demand rises slowly and predictably. In that case, the steps followed might be these:

1. Investors expect a rise in the demand for A.
2. In the hope of high profits when this rise in demand occurs, investors acquire funds, bid inputs into A, and increase the productive capacity of industry A.
3a. If the demand does rise as anticipated, then production will expand at the same rate as demand; and profits per dollar invested in A will remain the same as originally and as in other industries.
3b. If demand rises more (or sooner) than anticipated (i.e., if investors underestimated the rise in demand), prices and profits will rise when demand rises, and the process described above (steps 1 to 7) will operate to increase output, reducing prices and profits again.
3c. If the demand does not rise as much (or as soon) as expected (if investors overestimated the rise in demand), the increase in output which results from the new productive capacity in A will drive prices and profits below alternative levels, giving incentive to investors to curtail further investment in industry A.

Except from entrenched monopoly, the largest profits under private enterprise are made by those who can correctly anticipate changes in consumer demand before others do. These high returns may be regarded in several ways: (1) as higher investment returns, or (2) as payment for the investors' unique ability or luck in predicting consumer demand, or (3) as temporary monopoly profits which attract competition. Insofar as they result from luck, the high profits should be balanced with the low or negative profits (losses) of unlucky investors who also gambled or speculated on future consumer demand. This balance represents the expected return to such risky ventures.

Around most large cities in the past several decades, all three outcomes, 3a, 3b, and 3c, have occurred in the housing industry. Observing the rising population and incomes, investors forecast rising demand for middle-income housing. Where they underestimated the rise in demand, land values and apartment values rose substantially, giving high profits to the initial investors. Where demand was overestimated, excess building occurred, apartments went unrented, houses unsold, so rentals and prices decreased, causing low returns or losses to investors. The same has been true of investment in shopping centers. Thus, it is the search for profits—the relationships between input prices and output prices—which directs production from one use to another. Whether this works out well for society, we shall consider shortly.

Quality And Consumer Choice

Nearly every one would rather have better quality products than poor quality. Does production according to consumer choice mean, therefore, that the best quality should always be produced? For example, should more Cadillacs than Chevrolets be produced if nearly everyone would prefer a Cadillac to a Chevrolet? No. Under competition, the more expensive item costs more *because* more inputs are used in its production. But many consumers, given their limited incomes, would rather have the cheaper car and more of other things. Similarly, the production of low quality clothes, housing, appliances, watches, cameras, etc. are all entirely consistent with consumer choice, where the relevant choice is not simply whether you prefer first class to tourist class, but which you would rather pay for, given that in either case your payment must cover the cost of production.

Too Much Variety?

Some people complain that profit-seeking producers do not serve consumer interests because an excess variety of some products—too many styles of clothes or cars or houses—results in higher prices than could be realized from less variety, with larger volumes of those varieties produced. However, it is not obvious that reducing variety would lower costs, because most of the varieties (of, say, men's shirts) may already be produced on such a volume that further expansion of any one style would not lower production costs.

Besides, even if a reduction in variety did lower costs, it might not serve consumer interests. Everyone may not be enthusiastic about Chairman Mao's shirt style. Indeed, if less variety *would* mean lower production costs and if consumers would prefer the resulting lower prices with less variety, then the largest producers would find it profitable to expand output of one variety (lowering production costs), reduce prices below competitors', and expand sales, thereby eliminating high-cost producers of different styles. That this does not occur is evidence that consumers prefer variety, even if it means somewhat higher prices.

Too Much Uniformity?

Ironically, others complain that profit-based private enterprise creates too much uniformity, by catering excessively to the mediocre tastes of the masses, ignoring the more culturally refined tastes (of the complainers). These objections are leveled especially at house and apartment builders, TV programmers, and advertisers (for "creating" such tastes).

The question is: who should determine what is produced? The consumer or some elite group with culturally refined tastes? Those who are able and willing to pay the price can have custom tailored, culturally refined clothes, concerts, plays, houses, cars, etc. But if the dollar votes of others (Lucy fans) attract resources out of what you and like-minded people would prefer but can't or won't pay for (televised Senate hearings?), have you a legitimate complaint against the profit system? In order to achieve greater program variety or "public responsibility," should the government tax Lucy fans to pay for programs others would prefer but can't or won't pay for?[3]

Why Consumer Choice?

In the rest of this chapter and the next, attention is given to how output *is* geared to consumer choice, the roles of prices and profits, under socialism as well as private enterprise, the effects of interference with the forces that so direct output, and the difficulties of directing output through political means.

It is appropriate, therefore, to question first whether output *should* be based on consumer preference. The meaning of "producing what people want" will be clearer after demand and supply are explained. Suffice to say, it involves the freedom of each individual to spend his money, time, and productive efforts as he wishes, as long as he doesn't injure or impede the freedom of others. Thus, if some people enjoy bowling, they spend money on this and others find it worthwhile to accommodate these preferences. The basic argument then for gearing production to consumer choice is that such production is the consequence of individual freedom and that individual freedom is desirable.

One may wish to go one step further and ask: "Why is freedom desirable?" A pragmatic answer is that experience has shown that freedom is a necessary condition for such goals as human satisfaction, justice, dignity, welfare, progress, and enlightenment. It is quite beyond the scope of this book to demonstrate whether this empirical assertion is true and whether these goals are desirable. These are fundamental questions that a truth-seeker should apply to numerous fields of study, including economics. A religious or quasi-religious reply is: "By my values or God's values as I understand them,

---

[3] In 1966, one of television's most distinguished executives, Mr. Fred Friendly, resigned as president of CBS News, after CBS refused to pre-empt re-runs of *I Love Lucy* for Senate hearings on the Vietnam War. (The hearings *were* being shown on other stations.) Both at the time and in later writings, Mr. Friendly roundly castigated CBS for its concern over profits.

freedom is desirable per se, independently of its practical value." Most people approve of freedom on both pragmatic and religious grounds, though, to judge by actions, many want freedom for themselves, but not for others. So much for why output *should* be geared to consumer choice: the exercise of personal freedom by consumers and producers results in consumer-directed production (in the absence of monopoly) and freedom is desirable for practical and religious reasons.

Next, why not produce what consumers prefer? There are four familiar reasons. (1) Output based on consumer spending is wrong because incomes are unfairly distributed. (Income distribution is covered in Chapter 6.) This is an objection to the distribution of income, but not to the proposition that output should be based on the preferences of people. By implication, redistribute income, then let freedom determine output. (2) Another objection to consumer-directed production is that private spending does not correctly consider social goals (like national prestige), or public goods (like national defense), or neighborhood costs (like air and water pollution). These are valid criticisms of private spending decisions. (They are covered in Chapter 12.) However, their main thrust is not against production based on consumer choice, but that private spending decisions may incorrectly indicate consumer preferences where social goals, public goods, and neighborhood costs are involved. (3) A third objection is that people lack the knowledge to make sensible decisions. They don't know about all available goods and services and can't evaluate the quality of those they know about. (Knowledge of alternatives is discussed at length in Chapter 10.) Again, however, this is not an objection against producing what knowledgeable people really prefer.

(4) The most fundamental objection to consumer choice and consumer-directed production is that some peoples' tastes are wrong *and* such people should not be allowed to consume nor others allowed to produce in accordance with these tastes. The word "and" is italicized to emphasize this point: the mere fact that some tastes are "wrong" does not necessarily mean that individuals should be prevented from living by these "wrong" tastes. One must assert both the error *and* the desirability of prohibition to justify the prohibition.

There are three general bases for objecting to tastes: (a) moral, (b) aesthetic, and (c) pragmatic, though some choices are opposed on all three grounds. The moral objection is that some conduct, say, prostitution, or gambling, or suicide, is wrong per se. The source of this judgment may be religion, personal conviction, or popular consensus, or some combination of these. But in a society with religious freedom, even if one agrees that there are absolute moral principles, and even if the majority is opposed to certain behavior, it does not follow that any particular version of such principles should be imposed on everyone. The aesthetic argument is that certain tastes, as for pornography or acid-rock, are vulgar and degrading per se. Again, even

"How tastes change! Three years ago this shocked
the Cannes film festival."

so, so what, as long as the alleged vulgarity is not imposed on others? The pragmatic disapproval is that some tastes, as for gambling, liquor, cigarettes, drugs, stock-market speculation, cars without seatbelts and strong bumpers, inane TV fare, are harmful to the individual and that individuals fail to assess their harmful consequences and must be protected from their own alleged stupidity, short-sightedness, and foolishness.

Few people would deny that some tastes are immoral, vulgar, and foolish (though there would be less agreement as to which are). The question is whether freedom should be curtailed therefore. Are the basic goals (such as human dignity) of the moralists and aesthetes achieved if people behave properly only because they have no choice? Are the moral and aesthetic truths so clearly established that deviant, experimental behavior should be suppressed? Is the loss of freedom from well-intended regulations (as against marijuana) less harmful than the prevented harm (if any) to the individual? From a practical point, what are the costs of enforcing prohibitions against conduct admittedly harmful (to some people), such as gambling, drinking, drugs, and smoking? Can prohibition be achieved without oppressive force?

The libertarian (some would say libertine) does not have to wrestle with these questions, because he opposes all infringements of freedom where the individual does not harm others than himself by his conduct. He would say you may exhort and proselytize people to change their ways, but don't coerce. Others, however, must weigh these problems with each regulation and prohibition.

Some will claim that anyone who harms himself must harm others who depend on or care for him, and, therefore, all self-harm can justly be prohibited. The libertarian would answer that private, voluntary relationships can be dissolved and their preservation (on one party's terms) does not justify regulating conduct, except for general laws of parental and contractual responsibility.

Without presuming to have resolved these issues, we move on with the admonition that when production based on consumer choice is referred to as "correct," one should recognize why and why not. Why? Because freedom is desirable. Why not? Because of income distribution, social goals, public goods and neighborhood costs, poor consumer knowledge, and claims that some consumer tastes are immoral, vulgar, and/or foolish. Fortunately, most consumer choices do not involve these possible conflicts between freedom and "good taste."

A Digression On The Relevant Measure Of Profitability

Because of the importance of the role of profits and the public controversy over profit levels in some fields, it is essential to understand in what sense competition results in equality of profits. As used here, "profits" means the money a business has left over after paying its expenses, including depreciation of equipment.[4] The point we shall develop is that the relevant measure of profitability in a company or industry is the *return on investment*. There is no presumption that, under competition, every company will make the same profits. A company that makes a million dollars profits a year may be less profitable in the relevant sense than a small company with profits of only $50,000. Furthermore, there is no tendency or reason why different companies would have the same profits in relation to their sales.

Consider the seven companies in Table 2-1. Suppose you had $100 to invest in any one of these, or, if you had already invested in any one of them, you could shift your investment to any other company. Assume too that your investment would yield profits at exactly the rates shown, which means the ratios on the right would not be changed by your $100 investment.

In Co. A, profits are 20¢ for each dollar of sales—shown by column (4), which is (2) ÷ (1). Column (5), which is (2) ÷ (3), shows that it takes $2 of investment in equipment, inventories, etc. to get each dollar of sales. The return on investment is 10¢ profit for each $1 of investment. This means one investment of $100 in Co. A will result in a yearly return of $10 continuing indefinitely until changes in tastes, technology, or competition cause the relationships between sales, profits, and investment to alter. The wearing out

---

[4] In some economics texts, "profits" means "economic profits" or monopoly profits—returns *above* the competitive level. Our definition conforms to the popular usage and that used for accounting and tax records.

Any reader who is not familiar with elementary accounting should read Appendix A at this point.

Table 2-1   Sales, investment, and profits in seven hypothetical companies

Company	Sales[a] (1)	Profits[a] (2)	Investment[a] (3)	Ratios P/S (4)	I/S (5)	P/I (6)
A	$ 1,000	$ 200	$ 2,000	.20	2.0	.10
B	10,000	2000	20,000	.20	2.0	.10
C	10,000	1000	10,000	.10	1.0	.10
D	10,000	5000	50,000	.50	5.0	.10
E	10,000	100	1,000	.01	0.1	.10
F	10,000	4000	80,000	.40	8.0	.05
G	10,000	500	1,000	.05	0.1	.50

[a] Sales and profits are amounts per unit of time, say per year. Investment is not an amount in any one year, but is the total amount invested in the company from its beginning through the year to which the sales and profits refer, minus the accumulated depreciation or wearing out of the capital equipment and minus any investment sold by the company. Investment is usually measured as a company's assets less its liabilities. (See Appendix A.)

of the nonhuman input (acquired with the $100 investment) is covered by "depreciation," an amount which you would receive in addition to the $10 a year and which is not counted as part of the "return to investment." If the equipment were wearing out evenly at 5% a year, the depreciation would be $5 a year. By reinvesting the depreciation, you would maintain your investment in the company at $100 and so maintain the yearly return of $10 above depreciation, assuming constant prices and costs.

Is Co. B doing better than Co. A? Its profits are ten times as high, but so are sales and investment. Therefore, an additional $100 invested in Co. B would also earn you $10 a year. No difference.

Next compare Co. C with Co. B. Both have sales of $10,000 a year, but Co. C has profits of $1000 while Co. B has profits of $2000. So Co. B seems to be doing better. But no. These companies are in different lines of business. It takes a larger investment in Co. B to get a dollar of sales than in Co. C. Your $100 investment in Co. B would add $50 per year in sales. With a profit margin of 20%, you would get $10 profit. Invested in Co. C, the $100 would bring $100 in annual sales, but with a profit margin of 10%, you would get the same $10 profit. Thus, the return on investment is the same in both companies: they are equally profitable and there would be no gain by shifting investment from one to the other, even though the profit margin in B is twice that in C.

Conclusion: profit margins or profits relative to sales do not show the true profitability of companies. Why not? Because it takes a different amount of investment to get a dollar of sales in one industry than in another. The owners' objective is to maximize their return on investment. Firms do consciously strive for high profit margins, because, given the investment to get a dollar's sales, the higher is the profit margin, the larger are profits. But competition tends to equalize the returns to investment in various economic activities.

The relevant relationships are expressed by the following equation:

profits per dollar of sales	equals	investment per dollar of sales	times	profits per dollar of investment
$\dfrac{P}{S}$	=	$\dfrac{I}{S}$	×	$\dfrac{P}{I}$

Continuing down the table, we see that Co. D, also with $10,000 sales, has a whopping profit of $5000. Yet, because investment relative to sales is so high, the return to investment is just 10%, the same as for companies A, B, and C. Co. E has a very small profit from $10,000 sales, but in this business it takes only $1000 investment to get $10,000 sales, so again the return on investment is as good as in A through D. Finally, in Co. F with large profits relative to sales, investment returns are only 5%, a poor investment compared to the others, while in Co. G, despite small profits relative to sales, the return on investment as a fantastic 50%, by far the best.[5]

Incidentally, what do you think the average manufacturing company makes as a profit (after taxes) per dollar of sales? Guess. McGraw-Hill's Opinion Research Corp. has asked this yearly since 1945 and the average answer has never been less than 3½ times too high. In 1971, the average guess was 28¢, seven times the actual 1970 figure of 4¢ profit per sales dollar. Women guessed 34¢ and teenagers 33¢. (*Business Week,* Dec. 18, 1971.)

Two questions arise at this point: (1) Are there really large differences in investment per dollar of sales (and, therefore, in profit margins when investment returns are the same)? and (2) If so, why?

---

[5] In Co.A where P/S is .2, the profit margin is 20%. A related term, applied mostly to wholesalers and retailers, is the "mark-up." This is the difference between the sales price of an item and the cost of the item to the seller, as a percent of the cost. If an item costs the grocer 60c and he sells it for 80c, the mark-up is 20c as a percent of 60c, or 33%. This does not tell the profit margin, because it does not include the operating costs incurred by the grocer. Nor does it tell anything about the investment or the return to investment.

Table 2-2   Profits relative to sales and to investment in
selected industries, 1970

Industry	$\dfrac{P}{S}$	$\dfrac{P}{I}$	$\dfrac{I}{S}$
1. Meatpacking	1.0[a]	9.6[a]	.10
2. Telephone and telegraph	11.5	9.5	1.21
3. Soft drinks	7.2	23.8	.30
4. Petroleum refining	7.2	10.9	.66
5. Restaurants and hotels	4.8	15.8	.30
6. Glass products	4.5	8.5	.53
7. Railroad	5.5	3.6	1.53
8. Trucking	2.2	9.2	.24
9. All industries	4.8	9.9	.49

[a] The numbers in the first two columns are in percentage terms and, therefore, are strictly (P/S)100 and (P/I)100. The last two columns are in reverse order from Table 2-1. Source: *Monthly Economic Letter,* First National City Bank of New York, April, 1971, p. 7. These data cover only leading corporations, not all companies.

An affirmative answer to the first question is seen from Table 2-2. Compare the first two industries. Profits per dollar of sales are over eleven times higher in telephone service than in meatpacking. Yet returns to investment are about the same. In telephone and telegraph, it takes $1.21 investment to get $1 sales, while in meatpacking only 10¢ of investment is needed for each $1 of sales. In the next pair, both industries received the same 7.2¢ profit per dollar of sales, yet the return to investment is over twice as high in soft drinks as in petroleum refining. Again, the critical difference explaining this is the investment required to get a dollar of sales—30¢ in soft drinks, 66¢ in petroleum refining. The same contrast is evident in the third pair: about equal in profits per sales but a large difference in returns to investment, which again illustrates that P/S gives no indication of P/I.

Finally, railroads and trucking provide another interesting contrast. Railroads have over twice the profits relative to sales, but are one of the nation's least profitable industries, with a return to investment only 39% as high as trucking.

You might well ask how come soft drinks and restaurants and hotels are so well off and railroads so poor if competition tends to even out investment returns? The answer is that the equalization of investment returns occurs over time and does not necessarily show up in a cross-section of profits in any particular year.[6] The chronically poor profit performance of railroads results from government compulsion upon railroads to provide unprofitable services, especially passenger service, and from barriers against technological improvements set up by unions and state "full-crew" laws. Also, railroads have been prevented by the ICC from lowering rates to match competition from trucking.[7]

Now to the second question: *Why* might the investment required to get a dollar's sales differ among industries? Mainly because companies differ with respect to these three points: (1) inventory turnover, (2) value added relative to sales, and (3) the ratio of labor to capital.

(1) In some activities, companies must carry a large volume of goods ready for sale so they can make quick delivery and so fastidious customers (we shan't specify of which sex) have plenty of items from which to choose. Furriers, jewelers, and furniture dealers are examples. The money value of the inventory is an investment to the owner. In other activities, goods are sold quickly after their arrival, so the inventory is small relative to sales per month. This is characteristic of foodstores and meatpackers.

(2) In activities where most of the sales value of the product consists of the value of the materials the company purchased from other companies rather than of what the company itself did to these materials, the investment per sales will tend to be low. Thus, a shipper who buys goods from manufacturers and sells them to wholesalers will have a high sales relative to investment, because most of what he is selling was finished when he acquired

---

[6] Striking evidence showing this equalization over time is presented in George Stigler, *Capital and Rates of Return in Manufacturing Industries,* Princeton University Press. 1963.

[7] Why railroads haven't made much money is illustrated in the following Associated Press item from Valley Forge, Pa: "When the Reading Railroad decided to eliminate a commuter stop here, only one person— Willard E. Debus—protested. Mr. Debus, who travels by train to his job in Philadelphia, is the only commuter who uses the station. But his protest worked. The state Public Utility Commission voted yesterday 3 to 1 to uphold Mr. Debus's complaint. It ordered the railroad to continue stopping at Valley Forge just for him." *New York Times,* April 16, 1965. While the ICC and Congress have allowed railroads to abandon much unprofitable passenger service, local commuter operations remain a losing effort and long distance service is now conducted through Amtrak. However, even this seems destined for oblivion, given the consumer preference for travel by car and air. As to inefficient work rules, the 1971 railroad strike centered around union insistence that railroads continue to change crews every 100 miles at full-day's pay, a practice which dates from the turn of the century when a 100-mile trip represented an 8-hour freight trip, instead of 2½-hours today. On The Metroliner which speeds passengers 230 miles between New York and Washington in 3½ hours, crew changes were avoided only by paying the crew 2½ days' pay—one-way.

it. On the other hand, consider a manufacturer who changes raw iron ore into finished steel products. Most of his sales represent work done by the company, which will generally require more investment per sales than when the value added by the firm's operations is small relative to sales.

(3) If most of the value added by the firm is done by labor which the firm hires and in which the firm does not invest, the investment to sales ratio will be lower than where most of the value added results from nonhuman inputs which the firm owns and in which it has invested. This contrast is illustrated in Table 2 by restaurants and hotels, where labor does most of the producing and I/S is low, compared with electric and gas utilities, where the physical plant and equipment do most of the producing and I/S is high.

Since these factors—inventory relative to sales, value added relative to sales, and labor relative to capital—do vary among industries, the investment relative to sales will also vary, and so, therefore, must profits relative to sales vary if there is to be approximate equality in returns to investment. That is, recalling that P/S = (I/S)(P/I), if I/S differs between industries A and B, and if from competition P/I is to be the same in A and B, then P/S must also differ between A and B.

Two Characteristics Of Correct Prices

1. Market-Clearing

2. Cover Cost of Production

We have seen that prices (and profits) play an important role in determining what to produce: they act as signals directing businessmen to produce what consumers prefer. But not just any old set of prices will do this. *If* we assume that production should be based on consumer preferences, then the price of each good and service should have the two characteristics listed above. And, as we shall explain, for each good and service at a given time and place, there is *only one price* which can simultaneously have both of these characteristics. Furthermore, there is only *one* rate of production at which this one price will automatically prevail. Thus, when the correct price is determined (that which best gears production to consumer preferences), the correct production is also determined—what to produce is determined. But remember, this is "correct" or "good" only if production should be based on the choices of consumers as these choices are expressed by the way consumers spend their money.

The Market-Clearing Price: What It Is; Why It Should Prevail

The market-clearing price is the highest price at which the existing quantity can be sold. Imagine yourself in a group of fifty persons. One member says he has two identical new cars which he is going to sell to persons in the group (without regard to the cost of the cars to himself). What should be the price if all members are to have equal opportunity to purchase the cars and if we accept the distribution of purchasing power within the group? It should be the highest price at which the two cars can be sold. This is the market-clearing price. To accept a price below this level would (almost certainly) be to deny some members in the group the privilege of offering more to purchase a car. The freedom of all to spend as they wish means their freedom to bid against each other for the available cars; and the absence of discrimination or favoritism by the seller means his selling to the highest bidders. Such free bidding would push the price up to, but not above, the market-clearing level: the highest price at which two cars could be sold.

So it is with everything produced: the freedom of each consumer to spend his money as he wishes includes his freedom to compete with other consumers. This freedom will result in market-clearing prices. If prices were higher than the market-clearing level, people would not buy as much as produced; hence consumer spending would never bid the price this high and producers have no incentive to set prices so high that they are producing goods they cannot sell. So prices above the market-clearing level will not be brought about any more than will those below it.

The market-clearing price depends upon the quantity available: the larger is the quantity, the lower is the price which clears the market. So we still haven't found a way to decide what quantities to produce. All we've determined is the price to charge, once the quantity is determined.

The meaning of the market-clearing price can be seen with the demand curve of Figure 2-1. The curve shows the quantities of some item that people would like to purchase at various prices of the item. Specifically, it shows that if the price is $10, people would like to buy 2000 per year; if the price were $6 people would buy 5000; and at $3, 9000 would be demanded. (The fact that people want to buy doesn't mean anyone will sell. How much people will sell at various prices is given by "supply.") This downward slope of the curve illustrates a condition which seems to apply to all goods and services: the lower is the product price, the more people will want to buy.

Precisely how much people would like to buy at various prices—that is, what the shape and position of the demand curve will be—depends on consumers' tastes (how much they like and/or need the item), their incomes (how much they can afford), and the prices of substitutes (like margarine for butter) and of complements (like electricity and light bulbs). A change in any

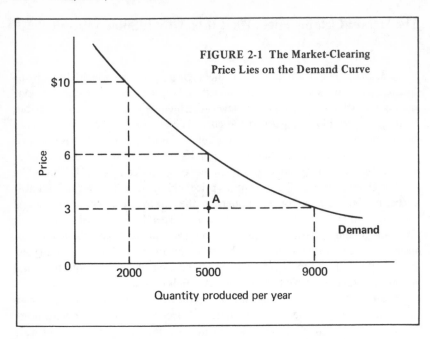

FIGURE 2-1 The Market-Clearing
Price Lies on the Demand Curve

one of these determinants (tastes, incomes, and prices of related goods) causes the whole curve to shift.[8]

Now back to the market-clearing price, as illustrated by the demand curve. If the quantity available happens to be 5000, then the market-clearing price is $6. At a lower price, people would want more than 5000. For example, consider point A: if the price were $3 and if only 5000 units were available per year, the goods would have to be rationed out by the sellers on some other basis than who pays the most. Discrimination, favoritism, waiting in line, and bribery would replace the freedom of consumers to compete with dollars. If the quantity were below 5000, say at 2000, the market-clearing price would be higher, $10. Thus, the market-clearing price depends upon the quantity available and will be the price on the demand curve which corresponds to the given quantity.

Examples Of Non-Price Rationing

When the price is at the market-clearing level, every one who is willing to pay this price can buy all he wants. The price is said to "ration" the item

---

[8] A more detailed explanation of demand and supply is in Appendix B, which could reasonably be read at this point and should definitely be read before the discussion of Figure 2-4.

amongst the population. When the price is below the market-clearing level, people want to buy more than is available. So there must be "non-price rationing" to determine who will get the available quantity.

A good example of the inefficiency and inconvenience which result from non-price rationing is the dangerous congestion in the air around major airports at peak hours, a congestion which, besides endangering lives and property, results in hours of waiting for an opportunity to land and occasionally forces some planes to land in other cities than their intended destinations. If landing fees were charged at market-clearing prices, these fees would be highest at the most popular hours (4−7 PM) causing fares to be higher for these flights and lowest at slack hours (1−5 AM) with consequent lower fares at these hours. The landing fees and plane fares would be bid up to where the limited landing privilege (based on airport capacity, consistent with safety) could just be sold. Everyone willing to pay the higher prices could be accommodated smoothly without dangerous congestion and without waiting. But with the privilege of landing at popular hours priced below market-clearing levels, more passengers seek to land then than can be accommodated and non-price rationing in the form of waiting and congestion occurs. The problem stems entirely from a failure to use the price system. While more airports might be a longer-run answer, this too might be hastened if market-clearing fees substantially raised the profitability of operating airports.[9]

During the World's Fair in New York, the most popular exhibits had lines several city blocks long, requiring complicated mazes of railings to channel the many impatient patrons. After hours of waiting, one man complained that if the companies couldn't reduce this inconvenience, he wouldn't have time to buy their products. Entrance fees, set at market-clearing levels, would have virtually eliminated the lines. Whoever was willing to pay the price could buy a ticket and enter without a long wait at the start of the show. Fairgoers would have spent more time watching exhibits and less time standing in line.

Another event priced below its market-clearing level was the 1965 concert by Vladimir Horowitz, his first in twelve years. People waited in line several days and nights in cold April weather, their spirits bouyed with hot coffee sent by Mrs. Horowitz. The line was so long, one passerby inquired whether it weren't "a Beatle thing." A year later before his next concert, the long cold waits were repeated. Each time, hundreds left empty-handed. About 200 of these frustrated music lovers received an atypical dividend

---

[9] To see how prices which reflect neither costs nor consumer preference are creating inefficiency in airport service, read "Landing Fees and the Airport Congestion Problem," by Michael Levine, *Journal of Law and Economics,* April, 1969. This article is an excellent application of the prime lesson of this book: the role of prices in directing economic activity.

from non-price rationing when in 1968 they were given tickets to the final taping of Mr. Horowitz's TV recital.

Much more serious are conditions in Russia, where for decades nearly all food, clothes, housing, and household appliances have been priced below market-clearing levels. The typical householder spends hours per week standing in lines. Indeed, one of those waiting to purchase tickets to a Horowitz recital commented that he had not done anything like this since he was in Russia and there it was for bread.[10]

What Is A Thing Worth?

The market-clearing price of a good measures what consumers would be willing to pay for another unit of that good. If an egg sells for 5¢ and an orange for 10¢ (both market-clearing prices), then to the consuming public one orange is worth two eggs. Value is measured by what a thing sells for.

Of course, many people have cherished items which they would not sell, mainly because their values to others—their market-clearing prices—are less than their values to their owners. And everyone knows of many goods and services which he feels are not worth their prevailing prices. But if one wants a measure of the value of something which valuation is independent of the tastes of a particular person, the market-clearing price gives this measure. Since all prices are expressed in terms of a common unit (dollars in America), relative prices measure how much, to consumers, one thing is worth in terms of another.[11]

In conclusion, what is the market-clearing price? It is the highest price at which the quantity available can be sold. It measures the value of an item to consumers. Why should this be the price? For two reasons: (1) because a lower price would deprive some consumers of an equal opportunity to bid for each good and service, and (2) if prices are below market-clearing levels by

---

[10] Non-price rationing also arises where local governments provide recreation services without fees or for below market-clearing fees. The five-hour wait to tee off at a municipal golf course on a summer Saturday morning is an example, as are long waits at tennis courts and swimming pools. Also for dock space at city marinas. A predictable result was described in *Newsweek*, June 22, 1970. Despite fees of over $500 per season, demand exceeds supply at Chicago's city-operated docks, so a like amount or more is paid to a Park District official, cash please, or one gets no mooring. One man who kept his boat in his backyard rather than ante up a $1500 bribe said, "Everyone knows it goes on."

[11] A sportswriter, complaining about 1969 World Series ticket prices, accused baseball owners of "running some kind of skin game aimed at dredging from the citizenry not what the show is worth, but what the market will bring." Well, what *is* the show worth, if not what the market will bring?

differing percentages, then producers, whether government-owned or private enterprise, lack the guide of price comparisons which reflect consumer preferences.

Why Price Should Cover Production Cost

A superficial answer is that if price is below production cost, private producers would not have incentive to produce the product. While this is true, it begs the question. After all, if private producers won't produce the product, then government can. But we seek a reason why price should equal production cost no matter whether private enterprise or government produces the product. In showing why price should equal production cost as well as being at the market-clearing level, we shall simultaneously demonstrate what the rate of production should be for each good and service.

First, it is necessary to develop two subordinate points: (1) the meaning of production cost, and (2) how the difference between production cost and market-clearing price changes as output varies.

(1) The meaning of production cost. In this discussion, production cost refers to the money cost of producing another unit of a given item. Economists call this the "marginal cost" to distinguish from "average cost" which is the cost per unit of output. For example, if total costs rise from $988 to $1000 when output expands from 99 to 100 (per unit of time), then the *marginal cost* of the 100th unit is $12, $1000 less $988, while the average cost at output 100 is $10, $1000 ÷ 100.

Unless a business is throwing money away, the production costs all represent payments to inputs. Furthermore, to acquire inputs, the firm will pay no more than it has to, which generally means it will pay no more than these inputs could earn working for (or invested in) other firms. On the other hand, to attract inputs, the firm will have to pay them as much as they could earn alternatively. So input payments equal what the inputs could earn in other employments.

For example, suppose an accounting firm wants to hire a 75-word-a-minute typist. It would have to pay as much as such typists are paid elsewhere (taking account of general work conditions, such as hours, vacations, and perhaps marital prospects) or it won't be able to hire the kind of typist it wants. On the other hand, it will not have to pay any more than the going rate for such typists. So it pays the going rate.

Now how much could inputs earn elsewhere? Answer: they could earn as much as their services are worth—surely no more or the firms elsewhere would be subsidizing the inputs, and surely no less if there is adequate competition for inputs. The proposition that input payments exactly equal value contributed to production is developed in Chapter 6.

The preceding paragraphs have developed the following three propositions from which we arrive at the main point about production costs:

1. The marginal cost of producing another unit of product A consists of the input payments necessary to hire the inputs.
2. The input payments in A equal the payments these inputs could earn elsewhere, in non-A.
3. In non-A, the inputs would be paid the money value of their contributions to production. (This applies to both human and non-human inputs.)

Therefore: the cost of producing the last unit (or one more unit) of any good or service equals the value of the other goods and services which could have been produced instead (had the inputs in A been employed in non-A).[12]

For example, if the marginal cost of producing a 12 cu. ft. refrigerator is $325, then the inputs which produced the refrigerator could have produced $325-worth of other goods. The other goods, the production of which is sacrificed to get A produced, are the "real" or "alternative" cost of producing A. This is important. The "real" cost of producing an item is the other things that could have been produced instead with the same inputs. And by propositions 1, 2, and 3 above, the marginal cost (which is in money terms) measures the value of this "real" cost.

(2) How production cost varies as output changes. This is the second of the two subordinate points required to show why the rate of production should be where the market-clearing price equals the marginal cost. The following diagrams show various ways in which marginal cost may vary with output. In A, the cost decreases as output expands; in B marginal cost rises with more output; in C it remains the same; and in D, which combines the patterns of A, B, and C, it declines, is constant, then rises. To understand these curves, consider diagram B. Point K says: The marginal cost of

---

[12] This conclusion may be developed more formally as follows (for a "translation" read the corresponding numbered statement above):

1. $MC_A = \sum_{i=a}^{n} W_{i,A}$, where $W_{i,A}$ is the wage paid to input "i" for producing the marginal unit of output A, there being n inputs employed, a, b, c, . . . , n.
2. $W_{i,A} = W_{i,non-A}$; therefore, $\Sigma W_{i,A} = \Sigma W_{i,non-A}$.
3. $W_{i,non-A} = V_{i,non-A}$; therefore, $\Sigma W_{i,non-A} = \Sigma V_{i,non-A}$, where $V_{i,non-A}$ is the value that input "i" would have produced if employed in non-A instead of A.

Therefore, by substitution, $MC_A = \Sigma W_{i,A} = \Sigma W_{i,non-A} = \Sigma V_{i,non-A}$; q.e.d.

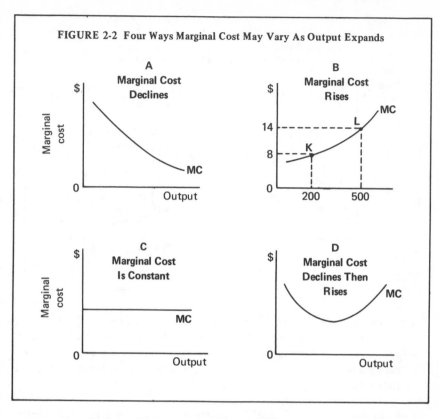

FIGURE 2-2 Four Ways Marginal Cost May Vary As Output Expands

producing the 200th unit is $8. Thus, whatever the total costs are for producing 199 units, these costs are $8 higher for producing 200. Point L says the marginal or added cost of producing the 500th unit is $14.

For our present purposes, it doesn't matter which is the case. But most studies suggest that D is typical and more advanced theory shows that, except for "natural monopolies" like local public utilities, all competitive firms operate at an output where marginal cost is rising as in B or in the rightward portion of D.[13]

Now let's turn to Figure 2-3, which shows the demand curve (the market-clearing price for any given output) and the marginal cost. According to the diagram, if 5,000 units are produced per year, the market-clearing price would be $14 a unit. But the marginal cost would be only $4. The difference between the market-clearing price and the marginal cost is $10 at output 5,000. This difference is the *vertical distance* between the two lines. Clearly,

---

[13] While we shall not prove it, marginal cost rises as output expands because of diminishing returns (discussed in Chapter 5).

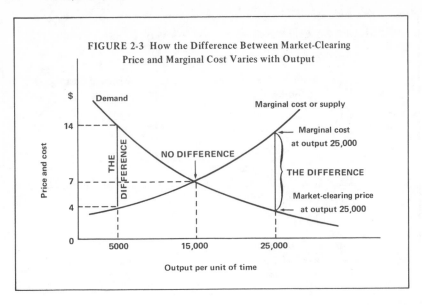

FIGURE 2-3 How the Difference Between Market-Clearing
Price and Marginal Cost Varies with Output

as output expands beyond 5,000, this difference declines, until, at output
15,000, market-clearing price equals marginal cost and both equal $7. After
output 15,000, marginal cost exceeds market-clearing price and does so by
increasing amounts as output expands, the difference again being the vertical
distance between marginal cost and demand.

**Why price should equal marginal cost: the determination of correct
output.** We are ready to explain, at last, why it is desirable that the output be
such that market-clearing price equals the cost of producing another unit.
This important conclusion follows from two propositions just developed:

(1) The market-clearing price of a good or service, A, measures the
value to consumers of another unit of A.
(2) The marginal cost measures the real cost, the value to consumers of the
output which must be foregone to get another unit of A produced.

Therefore: if A's output is at a level where the market-clearing price exceeds
marginal cost, consumers gain by an expansion of A's production (and
curtailment of non-A) up to the level where market-clearing price equals
marginal cost, and conversely, if marginal cost exceeds market-clearing price.

Consider output 5,000 in Figure 2-3. The value to consumers of
another unit of the product is $14, the market-clearing price. The cost of
producing another unit, which measures the value of goods foregone to
produce another unit, is $4. So consumers consider another A worth $10
more than the goods which the inputs required to produce another A could
have produced. Of course, consumers have no conscious thought of this,

because they have no awareness of marginal cost or its equality with value of goods foregone. But the real cost is present and unavoidable whether anyone is aware or not.

As additional units of A are produced beyond 5,000, what happens to this $10 difference? From the diagram, it clearly gets smaller. The market-clearing price declines and the marginal cost rises.[14] Consumers continue to gain from more A and less non-A as long as the market-clearing price exceeds marginal cost, as long as the value of another unit exceeds its real cost. This occurs until output is 15,000, where market-clearing price equals marginal cost; so any lesser output would be contrary to consumer choice as expressed by dollar votes.

Suppose output were 25,000 in Figure 2-3. There marginal cost exceeds market-clearing price. This means the value of the goods foregone to produce the last unit of A is greater than the value to consumers of this last unit of A. So consumers gain by a reduction of A's output (and a corresponding expansion of non-A). Obviously, this situation is true for all quantities greater than 15,000. Of course, output 25,000 (or any output where MC is greater than the price consumers would pay) would be unprofitable to produce. But this unprofitability is *not* the reason why such outputs are against *consumer* interest. To repeat, output 25,000 is undesirable *to consumers* because, for all outputs past 15,000, the value *to consumers* of the last unit, as shown by the demand curve, is less than the value *to consumers* of the alternative goods which could have been produced, which value is measured by marginal cost.

Thus, 15,000 would be the ideal output from the standpoint of consumers, as their tastes are expressed by their spending. At this ideal output and *only* at this output, market-clearing price equals marginal cost. We have finally proved why output should be such that price has the two characteristics, market-clearing and equality with marginal cost.

To recapitulate, we have shown:

(1) Prices *do* play a role in determining what to produce under private enterprise;
(2) For each good and service, price should equal production cost and be at the market-clearing level;
(3) When (2) obtains, output will ideally reflect consumer choice.

The next questions to be answered are:

(1) *Will* prices automatically be at market-clearing levels and equal

---

[14] The vertical distance between the curves would also decline as output expanded from 5,000, even if marginal cost did not rise, as long as marginal cost lay below the demand curve and eventually intersected demand. This is the reason for the statement that it does not matter which of the cost patterns of Figure 2-2 prevails.

marginal cost under private enterprise? The answer: Yes under competitive conditions, but not under monopoly.

(2) So what, if prices do not meet these conditions and output is different from the ideal? The answer: Society's productive capacity will produce goods and services less satisfying to consumers than available alternatives.

(3) Couldn't output just as well be determined without a price system, but through political ballots or by decisions by a government which tried to act in the public interest? Answer: Almost certainly not. (See Chapter 3.)

Price Determination Under Private Enterprise [15]

We have shown the characteristics prices *ought* to have (assuming output should be based on consumer choice as expressed by spending decisions). We have not shown that such prices *will* prevail under private enterprise. As every one finds out early in life, things do not always work out as they ought to.

In this case, however, it is easy to see that price and output *will* be "ideally" determined under competitive conditions. Please refer to Figure 2-4. The demand curve shows the quantities people would like to buy at various prices. The supply curve shows the quantities other people (businesses) would like to sell at various prices. With minor qualifications developed in an advanced treatment, supply is derived directly from marginal cost. In fact, for a single company, the upward-sloping portion of the marginal cost shows the quantities the firm would like to produce at various prices. And the supply for the whole industry (in Figure 2-4) is, with some qualifications, simply a horizontal summation of all the firms' marginal costs at each price.

We shall now explain why price and quantity *will* be at p_1 and q_1, whereas earlier we explained why they *ought* to be there. In the earlier discussion, we concentrated on the *vertical* distance between demand and marginal cost curves. In this discussion, we use the *horizontal* distance between the curves. We shall explain first why the price would not stay *above* p_1, then why it wouldn't remain *below* it, thereby explaining why private interest will bring about p_1 and q_1 under competition. This shows that p_1 and q_1 are the *equilibrium* price and quantity, the outcome that is brought about by the forces underlying demand and supply.

First, why the price could not remain above p_1. (It is essential that you refer back and forth between the discussion and the diagram.) If the price were above p_1, say at p_3, then according to the supply curve, producers would like to sell q_3. But at this price, p_3, the demand curve shows

---

[15] Be sure to read Appendix B before beginning this section.

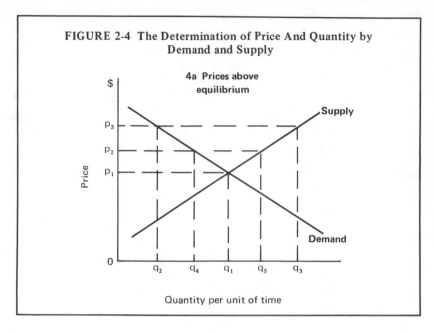

FIGURE 2-4 The Determination of Price And Quantity by Demand and Supply

consumers would buy only q_2. The difference, $q_3 - q_2$, between what suppliers would produce and consumers would buy is "surplus" production.[16] Suppliers, who could not sell what they would like and whose inventories would be growing, would offer to sell for less. This would drive down the price, say to p_2. At this lower price, consumers would buy more, q_4, and suppliers would produce q_5, less than at p_3. Still, there would be a surplus of $q_5 - q_4$ and the price would still be driven down by the competition of sellers for consumers. Only when the price fell to p_1 would the pressure for a lower price cease, for only at p_1 does the quantity demanded equal the quantity supplied. Thus, no price *above* p_1 could prevail.[17]

Now how about prices below p_1, such as p_4 in Figure 2-4b? If the price were p_4, then according to the demand curve, consumers would like to

---

[16] Why wouldn't suppliers just cut output back to q_2 and keep charging p_2? Perhaps they would, but only if they colluded monopolistically to restrict output. Under the *competitive* conditions assumed here, each supplier produces what his costs indicate is profitable at the prevailing price, so that the total produced by all is that shown by the supply curve at any given price. Monopoly is covered later.

[17] There is no implication that sellers refrain from charging as high prices as they can get. It is the competition among sellers and a desire to avoid surplus production that keeps price from rising above p_1, not any benevolence, fairness, or altruism of sellers.

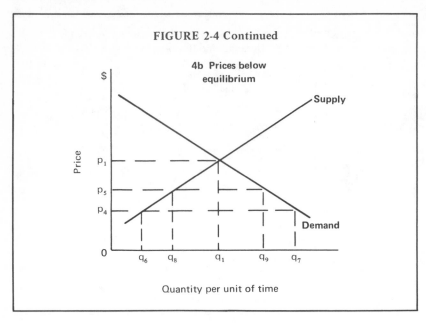

FIGURE 2-4 Continued

4b Prices below equilibrium

Quantity per unit of time

purchase q_7. But suppliers would produce only q_6. So there would be a "shortage" of q_7-q_6. Some consumers who could not obtain all they want at p_4 would be willing to pay more than do without. Either they would explicitly bid up the price or sellers, finding their shelves so quickly depleted, would know they could raise the price and still sell all they had on hand. As the price rose, the quantity demanded would decrease and the quantity supplied would increase. But at any price below p_1, the quantity demanded would exceed the quantity supplied and the competition among the consumers would bid the price up until p_1 was reached. This shows that no price *below* p_1 can prevail.

Thus we have shown that, given competition among sellers and buyers, the price will automatically settle at p_1 where quantity demanded equals quantity supplied. And this is the same one price at which the market-clearing price (on the demand curve) equals the marginal cost (on the supply curve). And thus competitive private enterprise brings about the ideal output, without anyone's being conscious of the ideal or striving to serve any interest but his own.

Interference With Competitive Prices

Notwithstanding the apparent beneficence of competitively determined prices and quantities, governments and private groups have frequently endeavored to bring about other prices and outputs. In this section, we consider five such interferences: (1) price ceilings, (2) price supports, (3) commodity taxes, (4) commodity subsidies, and (5) monopoly collusion. In a later chapter, interference with competitive wage determination is discussed.

Price Ceilings

A price ceiling is a law stating that a good or service cannot be sold for more than a specified price, the ceiling. Such laws are generally passed to curb inflation, though, as explained in Chapter 9, most economists feel that inflation is better combatted with monetary-fiscal policy to regulate overall consumer buying power than by price controls, because monetary-fiscal policy curbs total spending without interfering with competitive price determination of what to produce.

Consider Figure 2-5. Under competition the price would be p_1 and the output would be q_1. Suppose the government, by law, says the price cannot be above p_2. Then consumers will want to buy q_3. (Check it. If you read along lazily without referring back and forth between the text and the diagram, you probably won't understand a thing—unless at one glance you retain an indelible picture of the whole diagram, in which case we defer to your genius.) While consumers demand q_3 at p_2, suppliers will produce only q_2. So there is a "shortage" of q_3-q_2. As a consequence, there will be non-price rationing. The lucky ones who get the q_2 will be the friends and relatives of the sellers and those of their race, nationality, and religion, or those who stand in line the longest, or those who violate the law and pay more than p_2. And to prevent these illegal "black-market" prices, the government will need an army of inspectors checking on transactions everywhere.

As you surely observed, with price p_2 and quantity q_2, the price is way below the market-clearing level (on the demand curve at q_2). This means more of the given item should be produced and less of other things. Such controls over most goods and services completely destroy the ability of the price system to allocate production in accordance with consumer choice.

Then why do they exist? For the most part, they don't. Price controls were adopted during World Wars I and II and the Korean War, when government spending was creating inflationary pressure. With few exceptions, they were removed soon after the wars ended. In 1971, they were again introduced by President Nixon. In all cases, wartime inflation resulted from excess money creation by the government, which creation was avoidable without price controls, though it would probably have meant higher taxes to finance the war.

One instance where price controls have been kept since World War II is

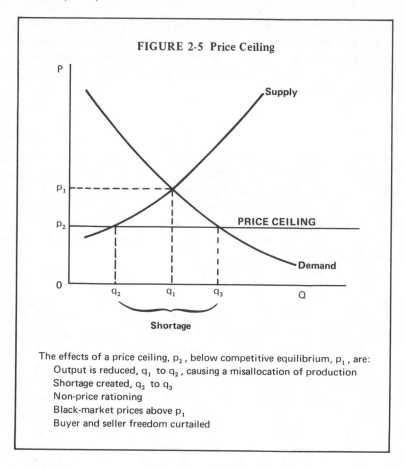

FIGURE 2-5 Price Ceiling

The effects of a price ceiling, p_2, below competitive equilibrium, p_1, are:
  Output is reduced, q_1 to q_2, causing a misallocation of production
  Shortage created, q_2 to q_3
  Non-price rationing
  Black-market prices above p_1
  Buyer and seller freedom curtailed

rent controls in New York City. And the consequence is disaster, mitigated only by the fact that, until 1969, rent controls did not apply to apartments built after the war. There is a terrible housing shortage in New York, huge illegal payments are commonplace to obtain a rent-controlled apartment, since the controlled rent is under half the market-clearing level in many cases (though not in post-war buildings), and the incentive to build new apartments or even maintain old ones has been virtually destroyed. (New York's rent controls are discussed further in Chapter 10.)

Another sort of price control is the law against ticket scalping, where someone sells a ticket for a larger mark-up than allowed to licensed brokers. Suppose you would like to attend the seventh game of the World Series, but couldn't decide long enough in advance to acquire a ticket, or weren't one of the lucky ones whose order was filled. Isn't it in your interest that someone is known to specialize in buying up such tickets and selling them at the gate?

Or suppose you purchased such a ticket and someone offers you $70 for it. If you would rather have the $70 than the ticket, why should the government prevent this exchange?[18] Or if you have an unexpected trip to New York and want to attend a hit play (whose ticket prices are below market-clearing levels and are, therefore, sold out for weeks or months to come), why should the government stop you from paying several times the box office price to a "scalper?"

If laws against scalping were abolished, returns to investment in this activity would be competitive, covering costs of the tickets, time and effort to sell, and balancing successful and unsuccessful speculations about the demand for future events. It would also result in greater efforts by producers of plays and sporting events to vary ticket prices with the demand for the event, a practice avoided somewhat because the public doesn't "appreciate" the allocative and distributive functioning of the price system. We trust you do.[19]

Suppose the price ceiling were set *above* p_1 in Fig. 2-5. What effect would this ceiling have? None. The price wouldn't be above p_1 anyway, so the law saying more than that can't be charged would be insignificant. However, if there were reason to predict that changes in demand and supply would raise the equilibrium to above the ceiling, then such a ceiling above the current equilibrium might discourage investment in the industry.

Usury laws. These laws set legal limits on interest rates, particularly on loans to consumers. They are price ceilings. Consider Fig. 2-6. It refers to the demand and supply for loans of a given type, say first mortgages on middle

----

[18] Some may react, "I'd sell it, and too bad about the law." But laws which rather decent people feel no compunction about violating cause disrespect for law generally; they lead less decent people to rationalize violating more important laws; they lead police to exercize discretion about which laws to enforce and which to wink at, which in turn leads to pay-offs and corruption and lax enforcement of all laws. Perhaps it would be better to repeal laws which are not worth enforcing to the letter. Wouldn't society's limited police, court, and prison facilities then be more efficiently allocated? See the provocative article, "Victimless Offenses Should Be Legalized, Some Officials Think," *Wall Street Journal,* August 25, 1971.

[19] See "The Price Is Wrong: Ticket Scalpers Reap Profit As Businesses Purchase For Clients," *Wall Street Journal,* December 31, 1970. Another *WSJ* article, "In Pro Football Today, The Real Scrimmage Comes In Battle For Seats," Sept. 16, 1971, reported that $98.50 season tickets to the Redskins sell for as much as $600 to $1000. A miffed Congressman threatened to vote against funds for Washington's R. F. Kennedy Stadium if he couldn't acquire tickets. Ticket-purchase privileges also figure in divorce settlements. One man was outraged to learn that his wife, separated for two years, had picked up two season tickets held in his name. All this because prices are below market-clearing levels.

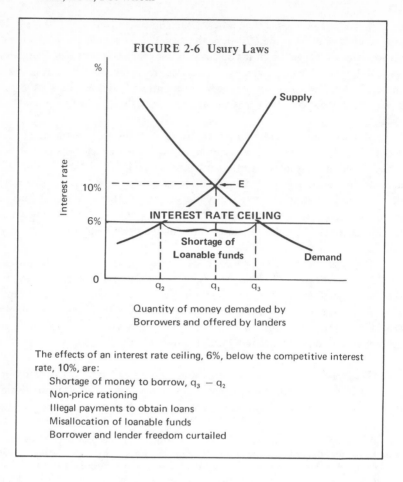

FIGURE 2-6 Usury Laws

The effects of an interest rate ceiling, 6%, below the competitive interest rate, 10%, are:
   Shortage of money to borrow, $q_3 - q_2$
   Non-price rationing
   Illegal payments to obtain loans
   Misallocation of loanable funds
   Borrower and lender freedom curtailed

class homes. We shall not go into the specific determinants of these curves. The downward slope of demand shows that the lower is the interest rate, the more money consumers would like to borrow to build homes. The supply curve shows that the higher is the interest rate on these loans, the more money will be offered by lenders. Under competition, the equilibrium, where there is no surplus or shortage, will be at E, 10% and q_1. But suppose there is a usury law which says banks cannot charge (nor borrowers pay) more than 6%. Such laws, which are found throughout the states and in most other countries, are enacted to protect consumers. But is this in consumers' interest? Borrowers want q_3, lenders offer only q_2. There is a shortage of money. Many consumers who are willing to pay 6% and more are prevented from buying the houses they want. There will probably be extra payments (such as "points" for placing the loan) which are quasi-legal devices to raise the interest rate. There will be non-price rationing, including race discrimination. Newcomers to the vicinity, without established bank accounts, will be especially hard hit. Loanable funds will be diverted away to other markets, such as corporate bonds, where no usury laws apply. Such was the case during the late 1960's when the equilibrium interest rates rose above usury limits. And predictably this caused great hardship for home buyers, for lending institutions like saving and loan associations which specialize in home mortgages and which experienced a severe loss of funds, and for those employed in the home construction industry. Would it not be better to let people pay higher interest rates, if they wish?[20]

Price Supports

A price support is a guarantee by the government to buy a product at a specified price. Suppose Fig. 2-7 refers to wheat and the government's support price is p_2. Note first that without the support, q_1 would be produced and sold to the public for p_1. There would be no surplus. But the government says to the farmers: "We guarantee you p_2. Whatever you can't sell to consumers at p_2, we'll buy." If farmers are assured of p_2, how much will they collectively produce? An infinite amount? Nonsense. The supply curve shows that at p_2, q_3 is the maximum amount farmers will want to produce. But at price p_2, how much will consumers want to buy? Answer: q_2, as the demand curve shows. If farmers produce q_3 and consumers buy q_2, the difference $q_3 - q_2$ is surplus production, which the government buys. The surplus occurs entirely because of the support price. Abolish the support, and the outcome will be p_1, q_1.

Are farmers producing more than consumers "need" when they produce q_3? In this context, "need" has no useful meaning. There *is* a price, shown by the demand curve, at which all q_3 would be bought by consumers. But farmers aren't willing to produce q_3 for that low price. There is no specific quantity that consumers "need." Their demand shows that they will buy different quantities at different prices. Of course, we "need" to eat. But, given substitute foods and the possibility of importing wheat, we don't "need" any particular quantity of American-grown wheat.

By earlier reasoning, the quantity that is appropriate is q_1, where the market-clearing price equals marginal cost. At q_3, the value of goods

---

[20] See "Would-Be Home Buyers Face Growing Difficulty in Arranging For Homes," *Wall Street Journal,* March 28, 1969. This discussion does not argue against recently passed laws which require that the true interest rate, in percent per year, be stated, so consumers know what they are paying, particularly on installment purchases of furniture, cars, and appliances, where there are different interest ceilings.

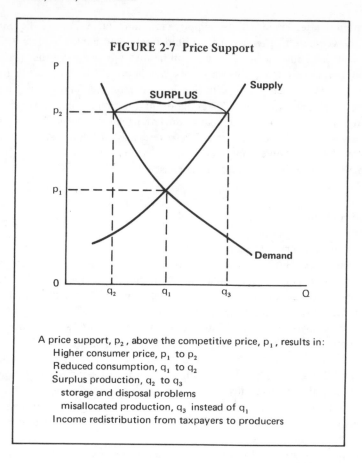

FIGURE 2-7 Price Support

A price support, p_2, above the competitive price, p_1, results in:
  Higher consumer price, p_1 to p_2
  Reduced consumption, q_1 to q_2
  Surplus production, q_2 to q_3
    storage and disposal problems
    misallocated production, q_3 instead of q_1
  Income redistribution from taxpayers to producers

sacrificed to produce the last bushel of wheat (measured by the supply curve) is greater than the value to consumers of that last bushel (measured by the demand curve).

Incidentally, what does the government do with all the surplus? It can't be sold to American consumers or the price for the q_2 that consumers do buy would be pushed down and the government would have to buy even more. So it is stored in rented silos and for many years in old World War II ships parked along the Hudson River, at costs which a few years ago came to over \$1-million a day. Or it is given away to poor countries or sold at a loss on the world market (thereby irritating other wheat-exporting nations). This is the essence of the farm support program that has existed since 1946 for most cereal grains, cotton, tobacco (yes, the government subsidizes tobacco production while it tries to convince people to stop smoking), peanuts, butter, wool, beets, honey, and sugar. Somehow, producers of fruits, vegetables, and meats, which are not so easily stored, have survived without these supports. The details do vary from crop to crop and include production quotas (which the farmers resent) and payments to take farms out of production (why not pay everyone not to produce?).

All this has been justified as help for low-income farmers. But since subsidies are based per unit of output (or per acre in the case of payments for not producing), it is the large affluent farmers, not the small ones, who have received most of the benefits. About five-eighths of all farm subsidy benefits go to the top one-fifth of farmers with annual sales over $20,000, most of this going to farms with sales over $40,000, hardly in the poverty class. The bottom 50% of all farms, with annual sales below $5000, receive only 10% of the subsidy benefits.[21] Every year for over 20 years a number of farmers, including members of Congress, have received subsidy payments in excess of $100,000, some over $1-million. Heading the list for several years has been California cotton producer J. G. Boswell, with a $4.1-million payment in 1970. The subsidy ceiling of $55,000 per farmer per crop, enacted in 1970 (a $20,000 limit was defeated in 1971) will have more effect on who in the family owns what part of the family farm than on the fact that most farm subsidies go to higher-income farmers.

While the Agriculture Department spends millions paying farmers not to farm, it also spends millions on irrigation projects to raise farm output.

---

[21] C. L. Schultze, *The Distribution of Farm Subsidy Payments: Who Gets The Benefits,* The Brookings Institution. 1971, pp 25-26.

"The Government is paying me not to plant anything this year."

Some farmers receive both payments. While it paid $2.5-million to farmers in the Texas Panhandle to encourage cotton production on land not suited to cotton, it paid millions more to California growers with favorable climate not to produce cotton. "The Salyer farm (in California) could have equalled all of the Texas county's production, with or without a subsidy. Yet the Government paid the Salyer family $942,000 to limit its cotton acreage."[22] Back in the 1950's, a *New York Times* editorial characterized America's farm policy as "Alice-in-Wonderland economics." In these changing times, isn't it reassuring that some things just go on and on?

Perhaps the politics of farm supports are worth discussing since they are so dominant. In the 1950's, President Eisenhower's efforts to phase out farm subsidies proved politically disastrous for Republican Congressmen and farm subsidies continued unabated despite Eisenhower's veto of even more generous grants enacted by a Democratic Congress. Shortly after President Kennedy's election, subsidy payments jumped 50% where they have remained for over a decade. Mr. Nixon has avoided Eisenhower's political mistake: see "Flood of Cash to Help Reelect Nixon Follows Hike in Dairy Supports," *Wall Street Journal*, Sept. 27, 1971. A month later, increased supports for feed grains were announced by the Administration. Asked if this would help Republicans in 1972, Agriculture Secretary Hardin "replied with a grin, 'Well I would hope so.' " Quoted from the *New York Times*, Oct. 19, 1971.[23]

This discussion of farm subsidies points out the consequences of having price and quantity, that is, what to produce, determined by political process

---

[22] This paragraph and the quotation are based on "Farm Policy Is Making the Rural Rich Richer," *New York Times*, April 5, 1970.

[23] The linkage between dollar voting and consumer choice may be wrenched occasionally by monopoly, misleading advertising, consumer ignorance, and fraud. But that between ballot voting and voter choice is not without its kinks either. Farm subsidies have been heavily influenced by Representative Jamie Whitten, Chairman of the House Sub-Committee on Agricultural Appropriations during five presidential administrations from Truman through Nixon. The chairman of each sub-committee of the House Appropriations Committee has immense power to give or withhold favors for individual Congressmen and thereby to enlist votes for his interests. Mr. Whitten, from rural Mississippi, supports farm subsidies. Says he: "If somebody . . . doesn't see that those who produce the food for the rest of us get a fair shake, there won't be any people to represent." What's fair? Aren't consumers sufficiently interested in eating to bid unsubsidized inputs into food production just as they do into other less essential outputs? (Quote is from an article about Mr. Whitten, *Wall Street Journal*, June 7, 1971.) The prospect: "For the foreseeable future—and I don't know the number of years—we are going to need price support programs for several of our commodities." So spoke Secretary of Agriculture Hardin in 1969. It is customary that the Congressmen on the agriculture committees and the top officials of the Agriculture Department either own large farms or were

rather than by dollar votes which reflect consumer choice. It also illustrates the political power of knowledgeable special interests over an unconcerned, economically uneducated electorate, a power which would not operate, despite economic ignorance, if farm prices and output were determined in the competitive market instead of politically. Many foreign nations, especially European, also have long histories of farmer subsidies, since agricultural interests are typically over-represented in legislatures. A similar picture of politically inspired inefficiency is given in Chapter 10 concerning rent controls in New York City and Federal import restrictions of oil.

One further ramification of farm subsidies illustrates the contagious nature of political interference with competitive markets. Because of support prices on cotton, American textile manufacturers must pay far more for American cotton (which they cannot import) than foreign manufacturers pay for American cotton. This creates a politically pursuasive case for restricting imported textiles made with American cotton. Once this is done, other producer-labor interests who would also like to avoid foreign competition say, "Why not protect us too?" And so it goes.[24]

Commodity Taxes

A commodity tax is a tax per unit (or per dollar value) of a good or service. Familiar examples are on gasoline, liquor, long distance phone calls, tickets to movies and sporting events, cigarettes, airline and train tickets, pari-mutuel betting, and electricity. There are many others; but we are not considering sales taxes which cover almost everything.

The effects are shown in Fig. 2-8. Without the tax, the price and quantity would be p_1 and q_1. Suppose the tax is the amount $(p_3 - p_2)$. In the diagrams, the tax is $1.20. If the tax is collected from the seller, his cost per unit is raised $1.20, causing the supply curve to move vertically by $1.20 to $S_{with\ tax}$. The new price paid by the consumer is now $2.40 in Fig. 2-8a or

---

employed by farm organizations. See "Who's Who in Capital's Farm Power Infrastructure," *New York Times,* April 5, 1970.

While the nation's farm population dropped from about 20 million in 1950 to 10 million in 1970, the staff of the Agriculture Department rose from 84,000 to 125,000. In Montgomery County, Md., outside Washington, while a third of the county's cropland was going to housing and industry, the county agent's staff rose about four-fold, with such new duties as counselling suburban children on puppy-training and pony care. In Abilene, Kan. county farm agents have finished teaching farmers about cover crops and now conduct programs on weight-watching, with movies like "The Oopsies," investing, air-conditioning, folk music, and famous women of Kansas.

[24] One can see why the field of economics used to be known as "political economy."

FIGURE 2-8 Commodity Tax

2-8a Buyer pays more of tax

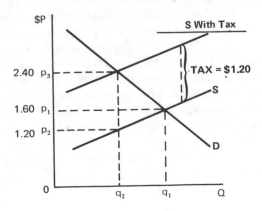

2-8b Seller pays more of tax

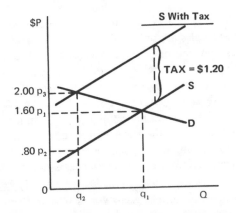

Effects of a commodity tax of $(p_3 - p_2)$:

Higher price to consumers, p_1 to p_3

Lower price to sellers, p_1 to p_2

Reduced output, q_1 to q_2, causing a misallocation of production

A special tax burden on the consumers and sellers of the taxed product

$2.00 in Fig. 2-8b. The difference between the two diagrams is in the slopes of the curves; pre-tax price and tax are the same. Concentrate for the moment on Fig. 2-8a. The price the seller has left after paying the tax is $1.20 (which only by coincidence equals the tax). In comparison with the pre-tax price, $1.60, the consumer is bearing 80¢ of the $1.20-tax, since he pays 80¢ more, and the seller is bearing 40¢, since he gets 40¢ less—even though the full tax is collected from the seller.[25]

In Fig. 2-8b, with the same starting price and tax, the consumer's price including tax rises only to $2.00, while the seller's net price after tax is only 80¢. So the burden is more on the seller. In general, the steeper the demand curve and flatter the supply, the more the burden is on the consumer, and conversely. As these slopes are not controlled deliberately by sellers or consumers, the distribution of the burden is neither a malicious conspiracy nor even a conscious effort by anyone.

As a means of gaining revenue, how do these commodity taxes compare with general sales or income taxes which do not bear on a particular good or service? In the case of gasoline taxes (and other user taxes on cars, trucks, and deisel fuel), if the proceeds are used to finance highways, the tax could be geared to make consumers of highways pay in proportion to their use of the highways. This makes some sense.

But how about taxes on liquor, cigarettes, etc., where the tax proceeds are used for the same general purposes as are sales and income tax revenue? Should consumers of the taxed items pay a larger share of the government's expenditures than do other people with the same incomes but with different consumer preferences? If so, why? Because their preferences for liquor, smoking and horse-racing are not as "nice" as those who consume less of these?

Besides taxing certain consumer tastes, commodity taxes cause a misallocation of production away from consumer choice (as expressed by dollar votes). The tax does not represent an input payment, so it cannot be counted as part of the "real" cost. At the output after tax, q_2, according to consumer choice, more should be produced (and less of other things), because the market-clearing price, p_3, is greater than the marginal cost.[26]

Where the tax is very large relative to the production cost (or supply price), serious problems of law enforcement arise, requiring expensive police efforts and often leading to corruption, disrespect for the law, and inequity in

---

[25] This division of the tax burden is unaffected if the whole tax is collected from the buyer instead of from the seller, the proof of which we leave to you.

[26] Sometimes Congress is less than candid about such taxes. In 1970 when it increased the tax on airline tickets, it prohibited, subject to fine, any airline from listing the increased tax on its tickets or in its ads. *Wall Street Journal* editorial, "The Little Things That Count," July 28, 1970.

who pays the tax. The 100%+ tax on liquor has inspired the famed moonshiners with their backwoods stills in Kentucky and Tennessee. Of more recent vintage is cigarette bootlegging. A carton of cigarettes that sells for $2.35 in North Carolina where more than half of America's cigarettes are made must sell for $1.60 more in New York City to cover the higher state and local taxes. So criminals are reaping great profits by purchasing cigarettes legally in North Carolina, then selling them illegally, but at bargin prices, to retailers in New York without paying the New York taxes, sometimes with counterfeit state tax stamps affixed.[27] In 1971, *Business Week* cited an estimate that one in five cigarettes sold in New York City was involved in an illegal transaction. Of course, most consumers still pay as much, but the state doesn't collect the tax. Such illegal sales are by no means confined to New York.

Commodity Subsidies

Commodity subsidies are payments by the government per unit bought or sold, in effect, negative commodity taxes. They have opposite effects from commodity taxes. (Some farm subsidies are of this nature.) Consider Fig. 2-9. The subsidy is $(p_3 - p_2)$, paid to the seller.[28] This acts as a negative cost and moves the supply vertically downward by the amount of the subsidy, bringing a new equilibrium. Q_2 is produced and sold to consumers for price p_2. The suppliers are willing to do this because, including the subsidy, they receive p_3, their supply price at q_2. The price-benefits can be ascribed to consumers and sellers again by comparing how much less consumers pay than if there were no subsidy, p_1 less p_2, and how much more sellers receive than without subsidy, $p_3 - p_1$. The taxpayers pay the subsidy, which would total q_2 times $p_3 - p_2$.

If commodity taxes misallocate production, do subsidies improve the allocation? No. They misallocate too. At q_2, the value of the last unit to consumers is p_2. But the real cost, which measures the value of the foregone goods to get the last unit, is p_3. So consumers would be better off if the units

---

[27] See "Organized Crime Thrives on Bootlegged Cigarettes," *New York Times,* May 9, 1971. In mid-1971, New York City imposed additional taxes of 3c and 4c on packs of high-tar cigarettes to induce consumers to smoke low-tar brands. And in 1972 the U.S. Surgeon General called for Federal adoption of such graduated cigarette taxes. Aside from problems with vending machines not geared for numerous different cigarette prices, this again poses the question about the government's role in protecting people from their presumed foolish consumer judgment.

[28] As with commodity taxes, the results are identical if the subsidy is paid to the consumer.

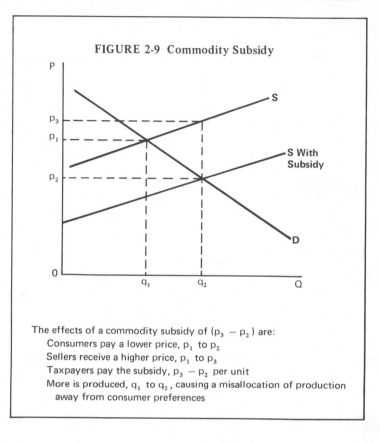

FIGURE 2-9 Commodity Subsidy

The effects of a commodity subsidy of $(p_3 - p_2)$ are:
Consumers pay a lower price, p_1 to p_2
Sellers receive a higher price, p_1 to p_3
Taxpayers pay the subsidy, $p_3 - p_2$ per unit
More is produced, q_1 to q_2, causing a misallocation of production
away from consumer preferences

from q_1 to q_2 were not produced and the resources were allocated elsewhere. Of course, "misallocate" and "better" are subject to the qualifications noted under the discussion, "Why Consumer Choice?"

Aside from farm commodities, subsidies have frequently occurred in the pricing of rail transportation, especially where a government operates a local bus or subway system, in setting postage rates, especially of second, third, and fourth class mail, and in the provision of museum, zoo, library, and national park services. And there is a growing inclination to subsidize artists, symphonies, operas, ballet, and the like. The fundamental justification for this is that consumer tastes are wrong and society, through government, should induce people to consume more of these things through subsidies (financed, of course, by taxing people—especially those who prefer naughty things like cigarettes and liquor?)[29]

---

[29] President Nixon's message on the arts of December 10, 1969, requesting that appropriations be doubled to $40-million, stated: "We would

Monopoly

Our final interference with competitive pricing is monopoly collusion. Again, the effect is production inconsistent with consumer choice. Consider Fig. 2-10. The competitive outcome would be p_1, q_1. Under monopolistic collusion, firms in the industry agree on a higher price, p_2. But, to avoid surplus production which, when sold, would drive the price down, they must restrict output to q_2. And to restrict output, they will generally divide the market amongst one another and try to prevent outsiders from entering the industry. All of these collusive arrangements regarding price, output, and entry are violations of the Federal anti-trust laws.

We shall not prove it, but in *any* competitive industry, firms would benefit from monopolizing—if we ignore the costs of maintaining the agreement and penalties for anti-trust convictions. But these costs and penalties are quite high. The misallocative effects of monopoly should be obvious. At p_2, q_2, the market-clearing price exceeds the marginal cost; so the value to consumers of more of this product is greater than the value of goods foregone to produce more.[30] In the final chapter, we return to the effects, extent, and remedies for monopoly. The curious are welcome to read ahead.

Another fault of monopoly besides missallocation of productive efforts is that, to sustain the output restriction, infringements of producer, consumer, and investment freedom are often required. Such limitations are frequently imposed by government. As already noted, the ICC restricts entry

---

be able to bring more productions in music, theater, literature, readings, and dance to millions of citizens *eager* to have the opportunity for such experiences. . . . We would be able to . . . support hard-pressed cultural institutions, such as museums, symphony orchestras, to meet the demands of new and *expanding audiences*." (Emphasis added.) If consumers are so eager and the audiences so expanding, why are subsidies needed? The $40-million was appropriated, but in 1971 the chairman of the newly formed Partnership for the Arts opened a campaign for a $200-million appropriation, pointing to higher per capita arts subsidies in other nations. (*New York Times*, Jan. 6, 1971). A *Times* article of July 29, 1971 noted the virtual absence of Congressional resistance to subsidies for arts and humanities. The demand for such subsidies is limitless, of course. America has 1100 symphony orchestras, many with expensive new halls, powerful labor unions, and long seasons. The big five each give about 200 concerts annually, compared with 20 by the Vienna Philharmonic. All this is in addition to the public's access to inexpensive records, tapes, and FM programming.

In a similar vein, a *Times* reader, lamenting the demise of *Look* magazine, called for Federal subsidies of periodicals to be financed by taxing television broadcasters. What does all this imply about consumer choice?

[30] The diagram refers to an *industry* with monopolistic collusion. The effect of monopoly in *one company* is essentially the same—lower output and a higher price than under competition.

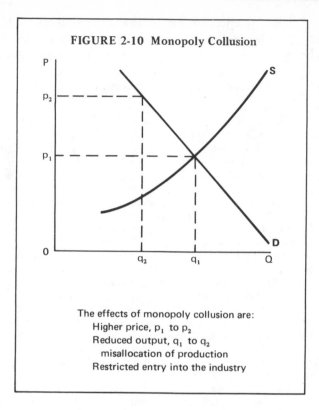

FIGURE 2-10 Monopoly Collusion

The effects of monopoly collusion are:
Higher price, p_1 to p_2
Reduced output, q_1 to q_2
    misallocation of production
Restricted entry into the industry

into the trucking industry, encourages trucking companies to collude in setting prices, and prevents railroads from competitive price cutting which would offend trucking (or barge) interests. The Interior Department sets quotas limiting oil imports, while state governments where oil is extracted restrict domestic oil production in order to keep prices above the competitive level.[31] Monopoly-like restrictions of consumer freedom also result from import tariffs which reduce imports and lead to higher prices.

It is interesting to compare monopoly, Fig. 2-10, with price supports, Fig. 2-7. What is the main difference? With price supports, the farmer not

---

[31] Testimony before Congress in January 1972 estimated that Federal oil import restrictions were costing the average American family about $100 annually in higher prices of gasoline and home fuel, a national total of some $5-billion a year. (*New York Times*, Jan. 11, 1972.) This is another example of a special interest policy with high benefits to a few and a small cost to many.

While the average American consumer can do little about higher oil prices, American producers of petrochemicals (which go into paint, plastics and other items) are talking of opening plants abroad so they can buy oil and

only gets a monopoly price, but can produce all he wants and sell it to the government. It's a better deal than any private monopoly could bring about. If monopoly is a crime if created by chemical, steel, or electrical equipment manufacturers, why is it public policy to bring it about in farm production, which without government action would be highly competitive?[32]

---

natural gas cheaper to compete with Japanese and European companies (whose oil costs are much lower than theirs). Interference with competitive pricing can have broad consequences. America's oil import quota program is discussed at some length in Chapter 10 under government by law.

[32] Another commodity where government promotes monopoly prices is milk. In 13 states (it used to be 32), it is a crime to sell milk below legal limits. In 1971, people paid $1.21 a gallon in Pennsylvania while across the border in Ohio milk sold for $1.02. (*Wall Street Journal*, May 24, 1971.) In spite of the law, intended to benefit dairy farmers, many store chains and coöps frequently receive illegal rebates and discounts and interest free loans from dairies competing for business, in effect lowering the price of milk illegally. New Jersey won't even allow S&H Green Stamps given for milk purchases, lest this constitute illegal price shading. So milk must be totaled separately at the checkout counter. In support of higher milk prices, one Congressman said in 1966, "Farmers are going out of dairying at a startling rate. We will find ourselves with an even greater shortage of milk unless something isn't done to make dairying more attractice." (*New York Times*, Nov. 18, 1966.) If there is a shortage, consumers will bid up the price, so why does the government need to hold it up? But if there's a surplus, what's wrong with an exodus from dairying?

If the Congressman needs a course in economics, he's not alone. In 1968, George Wallace's agriculture platform promised "to rely heavily on a competitive market structure rather than on prices administered or fixed by bureaucratic procedures." This, the platform explained, meant raising price supports about 30% to 50% above their prevailing levels.

In 1967, a Michigan dairy farmer wrote a plaintive letter to Ann Landers about his cows' unhappiness with low milk prices. Miss Landers got Agriculture Secretary Orville Freeman to reply: "Please don't give up. Tell this to your cows too." He promised to raise milk prices so more farmers would want to produce more milk. But what would more milk do to milk prices without laws preventing the prices from falling? And with such laws, who would buy the milk?

One more from the food area. U.S. Government advice and finance helped develop a thriving tomato industry in Mexico, much for export to America. But in 1969, the Florida Tomato Committee, a private grower group using authority granted by the Department of Agriculture, ruled that tomatoes picked *green* must be at least $2\frac{9}{32}$ inches in diameter, while those picked *ripe* from the vine had to be at least $2\frac{17}{32}$ inches in diameter. Although consumers prefer the tastier vine-ripened fruit, this ruling barred 30% to 50% of the smaller, vine-ripened Mexican crop, but affected only 15% to 20% of the Florida crop, more of which is picked green. Predictably, tomato prices rose sharply from the decreased supply, tons of Mexican tomatoes rotted, and America was roundly berated for bullying poor Latin American farmers. "Curbs on Tomatoes From Mexico Cause U.S. Prices to Rise," *Wall Street Journal*, March, 4, 1969.

In conclusion, why are there interferences with competitive prices and output? They derive from a combination of four sources: (1) the advantages to producers (including workers) of suppressing competition and freedom to get more income for themselves (true of monopoly and price supports); (2) inefficient pursuit by government of worthwhile objectives (price ceilings to curb inflation, commodity taxes to gain revenue, anti-scalping and usury laws to protect consumers); (3) deliberate efforts to redirect production away from that determined by consumer choice, on the grounds that consumer choice is wrong (commodity taxes and subsidies); (4) public ignorance of the existence and/or effects of such interference.

The Invisible Hand

It is widely recognized that if an individual pursued his own self-interest without any social restraint, he might harm others. To provide order, tranquility, and justice, society prohibits individuals from coercing others and from damaging others' persons or property.

Suppose then we assume that appropriate laws are enforced against violence, fraud, and contract violation. It has been asserted that under these conditions, if individuals do pursue their self-interest, as they will generally do if free, they will unintentionally serve the general interest of society, that there is not a conflict between pursuit of self-interest and the legitimate collective ends of society. In his famous work *The Wealth of Nations*, published in 1776, Adam Smith said that individuals, pursuing their own interests, were guided by an "invisible hand" to promote the welfare of others. The invisible hand is the price and profit system. This claim, applied mainly to economic activities—buying, selling, hiring, renting, lending, investing, and organizing businesses—has been a major argument for a "laissez faire" political philosophy, that government need not and should not interfere with economic activities.[33]

---

[33] In Smith's words: "As every individual . . . by directing that industry in such a manner as its produce may be of greatest value, he intends only his own gain, and he is in this, as in many other cases, led by an invisible hand to promote an end which was no part of his intention. . . . By pursuing his own interest he frequently promotes that of society more effectually than when he really intends to promote it. I have never known much good done by those who affected to trade for the public good.

". . . The statesman. who should attempt to direct private people in what manner they ought to employ their capitals, would not only load himself with a most unnecessary attention, but assume an authority which could safely be entrusted, not only to no single person, but to no council or senate whatever, and which would nowhere be so dangerous as in the hands of a man who had folly and presumption enough to fancy himself fit to exercise it." *The Wealth of Nations*, Book IV, Chapter II.

It is beyond the scope of this book to develop fully the arguments for and against such a philosophy. However, at several places, we shall point out where this invisible hand is said to operate. The most important qualification, besides laws against fraud and violence, is that there be adequate competition. Other qualifications also apply, some involving questions of fact (such as whether economic instability is inherent in private enterprise), others questions of value (such as whether government should try to improve the morals or tastes of people). Another qualification to the invisible hand idea (that self-interest serves the general interest) arises when the production of a product imposes costs, like air and water pollution, which are not automatically included in the consumer's price. All these points are taken up in Chapter 12. Indeed, while we don't generally recommend reading the end of a book before the rest, this might be appropriate here, so one is continually aware of the possible qualifications to the favorable picture of private enterprise described along the way.

The invisible hand is well illustrated from our discussion of what to produce. First we saw that it is desirable that prices and output be such that market-clearing price equals marginal cost. Then we found that when sellers seek profits, charging prices as high as possible, given the competition of other sellers, and when buyers seek goods they prefer, paying no more than they have to, given the competition of other buyers, that such pursuit of self-interest leads to *the* prices and outputs which are in the general interest.[34] Moreover, any outside interference with these prices and outputs conflicts with the general consumer interest. But is consumer interest the main end? In the next chapter, we consider whether worker and investor claims may justify altering what to produce.

Summary

Under private enterprise, consumer choice is the primary determinant of what to produce. Of the three groups, input owners, input organizers, and consumers, only consumers care much what is produced.

---

[34] As an example of the irrelevancy of personal motives (from society's standpoint), consider John Hallowell, whose engineering company in Dearborn, Michigan suffered a severe decline in business when auto companies cut back on model changes. Seeking other income, he developed a huge vacuum cleaner for clearing litter from parks and freeways. Many months' work were required to work out technical bugs, like trash floating against the blower's screen and blocking the vacuum. This $1500 to $2000 cleaner represents quite an advancement from the known alternatives—a man with a stick or a $50,000-machine. Mr. Hallowell denies being motivated by the environment movement: "I'm not trying to save the country. I'm just trying to make a buck." Does it matter? (*New York Times*, April 18, 1971.)

Prices and profits act as signals which direct input organizers to produce what consumers desire.

Consumer choice leads to both high and low quality output, according to what people are willing to pay for.

Individual freedom implies that production is based on consumer choice.

Consumer-directed production is criticized because of unfair income distribution; failure to account for public goods, collective goals, and neighborhood costs; poor consumer knowledge; and assertions that some consumer tastes are immoral, vulgar, and foolish.

The relevant measure of profits is not profits per dollar of sales, but profits per dollar of investment. Since the investment required to get a dollar of sales varies from one activity to another, when P/I is equal among various industries and companies, there will be differences in P/S. The investment per dollar of sales varies among industries because of differences among industries in inventory turnover, value added relative to sales (how much the companies do to the material they buy), and in the relative contributions of labor and capital to production.

If all consumers are to have equal freedom to spend as they wish, including the right to compete for the available output, the price of each good and service must be at the market-clearing level, that price at which the available quantity and no more can just be sold.

If the price is below the market-clearing level, non-price rationing will be required to determine who will get the available quantity.

The two rules, that price be at the market-clearing level and that output be where the market-clearing price equals the marginal production cost, determine for each good and service *the* price and output most consistent with consumer preference, as expressed by how consumers spend.

This conclusion is derived from these two points: (1) the market-clearing price measures the value to consumers of a given item, and (2) the marginal cost measures the real cost—the value to consumers of what else could have been produced instead of the given item.

Under competitive private enterprise, with prices determined by demand and supply, price and output *will* be the ideal just described.

Price ceilings below equilibrium cause shortages and lead to non-price rationing.

Rent controls, laws against ticket scalping, and usury laws are examples of price ceilings.

Price supports above equilibrium result in surplus production.

Most farm price supports have been paid to relatively high-income farmers.

Commodity taxes cause output to decline, price to rise, and sellers to receive less after paying the tax. The relative effects on buyer and seller depend on the slopes of demand and supply curves.

Commodity taxes cause output to differ from consumer choice and make tax payments depend on consumer preference.

Commodity subsidies lead to increased output of the subsidized product, lower consumer price, higher revenue to sellers, and a different output than consumer choice would indicate.

Monopoly collusion results in reduced output of the monopolized product, higher prices, and usually some restriction in freedom in order to keep outsiders from entering the industry. The reduced output is inconsistent with consumer preference.

The "invisible hand" refers to an alleged tendency for unregulated pursuit of self-interest to be consistent with the general welfare of society.

Study Questions Chapter 2

1. Who determines what to produce?

2. Explain the intermediary role of businessmen. Intermediary between what other two groups?

3. What are the relevant motives of each group?

4. How can an alleged indifference of businessmen about what to produce be reconciled with widespread advertising?

5. Even though some nonhuman inputs can be used to produce only one product, businesses are continually in a position to decide between producing one product or another. Explain.*

6. Explain the roles of prices and profits in determining what to produce by describing the adjustment following a change in consumer tastes.

7. Explain how the answer to #6 differs if producers have perfectly forecast the change in tastes, if they overestimate the change; if they underestimate it.

8. Does production based on consumer choice always mean the best quality products will be made? Explain.

9. Why should output be based on consumer choice?

10. Why is freedom desirable?

11. Explain what is meant by a pragmatic answer? A religious answer?

12. What are objections to consumer-directed production?

---

*Starred questions are answered briefly below.

13. Explain why allegations of unfair income distribution, neighborhood costs, and consumer ignorance are not really objections to consumer-directed output.

14. What are three bases for objecting to people's tastes?

15. Discuss reasons for and against allowing people freedom to act on "wrong" tastes.

16. If profits, sales, and investment are respectively 300, 10,000, and 2400, compute the numerical values in the equation $P/S = (I/S)(P/I)$.*

17. What is the percent of profit per dollar of sales? The percentage return on investment? The investment required per dollar of sales?*

18. In terms of profitability, which in Table 2-1 would this be better than? Worse than? Same for Table 2-2*

19. Explain why P/S is not a relevant measure of profitability.

20. In equilibrium among industries, what becomes equal—prices, profits, wages, investment, profit margins, returns to investment?*

21. Explain why I/S varies among industries—three reasons. So what?*

22. Define "market-clearing price."

23. Show the market-clearing price on a demand curve.

24. Why should price be at the market-clearing level?

25. What is "price rationing?"

26. What is "non-price rationing?" What forms does it take? What causes it to arise?

27. What does the market-clearing price measure?*

28. Define "marginal production cost" or MC.

29. Explain the term "real cost."

30. Justify by reasoning why MC measures the real cost of production.

31. Show with a diagram how the difference between the market-clearing price and marginal cost varies as output varies.

32. Explain with reference to a diagram why output should be at that quantity where market-clearing price equals marginal cost. (Explain why output should be neither more nor less than this quantity.)

33. At times the market-clearing price for a given quantity has been viewed as the value of the *last* unit purchased, at other times as the value of the *next* unit, even though the price must fall to sell another unit. Similarly, MC has been viewed as the cost of producing either the *last* unit or *another* unit. Is there any inconsistency in this?*

34. What critical and debatable assumptions underlie the conclusion that output "should" be at this quantity?

35. With reference to a diagram, explain why, under competitive conditions, output will be at this level. (Explain why price would be neither above nor below equilibrium.)

36. Explain what would happen if price were above equilibrium, then what would happen if price were below equilibrium, showing why in either case price would move toward the equilibrium.

37. What is meant by equilibrium?

38. What is a price ceiling?

39. What is its main effect?

40. Why is the resulting quantity inconsistent with consumer choice? Explain.

41. Draw a diagram which shows the effects of a price ceiling.

42. What is the effect of laws against ticket scalping?

43. Consider arguments for and against such laws.

44. Explain the effects of a price ceiling above equilibrium.

45. What are usury laws?

46. Show their effects with a diagram.

47. Who benefits and who is harmed by usury laws?

48. What is a price support?

49. Show with a diagram the effects of a price support.

50. On Fig. 2-7, if P_1 is $2.00, roughly what is the price at which consumers would purchase the full amount that farmers would produce at the support price, P_2?*

51. Does a price support cause more to be produced than consumers need? Explain.

52. What is amiss with the quantity produced under price supports?

53. Why can't the government sell surplus farm products to American consumers?

54. If farm price supports were abolished, would there be a shortage of food in America? Explain.

55. Show with a diagram the effects of a commodity tax.

56. Explain who bears the burden of this tax.

57. How does the burden vary with the slopes of demand and supply?

58. What are arguments for and against commodity taxes as a means of raising revenue?

59. Explain why a commodity tax is said to cause a misallocation of production.

60. What special law enforcement problems arise when commodity taxes are very large relative to production cost?

61. Show with a diagram the effects of a commodity subsidy. Who benefits?

62. From the diagram, explain why a subsidy causes "incorrect" production.

63. Evaluate the case for and against subsidies of the arts.

64. Using a diagram, show the consequences of monopoly collusion.

65. What is critical to the success of monopoly collusion?*

66. Explain from the diagram why monopoly causes "incorrect" production.

67. Compare monopoly with farm price supports.

68. Explain the meaning of Adam Smith's "invisible hand."

69. What are the qualifications or conditions under which the invisible hand process works for society's benefit?

Answers to starred questions.

5. Much nonhuman equipment wears out within 5 to 10 years and decisions must be made whether to replace depreciating equipment or whether to invest depreciation funds and profits in other activities.

16. $\dfrac{300}{10,000} = \dfrac{2400}{10,000} \times \dfrac{300}{2400}$, or .03 = .24 × .125, or 3% = 24% × 12½%.

17. 3%, 12½%, and 24¢.

"I know just what you mean. While you were circling up there waiting to land, I was driving around and around down here looking for a place to park."

18. Better than all but G in Table 1 and 3 and 5 in Table 2.

20. Returns to investment.

21. It is the variability of I/S that explains why P/S is not an indicator of P/I.

27. The value to consumers of another unit of the item.

33. Not really. If the output of a whole industry is in the thousands or millions, a movement of one unit does not perceptibly affect the price or cost, even though the demand and supply curves do slope downward and upward respectively. Those familiar with calculus may recognize that the ambiguity arises partly because we have discussed in finite terms what is actually a derivative and does not involve a movement along the curve: marginal cost is actually d(total cost)/d(output), where the equation differentiated, is how cost varies with output.

50. $1. At support price P_2, farmers produce Q_3. The price on the demand curve which corresponds to Q_3 appears to be about half as high as P_1, which was assumed to be $2.

65. Restriction of output to avoid surplus production.

3
What To Produce, Continued

Are Price And Profit Guides Necessary For Determining What To Produce?

We have discussed how what to produce is determined in a competitive private enterprise system. Clearly this is not the only conceivable arrangement for making this basic economic decision. But if private enterprise is to prevail, prices and profits *are* indispensable. After all, a price is simply the terms on which one thing (say money) is traded for another (a good or service). To abolish prices then means either to outlaw all voluntary trades or to ban the use of any one item as a medium of exchange (in terms of which other things are valued), i.e., to outlaw the use of money, leaving a pure barter economy. As explained in Chapter 9, this abolition of money would also cause most trading to cease. Without trades, but with each family trying to be self-sufficient, living standards would soon decline to the caveman level. So prices are necessary.

If we allow prices but not profits, then no one would have incentive to create, own, and organize nonhuman inputs; so again the unregulated economy would collapse. And even if people were somehow willing and anxious to create, own, and organize nonhuman inputs without profit—just to serve mankind—they would be unable to determine what consumers preferred without the guide of profits to spur production here and of losses to curb production there.

Thus, the necessity of prices and profits in an unregulated economy is quite obvious. Their role was indicated in Chapter 2 and will be explained further below.

Prices And Profits In A Regulated Economy

Suppose the government were going to determine what to produce. Would prices and profits be necessary then? Let us assume initially that the government wants to base production on consumer choice. Couldn't the officials run on political platforms stating what they will choose to produce if elected? Or couldn't the government estimate consumer choice by questionnaires or from a statistical breakdown of the population by age, sex, family size?

Counting people and "needs" to determine what to produce. Suppose, without using prices, the government makes a list of all the things people need and want, arranging items from more to less important. (How could they determine relative importance?) Given X men with foot-size 11, produce X size-11 pairs of shoes per year. And so on. The trouble is that everyone doesn't want or need the same number of shoes per year. Some walk a lot; others ride. Some people would rather repair their old shoes or buy second-hand shoes and spend their money on something else. Others want several styles of shoes and don't value other things so highly.

Or take food. There are great variations in tastes and "needs," so again you can't count mouths to determine what to produce, *if* you want the outcome to satisfy consumer choice as much as possible. Furthermore, after leaving "necessities," the variations in tastes and ability to pay are even more important. How many lodges on Wisconsin lakes should be build? Without a price system to determine the cost and how many people are willing to pay this cost, how could one tell?

It might be suggested that the government could ascertain consumer choices by noting which goods moved off the shelves and which did not. But if goods have no prices (are distributed free), nearly anything the government produced would appear wanted and move from the shelves. There would still be no basis for deciding how much of various things to produce or when the relative quantities of outputs should be changed. The same would be true if prices were all quite "low"—below market-clearing levels. And if prices were "high," people could not afford much, but this would not tell anything about what they prefer.

Dollar votes or political votes. When you spend money for a particular item, you are in effect voting to have inputs employed to produce that item, even though in most cases producers have (they hope) anticipated your vote, so the item is available when you want to buy it. Is it not just as much an expression of consumer or popular choice when legislators, elected by the people, make a decision as to what to produce? And if what to produce were determined entirely by an elected government without reference to consumer choice *as shown by* prices and profits, could it not be said that whatever they produce represents the preferences of the population, since the population elected the government? In what sense are the choices via dollar votes (consumer spending), either under private enterprise *or* socialism, preferable to the choices via political votes?

To answer this question, one must make some assumption about the appropriate distribution of income (and of political votes). Assume we have an acceptable or fair distribution of income (brought about, if necessary, by government redistribution policies). If this distribution is acceptable, then the determination of what to produce by dollar votes has the advantage that each person's vote is proportional to the amount of money he has (and spends). The political vote could also be made proportional to wealth or income, but it is not and perhaps should not be, because of the advantage this would give to wealthier people in setting government policy on matters other than what to produce. Thus, if we accept one-man-one-vote for political candidates and also accept an unequal distribution of income as fair, then elected political officials, in representing the views of those who elected them, would not represent the consumption preferences of those with far above average dollar votes.

The major drawback of political votes to determine what to produce is the practical impossibility for each voter's consumption preferences to be identified with him and assimilated by an elected official or group—unless the government uses dollar votes. The ballot cannot list separately all of the alternatives from which the consumer might like to choose, and indeed typically it lists none. The voter must generally select a candidate with whom he agrees on some things and disagrees on others. Thus, the voter never registers his preference on most specific issues. Through dollar voting, however, the consumer votes continuously on all "issues" (re what to produce) by how he spends and does not spend. Dollar voting, in political language, resembles a continuous referendum on what to produce.[1] But even ballot referenda to determine what to produce would be inferior to dollar voting, because, to vote sensibly, the individual must know how much of one good or service he must sacrifice in order to obtain how much of another; that is, he must know prices to decide intelligently. But without dollar voting the relevant prices could not be determined in advance of the political ballot vote.

In sum, the advantages of dollar voting over ballot voting to determine what to produce are: (1) dollar voting allows the outcome to reflect differences in income distribution; (2) each individual can vote specifically on the items, styles, and varieties of his choice rather than for a candidate who stands for a collection of things; (3) the individual can vote continuously, so that changes in preferences are registered, whereas under infrequent political

---

[1] Indeed, with computers and modern transportation, there is no technological reason why many political issues decided now by legislators could not be decided by direct referenda. Farm subsidies might fare differently under direct referenda than by Congressional votes.

ballots, if he could express his preferences at all, he must articulate and predict these preferences over an extended period; (4) no central organization has the impossible task of assembling and acting upon the totality of all preferences. Thus, political officials cannot know or act upon the specific and individual consumer preferences of the people they represent and thus dollar voting is superior to political voting for determining what to produce. This discussion has little to do with whether the economic system should be capitalist or socialist, but reinforces the importance of prices and profits determined by dollar votes under either system.

While most production in America *is* determined by dollar votes, there is a growing tendency for elected legislators to make decisions about what to produce. Of course, the government determines the size of military expenditures. But it also determines the quantity of many other goods and services: museums, parks, recreation facilities, housing, medical expenditures, religious activities (by exempting religious institutions from taxation), radio and TV programs (by setting program content requirements for licenses and limiting entry), education expenditures, and many others. The preceding reasoning suggests that either government should reduce its role in determining what to produce because it cannot judge consumer tastes as well as the private market does, or, if the government is going to operate a project (public park or dam or museum), it should charge market-clearing prices and set output to cover marginal cost. But in some cases there are sound reasons for not doing this—considered in the last two chapters.

"Either you come up with some better campaign promises or you'll be back where you were, writing used-car ads."

For an example of political decision-making about what to produce, consider the supersonic transport (SST). By Spring 1971, the Federal government had spent nearly $1-billion for research and development for this plane, to be used for private commercial flights. How many voters were conscious of this issue when they cast votes for Congressmen or President? Likely noise and air pollution made this a doubtful venture to start with. Aside from that, if consumer demand justified the SST, why would government funds be necessary? And if it did not seem profitable without subsidy, why produce it? Despite intense pressure from the Nixon Administration and others, in 1971 Congress narrowly rejected additional billions to finance the SST. After one defeat, however, the project seemed slated for revival when the question of aiding financially troubled Lockheed arose, though Lockheed was not associated with the SST (whose prime contractor was Boeing). On the second SST vote, one Congressman from a Georgia district with a Lockheed plant stated on TV that he shifted his vote from against to for SST funds after being promised that in return others would vote to aid Lockheed. The merits of the SST had nothing to do with his second vote. (The Lockheed aid is discussed below, fn. 14.)

The interests of producers (meaning investors and workers) often override consumer interest when what to produce is determined politically, though the SST's defeat did match consumer choice. When profits and jobs are lost because *consumer dollars* go elsewhere, little is done to prevent the adjustment. The producer interests have no one to blame. But when the decision to cut back is to be made by the government, then producer interests put blame and pressure on elected officials to, in effect, veto the choice of consumers. Producer interests are usually vocal and organized, consumer interests diffused and unorganized, there being a large impact per investor and worker and a small impact per consumer or voter. Add to this, consumer ignorance of the issues, and the winning political strategy is usually to favor the producer interests. The SST probably lost because of the environmental issue, though by consumer preference it should have lost anyway and should never have been a governmental concern at all (except to require pollution and noise control).

This discussion may seem to reverse completely our earlier contention that only consumers, not investors or workers, care what is produced. In the SST case, producers simply wanted to maintain their incomes (profits and jobs), whether by producing the SST or something else was secondary. In a short run view (not allowing for time to adjust to a different product), producer interests do relate to particular products. But in the long run or prior to any fixed investment or job situation, only consumers care what is produced. And regardless of their short run concern, producer interests will be dominated by consumer interests if dollar votes are allowed to determine wages and profits.

When we started this discussion of the political determination of what to produce, we assumed the elected officials wanted to base production on consumer choice. Suppose instead the government, perhaps a benevolent dictator, feels it knows better than consumers what ought to be produced. Would prices be necessary then? Yes. Presumably the government has priorities and wants more than can be produced—the basic economic problem still exists. To meet its objectives as much as possible, the government would still need prices and profits, at least for accounting purposes. Output prices would still show how much of one thing is worth how much of another (to the government, if not to consumers).

Profits Under Socialism

Why should a socialist enterprise, owned and operated by the government, earn profits? Couldn't the government, acting for society, pay inputs enough to develop and operate the enterprise, without earning profits? Yes. And if so, couldn't prices then be lower than under private enterprise, where the price includes the owners' profits as well as their costs for labor, materials. and fuel? Again, yes. Then what useful purpose would profits play? The answer, as we shall explain, is that unless competitive profits are included in product prices, the government will be unable to determine the output consistent with consumer choice and prices will be below market-clearing levels, thereby requiring non-price rationing.

It is a fact of economic life that nonhuman inputs (floorspace, machinery, desks, etc.) do contribute to producing the final output, just as does labor. (In subsequent chapters, we explain how to identify the separate contributions to output of each input.) It is also a fact that nonhuman inputs can, like labor, be shifted from one output to another (especially in the "longer run" to which our discussion applies, when a choice is made between using $X to create capital in one industry or another). Therefore, the "real cost" of producing output A is the non-A which both the human *and* nonhuman inputs could have produced elsewhere. So, if price is to equal real cost, it must cover not just the labor cost but also the value the capital or nonhuman inputs could have produced elsewhere. But this value *is* the competitive return to investment or competitive profits.

To understand what is meant by "real cost must include profits," consider the following. Remember, inputs are paid what they could earn elsewhere and elsewhere they would earn their value contributed to production (as explained in Chapter 6).

Marginal Cost of Producing Another X
If Output is 100,000 Per Year

Labor expense	$2.00	equals the value the labor could have earned and contributed if employed elsewhere
Materials, fuel	1.00	equals the value these items would have in alternative uses
Depreciation	.10	equals the gross (or, without depreciation, net) value the nonhuman inputs could have earned and contributed if employed elsewhere
Profits	.30	
	$3.40	

The real cost of producing the marginal unit of X is $3.40-worth of non-X, the value these inputs could produce elsewhere. A price of $3.40 would give the enterprise a profit on this item of 30¢. (Depreciation is considered an expense, not part of profit.) Thus, as long as capital contributes to production, a price which equals real cost will include a profit.

Now to demonstrate the necessity of profits under socialism, we must show why a price like $3.00, covering only labor and materials, will probably cause the government to select the "wrong" outputs, while a price of $3.40, including profits, would bring about the "correct" output—judging by consumer dollar votes.

For this, please refer to Fig. 3-1. Fig. 3-1a refers to a "capital intensive" product, where capital does most of the producing, such as petroleum refining. Figure 3-1b applies to a labor-intensive output where labor does most of the producing, hotel services. Demand has the same meaning as in previous diagrams. $MC_{capital\ and\ labor}$ is what was simply MC or S in previous diagrams. The new line is $MC_{labor\ only}$. The vertical distance between $MC_{labor\ only}$ and $MC_{capital\ and\ labor}$ is the marginal capital cost (which could be $MC_{capital\ only}$). That distance is relatively greater in petroleum than hotel service because capital is more significant in petroleum refining than in hotels.

For reasons explained in Chapter 2, the "correct" output is q_1 in each product. This is true regardless of whether p_1 is the price charged. Now let us assume these are socialist industries. The government follows Karl Marx's "labor theory of value" which claims that labor creates all value and that prices should be based on this labor value. This means that in petroleum, at

FIGURE 3-1 Pricing and Output Under Socialism Without Profits

3-1a Petroleum, where capital
does most of the producing

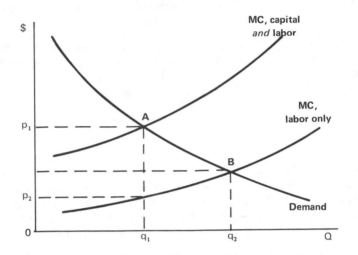

3-1b Hotel services, where labor
does most of the producing

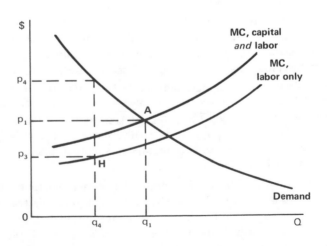

output q_1, the price would be p_2, covering labor cost only.[2] Clearly, if q_1 is produced and p_2 is the price, the quantity demanded is greater than q_1. There will be a shortage, requiring non-price rationing.

But the socialist's problem is more serious. How would the government know to produce q_1 in the first place? You may say they can see it from the diagram. But no. No one knows these diagrams under either socialism or private enterprise. We can be sure there is a downward sloping demand for petroleum and some marginal cost curve. Estimates could be made for small portions of these curves. But if market-clearing prices—*on* the demand curve—are never charged, no one would have any idea what the demand curve was and, therefore, there would be no way to determine q_1, the correct output.

Why wouldn't the socialist government expand every output beyond q_1 to where $MC_{labor\ only}$ intersects demand and charge the market-clearing price at that quantity, point B in Fig. 3-1a? Because with q_1 produced in each industry, there is full employment of resources. For every unit produced beyond q_1 in any one industry, resources must be moved out of another industry. That's the essence of a "real" cost. So if one industry expands beyond q_1, some other(s) must produce less than q_1. And the "wrong" outputs are produced in both cases.

So what *would* the socialists do? One can't be sure. Most socialist governments are not democracies which try to produce what dollar votes would suggest anyway. But suppose they were. Assume they follow the labor theory and set the price on the $MC_{labor\ only}$ curve. In capital intensive industries like petroleum, Fig. 3-1a, if q_1 were produced, the price p_2 would be much further below the market-clearing level than the corresponding price at q_1 in labor intensive industries, Fig. 3-1b. So there would be greater consumer pressure for more output in capital intensive industries than in labor intensive, there being shortages in either case. Quite likely then the socialists would expand output in 3-1a. But this means withdrawing inputs from elsewhere, 3-1b. This might lead to outputs such as q_2 in Fig. 3-1a and q_4 in Fig. 3-1b. In neither industry does this conform to consumer choice. At q_2 in petroleum, the real cost, measured by $MC_{labor\ and\ capital}$, of all units past q_1 is greater than the value to consumers of the added output. And at q_4 in Fig. 3-1b, more should be produced because the value to consumers of additional units would be greater than the value of what is given up. Thus, to locate and produce at q_1, the "correct" output based on consumer choice, the socialists must charge the market-clearing price, and that means the same price, p_1, that would be charged, under competitive private enterprise, which price includes a profit equal to capital's contribution to production.

---

[2] For brevity, materials and fuel are not in the diagram. Since socialist prices have usually covered these, you may assume they are included in "labor cost."

This reasoning is a bit involved. So, once again, why must prices under socialism be such that profits are earned if output is to conform to consumer choice? (Try to visualize the appropriate diagram with each statement.)

(1) Output should be at that quantity, q_1, where market-clearing price equals real marginal cost (labor *and* capital).

(2) Unless market-clearing prices are charged, the government probably could not ascertain what output this would be for each industry.

(3a) If prices are set to cover labor cost but not real capital cost, then prices must be below market-clearing levels, because it is physically impossible for all industries to produce quantities (like B in Fig. 3-1a) where labor-cost-only equals demand.

(3b) If prices equal labor-cost-only and are below market-clearing levels, then shortages will be greatest in capital intensive industries, creating political pressure to produce "too much" of these outputs and "too little" of others, the government having no way of knowing what the "correct" output, q_1, is for each industry.

(4) If the quantities produced *are* at the "correct" levels (based on consumer choice), and if market-clearing prices *are* charged, then the enterprises *will earn* the competitive profits of private enterprise, since price will cover not only the labor cost but also capital's net contribution plus depreciation.[3]

At an initial changeover from private enterprise to socialism, the government might have an indication of correct output, although, at any given time, output is moving *toward* but is not *at* equilibrium, so even prevailing output is not a reliable guide. However, after a few months, changes in demand (shifts in the curves) and changes in technology (causing shifts in the marginal cost curves) would require other rates of output. Thus a new set of prices and profits would be needed to ascertain correct outputs.

Another advantage of a profit system is that the individuals who make the immediate decisions about what and how to produce are *residual income recipients*. This means as owners they receive whatever money is left after paying contractual expenses. Therefore, they have incentive to seek higher

---

[3] For decades, postage rates on third and fourth class mail, while presumably not based on a labor theory of value, have been set below cost, the loss made up from Federal tax revenues. The result is that postal services are produced and sold at a point similar to B in Fig. 3-1a. (The postal authority which began in July 1971 is supposed to eliminate this.) Another item priced below cost is water in cities, especially where residents are not charged according to how much they use. Consumers have little incentive to economize on water use.

As we shall see, profits are also necessary under socialism to determine "how to produce" sensibly, as well as to determine "what to produce."

profits and to avoid low profits or losses. Under socialism, where all enterprises are government-owned, even if profits are earned by charging labor and capital costs, these profits usually go to the government rather than to the individuals in charge of the enterprises. Therefore, no one in an enterprise has incentive to improve products and cut costs. (At least not a selfish interest.) Indeed, the tendency in socialist firms is to avoid new and risky products with chances of failure and to avoid offending workers by introducing technological change. With such a don't-rock-the-boat attitude, one might say that socialism breeds conservatism! The result is inefficiency and lack of product innovation.

For this very reason, in order that those directly involved have incentive to serve consumers better, Russia and several other Communist countries have been experimenting with arrangements whereby workers and/or managements get more pay if their enterprises make more profits. By introducing a profit system, letting prices be set by the individual firms, by giving enterprises more autonomy from central planners, by allowing enterprises to compete with each other for inputs and for customers, by taking account of capital costs as well as of labor costs, and by having managers' and workers' incomes vary with enterprise profits, socialists are recognizing not only the necessity of *a* pricing system, but also the superiority of prices determined by competitive market forces (though "revisionism" hasn't progressed to where they would put it quite this way).[4]

---

[4] The positive attitude toward prices and profits in Communist countries can be seen from the following items:
"Soviet Profit Plan Seeks to Spur Efficiency"
New York Times headline, Oct. 20, 1962
"Soviet Economist Renews Drive for Profit Plan"
New York Times headline, Sept. 21, 1964
In 1962, Soviet economist Y. G. Liberman proposed a profit system to promote efficient production methods, to provide incentive to develop new products, and as a way to arrive at prices based on supply and demand. In spite of resistance by many industrial officials, his ideas have been given wide publicity in *Pravda*, the official government newspaper, and are gradually gaining acceptance in Soviet industry. (Paraphrase of the above articles.)
"Soviet Lawyers Urge Valuation of Land Resources"
Explaining why bulldozers had ruined a freshly plowed 200-acre farm for housing when other land was available, Soviet lawyers complained in a *Pravda* article: " 'Since land in our country has no valuation, it is much more 'advantageous' for [construction planners] to [use] level farmland rather than land which will require additional expenditure for preparation.' " (Quoted in the *New York Times*, June 11, 1966.)
"Hungarian Profit System Spurs Production"
"Finding that his peasants had no interest in working hard for fixed pay, the president of the Naduvdar farm [30,000 acres], Istvan Szabo, secretly introduced his incentive system in 1952. . . . Now it has spread to more than half of Hungary's farms." The average yield of wheat at Naduvdar more than

Can we conclude that a socialist government could not determine the output most consistent with consumer choice, while competitive private enterprise could? No. But to determine what to produce as effectively as does competitive private enterprise, the socialist government must charge market-clearing prices as done under private enterprise and must have each

---

tripled between 1950 and 1963. Speaking of his peasant workers, an official of the Ministery of Agriculture said, " 'The difference is they work even in the rain and on Sunday's, because they know it means profits.' " (*New York Times*, Nov. 1, 1964.)

Speaking in Swiss exile, Ota Sik, the Czech Communist economist and architect of reforms which were swept away by Soviet tanks, said, "From the contradictions, from the shortages, you can see the need for the functions of the market, which provide the objective criteria for planning. Without objective criteria you have arbitrary decisions by the bureaucracy. . . . For the time being in Czechoslovakia the political pressures are greater. But in the long run, without liberalization and use of market functions, the socialist economy cannot win." (*New York Times*, March, 9, 1970.)

Describing the move from central planning to decentralized decision-making using prices and profits, a top Communist economist who is Chairman of the Hungarian Board for Materials and Prices listed the following reforms for 1968:

1. Central programming of production is to be abolished and the production pattern is to be shaped by direct bargaining between enterprises.

2. The rationing system is to be abolished and a market for the means of production established.

3. Central allocation of investment is to be replaced by self-financing.

4. Enterprise incentives based on fulfillment of obligatory targets are to be substituted by profit maximization.

5. Centrally-fixed wages are to be replaced by a link between wages and enterprise profit.

6. The administrative price system is to be replaced by a market price system.

Quoted from Bela Csikos-Nagy, *Pricing in Hungary*, Occasional Paper 19, Institute of Economic Affairs, London. 1968, p. 12.

Finally, SDS radical leader Kathy Boudin, no friend of private enterprise, on returning from a trip to Russia, reported that young Russians were dissatisfied with Socialism. As for their young radicals, Miss Boudin noted unhappily, "Their solution is a free-market economy in which money translates people's wishes." Quoted in the *New York Times*, Mar. 19, 1970.

Thus it is clear that the roles of prices and profits in registering consumer preferences, in registering the availability and measuring the productivity of inputs, both labor and capital, and thereby providing the signals and incentives to organize production efficiently–these functions which are described in the first seven chapters of this book are recognized as basic and essential ingredients of economic organization in all modern economies, whether private enterprise or socialist. (A Red Chinese economist, who lost favor during the Red Guard ascendency, could also have been cited.)

For more on this subject see A. Balinky, *Planning and the Market in the U.S.S.R.: the 1960's*, Rutgers University Press, 1967, especially the chapter

government-owned enterprise earn the same profit as a privately-owned competitive company would earn, by charging a price which covers the capital cost, including the competitive return on the investment. Both prices and profits are necessary under socialism as well as under private enterprise to determine what to produce in accordance with consumer choice.

The benefits a socialist might still claim for his system are that the profits (or whatever he chooses to call them) would go to the general public, not to private owners of capital. In this case, however, the general public must also bear the risks of mistakened business decisions and changes in consumer tastes, which risks are born by private owners under capitalism. And in order to create nonhuman inputs, the required reduction in current consumption will be done by the general public rather than by the particular individuals who save and invest voluntarily in a private enterprise system. Thus, this public distribution of "profits" under socialism is not a bonanza without corresponding costs.[5]

Our purpose here has been to highlight the importance of prices and profits for deciding what to produce. In principle, the same results—prices, outputs, and income distribution—could be brought about under either economic system. However, the differences in the locus of decision-making power, risk-bearing, and incentives to innovate make it unlikely that the two systems would bring about the same results even if this were the objective.

Needs Versus Wants

Many people think that a benevolent dictator or elected legislature would, in contrast to private enterprise, produce necessities first and luxuries only after all needs are met. Much confusion is usually embroiled in attempts to distinguish between needs and luxuries or needs and wants, and especially to judge the economic system by whether this distinction is reflected in what is produced.

What is the difference between a need and a luxury? Are "needs" just

---

by Abram Bergson. Also read selections by Y. Liberman and V. Dyachenko in *Soviet Economy: Plans, Problems, Prospects, 1965-1970*, published by Novosti Press Agency, Moscow (no date given). On the early 1960's, see J. L. Felber, *Soviet Economic Controversies*, M.I.T. Press, 1966.

[5] At the initial changeover from capitalism to socialism, a bonanza of sorts might accrue to the government (and in principle to the general public) at the expense of the former owners of nonhuman inputs. This will occur if the privately-owned inputs are partially or totally confiscated rather than sold to the government at "fair market value." One wonders whether the lure of socialism in many countries is not this confiscation of property, especially foreign-owned, with its attendant wealth and power for government officials, rather than a belief in the superiority of socialism over capitalism.

those goods which are necessary to maintain life? If a family ate the cheapest foods available to give a nutritious (but not necessarily palatable) diet—home grown dandilion greens, algae, corn, vegetables, and perhaps chicken—and if it had no more clothes and shelter than necessary for healthy protection from the weather—no "need" for central heating, inside plumbing, electricity, autos—it could live on under $500 a *year* in the rural South. Medical expenses might add more, but insurance could even these out.

If "needs" include some additional comforts of modern life, how do we separate the comforts which are "needs" from those which are not? Is sirloin steak once a week a "need?" Once a month? How many square feet of housing per person? We encounter the same problem in defining "poverty." The "poverty" line itself moves upward as the average standard of living rises and it is largely a matter of how far below average one chooses to define it. What people "need" is a subjective matter, hardly distinguishable from what they want or what someone thinks they ought to have. Professor Stigler has aptly defined a "luxury" as "something that some people think others should do without." [6]

If people have incomes above the "poverty" level, won't they want what they "need?" If not, do they really "need" what someone thinks they need? Most of the complaints that private enterprise is not responsive to the needs of people should more candidly be stated as objections to the distribution of income or as assertions that people do not know what is good for themselves, that they squander on unimportant things while "needs" go unmet.

It is safe to assert that in an economy with incomes as high as in America if what to produce is determined by dollar votes, by what people *want,* then most personal *needs* will be met. Most people do have sense enough to give the children's milk adequate priority over Daddy's whiskey sour. To cope with those who don't have this sense, specific regulations and penalties, as for parental negligence, are probably more appropriate than an overall regulation of everyone's consumption. But if the portion without such sense were high enough, more sweeping consumption control might be appropriate. For example, one of the arguments for a compulsory social security system covering everyone, rather than only a subsidy program for indigent aged people, is that too many people wouldn't have sense enough to save voluntarily during their working years for old age.

Public Needs

Often one hears proposals for subsidies based on "public needs" which are not met by private enterprise following dollar votes. Consider for example

---

[6] George Stigler, *Price Theory,* Macmillan. 1947, p. 68.

commuter railroad service into New York City from the wealthy suburbs. For years, railroads have lost money on this, the loss being covered by higher freight rates or by less than competitive returns to stockholders or defaults on railroad bonds.[7] Railroads are required by law to provide commuter service, even though at a loss, because of an asserted "public need" for transporting these people into New York by railroad. If these people really "need" this transportation, why not raise the fares to cover the costs? The regulators (and commuters) claim such high fares would lead people to abandon the railroad for other transportation (or move to the city). Then do they really "need" the rail service? [8]

One related argument is that rail service should be subsidized to reduce auto traffic. But why not simply make sure car drivers are taxed enough to pay the costs of highways, parking facilities, pollution control, etc.—then let commuters choose among auto and rail and moving to the city, paying the full costs either way? That is, in what sense is there a "need" for commuter railroad service from Scarsdale to Grand Central Station, if there are not enough customers to pay the costs? Do not the same considerations apply to the use of general tax revenues (where one group pays and another benefits) for subway costs, public housing for people above the poverty level, rehabilitation of "rundown" business districts, or the operation of national parks? If voluntary spending will not bring these results about, why should government compel people to finance these activities through taxes? What is a "public need" in these contexts? [9]

Losers' Claims And Profit Equalization

Profit equalization is the process by which resources move into industries where profits are higher and out of lower profit industries. Through

---

[7] The present trend is for state and Federal governments (i.e., general taxpayers) to subsidize "necessary" commuter service. A new twist appeared when the Federal government told the Pennsylvania and New York Central Railroads they would not be allowed to merge unless they agreed to take over the losing commuter business of the bankrupt New Haven Railroad, thereby transferring the commuter subsidy from the hapless investors of the defunct New Haven to those in the Penn Central and to consumers who buy goods on this newly-merged line (now itself bankrupt). Shortly thereafter, the states of New York and Connecticut, with Federal assistance, purchased the line's New York commuter service and are paying Penn Central to operate it, with deficits financed by taxpayers, most of whom are much less affluent than the line's commuter customers.

[8] Sometimes it seems that a "public need" is little more than a desire by group A for someone else to pay for A's goods and services.

[9] A more sophisticated view of "public needs" is discussed in Chapter 12 in connection with divergences between public and private costs and benefits. Also, see Chapter 11 on basic research.

this process, production is geared to consumer dollar votes. What about the interests of workers and investors? As explained in Chapter 2, these two groups are largely indifferent about what is produced. Nevertheless, a change in tastes may impose losses on them. Indeed, it is the losses of incomes, jobs, and profits that provide part of the incentives which get production rechanneled in accordance with consumer choice.

So let us consider who gains and who loses when consumer choice changes. Then ask with respect to each gaining group: are they entitled to these gains? And ask of each losing group: are their losses justified? Should the gainers (or anyone else) compensate the losers? Should the adjustment to the change in consumer tastes be prevented, slowed, or otherwise altered for the sake of the losers?

Answers to all of these questions involve judgments of fairness. Now it is quite true that the fairness of a situation or the relative fairness of two alternatives will often be a matter for each individual to decide for himself. Nevertheless, people do evaluate social events in terms of fairness and where, as often the case, the events involve conflicting interests among people, some such judgment is inevitable. Furthermore, however subjective fairness may be, a substantial consensus exists on many important issues. Economic theory does not provide the ethical principles to determine fairness. On the whole, we merely highlight the normative issues, leaving the judgments to each reader.

Suppose there is a change in consumer preferences: a rise in the demand for product A and a decline in the demand for product B. If it helps, you may visualize a rise in the demand for television programs and a decline in the demand for movies (except on TV), or a rise in the demand for professional football and a decline in the demand for professional baseball, or a rise in the demand for petroleum products and a decline in the demand for coal. There will be a shift of resources out of B where demand declined and into A until profits are equalized in A and B.[10]

---

[10] It is easy to visualize workers shifting from one industry to another. But how can one shift nonhuman inputs to a different industry? Of what use is a textile loom in making steel or a dump truck in a beauty parlor? First, some nonhuman inputs *can* be used for producing different outputs. Looms can make different types of cloth; dump trucks can be used for moving land and materials in preparation for expanding many types of output.

But more fundamentally, the value of nonhuman productive capacity in one industry (textiles) can decrease simply because it is not replaced as it depreciates (wears out). And the cash flowing into that industry *can* be shifted to expand productive capacity in another industry (steel). Other things the same, if productive capacity expands in steel by $X and wears out in textiles by $X because money received in the textile industry is reinvested in the steel industry instead of being used to maintain the level of investment in textiles, then the result is the same as if textile machinery were converted

Tastes change. (Let us assume consumer choice itself cannot be regulated.) Before any shift in resources, profits rise in A and fall in B. Who gains and who loses by the adjustment to this change? The gainers are: (1) the investors who shift into areas where profits are higher; (2) the consumers who prefer the goods produced in the high-profit areas (since output will rise and either prices decline or quality improves or both); (3) workers and other input owners with skills specific to the expanding areas since their wages and prices may rise; (4) investors and input owners who remain in the low-profit areas, since after investment and output decrease there, profit rates will rise for those left.

The losers by this shift are: (1) investors already in the high-profit areas who would prefer that outsiders stay out and that insiders not compete, so profits will not be decreased; (2) consumers who prefer the goods produced where profits are lower and from which inputs are diverted and where output will then decline and prices rise; (3) laborers and other input owners whose skills are specialized to the fields where output is declining and who will receive wage cuts and perhaps have to shift to other jobs at lower pay.[11]

Would it be possible to arrange for the gainers (from an investment shift) to compensate the losers? No. In any given year, investment shifts occur among hundreds of industries and geographical areas. Nearly each individual, as a consumer, benefits a little from some shifts and loses a little from others. The exact gains and losses could not be identified with each consumer. Gains and losses to investors and workers could occasionally be identified roughly.

Still, even if all benefits and losses cannot be precisely identified person by person, we must consider whether the losers have any legitimate claims for compensation or for thwarting the change. Do the investors in an industry where demand has risen, in order to protect their profits, have a right to prevent or impede outsiders from entering and to prevent insiders from expanding production, cutting prices, or improving quality? You decide. If so, then the freedom of others is limited, and the insiders are given a special privilege not open to others—the privilege of operating in a given industry.

Do the consumers of particular products where demand has fallen have a right to require (a) that investors produce these products when returns are higher elsewhere, or (b) that workers stay employed in these industries when they could earn more elsewhere, or (c) that consumers who are bidding inputs

---

into steel machinery, while the total productive capacity of the economy did not rise. In this sense, one *can* think of nonhuman inputs shifting from one industry to another.

[11] Workers with skills not *specialized* to a particular industry will not be affected greatly by the shift in tastes. Even if they have to change jobs, their wages would not be reduced. In this context an airline pilot is specialized to an industry, a typist is not. Generally, any person with the ability to acquire one specialty can, with training, acquire another.

away from these products stop spending as they choose? If not, then the consumers who lose by a taste shift have no claim to thwart the resource shift. If so, why? If so, then these consumers are given a special privilege to interfere with the freedom of others to invest, work, and spend as they choose. Do workers, such as blacksmiths when cars were replacing carriages, have a right to prevent consumers and investors from changing products, in order to avert a decline in the wage of certain occupational skills?

Some people are bound to be harmed by the achievement of economic efficiency and the exercise of freedom by consumers, investors, and workers. So too does the exercise of free choice in the selection of friends or of a spouse often involve harm to others, such as to disappointed suitors. One may regard these possibilities as an acceptable price of freedom.

Or one may take a qualified position. For example, one may feel that consumers and investors who lose by the exercise of others' economic freedom have no valid claim for compensation, but that workers should receive partial compensation, such as severance pay, unemployment benefits, and/or subsidized retraining. Even so, it would be virtually impossible to identify the gainers and to charge them the costs of such worker benefits. Therefore, former employers or the general taxpayer would probably have to bear the burden of assisting workers. For example, the shift in consumer demand from coal to oil has adversely affected coal miners. In response, the Federal government (the taxpayer) is financing aid for these workers.[12]

Evaluation of the Determination of What to Produce

Let us now evaluate the determination of what to produce under competitive private enterprise by three criteria: (1) efficiency, (2) freedom, and (3) fairness. These are three goals of society by which economic activity is frequently judged, though other criteria, such as morality and esthetics, are also relevant.

Efficiency. Efficiency means deriving the most output from the available inputs (given the freedom of input owners to take leisure if they choose). To compare different goods and services, output is measured in dollars. As we saw earlier, when output is determined competitively, so that price equals

---

[12] Any such program faces the objection that it reduces the worker's incentive to improve his own condition. Well before the Federal program, most miners *had* moved to jobs in other areas. Moreover, unemployment among coal miners has been aggravated since the early 1950's by the miners' insistance (through their union) that miners' wages per hour rise substantially relative to wages elsewhere while the demand for their labor was declining. If miners are causing their own unemployment, should taxpayers still subsidize them?

marginal cost, any rates of production other than those determined by demand and supply would mean the value of the additional goods produced (moving to the right of the intersection of demand and supply) is less than the value of the goods given up (moving to the left of demand and supply intersection in some other industry). Thus, what to produce is determined as efficiently as possible.[13]

---

[13] Even on a simple notion like efficiency, confusion abounds. An official of the Colorado State Highway Department was quoted as saying: " 'American travel habits haven't a damn thing to do with efficiency. All I know are the facts: The number of people per unit of automobile keeps going down and down and down." *Business Week,* Oct. 20, 1962.

Economic efficiency does not mean consumers should engage in carpools any more than it means they should use railroads and buses instead of cars. Efficiency means maximum satisfaction of consumer preferences, whatever these preferences are. If people prefer the convenience of autos (and living dispersed in the suburbs rather than in high-rise apartments at mid-city), it would be inefficient to compel them to use mass transportation, which would require long walks and waits at the beginning or end of their trips. Nor is it "inefficient" to build homes so each child can have his own room and each family its own yard, if people are able and willing to pay for this. Nor is it "inefficient" to have a huge "underutilized" retail establishment most of the year, because consumers prefer to go on a vast buying spree each December rather than buying the same annual volume at a uniform rate throughout the year.

If anything is amiss about all this, it is consumer tastes. But it is a separate issue unrelated to efficiency whether consumers know what is good for themselves.

This is not to deny that urban transportation is inefficiently organized. It could hardly be otherwise, given the distorted prices used. Commuters from the suburbs are not charged the full costs of the highways they use. One economist estimated a subsidy of 10c a mile for one city. If these costs *were* born by the drivers, many comuters would readjust by (a) using mass transportation, (b) moving to the city, and (c) working in the suburbs (and employers would find it profitable to locate more in the suburbs).

Quite likely highway transportation around large cities is to the right of q_1 in Fig. 3-1a, where market-clearing price equals marginal cost. If so, the added cost of the last mile of highway exceeds its benefit. Why is this? Because local comuter expressways are not paid for locally. The Federal Government pays 90% of the cost if the highway is part of the Interstate System and 50% otherwise. So, to any community, the highway is a bargain at 10% or 50% of cost. Each locality reasonably feels that if it doesn't get the Federal highway money some other place will. So long as the benefit exceeds the *local* cost only, it's worth accepting. Therefore, people vote locally (by political ballot) for highways even though the cost (including Federal subsidy) is greater than the benefit. And on the Federal level, there is little restraint, as each Congressman wants to show his constituents how much "he" got appropriated for them. Along with this overinvestment, political influence inevitably dominates benefit-cost comparisons (i.e., consumer choice) in determining which localities receive how much of the funds

Freedom. Under competitive private enterprise, there is complete economic freedom for all individuals, except for restrictions against violence, fraud, contract violation, and monopolistic collusion. Furthermore, any outcome other than the competitive one will invariably involve impediments of freedom for some consumers, workers, or investors. Consumers will be

---

Congress appropriates for highways. In 1971, New York City's Transportation Administrator announced plans for a major rennovation of Manhattan's West Side Highway on the assumption that it would qualify as part of the Federal Interstate System and New York would pay only 10% of the cost. He noted at the time: "If I had a billion dollars [the possible cost] at my disposal, I'd spend it on mass transit, not highways, but the money for this program is earmarked for highways only and this may be the last chance we'll have to get it for the city." (*New York Times,* April, 4, 1971.)

Granted that local roads must be government financed and operated, because collecting tolls on private roads would be too expensive. But if Federal financing for local roads were ended and if those who benefit (drivers) were made to pay the full cost (by local taxes on gasoline, deisel fuel, and vehicle weight), they would not buy past the point where cost exceeds benefit. In short, where prices are distorted, inefficiency results. And inefficiency abounds in American transportation because decisions are made by political process rather than by dollar votes. Congressmen and regulatory agencies respond to special interests (including those of labor unions) and even where a genuine effort is made to serve the general interest, competitive market-determined prices are neither sought nor used.

"I'm sorry I'm late for my appointment -- I was held up
three hours by road construction -- watching
my tax dollars at work!"

prevented from bidding resources into some industries or workers prevented from entering or leaving certain occupations or investors prevented from entering or leaving some industries if output is other than that determined by competitive demand and supply.

Fairness. Most people, on considering the rights of gainers and losers from changes in consumer tastes, would probably feel that the competitive determination of what to produce is fair, though there is nothing in economics per se that leads to or against this conclusion.

Compulsory Profit Equalization

If profit equalization is desirable, why not pass a law assuring every investor the competitive return and prohibiting any profits above this? It is important to appreciate that this would completely destroy the beneficial effects of profit equalization. No longer would investors have incentive to shift inputs, human and nonhuman, out of areas of low returns and into areas with high returns. Thus, no longer would inputs automatically shift in response to changes in consumer tastes. Nor would businessmen have incentive to reduce costs, improve quality, or develop new products, if they were guaranteed the same rate of return, no more and no less, regardless of their costs or of consumer acceptance of their products.

Profit equalization is a *process* of adjustment, a process which will not operate unless people are free to strive for higher than normal profits and unless lower than normal profits can occur when products fall from consumer favor or when companies fail to operate as efficiently as their competitors. Profit equalization serves society, if it does, only because in the process of attaining it "what to produce" is determined in accordance with efficiency, freedom, fairness, and other goals. Eliminate the process by which it is achieved and its advantages will disappear also.[14]

---

[14] While no one was actually proposing compulsory profit equalization, the law passed in 1971 to aid the Lockheed Corporation is a move in that direction. The company alleged that, because of its inability to repay bank loans coming due, it faced bankruptcy, unless the Federal government would guarantee its loans. That is, banks would be willing to extend and make new loans, if the government would assure the banks that when the renewed loans came due the government would repay them if Lockheed could not. By a narrow margin, Congress approved a loan guarantee of $250-million. This followed the defeat of a broader $2-billion proposal to aid financially distressed companies.

Would not such assurances reduce the incentive of management to curtail unprofitable operations and reduce the incentive of lending institutions to withhold finance where profit prospects are poorer than alternatives?

Because this is a process which takes time and because tastes and technology are continually changing and new products being developed, we would not expect profits to be equal in all industries at any one time. However, if the economy is operating competitively, there should be a tendency for profits to fall where they are higher than usual and to rise where they are less than normal, while abnormally high or low profits arise elsewhere from the latest changes in tastes, technology, and new products. Experience shows this to be the case.[15]

These arguments against compulsory profit equalization apply to other regulations of prices and profits under competitive conditions (including the "Phase I" and "Phase II" regulations introduced in 1971). Such regulations thwart the process by which prices and profits and their changes direct production in accordance with consumer choice. This does mean that all such regulations are necessarily bad—is consumer freedom, or as often called "consumer sovereignty" always good? Moreover, under monopolistic conditions, such as a local water company, price and profit regulation may be appropriate to bring about competitive results consistent with consumer choice.

Why Differences In Profit Rates May Persist: Nonmonetary Goals

Suppose investing in some industry provides investors a nonmonetary satisfaction in addition to money returns. Investors in farming may enjoy the ownership of attractive land. Investors in professional sports may derive excitement, pride, and status from ownership that they could not receive merely as fans or as employees of the teams. In such cases, if the returns were at the competitive level attainable elsewhere, and if there were free entry into these fields, then more investment would flow into these areas, driving down returns until no further incentive existed to shift into them. Thus, lower than competitive returns would persist.

The same principle applies to wage differences: an occupation which provides nonmonetary pleasure in addition to salary will tend to have lower

---

If the government underwrites such unprofitable activities, will this not remove a major pressure toward efficiency and production in accordance with consumer tastes?

It was felt that bankruptcy would lead to unemployment. However, people *can* change jobs. Furthermore, when a large company goes bankrupt because it cannot pay its debts, unless its prospects are hopeless, its creditors will often favor its continued operation under court-appointed management as their best chance for repayment. Then unemployment is slight. This has been the status of the Penn Central Railroad.

[15] See the book by G. Stigler cited in footnote 6, Chapter 2.

wages than another occupation requiring the same abilities and effort but not affording the nonmonetary pleasures. Again, professional sports are an example. Also, art, music and perhaps teaching.

Likewise, an area of investment which entails nonmonetary dissatisfaction will have fewer investors, other things the same, causing returns to be higher than elsewhere by enough to compensate the least willing investor for the nonmonetary disutility he incurs. Some investment areas with nonmonetary disutility are the ownership of slum housing, garbage collection, junk, and some exceptionally risky ventures.[16]

It would be inappropriate to eliminate forcibly these profit (and wage) differences which reflect nonmonetary preferences. For there is no *a priori* basis for placing monetary objectives morally above or below nonmonetary preferences. Besides, for most people, money is a means to some nonmonetary ends anyway.

Nor have we suggested that a pursuit of profits is a moral obligation in a competitive private enterprise system. Pursuit of profits is what generally occurs when the organizers of business are free to act in their own interest: motivated perhaps from greed, perhaps by a drive for status and power, but also perhaps by a desire to provide comforts and security for their families, perhaps to serve consumers, or perhaps to acquire funds to support a college, church, the Red Cross, the NAACP, or some other social or political group. We expect most people act on all of these motives in varying degrees and would do so regardless of the economic system as long as they are free. An advantage of competitive private enterprise, given laws against violence, fraud, and monopolizing, is that any natural tendency of people to act in their own interests is channelled into socially beneficial ends—the provision of goods and services desired by others.

With this discussion of "what to produce" under competitive private enterprise, we have only begun to describe how a private enterprise system works and have not provided a basis for a final judgment of the system or of various governmental interferences with its operation.

Summary

In an unregulated economy without prices and profits, there would be no trades (since a price *is* the terms on which one thing exchanges for another), no incentive to create nonhuman inputs, and no incentive to organize inputs.

---

[16] On the nonmonetary factors in investment, see the long article "Owning a Sports Team Looks Like Fun, But it Isn't Always a Gold Mine," *Wall Street Journal,* Sept. 9, 1969. Former owner Bill Veeck asserted that

Consumer preferences cannot be ascertained simply by a central listing of what people need and of how many people there are by age, sex, size, etc., because people with given social-economic-physical characteristics have different preferences.

Nor can consumer preferences be ascertained through political ballots (or by elected government officials), because the ballots cannot be devised to register individual preferences or changes in preferences as effectively as does "dollar voting."

If production is to be based on consumer preferences in a socialist economy, the socialist enterprises must charge market-clearing prices and earn profits equal to what privately owned firms would earn under competitive conditions.

The Soviet Union and other Communist nations are making increasing use of market-determined prices, profits, and decentralized economic decision-making.

The distinction between "needs" and "luxuries" is arbitrary and of little use in evaluating the determination of what to produce.

Private enterprise produces according to desires, not necessarily according to "needs."

But if "need" is defined at all sensibly, and if people are adequate judges of their own interests, then people will desire what they "need," and where incomes are high enough (as in America for most families), they will acquire their "needs."

A public need refers to a good or service which voluntary consumer spending does not make profitable but which should be produced anyhow. Frequently, though not always, a public need is alleged where there is an intention that the good or service be paid for by taxpayers in general rather than by the beneficiaries of the good or service.

What to produce under competitive private enterprise is determined in a manner which is efficient, is compatible with individual freedom, and is fair, assuming those adversely affected by changes in consumer preferences have no legitimate claims for compensation or for impeding the adjustment to the changes.

Profit equalization achieved through setting and guaranteeing profits in various areas would completely destroy the beneficial effects of profit equalization. Without the freedom of prices and profits to change, up or

---

owners "like the prestige of associating with athletes and being on the inside of all the strategy talk before the big game." On the negative side, another *Wall Street Journal* article, Sept. 5, 1969 discussed the higher interest rates that tobacco and liquor companies must pay on their bonds because many investors, particularly funds of churches, insurance companies, and some pensions, refuse to lend to such businesses.

down, incentives and signals to adjust production in accordance with consumer choice would be lost.

Profit differences may persist under competitive private enterprise where there are nonmonetary gains or losses from investing in some areas.

Study Questions Chapter 3

1. Explain the shortcomings of determining what to produce by counting noses rather than by dollar votes.

2. Explain why dollar voting is superior to political voting for determining what to produce—i.e., to having elected officials make this decision. Give any reasons why political votes may be superior.

3. What, if any, contribution to output are competitive profits a payment for?*

4. What real cost do wages represent? Profits?*

5. If price equals real cost, why does that necessarily mean that the firm receives a profit on the marginal unit?*

6. Explain the meaning of "capital intensive" and "labor intensive" industries.

7. Show diagrams which separate the marginal cost into labor and capital costs, (a) for a capital intensive industry, and (b) for a labor intensive industry. Answer: Figure 3-1.

8. (Review from Chapter 2) Show on this diagram the output which best reflects consumer choice. Answer: q_1.

9. (Review from Chapter 2) Explain why this *is* the "correct" output.

10. Explain with this diagram the consequences of having price cover only the labor cost, if output is at the correct quantity.*

11. Explain why the expansion or contraction from this correct output will be contrary to consumer choice.*

12. In which industries will there be a tendency under socialism to expand production? To Contract?*

13. Show on the diagram the quantity where labor cost only equals market-clearing price.*

14. Why couldn't each socialist enterprise produce this quantity and then set price simultaneously to equal labor cost and be at the market-clearing level?*

15. So what if it cannot do this?*

16. Why could a socialist government which set price equal to labor cost probably not produce the correct output if it wanted to?*

17. What is meant by the term "residual income recipient?"

18. What is the advantage of having such a group?

19. Even if prices were the same under private enterprise and socialism, what might be claimed an advantage of socialism?

20. What costs go along with this advantage?

21. Try to distinguish a "luxury" from a "need" without imposing your (or a majority's) values on others.

22. "Production should be based on what people need, not on profits." Comment.

23. Explain how nonhuman inputs can shift from textiles to steel, even though textile machinery cannot be used to produce steel.*

24. Identify the gainers and losers from a change in tastes.

25. Evaluate the claims of each group of gainers and losers that output should not be redirected in accordance with the change in tastes.

26. What does it mean for a worker's skills to be "specialized to a given industry?"

27. Why are such workers more affected by a change in tastes than those with transferable skills?

28. What does efficiency mean?

29. What justifies the contention that what to produce is determined efficiently under competitive private enterprise?

30. Why is inefficiency likely to result from Federal appropriations for city highway construction?

31. Is the competitive determination of what to produce compatible with individual freedom? Explain.

32. With fairness? Explain.

33. Why is profit equalization desirable, if it is?

34. Why is the process of profit equalization as important as the end result?

35. Why would compulsory profit equalization not be desirable?

36. Explain how nonmonetary goals may prevent profit equalization.

37. Why is such profit inequality not inefficient?

Answers to starred questions.

3. The contributions of nonhuman inputs owned by the enterprise.

4. What the labor could have produced elsewhere. What the capital could have produced elsewhere.

5. Because part of the real cost *is* the value the firm's nonhuman inputs could have produced elsewhere, and this value, after payment for labor and materials and after depreciation, is by definition profits.

10. Non-price rationing. Unable to ascertain the correct output.

11. Same answer as to #9.

12. Expand: capital intensive industries where price is relatively more below the market-clearing price. Contract: labor intensive industries, where shortages are smaller, to provide inputs for the other industries. (This tendency depends on the relative elasticities of demand as well as on the relative input intensities.)

13. Point B on Fig. 3-1a.

14. To expand beyond q_1 in one industry, others must contract to provide inputs for the expansion.

15. Then if price equals labor cost only, prices must be below market-clearing levels for most goods and services, which leads to the problems of #10 and from that to the conclusion that, for ideal output to be determined, price must equal the real cost of both labor and capital, which means it must include profits, the same as under competitive private enterprise.

16. With prices below market-clearing levels, it would not be able to locate the ideal quantities, where market-clearing price equals real cost, labor *and* capital.

23. Depreciation funds not used to replace textile equipment could be used to expand steel capacity.

4

How To Produce

The Meaning Of This Decision

"How to produce" is the decision as to which method of production to use. Take a simple task like digging a square hole, say for a building excavation. We could list many methods, each employing a different technology and a different combination of inputs. Here are just a few: (1) common laborers with bare hands and no tools, (2) fewer laborers and some hand shovels and picks, (3) even fewer laborers and a mechanical shovel which lifts 200 pounds of dirt per scoop, (4) a fifteen-ton-per-scoop steamshovel, some dump trucks, and their operators, but no common laborers, (5) and (6) explosives, along with labor, with or without mechanical shovels. Clearly, there are many more choices, especially if we specify the quality of the equipment or the strength and experience of the workers, or the competence of the foreman or of the engineer who determines when the correct size has been reached or what to do about an underground creek. For a more complicated operation like building a house, making a TV set or a nylon shirt, the number of different methods of production is even greater. How is the choice of production methods made? Do the producers' interests and society's welfare conflict or coincide? Let us look first at the producers' interest.

The Businessman's Objective: Low Costs Per Unit To Maximize Profits

In each instance, the choice of production methods is made by the owners of businesses or by people hired to act in the owners' interest. An owner wants to maximize profits. Therefore, he will choose that method of producing a given output which costs the least. The smaller the production costs, given the sales price, the higher will be his profits. Of course, it costs more to produce more. We're not saying the producer wants to minimize costs altogether. The way to do this is to close down the business. Rather, he wants to minimize the costs of producing whatever output he produces. Frequently, the cost per unit of output varies with the level of total output. At low outputs, cost per unit may be very high; as output expands, this cost per unit may decline and then after some level of output may gradually rise in a given company. (See Fig. 2-2D.) The producer will not necessarily operate at that output where cost per unit is the least. However, whatever level of output he does select, he will want to produce that amount at the lowest possible cost. (That is, he will want to be *on* the cost curve of Fig. 2-2D, not above it.) So much for the producer's objective. Now society's.

Society's Interest: Minimize Real Cost To Maximize Total Output

The money cost of producing an item is the money paid for labor and materials plus the prorated cost of capital equipment and overhead used in producing the item. The real cost of producing the item, as explained in Chapter 2, is the goods and services which society gives up to get the item produced—the things that could have been produced instead of the given item. For simplicity, in this discussion, we assume there are no "neighborhood" costs like air or water pollution, which the consumers are not charged for. These are taken up in the last chapter.

Why should real costs be minimized? Since we have the basic economic problem of not enough to go around, the more output that is produced from a given employment of inputs, the better off people are. And the possible output of society will be highest if, in the production of each individual item, that method of production is used which minimizes the goods and services sacrificed to get the given item produced; that is, that minimizes the real cost of production.

Proof That In Minimizing Money Cost, The Producer Minimizes Real Cost

Having identified the producer's interest to minimize the money cost of production and society's interest to minimize the real cost, we shall now establish that it is also in society's interest for producers to minimize the money cost of producing, because in doing so, producers will simultaneously and unconsciously minimize the real cost of producing. The reasoning proceeds as follows.

1. To attract inputs into the production of A (say chairs), producers must pay these inputs as much as they could have earned in the production of

other goods and services, non-A; otherwise the inputs would go to work in non-A instead of A.

2. The payment which inputs, human and nonhuman, would have received in non-A equals the money value of their contribution to production in non-A. This says that a worker on the assembly line in a radio factory is contributing $1.75 worth of production per hour, if his wage (including fringe benefits) is $1.75 an hour. Also, the profits left for the owner equal the value contributed by the nonhuman inputs. These points are developed in the next two chapters.

3. Since each input in A receives what it could have earned in non-A and in non-A would have received the value of its contribution to production, it follows that the money paid to inputs in A measures the value of the goods and services which society gives up to get A produced.

4. Therefore, to minimize the money costs of producing A (which the producer has an incentive to do in order to maximize his profits) is also to minimize the goods and services given up to get A produced (which is what is in society's interest, because society wants as much as possible produced from a given input effort, so people will have the highest possible standards of living consistent with freedom to choose between work and leisure), q.e.d.[1]

Since this point is so important, we restate the reasoning in simpler but less rigorous fashion.

1. To get workers to work in a radio factory, you have to pay them as much as they could earn elsewhere (say in a bed factory).

2. In the elsewhere, they would be paid the value of their contributions to production, the value of the beds they produce.

3. Therefore, the payment to workers in the radio factory equals the value of the other things (beds) given up to get the radios produced.

4. Therefore, if we use that method of producing radios which costs the least, then as few of other things as possible are given up to get the radios produced. That is, if by method X it costs $100 to produce a radio, but by method Y it costs $80 for the same radio, method Y is in society's interest, because society sacrifices only $80 worth of other

---

[1] It is assumed here that inputs in any one use are paid no more than they could earn in another employment, which means that all employed inputs do have alternatives where they could earn as much as where they are employed. Also, for wage to equal value contributed, employers must acquire inputs "competitively," as explained later.

In Chapter 2, we used points 1, 2, and 3 to prove that marginal *money* cost measures marginal *real* cost. From that proof, it also follows that to minimize money cost is to minimize real cost.

things using Y rather than giving up $100 of other things by method X.[2]

Applied to all products and services, this procedure makes possible a maximum total output from a given use of our productive capacity and the highest possible standard of living from its use. Therefore, when producers minimize production costs, they serve society's interests as well as their own, even though they may be motivated to serve only their own.

One should appreciate that this reasoning depends crucially upon the assumed equality between input payments and value contributed to production. Without this, we could not assert that when money costs of production are minimized, real costs are also minimized. For example, to take an absurd possibility, suppose input payments were inversely related value contributed, that is, the greater the value contributed by an input, the lower is its payment. In this case, the production method which costs the least money will likely not be that which involves the least sacrifice of other goods. Similarly, if input payments were simply uncorrelated with value contributed, as, say, if a worker's salary were based on the size of his family, then again the production method of minimum money cost would not likely be that which minimizes real costs.[3]

Frequently when asked to explain why it is socially desirable for producers to adopt that production method which costs the least, students reply to the effect that when production costs are low, then prices will be low and consumers can then afford to buy more. This reply, while not incorrect, is incomplete and not to the point of the question because (1) it does not prove that the real cost is minimized by that production method which minimizes money cost, (2) it does not prove that lower production costs necessarily result in lower prices (though they do with competition), and (3) it leaves the false impression that regardless of production method (which *is* the issue), if money costs were arbitrarily lowered (say by wage or profit

---

[2] Of course, we are not suggesting that only the cheapest quality radios should be produced, but that any given quality radio should be made by the method which costs the least. Nor is it suggested that arbitrary wage cuts to lower production costs would do any good. Wages should equal value contributed in alternative uses and the production method should be adopted which minimizes these costs. The cheapest production method may employ common labor or expensive skilled labor: it is money and real cost per output, not per input, that is relevant here.

[3] For the above reasoning, we *could* replace the assumption that input payments *equal* value contributed with a broader assumption that input payments are *proportional* to value contributed, say all input payments equal k times value contributed, where k might be .8 or 1.1 rather than 1.0 as equality assumes. However, we shall stick with equality rather than proportionality, because equality is simpler and is the result of competitive wage and profit determination anyhow.

controls), consumers could acquire more goods and services. But in fact no arbitrary rigging of input or output prices will raise society's productive capacity and increase total output. The correct answer given above shows that regardless of the prices charged for the outputs, that production method which minimizes money costs will minimize the sacrifice of other things and therefore will maximize the total goods and services available to society from a given rate of input utilization.

Evaluation Of How To Produce Under Competitive Private Enterprise

Again, we use the three criteria: efficiency, freedom, and fairness.

Efficiency. By definition, the most "efficient" production method is that which maximizes the ratio: $\frac{\text{output}}{\text{input}}$. Mathematically, when the ratio, $\frac{\text{output}}{\text{input}}$, is as high as technically possible, then the inverse ratio, $\frac{\text{input}}{\text{output}}$, is as low as possible. The preceding discussion has just shown that when money costs are minimized, the use of inputs (in real terms) to produce a given output is also minimized, which is simply another way of saying the ratio, $\frac{\text{input}}{\text{output}}$, is minimized. Therefore, insofar as producers minimize money costs of production, they will have adopted the most efficient production method.

Freedom. The determination of how to produce by minimizing money costs is consistent with the freedom of businessmen to hire and purchase inputs of their choice, at prices agreeable to the input sellers, and to decide the use of these inputs, subject again to the freedom of workers to quit if they are dissatisfied with the tasks assigned to them.[4] Strictly, the entrepreneur is free to adopt a method which does not minimize costs, but this will cost him profits if he must compete with others who do minimize costs. Since this exercise of entrepreneurial freedom does not infringe on the freedom of consumers or workers, we conclude that the determination of

---

[4] Freedom here means workers can quit if they don't like their jobs. But it does not mean employees can collectively say to their employer: you use *this* method of production or else we shall refuse to work *and* we shall forcibly prevent you from hiring other workers who are available and from using another method with them. The latter is a form of private coercion which infringes on the freedom of the employer and of the potential "strikebreakers." "Freedom" does not mean the freedom to interfere with the freedom of others to make mutually satisfactory agreements about the terms of employment.

how to produce under competitive private enterprise is compatible with personal freedom for everyone.

Justice or fairness. For this evaluation, we first identify the gainers and losers from money-cost minimizing, say, from the introduction of a new method of production which reduces costs. The gainers are: (1) owners of business who maximize profits by minimizing costs, (2) consumers who benefit from the higher output (and lower prices) which must result from any reduction of *real* costs, and (3) any input sellers whose inputs (skills) are made more valuable by the cost-reducing technological change (such as computer programmers when computers are widely adopted). The losers are input owners (mainly laborers) who, when the new method of production is introduced, may have to find alternative employment, and especially laborers whose skills are made less valuable by the technological change and whose alternative employment may be at a lower wage.[5]

Do the losers, the displaced workers, have any rightful claim against anyone? If Company A hires Mr. X (on mutually acceptable terms since neither forces the other into the employer-employee relationship), and if at the outset there is no explicit or implied understanding about the duration of the employment, and if Mr. X is free to quit whenever he chooses, then is Company A under any obligation to employ or pay Mr. X after Company A decides it no longer desires the service of Mr. X? If the answer is yes, then should not this obligation be made explicit in the first place? Clearly, to the extent that the company is liable for Mr. X's losses, it will refrain from introducing cost reductions unless they more than cover this liability. This hesitancy will reduce total output from what it could be, because real costs of production are not minimized.

If Mr. X, displaced by a new production method, has no justifiable claim against the company, does he have a claim for compensation for his job loss against the consumers who benefit or against society in general? To the extent that Mr. X is compensated, his personal incentive to adjust by finding another job may be reduced, thereby raising the loss for which he is to be paid.

The problem of technological displacement is often exaggerated. Over the past two centuries of the industrial revolution, technological advance has

---

[5] Generally, workers displaced by technological change can get other jobs without taking wage cuts: their former employers would not have paid them more than what they could earn elsewhere. However, in some firms, a union or a seniority system may have pushed the wage for some workers above what they could earn elsewhere. Also, if a technological change is applied simultaneously throughout an industry (say coal mining), there may be a general decline in the demand for certain skills, which skills are not used outside that industry, in which case the displaced workers would likely have to accept lower-paying jobs.

created more jobs than it destroyed. Further, major changes in an industry are generally introduced at a rate not much greater than the gradual attrition of employment from voluntary quits, so that few workers are actually laid off. During prosperous periods over 15% of all manufacturing workers voluntarily quit their jobs every year (not counting layoffs and discharges). Also, when they have to, workers can and do shift from one industry to another. The amazing adaptability of the labor input is forcefully illustrated by the fact that for over thirty years the net migration off farms in America has averaged over 700,000 people per year, only a small fraction of whom have experienced prolonged unemployment. This high mobility among industries and occupations suggests that in most cases technologically displaced workers can and should find alternative employment without outside assistance.

The fact that cost minimization causes unjust hardships, if it does, does not necessarily mean that it should be prevented or that the Mr. X's should be compensated. The prevention of cost minimization may be more undesirable than the injustice, and the compensation by society to the X's may also be regarded as an unjust imposition upon society. A compromise solution which concedes injustice to displaced workers might be partial compensation by society for a limited period and only after some initial period of unemployment. This allows cost minimization to occur without hindrance and preserves the incentive of displaced workers to become self-supporting again as soon as possible. We leave it to the reader to judge the fairness of cost minimization: whether its beneficiaries are entitled to their gains and what, if anything, should be done to assist technologically displaced workers.[6]

---

[6] Here are two technological advances in the offing which will mean lower prices and elimination of particular jobs. Should they be prevented? (1) Replacement of the gas and electric meter man by a computer-equipped truck

"I have been replaced by a machine -- except for this little part of it!"

The Roles Of Prices And Profits

Just as in the decision "what to produce," so in "how to produce" prices and profits are indispensible for sensible decisions. Pursuit of profits is the goal which induces producers to minimize money costs and, therefore, real costs.

Prices, especially in this case the prices of inputs, enable the producer to determine which method of production does in fact minimize the money cost of production and hence the real cost of production. Without price tags on various inputs, which prices reflect the contribution of these inputs in alternative uses, it would be impossible to know which production method costs least in real terms.

Once again, this is as true under socialism as under private enterprise. For many years, Communists did not count capital expense as a cost of production. Therefore, an enterprise which sought to minimize costs sought only to minimize labor costs. Capital was arbitrarily allocated by a central agency. Each enterprise had incentive to ask for as much capital as it could get, thereby to reduce its cost per unit of labor, even if the cost per unit of capital *and* labor were raised. Thus, capital was wastefully used in the selection of production methods. Since the early 1960's, through a greater use of prices and profits and the virtual abandonment of the labor theory of value, such wasteful practices have declined, as noted in the preceding chapter. But this has not occurred without controversy and without attempts to couch economic reforms in words that appear to adhere to Marxian principles, even if they do not.

Points Of Confusion

Some people react to this discussion with questions like these: (1) Minimizing costs to maximize total production may be important, but is it all important? (2) Shouldn't consideration be given to whether people want the additional production or (3) to what kinds of jobs people prefer or to other work conditions? (4) Instead of minimizing costs, shouldn't costs be raised sometimes to give workers decent wages, especially if profits are high?

Let's take these points in order. (1) and (2). We don't say production should be maximized regardless of consumers' desire for output or for leisure

---

which reads and records radio signals from home meters—100,000 per month—at 10% of the present meter-reading costs. (2) Development of dwarfed apple trees, 8 feet wide, 10 feet tall, planted in hedgerows and picked by a machine which straddles two rows and shakes apples off into conveyer belts, thereby eliminating most migratory farm jobs in apple picking. To prevent such changes in order to preserve certain jobs is to retard the growth of real income for everyone.

over work. Certainly not. We merely say that for the same level of input utilization, it is better to produce more output than less (which means give up as little as possible to produce any given item), because we do have the basic economic problem of not enough to go around. (3) Certainly preferences about employment conditions are relevant. They are reflected in the input (labor) costs which are used to choose among production methods. To the extent that task A is more distasteful than task B, employers will have to pay workers more to do A than B, and will have added incentive to mechanize task A. Also, the higher cost of getting A done will raise the price consumers have to pay for outputs which require task A. (4) As to raising wages to improve living standards, if wages are arbitrarily raised without a corresponding improvement in worker productivity, some workers will lose their jobs; so *their* incomes and living standards will be reduced, not raised by the wage rise. This has been the effect of both labor unions and minimum wages. When there really *is* an improvement in worker productivity, wages will rise automatically, because the demand for labor will have risen.

Simultaneity Of "What" And "How" Decisions

The decision "what to produce" is not first made and then the decision "how to produce" made. Rather, both are made simultaneously and for the economy as a whole both entail millions of individual decisions every day.

These decisions are interdependent because both depend on the various quantities of different inputs. For example, consider two economies, A and B, both with the same consumer preferences for goods and for work versus leisure and both with the same knowledge of production methods. In A there are abundant nonhuman inputs—machinery, waterpower, minerals—but not much labor, while in B there are few nonhuman inputs, but abundant labor. In spite of the similarities in consumer tastes and producer knowledge, there will be differences in both what is produced and how it is produced. The ratio of the price of nonhuman inputs to the price of human inputs will be lower in A than in B.[7] Therefore, in A, production methods will be adopted which utilize relatively more capital and less labor (steamshovels and dump trucks to dig a hole), while in B the same output would be produced with less capital and more labor (laborers with hand shovels)—both being the most efficient in each economy.

---

[7] As practice for thinking in terms of ratios and symbols, write the preceding statement in the form of unequal ratios: $(?/?) < (?/?)$. Also, restate the sentence verbally three other ways to describe the same relationships by reversing the order of "nonhuman" and "human" and A and B. Rewrite the inequality for each version. An ability to do this will prove quite important for studying economics. This ability *can* be developed.

Furthermore, in A there will be relatively more outputs produced which emphasize nonhuman inputs and in B relatively more which utilize human. Thus in A there would be more vacuum cleaners, telephones, and police cars, while in B more servants, messengers, and ambulatory policemen. These contrasts apply to America as A and India as B and to a lesser and declining extent to the North versus the South within the United States. Thus, the relative abundance of different inputs—the same could be applied to skilled and unskilled workers—affects both "what" and "how" to produce.

Labor Or Machines?

Is it always more efficient to use machines instead of labor wherever possible? Clearly not. The best method is that which costs the least. This says nothing about the relative use of human and nonhuman inputs. Where labor is highly abundant relative to capital (India), wages relative to capital costs will be lower than where labor is less abundant relative to machines (U.S.). So in India it will be cheaper to employ more labor-intensive production methods than in America.

Government policy has raised wage costs of tomato pickers by restricting the use of seasonal Mexican labor. This has resulted in the rapid development and adoption of mechanical tomato pickers and the development of newly shaped tomato plants which can more readily be picked by machine.[8] Does this mean tomatoes are now picked more efficiently? Not if the costs per tomato have risen. The higher costs mean more of other things are sacrificed to get the tomatoes.

The same is true of a labor-saving change induced by a union or minimum wage. The only possibility that greater efficiency might result from the wage increase is that the producer was led to adopt a new method which would have been cheaper all along but which he failed to recognize. Or perhaps the workers displaced by the machine were forced into higher paying alternatives which were available all along. But if so, why didn't the employer or the workers adopt the better alternative in the first place? There may indeed have been such situations where knowledge was deficient. But more

---

[8] In 1965, the first year of the restrictions, "more than 20% of the California tomato crop—which supplies some 60% of the nation's tomatoes for canning—were harvested by machine . . . next year the machines are expected to do 85% of the picking, and eventually all of it." *Business Week,* January 8, 1966, p. 108. In 1964, only 3% of the crop was machine-picked. Partly explaining the rapid adjustment to machines, are the several years of Administration-Congressional promotion which preceded the repeal of the law which permitted "bracero" labor and the threat of unionization of farm labor soon after repeal took effect.

generally, if a union forces up the price of labor and the employer is thereby induced to use fewer laborers and more machines to produce given outputs, the resulting production method will be more costly per unit of output and hence less efficient.

Summary

How to produce involves choices among alternative methods of production. While producers want to choose the method that costs the least in order to maximize profits, society prefers that method which requires the least sacrifice of other things, in order that as much as possible will be produced from the inputs used. Under competitive private enterprise, these two objectives coincide. Therefore, given competitive conditions, in the determination of how to produce, individuals can be left to pursue their own interests. Adam Smith's "invisible hand" again operates to promote economic efficiency.

Under private enterprise, the "how" decision is made in a manner that is compatible with personal freedom. Whether the determination is fair depends upon whether technologically displaced workers should be assisted or should be expected to make their own adjustments.

Under any economic system, inputs must have price tags which reflect their value to production, if efficient production methods are to be selected.

Both "what" and "how" to produce are determined simultaneously and both depend upon the relative abundance of various types of inputs.

Before discussing the next basic economic decision, who gets what is produced, we shall first explain the principle of diminishing returns. This concept will then be used in the explanation of income determination, upon which the distribution of output depends.

Study Questions Chapter 4

1. What is the businessman's objective in choosing a method of production?

2. What is society's (or consumers') interest in the selection of production methods?

3. Explain why in adopting the production method which minimizes money cost, the producer will unconsciously minimize real cost.

4. Evaluate the decision how to produce by three criteria: efficiency, freedom, and fairness.

5. Explain the roles of prices and profits in determining how to produce.

6. Explain how the "what" and "how" decisions are related: compare the

two decisions in A and B, where A has the same consumer tastes as B, but has a higher capital/labor ratio.

7. How would relative input prices, capital/labor, differ in A and B?*

8. Is the production method which uses the least labor always the most efficient? Explain why or why not.

Answer to #7. The capital/labor input price ratio would be lower in A.

5

The Principle Of
Diminishing Returns

The principle of diminishing returns describes a relationship of profound importance to economic understanding. It describes how output changes when one kind of input is added to a fixed quantity of other inputs—say, how corn production changes as more laborers are added one by one to a 1000-acre farm.

A Hypothetical Illustration

We shall illustrate the principle with a hypothetical example, then state it formally. Suppose we have a corn farm of 1000 acres with a specified number of tractors, barns, silos, fencing, and other equipment. What would be the output of the farm if there were no laborers? Since plants might grow anyway, there might be some production. But without laborers the farm would be quite a mess after a few years. So let's assume that, without labor, the output of corn per year would be zero. The first row of numbers in Table 5-1 shows this. Next, suppose with the same acres and other farm inputs, we have one laborer (working some specified hours per year). Then the output might be 8000 bushels per year.

Now suppose a second laborer is added and output per year instead of being 8000 is 19,000 bu. Why might the output more than double when the labor input just doubled and when total inputs (labor, land, and capital) rose less than two-fold? There is no assurance that this more than doubling of output would happen. But it might. If it did, it would be because when there were two laborers instead of one, each laborer could specialize in certain chores and become more proficient in these, whereas the one laborer on the farm had to be a "jack-of-all-trades" and did not develop skills as highly in a narrower range of activities. A second reason is that some important tasks, such as lifting or moving heavy loads, are readily done by two people, but require cumbersome, time-consuming methods when one person does them.

Table 5-1   Illustration of the principle of diminishing returns with a hypothetical 1000-acre corn farm

Number of laborers (1)	Total output (2)	Marginal physical product (3)	
(per year)	(thousands of bushels per year)		
0	0	–	increasing returns
1	8	8	
2	19	11	constant returns
3	30	11	
4	39	9	
5	46	7	
6	51	5	
7	55	4	diminishing returns
8	58	3	
9	60	2	
10	61	1	
11	61	0	zero returns
12	60	–1	negative returns

Now let's add a third laborer and note the output per year. The table shows output rising to 30,000 bu. per year. Continuing down the table, we assume with four workers output would be 39,000, with five workers it would be 46,000, with six 51,000 and so on, rising by less and less with each additional worker until another worker adds nothing to output (the 11th), after which more workers cause output to decline.

The Marginal Physical Product Or MPP

Look at column (3). The *marginal physical product,* is *the additional output which results from one additional unit of an input.* As you can see, the size of the MPP depends on how many of the laborers we start with when we add another. When the first worker was added, the output went from zero to 8000, so the MPP was 8000. When the second laborer was added, output rose from 8000 to 19,000, so the increment attributable to the second laborer is 11,000, the difference between 8,000 (with one worker) and

19,000 (with two workers). The MPP for any input is the amount by which output changes as a result of the addition of that input.[1]

Statement Of The Principle

Let us now state formally **the principle of diminishing returns**: with given technological knowledge, as additional units of a variable input are added to a fixed quantity of other inputs, after some point the increments to output will become successively smaller. This means, in terms of our example, as we added additional laborers to the 1000-acre farm the output of corn would rise by less and less from the added labor, after some number of laborers (after three in the table.)[2]

The hypothetical example represents five different ways in which output may change as variable inputs are added:

1. increasing returns, where the MPP is rising;
2. constant returns, where the MPP is constant;
3. diminishing returns, where the MPP is decreasing;
4. zero returns, where the MPP is zero;
5. negative returns, where the MPP is negative.

(Since numbers 4 and 5 could occur along with any of the first three, there are perhaps only three different ways in which output changes with respect to the variable inputs.) The principle of diminishing returns does *not* say that the MPP will go through all five of these possibilities as the variable input is increased from zero toward infinity. Read it carefully. It merely states that stage 3, diminishing returns, will be reached. There could be diminishing returns after the first unit of the variable input, hence no increasing or constant returns. MPP could always decline with added laborers, but never become zero or negative. Thus, there may be diminishing returns from the start but no zero or negative returns. For example, with each successive laborer, the MPP might follow a pattern like this: 64, 32, 16, 8, 4, 2, 1, ½, ¼, ⅛, etc., getting smaller and smaller, but never reaching zero. Finally, the

---

[1] If the output is zero when the variable input is zero, then total output for any number of the variable input is the sum of the MPP's up to that number of the variable input. For 7 laborers, total output (in thousands) is 0 + 8 + 11 + 11 + 9 + 7 + 5 + 4 = 55. Thus, column (2) could be derived from column (3) or (3) could be derived from (2).

[2] In the principle of diminishing returns, the word "returns" refers to changes in *units of output,* not to profits or money. In other contexts, such as *returns* to investment, "returns" means dollar profits.

MPP could decline asymptotically toward some number above zero, again giving diminishing returns without zero or negative returns.[3]

Why There Are Diminishing Returns

So far we have stated the principle of diminishing returns. Now let's consider why production follows this pattern. Actually, given that the principle is observed to operate, why it operates is of secondary importance, but worth considering nevertheless. We have already noted that increasing returns may result from specialization of inputs and from cooperation among inputs.

Diminishing returns will occur because as more of the variable input (labor in this case) is added to a fixed quantity of other inputs (land and equipment), each unit of the variable input (including those already there) has less and less of the fixed input with which to work (there is less land and equipment with which each laborer can work). This means there is less useful work for the variable inputs to do. They are assigned less important tasks. So output does not rise as much. Eventually, the variable input may become so numerous relative to the fixed inputs that more of the variable inputs add nothing to output (MPP = 0). After that more variable inputs may simply get in the way of those already working and cause output to decline, in which case the MPP is negative.

The above reasoning should convince you that returns will diminish as variable inputs are added to a fixed quantity of others. Another convincing argument is to imagine the logical consequences of asserting that the principle does not operate. (Note, however, that whether the principle does operate is an empirical question to be ascertained by observation, not a proposition which can be proved by pure reasoning.) If there were no diminishing returns, then there would be indefinitely continuing increasing or constant returns. Consider what this implies. Suppose, in the table, there were constant returns after the third worker. Then each additional worker would add 11,000 bu. − the 100th worker, the millionth, the billionth, etc., all on a 1000-acre farm. This result is so palpably absurd as to convince intuitively that somewhere diminishing returns must set in. Indeed, if we started with a 100-square foot

---

[3] Table 5-1 is strictly hypothetical and does not pretend to represent a likely farm. Our urbanite's guess is that the MPP on a 1000-acre corn farm with modern equipment would diminish rapidly after the first laborer, but would not become negative until there were well over 5000 laborers. That is, we expect the MPP's for successive laborers would be something like this (in thousands of bushels per year): 45, 15, 3, 2.5, 2, 1.5, 1.2, 1.0, 0.9, 0.85,.... The table was set up to show all possible stages.

farm and never had diminishing returns, we could grow trillions of bushels of corn just by adding more labor.

Diminishing Returns Applies To Nonhuman Inputs Too

The principle of diminishing returns simply mentions variable and fixed inputs, not land, labor, or capital. The illustrative example showed diminishing returns from additional labor to a fixed quantity of land and capital. We could just as well illustrate the principle by varying land (or a type of capital), keeping constant labor and other inputs. Imagine starting with 10 laborers, a specified quantity of equipment, and one acre of land. There would be some output per year. Next, suppose we have the same 10 laborers, but two acres. Output would be larger. Then three acres, 4, 5, etc. Each additional acre will increase output. After some point, there would be diminishing returns from additional acres.

In this example, there might not be increasing returns, although if we started with a very small piece of land (just enough to pile the laborers and equipment on) and increased land from there, there would probably be increasing returns to the land. But would there ever be negative returns to land? It is hard to see why. As acreage increased, increments to output would gradually fall, because the variable input would be combined with less and less of the fixed inputs; that is, each acre would be worked by fewer men and less equipment. However, acres would not get in each other's way; so the worst that would happen would be zero MPP, when an additional acre is simply ignored because the men and equipment cannot use it along with the land already used.

Most economists feel that the principle of diminishing returns applies to all productive processes. Vary any type of input in a company—typists or desks or lathes or trucks—keeping constant all other inputs, and there will be diminishing returns.

How Many Laborers Would You Hire?

Before reading further, try to answer this question with reference to Table 5-1. This leads to an important application of diminishing returns and to the third basic decision: who gets what is produced. Actually, the question cannot be answered from the information in the table. You need two additional pieces of information: (1) how much the corn sells for and (2) the cost of hiring laborers. Well, suppose corn sells for $1 a bushel and labor costs $3500 per year. How many laborers would you hire?

Many people suggest hiring 2 or 3 workers, where the MPP is highest, or hiring 3 where the output per worker is highest. Others suggest 10 workers, where the total output is highest. None of these is correct. What is the firm's objective? To maximize profits. We can't tell what the firm's profits are in this example, because we don't know the costs of the other inputs (land and equipment). But we can tell when it is or is not profitable to hire workers, knowing the table and the prices of corn and labor. Suppose we had 4 workers. Would a 5th be worth hiring? He would add 7000 bu. of corn, hence, at $1 a bu., $7000 in revenue to the company. Since the wage is $3500, the company clearly gains from this 5th worker. But why stop there? A 6th worker adds 5000 more bushels, worth $5000 and also costs $3500, so he is worth hiring. A 7th adds 4000 bu. or $4000, but costs $3500. So hire him too. The 8th worker, however, adds only 3000 bu. or $3000. At a wage of $3500, the firm would lose $500 by hiring him. Answer: hire 7 workers.

If the wage rate were $6500 per year, the firm would hire only 5 workers, because the 5th adds $7000, while the 6th adds only $5000, not enough to warrant spending $6500 to hire him. Later discussion of wage determination will show that the MPP times the product price tells the maximum wages the firm would pay to hire any given quantity of labor, or, it tells the quantities of labor the firm would hire at various wages: it is the firm's demand for labor.

Operate In Diminishing Returns

The term "diminishing returns" has a connotation of something undesirable, to be avoided. But, as in our example, a firm will always find it most profitable to operate where there are diminishing returns. The unlikely exceptions are (1) if the inputs were free, the firm would hire until MPP = 0; or (2) if the inputs actually paid the company to be hired—negative wages—the firm would operate in negative returns. But then the company's output is not merely the product, but the privilege of working for the company. Perhaps some dude ranches would qualify.[4]

Clearly, with positive input costs, the firm would never add an input which actually caused output to decline or to remain the same (assuming the

---

[4] Here's a possible example of negative wages. Several years ago, a man in South Carolina found rubies and sapphires along a stream on his property. After prospecting proved unprofitable, the enterprising owner decided to sell the privilege of looking for gems. Now on any warm weekend, people by the hundreds come to the "Gem Capital of the World" and buy buckets of mud which they sift by hand through screens provided by the owner. If the average value of gems recovered per bucket is less than the price per bucket of mud, then people are paying to work on their leisure time—negative wages! Does the fact that *any* gems are found mean the MPP of labor is positive? No. The MPP is not the average gems per bucket, but is the additional gems found

firm is not coerced to hire against its will). This eliminates the operation in stages with zero or negative returns. We can eliminate operation in stages with increasing or constant returns by demonstrating that these stages imply zero or negative returns with respect to the fixed input. That is, if there are increasing returns when labor is increased relative to land, there are negative returns to land: output could be raised by using less land.

This point is proved mathematically in advanced texts. However, for your amusement, we illustrate it with the numbers in Table 5-1 where increasing returns exist:

	Land	Labor	Output	MPP of Labor
(1)	1000	0	0	
(2)	1000	1	8,000 bu.	8,000 bu.
(3)	1000	2	19,000 bu.	11,000 bu.

As labor rises from 0 to 1 to 2, the MPP of labor rises from 8000 to 11,000, showing increased returns. We now show that this implies negative returns to land, that is, more land means less output. To show this, we adopt the reasonable assumption that if *all* inputs are doubled, output would also be doubled. Therefore, if we double both land *and* labor in row (2), we get twice the output of row (2):

(4)	2000	2	16,000 bu.

Row (4) is twice row (2). But compare row (4) with row (3). The increase in acreage from 1000 to 2000 (with the same labor) has *decreased* output by 3000 bu.—the MPP of land is negative where the MPP of labor is rising, q.e.d. This would imply that the second 1000 acres caused men to be spread too thinly over the land. This illustrates the point that where there are increasing returns to a variable input, there are negative returns to other inputs. And since firms would not operate in negative returns, they will not operate in increasing returns. Therefore, firms always operate where there are diminishing returns to all inputs.

Assumptions Of The Principle

The principle of diminishing returns says increments of a variable input will cause successively smaller additions to output under the following four conditions:

---

by the marginal sifter. By selling buckets of mud instead of letting people pay to prospect as they wish, the owner is probably preventing the congestion that might otherwise drive MPP below zero and reduce his business. Reported, appropriately, on CBS News with Roger Mudd.

(1) The quantity of other kinds of inputs is fixed.

(2) The units of the variable input are of equal competence. When we add laborers to acres, each laborer is as skillful and industrious as the others. The declining MPP occurs because, with more workers, each worker, the others as well as the new one, has fewer other inputs with which to work. When we have 7 workers in the table, any one could be considered the 7th; and the productivity of all 7 is 7 times the productivity (MPP) of the 7th. Likewise, for the MPP of land, the additional acres are of equal productivity. The MPP of an acre declines when more acres are added to a fixed quantity of labor and equipment because less labor and equipment are used with each acre.

Of course, laborers do differ and so do acres. In principle, a different table applies for each different occupation and for each skill within each occupation. For small differences in ability within a given occupation, one might define a unit of labor (or land) in terms of certain abilities and view a person with less or more ability as less or more than one unit of labor. But carpenters and typists would be two separate kinds of inputs, unless anyone with one skill had the other.

(3) A given state of technological knowledge. The same knowledge of production methods does *not* mean the same method of production is used no matter how many laborers are hired. Indeed, we presume that as each laborer (or acre) is added, other inputs constant, all inputs are rearranged and reassigned in the best possible way. The MPP is found after the rearrangement.

Nor is it assumed that when firms hire workers they do in fact hire one at a time and construct something like Table 5-1. Firms start with a combination of inputs and grow by adding to all inputs. Still, to decide how many of each to hire, they have vague notions of a small but relevant portion of such tables for each input—that is, the firm does estimate whether an additional typist or accountant or 1000 square feet of floor space is worthwhile, also whether one or two fewer might be profitable.

(4) The proportions in which inputs are combined can usefully be varied. In terms of our hypothetical farm, consider how production conditions would be described if the proportions in which inputs are combined could *not* usefully be altered. There would be some necessary ratio of labor to land (ignore equipment for simplicity), say one man for each 20 acres. Starting with this combination, if we added more acres without more men, output would not change. If we added more men without more acres, there would also be no change in output. To increase output at all, we must add one man *and* 20 acres. Clearly, this does *not* describe true production conditions. We *can* add men to acres and raise output, or add acres to men and raise output. And similarly for capital equipment. There is no set proportion or ratio in which inputs must be combined.

Even in situations where the proportions seem fixed, they can generally be varied. The ratios of typewriters to typists, lathes to lathe operators, trucks to truck drivers—all these can be varied by more or less intensive use or by changing the quality of one kind of input, keeping constant the other. Some of these changes do not fit neatly into the table, but they do mean the principle of diminishing returns applies quite generally.

Here as elsewhere in economics one must distinguish the short run from the long run. In the short run, input proportions may be somewhat fixed because changes in work assignments or type of machine or size of classroom (teacher/class-space ratio) cannot be made overnight. But in the longer run (a 5 to 10 year horizon) that is more relevant for economic decisions, nearly all input proportions can be altered.

Effects of a change in assumed conditions. Some insight into the meaning and significance of diminishing returns is gained by asking in what direction would the numbers in Table 5-1 change under either of these situations: (1) the variable input, labor, is added to a larger quantity of other inputs, say, to a 5000-acre farm with more equipment instead of the 1000-acre farm; or (2) with the same combination of variable and fixed inputs as in Table 5-1, there is improved knowledge about how to combine inputs—a new method of production is discovered.

For either situation, the effect is about the same. Both the total output and the MPP's would be higher for given quantities of labor. Probably, but not for sure, the point of diminishing returns would come further down the table (at a larger number of the variable input) and more certainly the point of zero returns would occur at a higher quantity of laborers.

Table 5-2 illustrates the effect of increasing the "fixed" input, land. The MPP's for 1000 acres are repeated from Table 5-1. Notice that any given number of workers have a larger MPP when combined with 5000 acres than with 1000 and larger yet with 10,000 acres. This is the general effect of raising the "fixed" input, land in this example. Similar rises in MPP would follow from improved production knowledge, with land constant.

Thus, we can say: (1) the greater the quantity of the fixed inputs (land and equipment in Table 5-1), the higher will be the MPP's of the variable inputs, and (2) the better the technological knowledge, the higher the MPP's. Therefore, since the demand for labor and hence the wages paid depend on the productivity (MPP) of labor, the larger the amount of capital with which labor is combined and the more advanced the technology, the higher will be the average wage rate. One does indeed find, comparing various countries, that wages are higher where capital per worker is higher and where technological know-how is greater. Thus, workers in America are more productive and get paid more than in India because they are combined with

Table 5-2   Effects of increasing the "fixed" input: hypothetical MPP's of labor for various farm sizes

Number of workers (per year)	Number of acres		
	1000*	5000	10,000
	(thousands of bushels per year)		
0	–	–	–
1	8	10	14
2	11	16	22
3	11	24	28
4	9	25	32
5	7	25	36
6	5	21	36
7	4	18	34
8	3	15	31
9	2	13	27
10	1	11	23
11	0	9	20
12	–1	8	17

* From Table 5-1.

more capital, not because they work more diligently. (Their higher education in America also raises their productivity.) And over time, countries like America and Western Europe and recently Japan where capital investment per worker has risen most are those where wages have risen most too. In effect, this reflects movements to the right in Table 5-2: more capital per worker, higher MPP of workers, and, therefore, higher wages.

Another View Of The Principle: The Law Of Variable Proportions [5]

This alternative and more complicated statement of the principle emphasizes an important point: the MPP of an input will decline, not only (a)

---

[5] The designation of one as a "principle" and the other as a "law" is arbitrary and insignificant. For the curious, the "law" would read: As one input is increased *relative* to others, after some point, the rate of change of output with respect to the relatively increasing input will fall—which means the MPP of the relatively increasing input will become less and less. The "principle" is a special case of the "law."

when more of the input is added to a *fixed* quantity of other inputs, but also (b) when the variable input is increasing *relative to* the other input. This distinction is shown in the following numbers.

Quantities of Inputs

(a)	Labor	1	2	3	4	5	Increasing labor to a fixed quantity of land
	Land	10	10	10	10	10

(b)	Labor	1	5	9	16	30
	Land	10	25	30	40	60

Increasing labor relative to land, with the same labor/land ratios as in (a)

(c)	Labor	1	10	6	100	1
	Land	10	50	20	250	2

(d)		.1	.2	.3	.4	.5	Labor/land ratios common to (a), (b), and (c)

In all three examples labor is rising relative to land in the same proportion. The law of variable proportions states that the MPP of labor under (b) or (c) will decline moving from left to right the same as under (a). This means the assumption of a fixed quantity of some inputs is not necessary, merely that the variable input rises relative to other inputs. A prediction from this is that for a given technology and labor ability, the average wage level will rise if nonhuman inputs increase over time at a faster rate than human inputs and that the wage level will fall if labor rises faster than capital and land. It also means that, given the growth in capital and technology, the greater the population, the lower the standard of living.

Population Growth, Malthus, And Diminishing Returns

Early in the 19th Century, Thomas Malthus, British philosopher and economist, predicted that unless people took deliberate steps to curb births, population would grow faster than the food supply.[6] He judged that this tendency had occurred in the past and that the rise in people relative to food caused a gradual decline in wages toward, then below, the subsistence level. Then population is reduced by famine, disease, and/or wars, leaving a lower ratio of people to food and higher wages, only to be followed by another cycle of rising population relative to food, lowering wages to below subsistence level, and again decimation through famine, disease, and/or war.

---

[6] He stated that population grows at a geometric rate, food at an arithmetic rate, and, therefore, the ratio of people to food becomes larger over time, without population checks.

It is from such forecasts that economics acquired the reputation as a "dismal science."

Let us reformulate Malthus' theory in terms of the principle of diminishing returns. If labor increases relative to land, the MPP and hence wages of labor will gradually decline to below subsistence level. At that point, if population is decreased by disaster, the ratio of labor to land will be smaller, the MPP of the remaining labor will be higher (we move up Table 5-1), and wages will be high enough to live and reproduce on. Then, the labor/land ratio begins to rise again by population growth.

Since things have not worked out as Malthus predicted, has the principle of diminishing returns been shown invalid? No. While population has been expanding in the Western world, the conditions which must be held constant for the MPP of labor to decline have not been constant. Also expanding greatly for the past 150 years have been the quality of labor (through education), technology, and capital per worker. In effect, we have experienced a movement to the right in Table 5-2, so that subsistence wages would not be reached (for most occupations) unless population were much higher than it is. Still, Malthus's predictions seem unfortunately correct for China, India, Indonesia, and parts of Latin America—over three-fifths of the world's population.

"Listen to this. 'At the present population growth rate, soon every square mile on earth will be inhabited by an average of 683.2 people'."

Summary

The principle of diminishing returns states that as additional units of a variable input are added to a fixed quantity of other inputs, the increments to output will decline after some quantity of the variable input. These increments to output caused by the variable input are called the marginal physical product, MPP. The principle applies to all productive processes and to all inputs, human and nonhuman. The demand for an input is derived from its MPP's and the price of the product. Firms will always hire inputs under conditions of diminishing returns.

The principle operates under these assumptions: (1) the quantity of inputs other than the variable is (relatively) fixed; (2) all units of the variable input are of equal competence; (3) a given state of technological knowledge; and (4) the proportions in which inputs are combined can usefully be varied. An increase in the quantity of the "fixed" input or a technological improvement will bring about both higher total output and higher MPP's of the variable input for all quantities of the variable input. This means that the higher is the ratio of nonhuman to human inputs, the higher will be the productivity and hence the wages of labor.

Malthus predicted population would grow relative to all other things. By the principle of diminishing returns, this implies a rise in labor relative to other inputs and, therefore, by diminishing returns to labor, lower wages. The main reason why real wages have risen despite population rise is that technological advance, improved education, and increased capital per worker have more than offset the downward pressure on wages of rising population.

Study Questions Chapter 5

1. What in general does the principle of diminishing returns describe?

2. State the principle of diminishing returns.

3. Illustrate it with a hypothetical example.

4. Define "marginal physical produce"—MPP.

5. What are the five stages which MPP may go through?

6. Give a numerical example showing all five stages.

7. Does the principle of diminishing returns say that MPP *will* go through all stages from increasing returns to negative returns? Which?

8. Explain how there could be diminishing returns as the variable input increases without there ever being zero or negative returns.

9. Explain why diminishing returns will always exist in a productive activity.

10. Phrase the principle of diminishing returns so that the variable input is nonhuman.

11. Reason out why the principle will apply from increasing nonhuman relative to human inputs (as well as human relative to nonhuman).

12. Explain the quantity of laborers to hire from the table you made for #3.

13. What general rule is used to determine the quantity to hire?*

14. Why would a firm never operate in negative returns?

15. What strange condition would make a firm willing to operate in negative returns?*

16. Explain with a hypothetical example why a firm will never operate in increasing returns. (The next three questions lead to the answer.)

17. If A and B are types of inputs, and if there are increasing returns to input A, what can be said about the MPP of input B?*

18. What key assumption underlies this proof?*

19. From the following numbers, show that increasing returns from more of input A implies negative returns from input B.*

Row	A	B	MPP_A	TP
a	0	1	–	0
b	1	1	10	10
c	2	1	12	22

20. What assumptions underlie the principle of diminishing returns?

21. What does it mean to "vary input proportions?"*

22. What numerical effect on the MPP's results from raising the "fixed" inputs or from technological advance?*

23. What does this imply about the standard of living over time as both technology and capital per worker rise? Explain.

24. Is the same method of production employed as input proportions are varied (as one moves down Table 5-1)?*

25. What is the law of variable proportions?

26. Explain why the principle of diminishing returns is a special case of the law of variable proportions.

27. Explain the Malthusian population theory. Phrase this theory in terms of the principle of diminishing returns.

28. Explain why population growth has not caused living standards to fall in the Western World over the past 200 years.

29. Does the principle of diminishing returns tell which quantity of inputs is most profitable to hire?*

30. What additional information besides that of Table 5-1 would be needed to determine the most profitable quantity to hire?*

31. Given Table 5-2, what more information would you need to pick the most profitable input combination?*

Answers to starred questions.

13. Add another worker as long as the value of its MPP exceeds the wage rate, because this difference adds to profits (or to the money available to pay the fixed inputs).

15. Negative wages—workers pay the employer.

17. It is negative.

18. If *all* inputs are doubled, output will be doubled.

19. Double row b to get row d:

Row	A	B	TP
d	2	2	20

Compare rows d and c: both have two A's, but d has 2 B's and c has 1 B; yet d's output is less than c's, so MPP_B is -2.

21. To change the quantity of one input relative to another (or others); or, stated differently, to change one input without changing all others by the same proportion.

22. They are raised, as shown by moving across the rows of Table 5-2.

24. No. While the state of technological knowledge is unchanged or given (as one moves down Table 5-1), the actual method of production used will vary with changes in input proportions.

29. No. The principle relates to units of output from units of input. It is not in dollars and says nothing specific about profits. "Returns" does not mean profits in "diminishing returns."

30. Price of the output and price of the variable input.

31. Same as #30, plus the price of land.

6

Who Gets What Is Produced

There are many ways in which the output of society could be divided up among the population. The private enterprise system receives much criticism for the unequal and, some say, unfair distribution of society's output, especially from the "have-nots" but also from others who sympathize with low-income groups.[1] How is this division determined under private enterprise? Is there any rhyme or reason to it? We turn now to the third basic economic decision: who gets what is produced.

Distribution To Highest Bidders

In effect, goods and services are auctioned off to the highest bidders. This has two tendencies: (1) things go to those with the most dollars; (2) things go to those with the greatest desire for them. Each tendency prevents the other from being fulfilled. Obviously, even if everyone had the same tastes, the inequality of purchasing power would cause those with more dollars to get more of society's output than those with less. The second tendency is less obvious. To appreciate it, assume that dollars were distributed equally. Would everyone then receive the same goods and services? No. Because people have different tastes, the bidding process would still operate. Individual items (golf balls) would still go to those with the greatest desire for these items relative to their desire for other things (say, mystery books).

It is important to look further into the basis by which goods and services are distributed. We have said so far that goods and services go to those who will pay the most. But what determines the distribution of the ability to pay? This depends mainly on the distribution of income. Some

---

[1] However, there are many who generally approve of this distribution and still sympathize with low-income people.

people may draw on savings or borrow, but these possibilities reflect past or expected income, so it is still income which determines the possession of purchasing power.

Income Depends On Contribution To Production

In this section, we show that each input's contribution to production can be isolated from the contribution of other inputs, and that, under competition, each input receives the money value of his contribution to production.

How to measure an input's effect on output. Is it really possible to ascertain the contribution to output of a typist in an auto company, a janitor in a shoe manufacturing firm, or the contribution of a typewriter, or of 100 square feet of storeroom space for cleaning equipment? The answer is yes, for all practical purposes. In all cases, this contribution is the marginal physical product, MPP, discussed in connection with the principle of diminishing returns.

A firm could measure the MPP of any input by the following experiment. First, measure the output of the firm before adding an additional unit of the input. Then measure the output after the input has been added. The change in output after the additional unit of the input is the MPP of that input. For each measurement, all inputs are assigned duties so they produce as much as possible. Thus, there may be a reassignment of duties. For example, an additional clerk-typist may free some accountants from clerical work they were doing and enable them to do quicker and better accounting, which in turn enables the plant manager to make more effective decisions. This in turn may mean the workers and machines produce more or better outputs. Of course, one clerk-typist in a large company won't make much difference to final output. But, there must be some difference or it was not worthwhile to hire the typist.

It is not enlightening to identify the MPP of an input from the specific tasks of that input. Consider the operator of a machine that stamps holes in the front of radio cabinets. He performs this operation hundreds of times a day. How much of each radio did this operative make? How much did the machine make? There is no useful answer to either question, except to describe the task, which provides no clue to the percentage of the radio made by the operative or the machine. The only way to measure the contribution of either in terms of whole radios is to perform the hypothetical experiment described above. In the case of the laborer, think not of one who operates a particular machine, but of a certain quality of labor abilities which could be trained and assigned to many different tasks (including the operation of the hole-stamping machine). The MPP of this machine operator is the MPP of any worker of that general ability no matter what his task (as long as he works steadily) and this *is* so many radios per hour or per day, because a change in the quantity of such labor (with *appropriate* rearrangement of tasks) will affect whole radio output. The added laborer will not result in a lot of radio frames without holes for the dials or a lot of tubes and wires without frames to put them in, if tasks are reassigned sensibly.

These points also apply for identifying the MPP of a unit of capital. If capital in the form of a particular machine is added, its MPP is calculated only on the assumption that other inputs (mainly labor) are reassigned appropriately (so the machine is not idle). Moreover, an increment of capital may take the form of a better machine replacing a poorer one. More or less labor of a given quality means more or fewer hours of labor service performed, however assigned. More or less capital means more or fewer dollars worth of capital equipment used per hour (assuming no changes in the prices of capital equipment).

Two incorrect measures of MPP. To avoid confusion, let us describe two other experiments which do *not* identify the MPP of an input, but which sound quite similar to the one which does. Suppose we wish to identify the MPP of farm laborers on a 5000-acre farm which has 10 laborers and some capital equipment. First measure the output of the farm *with the 10 laborers*. Then measure the output of the farm *without any laborers*. This difference in output is *not* the MPP of the 10 laborers. Rather, the MPP of *all 10* of the laborers is *10 times* the MPP of the 10th laborer, ten times the change in output which occurs between the 9th laborer and the 10th. If it were the difference in output between zero laborers and 10 laborers, then the MPP of the 10 laborers would amount to almost the entire output (assuming there are no other kinds of laborers used and that the output would be about zero without any labor).

If we calculated the MPP of capital the same way—measure the difference in output with no equipment and with whatever equipment is actually used—the MPP of capital would also amount to almost the entire output under modern farm technology. And by this incorrect method, we would calculate the MPP of land as the difference in total output with no land and with all 5000 acres, and again attribute the entire output to land, since without land there would be no output. More correctly, the total contribution of land is 5000 times the MPP of the 5000th acre. And 10,000 times the MPP of the 10,000th half-acre would be a better measure of the total contribution of the land. In general, the MPP of any input is found by observing the output change from a small increment of the variable input. That change in output is the MPP of all such units of the variable input (all 10,000 half-acres), since any one of these units could be the marginal unit added. In this way, we avoid the absurd result of this incorrect experiment, namely that the sum of the outputs ascribed to each of the inputs exceeds the total output.

A second incorrect experiment is to change the quantity of a variable input without reassigning other inputs. For example, suppose we are to measure the MPP of a particular laborer who is a night guard and whose final duty is to unlock the plant entrance in the morning. If we assume (absurdly) that without this particular input, no one else would be assigned this task, and, therefore, the plant would remain locked and nothing would be produced, the MPP of this person becomes the whole output. In fact, however, if the company employed all other inputs except this guard, it would reassign others so the entrance would be unlocked, while some other less important things would not be done (as effectively). To repeat, the MPP of any input is the change in output when a small increment of that input is added to a given quantity of other inputs and where, both before and after the addition, all inputs are assigned to be used as effectively as possible.

With the correct experiment in mind, one should have no difficulty understanding that output is affected by inputs like janitors, typists, engineers, and plant managers who do not work directly on the final product. A janitor whose cleaning causes others to work more effectively has an MPP equal to the added effectiveness (added output) caused by his services. An industrial engineer whose ideas reduce the inputs required to produce a given output has an MPP whose value is the savings in costs caused by his services.

However, one might question whether inputs devoted to sales and advertising contribute toward output. They certainly would not affect the number of radios a factory could produce, though they would presumably affect the price and quantity that can be sold. Several approaches are possible regarding sales inputs. Sales efforts provide information. It could be argued that the company is selling information as well as product (radios). The MPP of salesmen would be the value of this information. Alternatively, sales and advertising may add to the value of a product (in consumers' eyes). One might argue that the radio company is really selling radio services and, having enhanced their value by advertising, they are selling more services per radio. Some would regard this as stretching the notion of radio production rather thin. Finally, one may acknowledge that, except as it does provide information, advertising is indeed no part of production of the radio company. Still, advertising inputs do add to the revenue of the company and their marginal units will be paid the value of their contribution to company income just as are all other inputs, as we shall see shortly. (The services of wholesalers, retailers, and transporters from the factory *are* part of radio production, since the consumer prefers radios at the store when he wants them, rather than more cumbersome alternatives, such as a trip to the factory to buy a radio.)

MPP and VMP: VMP = MPP X Product Price. The marginal physical product, MPP, is the addition to output from another unit of a variable input. It is stated in units of output, not dollars. *The value of the marginal product,* VMP, is the *revenue* the company takes in from the sale of the MPP, or stated differently, the VMP is the additional revenue from an additional unit of a variable input. It is in dollars. If the company can sell the MPP without lowering the product price, the VMP equals the MPP times the price of the product. For example, the MPP of the 7th laborer in Table 5-1 (on diminishing returns) is 4000 bushels of corn per year. With the price of corn $1 a bushel, the VMP of the 7th laborer is $4000. If corn sold for $1.50 a bushel, his VMP would be $6000.[2]

Proof that inputs are paid the value of their contribution to production. This outcome occurs only under *competitive* private enterprise. In this proof, we assume the firm can acquire additional inputs of a given kind without changing the price of the input. This is part of "competition." This means, for example, that if the wage rate for farm laborers is, say, $4000 per worker per year, the firm can hire as many workers as it wants at $4000 per worker.

1. As successive units of a given kind of input are added to a fixed quantity of other inputs, output rises and so, therefore, does revenue. That is, the input has a positive MPP, so MPP times product price is positive. (If product price itself declines as output rises, the wording is altered, but the conclusions are the same.)

2. By the principle of diminishing returns, these additions to output become successively smaller as additional units of the variable input are added. Therefore, the additions to revenue also become smaller. (As we move down Table 5-1, of Chapter 5, both the MPP and the VMP are decreasing).

3. To maximize profits, the firm will hire additional units of the variable input as long as the revenue gained (the VMP) exceeds the cost of the inputs (the wage).

4. Since the VMP gradually declines with additional units of the variable input and the wage per input stays the same (by the competitive assumption), if the firm can vary the inputs gradually, it will hire up to but not past the quantity of the input where the wage equals the VMP, the value of the input's contribution. If the firm stopped hiring before this, it could gain by hiring a little more, because the VMP, the increase in revenue, would exceed the wage, the addition to cost. If the firm hired past this quantity, it would lose on the added unit of labor, because the VMP would be less than

---

[2] If the product price falls as more output is sold, the added revenue from an additional unit of input is called the marginal revenue product, MRP, and equals the MPP times the "marginal revenue."

the wage rate. So it hires exactly the quantity at which the wage equals the value of the worker's contribution to production, the VMP, q.e.d.

In the case of an input owned by the company and not hired, the same principle applies but the wording is different. The firm would purchase such an input as long as its VMP over the life of the input exceeds the cost of the input, prorated over its life.

We do not allege that firms in fact hire inputs one by one. But whatever quantity they do hire they can vary slightly relative to other inputs. In so doing, they end up with wage equal VMP; for, if not, a firm can raise its profits by changing the quantity it hires, as point 4 shows.

This proof can be illustrated with a diagram. In Table 6-1, the VMP is derived from the MPP by the formula VMP = MPP times product price. In Fig. 6-1, columns (1) and (4) from the table are plotted and the points connected to get the VMP curve, which is the firm's demand for labor. Point A is the point of diminishing returns. Suppose the competitive wage is $78 per week (for the type of labor in the diagram). How this wage is determined is discussed later in this chapter. We want to show that this wage will equal the value of each worker's contribution to production. Since the VMP measures this value and the wage equals the VMP at quantity 16 (point E), we need to explain therefore why the firm will want to employ 16 workers, no more and no fewer.

Suppose it hired fewer than 16, say 12. Then by adding a 13th worker

Table 6-1. Derivation of the value of the marginal product from the marginal physical product

(1)	(2)	(3)	(4)	(1)	(2)	(3)	(4)
Quantity of Labor	Marginal Physical Product	Product Price	Value of Marginal Product (2)x(3)	Quantity of Labor	Marginal Physical Product	Product Price	Value of Marginal Product (2)x(3)
0	–	$2	$ 0	11	67	$2	$134
1	22	2	44	12	60	2	120
2	42	2	84	13	54	2	108
3	54	2	108	14	48	2	96
4	65	2	130	15	43	2	86
5	72	2	144				
6	78	2	156	16	38	2	76
7	81	2	162	17	34	2	68
8*	82	2	164	18	31	2	62
9	79	2	158	19	27	2	54
10	73	2	146	20	25	2	50

* Point of diminishing returns

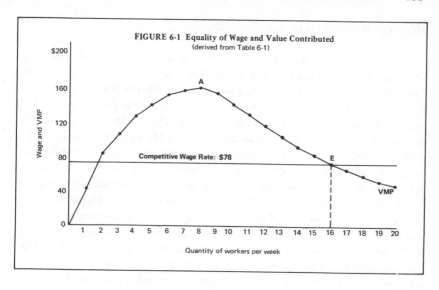

FIGURE 6-1 Equality of Wage and Value Contributed (derived from Table 6-1)

it would raise revenue by $108 while costs rose by only $78. The firm would be better off by $30. Such a gain is true for any quantity back of 16. On the other hand, if it hired 20 workers, the added cost of the 20th, $78, would exceed the added revenue therefrom, $50, causing a loss of $28 on this worker. Similar statements apply to all quantities over 16. For quantities under 16, the *vertical gap* between the VMP and the wage line measures the gain derived from hiring another. Beyond 16, this vertical gap is the loss from each additional worker.

Why not stop at 15, since #16 adds the same in revenue and costs? If the firm could hire fractional workers (perhaps part-time), it would gain by hiring beyond 15 toward 16. If not, the 16th would be a matter of indifference. Exact equality between wage and VMP presumes an ability to move continuously along the curve. In the real world of finite (rather than infinitesimal) adjustments, the firm would come as close as possible to equality between wage and VMP. Furthermore, if the equilibrium quantity of workers is 50 or more where VMP equals the wage, then one may expect that the VMP for just one worker before the intersection of VMP and the wage line would be very little different from that at the intersection. Imagine all the quantities in Fig. 6-1 multiplied by 10. Equilibrium would be 160. Obviously, the VMP for #159 would not be noticeably different from that at 160. This adds to the expectation that equality between VMP and wage is virtually achieved under competitive conditions.[3]

---

[3] Similar reasoning was used in Chapter 5 to determine the quantity to hire in Table 5-1 on diminishing returns, except that this time, the product price and wage rate are given. Suppose the wage were $120 per week. What

Motives Of Employers And Workers

The equality of wage with value contributed does not result from any deliberate efforts by the firm (or workers) to arrive at "fair" wages. It results from efforts of firms to maximize profits—to hire when it pays and not when it doesn't—under these conditions (1) input proportions can be varied; (2) increments from a variable input are subject to diminishing returns; and (3) for reasons the firm cannot control, the firm hires inputs competitively. If the firm does not have to compete with other employers to get its workers, the same efforts at profit maximization will result in wages that are below the value contributed by workers, and one might say the workers will be "exploited" as explained under "monopsony" in Chapter 7. To reiterate, the forces that bring about equality between wage and value contributed are the variability of input proportions, diminishing returns, competition among employers to get workers, and employer efforts to maximize profits. The main condition acting against this result is employer monopoly power in hiring workers. Employer motivation is the same in either case—profits.

Can Input Proportions Be Varied So Finely? [4]

The above discussion assumed that if VMP exceeded the wage by a small amount, the company could add a small quantity of the variable input (or reduce the other inputs by a small quantity) and thereby raise profits. Otherwise, it would not end up precisely where wage = VMP. But can this be done? Or are not most inputs "lumpy" so they cannot be varied by small amounts? To some extent, lumpiness does preclude perfect adjustment. But remember, by the law of variable proportions, the effect of raising input A keeping B constant is also achieved by reducing B keeping A constant, which adds to the possibility of fine variations.

Also, are there not frequently input combinations which cannot be varied at all? One typist to one typewriter; one machinist to one machine. Again yes and no. Since what is desired from both typist and typewriter is certain services, the inputs can be defined in terms of the ability to provide these services. In this way the company can in effect raise the ratio of typist to typewriter by hiring a more skilled typist, or raise the ratio of typewriter to typist by acquiring a better typewriter (on which any typist could do

---

would be the quantity employed? (Answer: 12) If wage = $50, how many? (Answer: 20) The lower the wage, the more it is worth hiring. Total profits cannot be determined from the diagram because the costs of hiring other inputs besides the variable labor are not given. Some of these other inputs are presumably other types of labor.

[4] This section is more difficult and of lesser importance than others.

better work). Furthermore, depending upon the cost of typewriters, it might be worthwhile to have extra typewriters on hand for other employees' occasional use or in case of breakdown, thereby altering the one to one ratio of typist to typewriter.

One might expect that if the proportions between inputs A and B really cannot be varied, then it would not be possible to isolate the MPP of A from that of B. But advanced theory shows that, even if inputs must be combined in fixed proportions within each company, if these proportions are different from one product to another (1A + 1B produce 1X, while 1A + 2B produce 1Y), there may still be a VMP for each input which declines gradually as the quantity of one input rises relative to others.[5] This possibility adds to the expectation that input proportions can be changed by small amounts and that firms reach a profit maximizing position where each input payment equals VMP.

All Incomes Are Value Contributed

Consider the following equation:

$$(1)\ MPP_a Q_a + MPP_b Q_b + \ldots + MPP_n Q_n = \text{Total Product.}$$

"a" is a kind of input (such as a typist, or a lathe operator, or a square-foot of floorspace). MPP_a is the marginal physical product of input "a" and Q_a is the quantity of the "a"s employed. As described above (p. 129), $MPP_a Q_a$ is the total contribution to output of all the "a"s employed. Similarly for "b" and the other inputs. Equation (1) says that the total output of a firm is the sum of the contributions to output of each input, where an input's contribution is defined as its MPP.[6]

---

[5] See *Price Theory*, Chapter 8, by Milton Friedman, Aldine Publishing Co., 1962, or *Economic Theory*, pp. 144-154, by Gary S. Becker, Alfred A. Knopf, 1971. Neither is a book for beginners.

[6] Equation (1) does not state an obvious truth, even though it may seem obvious that the total output is the sum of contributions of each input. Equation (1) holds only under the production conditions that if the quantity of all inputs is increased by any proportion, then output will expand by that same proportion. This means, for instance, if all inputs were doubled, output would be twice as great (an assumption we used on p. 118). While these production conditions are plausible, others could prevail and then the sum of MPP's of all inputs might not equal total product. These mathematical relationships are discussed in advanced texts where MPP_a is expressed as a partial derivative, $\dfrac{\partial \text{ output}}{\partial \text{ input a}}$, of a "production function" relating output to the quantities of inputs, output $= f(Q_a, Q_b, \ldots, Q_n)$.

Now let us multiply each side of equation (1) by the price of the product,

$$(\text{product price}) \times (MPP_aQ_a + MPP_bQ_b + \ldots + MPP_nQ_n) = (\text{product price}) \times (\text{output}) \text{ to get:}$$

$$(2) \; VMP_aQ_a + VMP_bQ_b + \ldots + VMP_nQ_n = \text{total company revenue.}$$

(Remember, $VMP = MPP \times$ product price.) The term VMP_aQ_a is the *money value* of the contribution to production of all the "a"s hired. We explained earlier that under competition each input is hired until its VMP equals its wage. (Note, however, that equation (2) does not show or prove this.) It follows from equation (2) that, *if* each input is paid its VMP (the value of its contribution to production), then the sum of all these input payments (equal to inputs' VMP's) exactly equals the firm's total revenue.

One may wonder then—where are the firm's profits? The answer is that if the firm owns any inputs—most companies do own their plant facilities and machinery—it will have left over, after paying each hired input its VMP, an amount equal to the VMP's of these owned inputs. Thus, profits are the value contributed to production by the inputs owned by the firm.[7]

This equation tends to refute a cornerstone of Marxian economic theory. Marx held that under capitalism, after wages are paid, there is left a "surplus value" which the workers created but which they are cheated out of. But we see that this "surplus value" is really the contribution of nonhuman inputs, not of labor. Marx failed to recognize that capital also contributes to production and that the contributions of labor and capital can be separated. The "marginal productivity theory" which underlies this chapter had not been developed during Marx's lifetime. To justify their contention that labor creates all value and should receive all income, some Marxists claim that capital equipment is really "embodied labor" having been produced by prior labor. This is discussed in Chapter 12.

Are all expenses for inputs? One implication of equation (2) is that all the company's income is used up paying inputs for their contribution to production. But are there not some payments which are not for inputs? If so, where does this money come from? The money would come from the company's profits, which are the payment for the contributions of the inputs owned by the company. Some examples of such expenditures are: (1) the

---

[7] In some cases where the firm's owners also work for the firm (a family-owned store or law firm) the salaries paid to the owners may be less than the VMP's of these worker-owners. Then, profits will be partly the contribution of owned nonhuman inputs and partly the contribution of underpaid worker-owners, who for various reasons (such as tax considerations) might prefer low salaries and higher profits to higher salaries and lower profits. (The opposite could also be true.)

purchase of goods and services for the direct use by the owners, such as "free" dinners at stockholders' meetings, (2) deliberate subsidies by the firm to others—employment of friends or relatives of the owners at wages above their value to the company, or donations to charity (where a gain in sales is not the primary objective). These two items are generally a very small part of most firms' expenses. (3) Another expense, quite large, for which the company usually receives nothing that contributes to production, is taxes. But if taxes were repealed, all of the former taxes would not go to the owners for long. Rather, competition for the higher profits would increase investment and force prices down, reducing profits.

Finally, there are many expenses which seem to have no relation to production, but which really are wage payments to inputs. We refer to the purchase of goods and services which make working conditions more pleasant (air conditioned offices). These may increase the productivity of workers. Or they may simply make the job more pleasant, thereby enabling the company to pay lower wages than without these conditions. Other examples are expenditures for some safety features, landscaping, comfortable rest rooms, nurses in attendance, company parking lots, company athletic facilities, and luxurious executive suites. The cost of these would come from the VMP's of the workers who benefit from them. And the same is true of other fringe benefits such as paid vacation, holidays, pension funds, social security taxes, jury pay, and paid sick leave—they are all part of wages. If workers did not receive these fringe benefits, their money incomes would be higher by the cost of the fringe benefits.

Do Companies Perform The Relevant Experiment?

We have explained that wages equal value contributed because firms hire additional workers until the value of their MPP's falls to the wage rate. And we explained how the MPP is measured in principle by comparing output before and after hiring a unit of the input, with appropriate reassignment of tasks. Now we suggest that companies really do not hire inputs one by one nor perform this experiment when hiring inputs. Have we then failed to show that wages tend to equal the value of the MPP's of workers? No.

All the company need do to bring about the equality between wage and value contributed is to ask, when deciding the quantity of any input to hire, "Will it pay to hire another?" True, to answer this question perfectly, the relevant experiment is necessary. But, without it, the employer (who can survive in business) undoubtedly can estimate with reasonable accuracy whether another janitor or typist or 1000 square feet of floor space will be worth the cost. Whether it is "worth the cost" means whether the added revenue, the VMP, exceeds the input cost. The employer need not be familiar with our economic jargon—diminishing returns, MPP, VMP—to act as economists, using these terms, predict.

Wage Determination By Demand And Supply

A wage is the price of a labor service. Like other prices it is determined by demand and supply. If you have mastered the appendix on demand and supply (don't worry about elasticity), this part should be easy. If not, a review of that might help before proceeding.

Figure 6-2 shows the demand for and supply of labor for a given occupation and degree of skill and in a given geographical area. Suppose it refers to 80-word-a-minute typists in Chicago. The demand curve shows the quantities employers would like to hire at various wage rates. It refers to a labor market with many employers, not just to one company. Its slope follows the law of demand—the lower is the wage, the more workers employers will want to hire. The main reason for the downward slope is our old friend diminishing returns—as more typists are added relative to other inputs, their MPP's and hence VMP's decrease, so it won't pay to hire more workers unless wages are lowered. The supply curve shows the quantities of labor offered at various wages. The higher are the wages of typists in Chicago, the more people will seek jobs there as typists, hence the upward slope.

Just as with product demand and supply, labor demand and supply have "determinants," forces other than wage which determine the quantity demanded or supplied, forces which are held constant along the curves, and forces changes in which cause the whole curves to shift. The demand for labor by *a* firm is the VMP and that by all firms in an area is (with some technical qualifications) a sum of firms' VMP's. Thus, three of the five determinants listed are directly derived from the relationship, VMP = MPP X Product price.

The determinants of the demand for labor are:

1. The price of the product (or products) produced by the labor.
2. Technology. How MPP changes as the quantity of labor changes. In other words, what the numbers are in Table 6-1.
3. The quantity of other inputs used along with the given input. The more other inputs used, the higher generally will be the MPP or productivity of the given type of input.
4. Prices of other inputs: substitutes and complements. The effect here is the same as for product demand.
5. Employer tastes (if any) for discrimination. If employers prefer blue-eyed blonds, they may pay a bit extra for them and the blond's productivity will include good looks as well as typing. Of course, the stockholders or top officials of a company would rather not waste money catering to such preferences of their subordinates. An employer

discriminates *against* a group if he fails to hire them even though their productivity would justify doing so. Stockholders lose from that too. If most employers discriminate against a group (by race, sex, religion), then demand will be less for that group and their equilibrium wage will be lower. What appears as employer discrimination is often worker discrimination. If employers hire those with whom other employees dislike working, they may have to pay more to get their other workers, unless the discriminating employees have virtually no alternatives where they can avoid the disfavored group. Rather than offend the discriminating employees (or pay them more), the employer may refuse to hire the disfavored group, unless their supply price is low enough.

The determinants of the supply of labor to a given occupation and area are:

1. Worker tastes for the occupation. This includes all the non-wage aspects such as danger, excitement, interest, glamour, status, marriage prospects, personalities of fellow workers, their race and religion, if relevant to the worker, character of the neighborhood, etc.
2. Wages in alternative occupations. A rise in wages elsewhere causes the whole supply curve to decrease and conversely. The alternatives must be relevant. For most typists, wages in sales, modeling, and bookkeeping are relevant; those of airline pilots, quarterbacks, or operatic tenors are not.
3. Costs of entry. This is mainly the time and expense of training required. The supply is affected by the extent of subsidization of such training, as by free tuition or living expenses (for students at West Point or Annapolis).
4. The overall price level. An inflation of 25% means workers will demand 25% higher wages (supply will decrease), since people work for command over goods and services, not for money per se—they work for real wages rather than for money wages.

Now let's turn to Fig. 6-2. As you might guess by now, the wage and quantity employed will be w_1 and q_1 where the lines intersect. But let's see why. In 6a we show why the wage could not be *above* w_1 and in 6b why it could not be *below* w_1, proving that it must be *at* w_1.[8] For this we must assume that no unions or minimum wage laws hold wages up and no wage ceilings hold them down. These are covered later.

---

[8] We have used this technique several times. So we'll give it a name: the equilibrium explanation technique, EET. To explain why a given outcome is an equilibrium, show why, if the price or quantity were on one side of the equilibrium, there would be a tendency to move toward equilibrium. Then take a point on the other side of the equilibrium and explain again the forces that would push toward the equilibrium.

FIGURE 6-2 Wage Determination by Demand and Supply

6-2a Wages above equilibrium

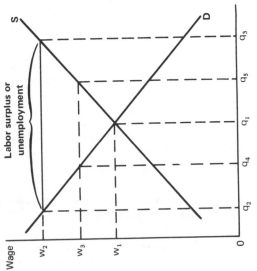

Equilibrium wage and employment: w_1 and q_1
Wage above equilibrium, w_2, causes
labor surplus or unemployment, $q_3 - q_2$
Competition among workers for jobs drives wage
down to w_1, eliminating unemployment

6-2b Wages below equilibrium

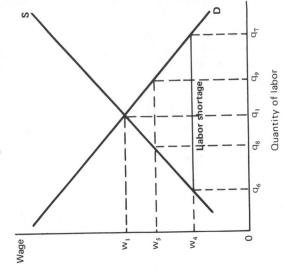

Wage below equilibrium, w_4, causes
a labor shortage of $q_7 - q_6$
Competition among employers for workers pulls
wage up to w_1, eliminating labor shortage

First, Fig. 6-2a. If the wage were at w_2, then according to the supply curve q_3 would want to work in the occupation and area. But the demand curve shows that employers only want to hire q_2 and wage w_2. So there will *be a labor surplus* of q_3-q_2. Either or both of two results will follow: (1) some of those not employed will offer to work for less than w_2 and employers will then lower the wage (for them *and* those already employed); or more likely (2) employers, noting an excess of applicants for jobs, will reduce wages, since employers, we'll assume, aren't going to pay any more than they have to. They're not in business to play Santa Claus. At a lower wage than w_2, say w_3, the quantity demanded (not the demand) rises to q_4, while the quantity supplied would be less, q_5. But there would still be a labor surplus, q_5-q_4; the same pressure to reduce the wage exists for any wage above w_1. Thus, no wage above w_1 will prevail.

Now turn to Fig. 6-2b. Our Simon Legree employers are free to push the wage down as much as they like. Will they pay starvation wages then? Not if there is competition among employers for workers. If the wage is below w_1 at w_4, then employers will want to hire q_7. But only q_6 are willing to work at this low wage. (What happened to the others who were available at higher wages? Some left the labor force for school, housework, and retirement. Others seek jobs in alternative occupations. Remember, on a supply curve, wages elsewhere are given; so high typist wages relative to wages in other occupations attract workers from elsewhere and low wages induce some Chicago typists to seek other jobs.) At wage w_4 there is a labor *shortage* of q_7-q_6. Employers want more workers than they can get at w_4. So some employers who would rather have more than do without (as the demand curve shows) will raise the wage to get more workers. Others will have to follow suit or lose workers to those who pay more. Suppose the wage rises to w_5. Then q_9 are demanded but only q_8 supplied; there's still a shortage which will induce employers to raise wages again, until the wage reaches w_1; q.e.d.

Thus, w_1 is the only wage compatible with the forces underlying demand and supply—the determinants of demand and supply. This is brought about because competition among workers for jobs prevents the wage from remaining above w_1 and competition among employers for workers prevents the wage from remaining below w_1. There is no effort to be fair or reasonable or altruistic, even though as explained earlier, the wage does equal the workers' contribution to production. It's the invisible hand again.[9]

One should appreciate the connection between Fig. 6-2 and Fig. 6-1. The wage w_1 determined in Fig. 6-2 is the competitive wage line of Fig. 6-1.

---

[9] Some people rebel at the fact that wages are determined by demand and supply like product prices. Others choose to deny it. In fact, in 1965, the Secretary of Labor, Willard Wirtz, prohibited the use of the term "labor market" in any Labor Department speech or publication.

The equality of wage with value contributed is seen from Fig. 6-1; it cannot be seen from Fig. 6-2.

Unemployment. Who are the unemployed? Not housewives, children, retired people, or society's drop-outs, who are neither employed nor looking for work. The unemployed are those without jobs who are seeking work and are willing to work for the going wage or less. At w_1, everyone who wants a job has one: quantity demanded equals quantity supplied. Only if the wage is *above* the competitive level is there unemployment. Unemployment is synonymous with labor surplus. Any unemployment in an occupation or area can be eliminated by wage reductions to the competitive level. However, even in prosperous times unemployment is normally about 4% of the labor force, because there are always people changing jobs and entering the labor force from school or housework. And while the widespread unemployment of a recession would be reduced by wage cuts, most economists also recommend expanding total spending power through monetary-fiscal policy. However, monetary-fiscal policy is not useful against localized unemployment covering only one or a few industries, localities, skills, occupations, or one broad category like young unskilled people ages 15-21, where unemployment is often several times the level of the whole economy. A rise in total spending through monetary-fiscal policy when unemployment is 15% among teenagers and 3% among others would only create inflation. If teenage unemployment were reduced at all, it would be only because prices and others' wages rose relative to teenage wages, which, in terms of unskilled teenagers' real wages, is the same as if their wages were reduced without the inflation. Thus, the solution to localized unemployment is wage reduction. For unskilled teenagers, improvements in skills would help, but for those who don't benefit from high school or college this improvement comes mainly through work experience, which requires a start at a low wage.

One competitive wage? The equilibrium just described and the earlier reasoning about real cost and wage payments in alternative uses has implied that for a *given skill and area*, all employers pay the same wage. Many people reject all of economic wage theory because they are sure that even for the same occupation and area different employers do pay different wages and in fact some individual employers pay different wages to workers doing the same thing. First, some apparent wage differences are deceiving. People in the same occupational title—typist—have great variations in skills, duties, knowledge of the job, potential for advancement, ability to get along with others, absenteeism, honesty, dependability, etc. All these factors affect one's economic worth, hence one's MPP. Also, fringe benefits, such as paid vacations, sick leave, and employers' social security and pension contributions, have to be counted in with wages. So part of what looks like different pay for the same work is not.

But some is. In part, such differences may reflect poor knowledge of alternatives by workers and employers. They may also reflect the effects of labor unions (discussed in the next chapter). More to the point, however, a uniform competitive wage for a given skill and area is something, like profit equalization among industries, that *tends* to be brought about by people acting freely under competitive conditions. At any given time, there will be differences. But over time, lower paying employers will have to pay more or they will lose employees. Higher-paying firms will slow down the normal rate of wage rise or lose business to lower-paying, lower-price competitors. And before this works out, changes in consumer tastes, technology, worker supply, and nonhuman input supply will cause shifts in the labor demand and supply curves, calling for a new set of equilibrium wages in various occupations and shifts of employment among workers. Thus, at any time, there are movements toward equilibrium wages, but before one equilibrium configuration is attained, changes call for different movements. Declining industries may pay lower wages as some workers prefer not to switch to other areas; expanding industries or employers may pay premium wages for a time to expand rapidly.

Without claiming to explain all of the variations in wages within occupation and area, a recent study has shown that these variations *are* affected by productivity-related forces, such as seniority, prior experience, and education, as well as taste factors such as discrimination by race and sex, and location of employer.[10] The study covered plants in the Chicago metropolitan area and workers in 12 occupations including accountant, typist, janitor, punch press operator, truck driver, and tool and die maker. The authors conclude with this comment:

> ... employers and workers seem to pursue reasonable goals in appropriate ways. If at first their behavior does not appear to make sense, it may be simply because the employment of a worker is a much more complicated transaction, and one with many more dimensions, than the purchase of a contract in the wheat futures market. Perhaps, despite the large body of sound research in labor markets of the postwar period, economists and other social scientists have not yet tried hard enough to understand this behavior fully.

Evaluation Of The Competitively Determined Distribution Of Income

Under competitive private enterprise, incomes are distributed in accordance with contribution to production. Is this socially good, bad, or

---

[10] Albert Rees and George P. Shultz, *Wages and Workers in an Urban Labor Market*, University of Chicago Press, 1970. The quotation is from p. 222.

neutral? Certainly, the fact that it occurs does not make it good or bad. We shall evaluate this basis of payment—contribution to production—by four criteria: (1) efficiency, (2) fairness or justice, (3) the standard of living of income recipients, and (4) individual freedom.

Efficiency of input utilization. Efficiency is a comparison of output to input. An input is used more efficiently in use X than in use Y if it produces more value in X than in Y per unit of time. Payment according to value contributed plays a vital role in achieving efficiency of input utilization. Owners of inputs, human and nonhuman, want higher standards of living and therefore higher incomes. To achieve this, they will generally sell their input services for the best price. Thus, in serving their personal interests for higher living standards, they will seek out the careers and employments where their inputs contribute the most.[11]

The employer or businessman, serving his interest to maximize profits, will, as we discussed earlier, use the input combination which costs the least. This cost minimization serves to minimize the goods and services society sacrifices to get given items produced *only because* input prices do reflect the value inputs contribute in alternative uses. Thus, payment according to contribution serves a double role in efficiency: (1) it gets input owners seeking higher pay to produce more rather than less, and (2) it shows input organizers how to select the method of production which costs the least in terms of things sacrificed.

The efficiency of competitively determined input prices (and income distribution) and the less efficient results of departures from these prices are reasons for accepting this method of income distribution. Even one who has misgivings as to the fairness of competitive income determination should consider whether any proposed alternative basis of distribution will have an adverse effect on allocative efficiency and so reduce incentives that the total output and economic growth will be held down.

For example, the Marxist rule of income distribution is: *to* each according to his needs, *from* each according to his ability. Since needs have virtually nothing to do with value contributed to production, income payments would be unrelated to production. But would people really contribute according to their ability then? Would they undertake difficult and expensive training, would they strive for promotion, or shift employers

---

[11] Even altruistic input owners seeking society's interest rather than their own would need the guide of input payments related to value contributed—unless (as usually the case among altruists) they chose to do what *they* felt society needed rather than what consumers apparently want. An altruist who did not want to impose his values on others should maximize his personal contribution and income, then give away as much as possible to the general public.

or occupations to contribute more, though receiving no more pay? And, without payment equal to contribution, how would the workers or planners or commissars know where input contributions are the most? This Marxist rule has never worked and has been quickly abandoned where tried, to be replaced by incentive pay systems in which more and better work means more pay. Even an avowed Marxist like Mao Tse-Tung has reiterated: those who don't work don't eat—a far cry from the Marxist rule.[12]

Fairness. What is fair is a matter of individual judgment, unless one accepts the determination of another, such as church, family, majority rule, or political leaders. It seems a widely held view that it is fair for an individual to receive from society as much as he gives. In fact, some socialists base their opposition to private enterprise on the claim that workers are "exploited," get paid less than what they produce, thus implying that workers ought to receive the value of their contribution.

If this outcome is not fair, then what is? Who should receive more than his contribution and who less? Remember, by equation (2), since the sum of values contributed equals total income, if anyone receives more than his contribution, this addition must come from the contribution of someone else who will then receive less than his contribution. If one insists that wages should not be below a certain level, say, $2 an hour or $100 a week, but the employer is still allowed the freedom to hire or not, then the employer will simply not hire those whose VMP is less than the minimum wage, which leaves these people with no wage instead of a "substandard" one. Therefore, it is probably better, if someone is to receive more than his contribution, that

---

[12] Consider this analogy: suppose a teacher, after grading test papers, in order "to equalize things," took 10 or 20 points off the grades in the 80's and 90's and "gave" them to those with grades in the 50's and 60's. Aside from fairness, what would be the effect on incentives of both high and low grade students? Do the same effects arise with income redistribution?

While we're on the question of incentives, perhaps the following sentiments are appropriate. Though some may agree with George Sand that "Work is not man's punishment. It is his reward and his strength, his glory and his pleasure," more would probably join with Honore de Balzac who said "Where will you find a man who is in love with his means of earning a livelihood? For it is with a profession as with marriage; in the long run you are sensible of nothing but the annoyances," or Aldous Huxley, "Like every man of sense and good feeling, I abominate work." (Taken from "Quotes: Labor" compiled by E. F. Murphy, *New York Times Sunday Magazine,* September 6, 1964.)

Back to education—In St. Louis, experimentors have raised the achievement of grade-school pupils by paying them in play money for good academic and personal performance. The children use the money to purchase privileges, such as to play checkers during class time. *New York Times,* April 26, 1970. Will the wonders of the price system never cease! In a similar vein, see footnote 18 of Chapter 11.

the government make the payment from tax proceeds rather than to expect the employer to make the payment.

One need not make a categorical judgment on the question of fairness. One might say everyone should receive the value of his contribution except that _____. The possible exceptions are limitless. Most people agree that dependent children, the physically handicapped, and aged people with little or no savings should be supported by society without having to rely (entirely) on their own earnings. Another exception might be to say that incomes above a certain level should not be allowed or should be taxed heavily. But how would this affect incentives? Actually, very high incomes do not amount to enough in total to affect average incomes much anyway. Or, one might say let labor be paid the value of its contribution, but not nonhuman inputs. Those who advocate this often feel that property owners do not deserve their income because they do not put forth effort as do workers, or because they feel most property is owned through inheritance. But if property was not acquired through gift or inheritance (or fraud), then it came from saving and investment out of labor income. The property exists because its owner refrained from consuming as much as he could and released productive capacity from consumption to investment.

Even property which came from inheritance was created by some abstention from consumption, but by someone else who chose to give it to its present owner. It is true that inherited property gives some people a better chance to enjoy goods and services than others. But so do inherited beauty, athletic ability, health, intelligence, and so do vast differences in the competence of parents and teachers to develop the potentialities of their children. Our guess is that these aspects of "undeserved" benefits, stemming from one's "choice" of parents, create far more income inequality than does inherited property. (But perhaps nothing can be done about any of these except property inheritance.)

We are led to this question: Is inequality of income and of living conditions something to be avoided? Or is it sufficient that each individual be assured opportunity through education to develop his potentialities and that society provides some minimum standard of living to those who cannot work? Should inequality be reduced in addition to these measures? One must weigh the costs and benefits of various interferences with competitive income determination. Not only may one inequity replace another, but interference may seriously affect incentives to work and produce, lowering society's total output and making even more difficult a permanent alleviation of poverty.

If redistribution policies impair incentives to produce and especially to invest, then we may have to choose between (a) dividing a smaller and stagnant pie more evenly (through redistribution policies) and (b) dividing a larger and growing pie less evenly (with less deliberate redistribution of income). It is entirely possible that while (a) could raise the lowest incomes more within a given year or two, (b) would raise them more over the long run, as well as allowing incomes of everyone else to rise more. For example, if (because of impaired incentives to work and invest) the economy's per capita growth rate were reduced by one percentage point, say from 2% per year to 1% a year, then an income level which would have grown in 20 years from $3600 to $5400 at 2% per year would only grow to $4400 at 1% per year. Over 50 years a $3000 income level would rise by 64% at 1% per year, against 169% at 2% per year. (The average annual rise in real income per person is 2%.)

The fairness of non-input payments. Besides input payments, other forms of income which may occur in a competitive economy are gifts, inheritances, and government transfer payments—welfare payments, subsidies—which are also essentially gifts. Another is interest on loans. The interest rate (such as 6% per year) is determined basically by how much is earned by money invested in nonhuman inputs, because those who receive interest could have invested in such inputs instead of lending money to others. Gambling earnings are transfers from losers to winners and represent no contribution to production.They are paid out of the incomes or wealth of the losers.

Finally, there is income (or loss) which results from unexpected changes in tastes or technology and occurs largely in the form of increased (or

"Some day, Ronald, all of this will be yours!"

"What do you mean you want it now?"

decreased) property values. Suppose you purchase some land or shares of stock in a company. The purchase price reflects the *then* expected productivity of this land or company. But afterward an unexpected change in tastes (including a government decision to build a research complex near your land) causes the value of the property to rise—because its productivity has now increased. As owner, when you sell the land, you would receive a windfall gain which represents no contribution by you or your property. Another kind of change—say cancellation of a development which was expected when you purchased the property—could cause a windfall loss. Such gains and losses result from sheer luck (good or bad) or from making good or bad guesses that the future will be different from what most people expect (which expectations determine the market price of the property). This income (or loss) is generally a minor part of incomes to most people, though, to the very lucky or shrewd, it might be substantial.

All increases in property value, especially of stock prices, are not of this nature. If the owners of a company reinvest part of their earnings in the company (as is quite common), a share of stock in the company will then represent ownership of more income-earning equipment than before, so its price will rise. During inflation, when prices are rising, VMP's (MPP's times product prices) are rising; therefore, property incomes rise and so do property values and thus stock prices. If property incomes and stock prices rise by the same proportion that prices have risen throughout the economy, stockholders are no better off than before the inflation. In fact, during the past decade, stock prices have lagged behind the rate of inflation as have corporate profits.

Our discussion of competitive income determination based on value contributed to production does not apply to gifts and inheritances (except that the donor probably acquired the property through contributions to production) and does not apply to changes in property values caused by unexpected events (except that property values reflect expected productivity of property). We leave to the reader to think through the fairness, efficiency, and freedom aspect of gifts, inheritances, and windfalls.[13]

Worker satisfaction and payment equal to value contributed. Would we find under competitive conditions that workers are satisfied with their wages

---

[13] Concerning the fairness of high incomes, consider this comment in a letter to the editor of the *New York Times,* April 18, 1969. Responding to an article on pampered pets of wealthy owners, a reader wrote indignantly: "When one well-heeled dog eats more meat in one day than some poor large families consume in one week, it is time to change the tax system which permits this hideous injustice."

Well, what kind of change? Eliminate all high incomes? Allow high incomes, but regulate the consumption choices of the rich? What about the consumption choices of the non-rich who spend on cigarettes, liquor, drugs, and gambling, not to mention family pets? At least one should think through the consequences of his plans to eliminate alleged social injustice.

because they see that the wages equal value contributed? Definitely not. Even if a person knew he was being paid the value of his contribution, he might still not be satisfied, though instead of feeling he should be paid more for his work, he might feel the way to higher pay lies in his doing better work or acquiring more skills and seeking another job.

However, more fundamentally, workers are not able to measure their value to production. It takes considerable knowledge of a company's operations even to guess how output will be affected if another typist or another janitor is hired. The employer has a feel for whether another is worthwhile, but in many cases it is not precise. The worker with less knowledge has even less idea of his worth. He will be inclined to exaggerate his contribution because he does not allow for the contribution of other inputs with which he works and does not visualize how tasks could be assigned to minimize the effects of his departure, other things the same. The worker is also apt to exaggerate his contribution by incorrectly considering what would happen to output and revenue if not only he were not there, but if all workers in his occupation left, and to feel he should receive his share of that difference. But, as we pointed out earlier, this method of calculating input contribution is wrong and ends up with all inputs "contributing" more than the total output.

Payment equal to contribution is a result of the competitive process, the invisible hand; it is not something that is consciously observed or sought or even realized by workers or employers. The worker seeks to maximize his income, the employer to minimize the cost of producing a given output and to maximize profits. Whether or not anyone is aware of it, the equality of wage and VMP is an outcome which must occur if employers do maximize profits and acquire inputs under competitive conditions. In fact, no one consciously seeks competitive conditions. Quite the contrary. Workers, employers, and sellers all strive for monopoly advantages. It is up to government to make sure that competitive conditions prevail.

Furthermore, even if workers knew they were being paid according to contribution, they would still stand to gain by restricting the entry and employment of people in their occupation, thereby reducing the ratio of themselves to other inputs and thereby raising their MPP's and wages. (See the discussion of collective bargaining in Chapter 7.)

Value contributed and a person's worth. Let it be stated emphatically that the value of an input's contribution is a value placed by consumers through dollar votes (the VMP is the MPP times the product price). There is no implication that he who contributes more value than another is morally or intrinsically better or superior to the other. Indeed, it may be quite the contrary, depending on one's personal values as contrasted with the more impersonal market. The market may rate the services of a liquor salesman at

$30,000 a year, while a preacher's services are worth only $8000, a heavyweight champion's services at one million dollars a fight, a nurse at $8500 a year. But complaints should be directed at consumers, not to the employer and not to the private enterprise system, unless it is the freedom of producers to do what consumers want that is judged a fault.

The standard of living of income recipients. Under competitive private enterprise the standard of living families will have depends on the incomes earned within the family and this in turn depends on the contributions made by the workers and their property. There is no assurance that everyone will have a "decent" standard of living or will receive at least "subsistence" wages. It depends on value contributed to production.

The reason for listing this as a separate criterion for evaluating wages is that many people rather inconsistently say it's fair that people be paid the value of their contribution to production, but it's not fair for people to be paid less than enough to live on. If payment equal to contribution is fair, then the level of living has nothing to do with the fairness of wages. Mr. Jones and Mr. Smith who contribute the same get paid the same, even though Smith is a bachelor and Jones has ten children to support. It is unfortunate that some people are unable (or unwilling) to contribute enough to earn enough to live adequately. But it serves no useful purpose to deny this and say everyone who works one hour does at least $2 worth of production when that is not so. This is not to say that society should ignore the problem of low incomes. But the basic remedy is to raise the productivity of people in low-income families.

Freedom. Competitive wage determination is compatible with the freedom of each individual to pursue the occupation of his choice, to seek employment where he wishes, to change jobs as he wishes, and with the freedom of employers to hire and fire as they wish. Indeed, any departure from the competitive determination necessarily infringes on employer and employee freedom.

This is seen in Fig. 6-3. Any point in the diagram, such as A, refers to the wage and quantity of labor directly to the left and below it. We shall go through every possible wage-quantity combination and show that the *only* combination compatible with personal freedom is E, the competitive equilibrium, which will naturally prevail in a competitive market. For this discussion, we assume that "freedom" does *not* include the freedom of workers or employers to collude monopolistically. Such collusion is covered in the next chapter. This means no third party, such as a union or government, interferes with the freedom of a worker and an employer to get together on mutually agreeable terms.

In all, besides the equilibrium, E, eight points are designated on the

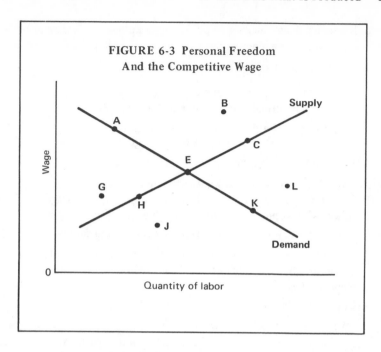

FIGURE 6-3 Personal Freedom
And the Competitive Wage

diagram, two on the demand curve above and below E, two on the supply curve above and below E, and one in each space bounded by the intersecting lines. These eight points represent every possible wage-quantity pair except E. To follow this, you must understand clearly what each curve shows: Demand is the quantity of workers employers want to hire at various wages; Supply is the quantities of workers seeking jobs in the occupation at various wages. For each point, assume the outcome is ordained by law. Then ask: whose freedom must the law conflict with? Employers'? Workers'?

Consider Point A (and any point on the demand curve above E):

1. Employers can hire all they want at this wage, since it is on their demand curve.
2. But workers want more jobs than employers provide.
3. A can be maintained only if the unemployed workers are prevented from offering to work for less and if employers are prevented from hiring them for less. Thus both employer and worker freedom are abridged.

Point B (and any point above E bounded by demand and supply):

4. Employers are forced to hire more workers than they want to hire at this wage.
5. Repeat #2.

6. B can be maintained only by forcing employers to hire and preventing workers from competing.

Point C (and any point on the supply curve above E):

7. Repeat #4.

Point G (and any point back of both demand and supply curves):

8. Here employers are prevented from hiring workers who are willing to work for them at wages employers are willing to pay.

Point H (and any point on the supply curve below E):

9. Here all the workers who want work are employed.
10. But employers are prevented from bidding up the wage and hiring others who would like to work at the higher wages.

Point J (and any point below E between the demand and supply curves):

11. Here workers are forced to work involuntarily—any point to the right of the supply curve must involve forced labor.
12. Repeat #10.

Point K (and any point on the demand curve below E):

13. Employers get all the workers they want, but only by forced, involuntary labor. Not anything that would exist in America. Right? Wrong! Suppose the demand is that by the U.S. Army for soldiers; the supply curve shows those willing to volunteer for Army jobs. At K, a wage below E, the horizontal distance between demand and supply is the quantity drafted against their choice into the army.

Point L (and any point beyond both demand and supply curves):

14. Here employers are forced to hire workers they don't want and workers are forced to work involuntarily.

Thus, no outcome except E is consistent with employer and worker freedom. At E, employers can hire all they want and are not forced to hire more and all workers who want work at the going wage can get jobs—no forced labor and no labor surplus.[14]

---

[14] An analogous discussion could show that the competitive price and quantity of a product is the only outcome compatible with consumer and producer freedom, again disallowing monopolistic collusion. You might try going through it. This could also be done with the usury law diagram determining the interest rate. The non-equilibrium quantities of Fig. 6-3 could be brought about through taxes and/or subsidies on particular occupations similar to commodity taxes and subsidies discussed in Chapter 2. But these would still involve infringements of freedom, including that of taxpayers. While the discussion concentrated on the parties to the wage agreement, one could also point to infringements of consumers' freedom to bid inputs into preferred uses. This would be particularly true if non-E outcomes were achieved through tax-subsidy means.

Freedom and efficiency. When input payment equals value contributed, the individual has *incentive* to use his inputs where they contribute as much as possible, because the individual prefers more goods for himself. But suppose the individual prefers a lower-paying occupation or prefers to work less than he could so he can have more leisure? Under private enterprise, the individual is free to choose among jobs and to take leisure instead of work. Is this a fault which causes inefficiency? If personal freedom and satisfaction are the basic ends of conduct, and if production is only a means to satisfy these ends, then there is no presumption that the individual should produce as much as possible. Efficient production means getting as much as possible from inputs, subject to the freedom of input owners and employers to choose between monetary and nonmonetary personal goals.

Thus, it is consistent with efficiency so defined for a bank vice-president in a large city to quit and become a groundskeeper for a small college (as did happen), or for an individual to prefer teaching math at $7500 to working for IBM at $12,000, or to prefer housekeeping to a career.[15] In spite of the ubiquity of these preferences—hardly anyone works as long hours as he could—payment by contribution does play a vital role in allocating people

---

[15] The pursuit of non-monetary aims (along with monetary) comes up continuously: (1) A school janitor in Akron, after graduating from night school at the University of Akron, quit his janitorial job at $6000 a year to teach in the same school for $5650. (*New York Times,* November 1, 1965.) (2) The owner of a laundry in Bournemouth, England had difficulty recruiting women employees until he advertised: "Strong fat women who wish to lose weight wanted for hard but well-paid work." His recruiting problems were over. (*Reader's Digest,* May, 1968, p. 106.) (3) Starting in 1958, a young California couple would buy a run-down house, fix it up in their spare time, sell for a profit, move to another house, and start over again. Objective: to save enough money to retire for five years at age 30 in the Canary Islands. (*Reader's Digest,* December, 1966.) Fans of Mr. Tinguely, no doubt. And here are others. (4) Frederick Loewe, composer of "My Fair Lady," "Camelot," "Brigadoon," and other hits, said: "I haven't the slightest intention to write another note. . . . I'm having a wonderful time and writing a show is no fun. There is no reason for me to work now. I don't need glory. I don't need money. I can use the time better. . . . This after all is what we're striving for . . . to be happy." (*New York Times,* Oct. 1, 1964.) Nevertheless, in 1971 Lerner and Lowe did start collaborating on a new musical, their first since 1960. (5) Jack Fuller quit as a $30,000 salesman of caps and gowns in Akron to work for less than half that above the Arctic Circle in Alaska. (6) Iver Brook quit as a stockbroker in his 40's to study and work in ecology. (7) Mike Mitchell, former $35,000-a-year Wall Street insurance broker makes under $10,000 operating a lodge in Maine. (The last three are from "Beginning Again In The Middle," *Life,* Jan. 12, 1970.) None of this is incompatible with economic efficiency or with economic theory. But neither is the pursuit of careers in sales or brokerage lines. Other accounts of people who have left the corporate "rat race" are in the *Wall Street Journal,* Feb. 19 and 21, 1971.

among jobs. People do want money and what it buys. *Other things the same about jobs,* they will select the occupation or employer who pays the most.[16]

Summary

Under private enterprise, goods and services are distributed to the highest bidders, to those with the most money and with the greatest desires. This distribution depends on the distribution of income. Income depends on value contributed to production.

(a) The amount contributed by each input is its MPP.

(b) Distinguish correct and incorrect measurements of MPP.

(c) The *output* contributed by all q_a units of input A is MPP_a times q_a.

(d) The *value* contributed by an input is its VMP, where VMP = MPP times product price.

The quantity employed of any input is such that its wage equals its VMP, which means each input is paid the value of its contribution to production.

A company's sales revenue equals the sum of input payments and equals the sum of values contributed: $TR = \Sigma VMP_i Q_i$.

Therefore, when wages equal value contributed, profits are the value contributed by the firm's nonhuman inputs.

Under competition, there is no "surplus value" contributed by workers but not paid to them.

---

[16] If a person chooses a lower-paying occupation than another he could succeed in, and thus contributes less, does he have a valid claim for a subsidy from his employer or from society because his standard of living is too low? Who does this? How about people in Appalachia who refuse to move to where jobs are available? Or many farmers? How about some artists, musicians, writers, and actors who seek Federal support for their professions, pointing to their low incomes? Teachers too. If their claims are just, it must be that consumers err in not valuing their output highly enough. But raise their incomes by subsidy, and won't a lot more people select these relatively pleasant occupations and drive down prices and incomes in them again, requiring even larger subsidies for adequate living standards? Then to avoid this, the government may establish artificial barriers to entry into the occupations or deny subsidies to some who are just as qualified as others who receive subsidy, or set up standards independent of consumer choice as to whose past or potential performance seems more deserving. It is not unusual that one interference with the workings of the price system leads to consequences which "justify" additional regulations and which impinge further on personal freedom.

Neither companies nor workers need know economic theory for the results described here to prevail.

Under competition, wages are determined by demand and supply and more fundamentally by the forces or determinants underlying demand and supply.

The demand for labor in a given occupation and area is determined by (1) product price, (2) technology, (3) quantity of other inputs employed, (4) prices of other inputs, (5) employer tastes for discrimination.

The supply of labor is a given occupation and area is determined by (1) worker tastes, (2) wages elsewhere, (3) costs of entry, (4) the general price level.

Wages above equilibrium cause unemployment.

Wages below equilibrium cause labor shortages.

Wage differentials within an occupation and area occur despite the theory's prediction that they should not. Some reasons are: (1) productivity differences within occupational titles, (2) worker and employer ignorance of alternatives, (3) labor unions, (4) temporary movements toward equilibrium, (5) continual shifts in the equilibrium.

Evaluation of the competitively determined distribution of income—payment equal to value contributed—as to efficiency.

(a) Payment equal to contribution gives input owners incentive to employ their inputs (themselves) where they contribute the most.

(b) Payment equal to contribution means that when input organizers choose the method of production which costs the least money, they will minimize the real cost of production.

"The Establishment awaits."

Evaluation as to fairness.

(a) Should people receive the value they contribute to production?

(b) Who should receive more, or less? Why?

(c) Is inequality of income undesirable?

(d) The justice of incomes which are not income payments—inheritances, gifts, windfalls.

Worker satisfaction and payment equal to contribution.

(a) Workers and employers cannot tell when payment equals value contributed.

(b) In any case, workers could gain by restricting entry and raising the wage.

(c) Payment equal to contribution is an incidental outcome of competition, not a consciously sought objective.

The standard of living of income recipients depends on value contributed. There is no guarantee that competitive income will be at least some minimum or at least at subsistence level.

Evaluation as to freedom: the competitive wage and quantity employed is the only outcome compatible with worker and employer freedom, disallowing freedom to monopolize.

Freedom and efficiency. The situation that input owners have incentive to contribute as much as possible in order to get higher incomes than otherwise does not imply that they *should* pursue monetary objectives, ignoring leisure or the nonmonetary aspects of different jobs.

Study Questions Chapter 6

1. What two tendencies follow from the distribution of goods to the highest bidders?

2. Explain thoroughly the hypothetical experiment by which an input's contribution to production is measured.

3. Why *not* identify a riveter's MPP as so many rivets or a typist's as so many pages typed?*

4. In what units are the MPP's of such inputs defined?*

5. How are activities like riveting and typing converted into units which can be valued?*

6. Explain the two incorrect measures of identifying the MPP of an input. Why are they incorrect?

7. Suppose, with 200 workers of a given occupation, output is 4000 per month, and with none of these workers, output would be only 150 per

month. The MPP of the 200th worker is 8. What is the contribution to output of all 200?*

8. Why not 3850?*

9. Is the method of production changed as the variable input is changed in quantity?*

10. Explain in words how a typewriter or an additional 500 square feet of office space has an identifiable MPP.

11. Define VMP. Relate it to MPP in both words and with an equation.*

12. Prove that inputs are paid their value contributed to production.

13. Illustrate this proof with a diagram.

14. In the diagram, why does the curve slope upward over a range?*

15. What is its maximum?*

16. What does the downward slope represent?*

17. In the diagram, how is the height of the wage line determined?*

18. Why not hire more than E in Fig. 6-1?*

19. Why not hire less?*

20. When quantity E is hired, what is true?*

21. On the diagram, what area represents wages paid to the variable input under consideration?*

22. On the diagram, what area represents profits?*

23. (The next two questions are relatively technical and unimportant.) What does the area bounded by the VMP above the wage line show?*

24. What area represents the total revenue of the firm?*

25. Are workers paid value contributed because employers try to be fair? If not, then why?*

26. What is the main point of the discussion entitled "Can Input Proportions Be Varied So Finely?"*

27. Explain the meaning of the equation:

$$MPP_a Q_a + MPP_b Q_b + \ldots + MPP_n Q_n = TP.*$$

28. What does "a" represent?*

29. What does Q_a represent?*

30. What does $MPP_a Q_a$ represent?*

31. Under what assumed production conditions does this equation hold true?*

32. Explain the equation:

$$VMP_a Q_a + VMP_b Q_b + \ldots + VMP_n Q_n = TR.*$$

33. What does $VMP_a Q_a$ represent?*

34. Where are the firm's profits in this equation and what do they represent?*

35. How does this equation relate to the Marxian theory of surplus value?*

36. Does the equation say or prove that wages equal value contributed?*

37. Must companies hire one by one to bring about the result that $W = VMP$? If not, explain.*

38. What does the demand for labor show?

39. What follows from its downward slope?*

40. Why does it slope downward?*

41. What does the supply of labor show?

42. What is meant by a "determinant" of the demand for or supply of labor?

43. What are the determinants of the demand for labor?

44. What are the determinants of the supply of labor to an occupation?

45. What happens to which curve if most employers discriminate against a group?*

46. If employees discriminate?*

47. Describe the equilibrium explanation technique, EET.

48. Relate it to the equilibrium of Figs. 2-3 (why output should be 15,000), 2-4, and 6-2.

49. Using the EET, explain how wages and the quantity employed are determined by demand and supply, giving detailed explanations of why wages could not be other than equilibrium and what actions people would take if wages were above or below equilibrium.

50. With a diagram, show a labor surplus.

51. What is another name for labor surplus? What causes it?*

52. Is everyone without a job considered unemployed? Who is? Who isn't?*

53. Distinguish the remedy for widespread unemployment in a major recession and for local unemployment in a few occupations or industries.*

54. Why the distinction?*

55. How can wage differences within a given skill and area be reconciled with the theory which says they should not exist?*

56. Give two reasons why competitive income distribution ($W = VMP$) contributes toward economic efficiency.*

57. Discuss the fairness of competitively determined income distribution.

58. Should different criteria be applied in evaluating the fairness of wage income and property income? Why or why not?

59. What are the various sources of income inequality?

60. Is income equality a reasonable goal? Why or why not?

61. Will workers be satisfied to receive the competitive wage? Explain.*

62. Contrast wage or VMP with the moral worth of a person.

63. Whose fault is it if the average liquor salesman earns three times as much as the average nurse?*

64. Evaluate the competitive income distribution by the standard of living competitive income recipients will have.*

65. Evaluate competitive income distribution as it relates to individual freedom.

66. Using a diagram, explain why the only wage-employment combination compatible with worker-employer freedom is the competitive equilibrium.

67. With a diagram, show the quantity drafted into the armed forces.

68. Does efficiency require that everyone maximize income? Explain.

Answers to starred questions.

3. Only units of output have ascertainable value; activities which contribute to output do not.

4. Units of output.

5. In principle by the correct experiment for determining the MPP: how revenue or output changes from a change in the quantity of the input, with all inputs optimally assigned before and after the change.

7. $8 \times 200 = 1600$; not $4000 - 150 = 3850$.

8. If all other human and nonhuman inputs' contribution were so calculated, the sum contributed by all would greatly exceed the actual output. By the correct method, MPP_aQ_a, the total contributions attributed to each input equal the total output, according to the equation of #27.

9. Yes, though perhaps slightly. Optimal reassignments are assumed.

11. VMP is the money value of the MPP. VMP is in dollars; MPP is in units of output. VMP = MPP times produce price.

14. Increasing returns.

15. The point of diminishing returns.

16. Diminishing returns.

17. The wage line is the competitive wage determined outside the firm by demand and supply, Fig. 6-2.

18. The cost of another worker (wage line) exceeds the revenue (VMP).

19. The revenue from hiring another worker (VMP) exceeds the cost (wage line), so profits (revenue less costs) are raised by adding another.

20. Profits are maximized and wage equals VMP; each worker is paid the value of his contribution to production.

21. Wage times quantity hired: the area of a rectangle formed by the height of the wage line and the distance on the quantity axis up to E.

22. No area shows this.

23. This area, minus the triangular area between W and VMP before W cuts VMP, equals profits plus the value contributed by other hired inputs. (This point was not explained in the text.)

24. The area under the VMP, between VMP and the quantity axis up to the quantity employed, E. This is another way of saying that total output is the sum of the MPP's up to any given quantity of the inputs. You can see this from Table 5-1. Derive column (2) by adding up the numbers in column (3).

25. No. Because employers must compete for workers and they maximize profits where W = VMP.

26. That a VMP can be derived and W = VMP even if input proportions could not be varied in producing individual products, as long as input proportions differ from one product to another. The proof is not given in this book.

27. The total product (TP) exactly equals the sum of the MPP's of each input, where for any type of input, a, the MPP of every "a" is viewed as the MPP of the last "a" employed.

28. A type of input like typists or unskilled labor or accountants.

29. The quantity of the "a"s employed.

30. The total contribution to output of all the "a"s employed.

31. Production technology is such that if all inputs are increased or decreased by the same proportion, output will change by this proportion. (Mathematically, this implies that a production function, relating output to quantity of inputs, is homogeneous of the first degree.)

32. The sum of values contributed by each input exactly equals total revenue of the firm, where each input's contribution is measured by its VMP.

33. The value contributed by all the "a"s employed.

34. The profits will be the value contributed by the inputs owned by the company (minus interest on loans used to purchase these inputs).

35. When, as under competition, each input is paid the value of its contribution to production, profits being value contributed by nonhuman inputs, no surplus is left which represents value workers contributed but did not receive.

36. No. This is reasoned separately and is true only if employers hire competitively, whereas the equation will be true anyway.

37. No. Companies merely have to follow the rule: hire inputs if it pays and don't if it doesn't pay. If they hire competitively, wage will equal VMP

without their being aware of it. Employers do not have to understand the economic theory explained here. In fact, few do.

39. The lower is the wage, the more employed.

40. Mainly diminishing returns.

45. The demand for the disfavored group declines, so their wage will be lower.

46. There will be a decrease in the supply of labor to the occupation or to the employers who hire the disfavored group.

51. Unemployment. The wage is above equilibrium.

52. No. Unemployed: without job and seeking work at the prevailing wage or less.

53. Monetary-fiscal policy for widespread unemployment to raise total spending; wage reductions for localized unemployment.

54. Wage rigidity makes overall deflation an impractical goal against a recession; monetary-fiscal policy against localized unemployment would cause inflation without reducing the unemployment much, if any.

55. Within-occupation differences in productivity, differences in fringe benefits, ignorance of alternatives by employers and workers, movements toward an equilibrium.

56. (1) Workers seeking higher income will contribute more; (2) Employers who minimize money cost will also minimize real cost.

61. No. Neither workers nor employers are aware that wage equals value contributed to production.

63. Consumers'.

64. Competitive income and the living standard provided depend on value contributed; they may be high or low.

7

Who Does What Jobs

The Meaning Of This Decision

So far, we have discussed three basic decisions of economic organization: what, how, and for whom to produce. Now we turn to "by whom," the problem of labor allocation. What determines the number of people who will be lathe operators in Cincinnati, fishermen in San Diego, metalworkers in Atlanta, or typists in Boston? What assures that there will be enough but not too many in each occupation, industry, and area? What brings about appropriate changes in input allocation and makes appropriate adjustments for retirements, migration, and changes in population size or age distribution? What determines the flow of nonhuman input services from owners to users? Again, under competitive private enterprise, important roles are played by the search for personal gain, guided by prices (including wages) and profits.

One might well ask whether this decision was not covered in who gets what is produced. However, "who is going to do what" and "who is going to get what" are separate questions. The answer to one need not depend on the answer to the other, though it does under private enterprise. Indeed, as we saw, the demand for and supply of labor determine both the wage rate and the quantity employed. And shifts in demand and supply cause shifts in both wages and employment.

In this chapter we explain further the role of worker preferences (labor supply) in affecting labor allocation and wages. Then we consider the effects on wages and labor allocation of occupational licensing, labor unions, and monopsony.

Worker Preferences And Labor Allocation

Occupational choice. Freedom of occupational choice is one of the basic libertarian developments which characterised the transition from the feudal society of privilege, class, and status to the capitalist society of personal initiative, social mobility, and economic growth. Throughout much of recorded human history, one's occupation was determined by that of his parents—peasants remained peasants, slaves remained slaves, craftsmen's sons learned their fathers' skills, and the nobility's progeny remained noble. To aspire otherwise was often regarded as a blasphemous rejection of God's choice of one's station in life. An individual's freedom to improve his lot in life was largely denied.

The same suppression of initiative has occurred under the caste system of India, where occupations were alloted to certain castes. In modern times, occupational choice has been restricted in Communist nations, especially under Stalin and Mao, where the government allocated people in accordance with national objectives without regard for individual preference. And one aspect of South Africa's Apartheid policy is to preserve certain occupations as the privilege of white people only.

Since income depends on occupation and the standard of living depends on income, the freedom to select occupations, taken together with subsidized public education, provides one from a low-income family and with normal capabilities the opportunity through individual effort to improve his position in life. In an era of concern about eliminating poverty both in America and abroad, it is well to recall these past impediments to occupational choice and their negative effects on initiative and advancement. For there are indications today of increasing barriers to occupational choice in America.

Freedom of occupational choice, which is characteristic of competitive private enterprise, does not mean one is guaranteed a job or a particular salary in the occupation of one's choice. It means the freedom to make employment agreements with others. But with this freedom, anyone with the skills required in an occupation (and without severe personal shortcomings like an uncontrollable urge to punch the boss in the nose) will be able to find employment in the occupation of his choice at about the going wage.

Of course, worker preference is not the only determinant of labor allocation. As noted in Chapter 6, worker preference is one of the determinants of labor supply. But the quantity actually employed is determined by supply *and* demand, neither one alone.

Worker preference and wage differentials. Worker preference is frequently the cause of wage differences between occupations or areas, as between teaching (generally regarded by those in other occupations as a soft job with no ulcerating pressures) and work in private industry, or between working in a large city with high commuting and housing costs and work in a small town where inexpensive single-family houses are available on large lots only a 15-minute drive or walk from work. (Such pedestrian aspirations assume increasing importance with the disillusioning force of age and experience.)

The effects of worker preferences on labor allocation and wages are seen from Fig. 7-1. Suppose we start with accountants' wages the same in big cities and small towns, both w_1. Then there is a change in worker preference (which does not affect demand) against big city sophistication and for the simpler amenities of small towns. A movement of workers from the big cities to the small towns will cause shifts in supply. Supply decreases S_1 to S_3 in (a), the big cities, and increases, S_1 to S_2 in (b), the small towns. The resulting wage differential, w_3/w_2 now reflects workers' residential preferences. Given these preferences, any attempt to eliminate this differential, by law or by unions, would inevitably infringe on some workers' living and working where they prefer. That is, given the new supply curves, a forcible return to the original equilibria at w_1, q_1 would curtail personal freedom, as explained with Fig. 6-3. In both areas, workers will be paid their value contributed. Competing employers will still hire quantities up to where W = VMP, in big cities were VMP = w_3, in small towns to where VMP = w_2.

The same principles apply to wage differences by region. If everyone (or most everyone) wants to live in sunny Florida, supply will rise, driving wages down until an equilibrium is reached where there is no incentive to shift further. And between two occupations, such as science teacher and engineer (assuming the required abilities are the same), a differential w_3/w_2 would again reflect preferences for teaching. And an attempt to eliminate the differential by raising the wages of teachers relative to engineers would reduce the quantity of teachers employed (mainly by failures to replace those who quit) and deprive some prospective teachers of their freedom of occupational choice.

Another reflection of worker preference is the movement toward a four-day work week. TGIF, Thank God It's Friday, is giving way to TGITh. This is simply a continuation of the trend of over 100 years for people to take some of their higher real income in the form of leisure as well as more goods and services. In many companies, this trend now shows up as 4 days at 9 or 10 hours a day. This means fewer commuting trips and may also bypass the worst rush-hour traffic. In fact, some companies are trying three 12-hour days. As this catches on, it will expand rapidly. And so will "moonlighting" by those who prefer a second job on their long weekends. In West Germany, many firms, including the airline Lufthansa, allow some employees to set their own hours for arriving and leaving work (within reason). This is especially convenient for working mothers, but also for those with a strong preference for arising early or sleeping late.[1]

---

[1] An article on the short work week is in the *New York Times Magazine*, May 16, 1971. For variable hours in West Germany, see the *New York Times*, July 12, 1971.

FIGURE 7-1 Worker Preferences Cause Wage Differentials

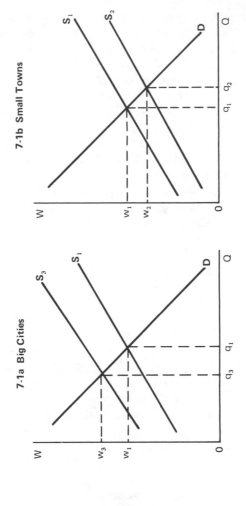

Demand and Supply of Accountants

7-1a Big Cities

7-1b Small Towns

Workers move from big cities to small towns

Initially big city wage
equals small town wage: w_1

Worker preference for
small-town living causes:

In big cities (a)

Decrease in labor supply, S_1 to S_3
Rise in wage, w_1 to w_3
Decrease in employment, q_1 to q_3

In small towns (b)

Increase in labor supply, S_1 to S_2
Reduction in wage, w_1 to w_2
Increase in employment, q_1 to q_2

The unpleasant jobs get done. If worker choice is important in determining labor allocation, why does anyone do the more unpleasant jobs—the physically hard, dirty, dangerous, and those at inconvenient places and hours? Because if "too many" entered the pleasant jobs and left the unpleasant ones, then from diminishing returns and declining product prices, wages would fall in the pleasant jobs and rise in those which workers abandoned. Eventually the wage difference between unpleasant and pleasant jobs would be great enough so some people would feel it worthwhile to do the unpleasant tasks. An equilibrium allocation occurs when the wage difference just compensates the least willing workers in the unpleasant jobs so they have no incentive to shift. Still, many of the unpleasant jobs seem to have low pay. This indicates that those in them have low productivity and are not qualified for many other occupations (or they just don't mind the conditions as much as others would).[2]

The Lump Of Labor Fallacy

There has been much concern whether "enough jobs will be created" to provide employment for the rising numbers of people reaching labor force age, 18-22, and for those displaced by automation. Some people apparently feel that at a given time there are just so many jobs to go around. In his *Economics,* Professor Samuelson calls this the "lump of labor fallacy." But as the downward-sloping demand curve shows clearly, the quantity of labor employers want to hire varies inversely with the wage rate; so the number of jobs depends on wage rates: the lower the wages, the more employers will hire. If the supply of labor in any occupation rises, there will be jobs for all at *some* wage.

---

[2] Fortunately, everyone doesn't have the same tastes about non-monetary job conditions. For example, Tom West earns $8.40 an hour plus fringe benefits as a "top connector," doing the most difficult and dangerous work placing steel beams in the construction of high rise buildings. He says, "The money is pretty good, I'm out in the air and I like the guys I work with. I like being able to do something that scares the hell out of other people." Quoted from a *Wall Street Journal* article, March 4, 1971.

On the other hand, non-monetary job attractions are so great at Colorado ski resorts that college graduates are found washing dishes and sweeping floors at low wages. Even so, wages are above equilibrium and jobs are chaotically allocated, with over 20 applicants for each opening. Some unemployed people hang around restaurants and hotels and snap up the jobs of late or absent workers. (*Newsweek,* Dec. 20, 1971.)

Another *WSJ* article of July 22, 1971 describes the resigned acceptance of boring jobs like coin-changer in a subway booth, traffic monitor in a tunnel, charwoman, laundress, and seamstress. Some people prefer a simple routine without much responsibility.

However, this does not mean that wages will in fact have to fall as labor supply rises over the next decade, because other forces—better education, more capital per worker, and technological advances—are tending to raise worker productivity and wages, while increased labor supply tends to lower wages. Experience suggests that the forces pushing upward will predominate. Anyway, if wages are left to competitive market forces, there will automatically be "enough jobs."

The lump of labor fallacy crops up occasionally in proposals to compel students to remain in school and older workers to retire before they wish, in order to "preserve jobs" for people ages 20-65. Another target of this fallacy is "moonlighting"—holding a part-time job along with a full-time one. An AF of L convention in Washington, D.C. condemned teachers in nearby Maryland for helping paint schools, on the grounds that this deprived painters of work as well as having undercut union wage rates.

Adjustments in Input Allocation to Changes in Consumer Tastes[3]

The joint roles of consumer and worker choice as well as the signalling effect of wages in allocating labor can be seen in tracing the effects on input allocation of a change in consumer tastes. Suppose consumer preferences switch from guitars (G) to banjos (B). For simplicity, assume the same skills are employed in making each product and that companies which make one product don't make the other. The following sequence may occur to get labor shifted from G to B:

1. Consumer preferences shift from G to B.
2. The rise in the demand for B will raise B prices, thereby raising the VMP of labor in B, thereby raising the demand for labor in B.
3. The rise in the demand for labor in B will lead to a rise in wages in B.
4. Simultaneously, the decline in the demand for G results in a reduction in G prices, therefore a reduction in the VMP of labor in G and a reduction in the demand for labor in G.
5. The reduction in the demand for labor in G leads to a reduction in wages in G.
6. The rise in wages in B and decline in G gives workers incentive to shift from G to B.
7. As labor supply increases in B, wages there will start to fall (from the higher level of step 2) and so will prices of B.
8. As workers leave G, wages will start to rise from the lower level of step 5.

---

[3] This elaborates on the seven steps of Chapter 2, depicting how price and profit changes lead to shifts in production when consumer tastes change.

9. An equilibrium will be reached when no one has incentive to shift further. If there are no nonmonetary preferences, wages will be the same in both G and B for a given occupation, as they were before the change in consumer demand.

Thus, through the forces of the "invisible hand," inputs are employed in accordance with consumer tastes, without central direction and even though input owners are seeking their own ends, not explicitly those of consumers. Any impediment to the above wage changes will thwart the adjustment of inputs and outputs based on consumer choice.

Actually, a shift of employment from G to B might occur with much less explicit movement from G to B and with less wage adjustment. Since well over 10% of production workers quit jobs every year anyway, and many people enter and leave the labor force every year, employment can contract simply because those leaving (from G) are not replaced and employment can expand (in B) from new entrants into the labor force and from those who have quit other jobs for various reasons.

Now let us expand the directional arrow technique to describe the adjustments in prices, wages, employment, and profits by which inputs and output adjust to a change in consumer tastes. This time we'll use ratios: $\dfrac{P_B}{P_G}$ refers to the price of banjos relative to the price of guitars. Therefore, $\uparrow \dfrac{P_B}{P_G}$ means P_B is rising and/or P_G is falling. Similarly, $\dfrac{Q_B}{Q_G}, \dfrac{W_B}{W_G}, \dfrac{E_B}{E_G}, \dfrac{D_{iB}}{D_{iG}}$ refer to respective banjo/guitar ratios of output, wages, employment, and demand for inputs, and $\left(\dfrac{Pr}{I}\right)_B \Big/ \left(\dfrac{Pr}{I}\right)_G$ denotes the ratio of respective investment returns (profits/investment) in making banjos and guitars.

We start at an equilibrium where $\left(\dfrac{Pr}{I}\right)_B = \left(\dfrac{Pr}{I}\right)_G$ = the competitive return on investment and $W_B = W_G$ equals the competitive payment for each kind of input (assuming there are no inputs completely specialized to B or G).

There is a rise in consumer preferences $from$ guitars to banjos. The following will then occur to bring about a new equilibrium:

$$\uparrow \frac{D_B}{D_G} \rightarrow \uparrow \frac{P_B}{P_G} \rightarrow \uparrow \left[\left(\frac{Pr}{I}\right)_B \Big/ \left(\frac{Pr}{I}\right)_G \right] \rightarrow \uparrow \frac{D_{iB}}{D_{iG}}$$

$$\downarrow \frac{W_B}{W_G} \text{ until once again } W_B = W_G.$$

$$\rightarrow \uparrow \frac{W_B}{W_G} \text{ and } \uparrow \frac{E_B}{E_G} \nwarrow \atop \searrow \uparrow \frac{Q_B}{Q_G} \rightarrow \downarrow \frac{P_B}{P_G} \rightarrow \downarrow \left[\left(\frac{Pr}{I}\right)_B \middle/ \left(\frac{Pr}{I}\right)_G \right] \text{ until once again}$$

$$\left(\frac{Pr}{I}\right)_B = \left(\frac{Pr}{I}\right)_G.$$

When the process is complete, E_B and Q_B per year will be higher than before the taste change, while E_G and Q_G will be at lower rates. The price ratio, $\frac{P_B}{P_G}$, may end up higher, though not necessarily. The same qualifications mentioned on p. 26 apply in case investors correctly anticipate the change before it occurs or if they overestimate it or underestimate it. Of course, in the real economy, thousands of such changes, not only in consumer preferences, but also in worker preferences, technology, and availability of nonhuman resources, occur continuously. Ideally, changes in relative prices of inputs and outputs and in profits guide economic activity toward the equilibrium consistent with consumer, worker, and investor choice.[4]

Efficient input allocation does require knowledge of alternatives on the part of input owners. However, if in each occupation a core of workers are aware of a few alternatives, this diffused but overlapping knowledge may be sufficient. (See Chapter 10 on knowledge of alternatives.) One economist has stated that, except for choosing a spouse, the selection of an occupation is probably the single most important decision required of a free individual. But selecting an occupation is not quite as irrevocable as getting married, though both are becoming less so all the time. It is quite common for young people to shift jobs frequently in their first few working years, just as it is not unusual for college students to change "majors" once or twice. The past few years have seen greatly improved testing and counselling services to aid in occupational (as well as marital) choices.

Short Run, Long Run Adjustments

Another view of how changes in demand and wages redirect workers is seen in Fig. 7-2. $S_{Long\ run}$ is the long run supply curve of labor in the occupation. It is what heretofore has simply been *the* supply. But people can't conveniently change jobs on short notice, though some do. $S_{Short\ run}$ shows the quantities of labor willing to work at various wages with only a short time to adjust to a wage change and assuming that the wage starts at w_1 and the quantity employed at q_1. The steep slope of $S_{Short\ run}$ indicates

---

[4] It bears repeating that wage and price controls such as instituted in 1971 severely impede the changes in relative prices and wages which guide inputs and outputs to produce what consumers prefer.

FIGURE 7-2 Short-Run, Long-Run Adjustments

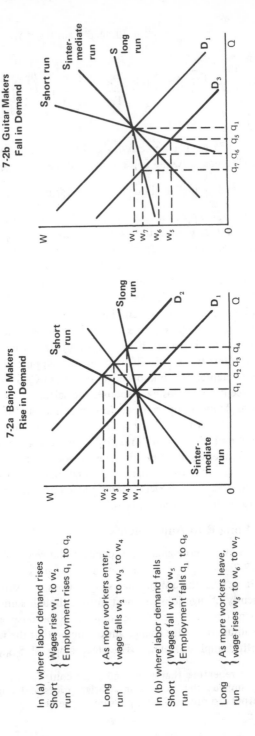

7-2a Banjo Makers
Rise in Demand

7-2b Guitar Makers
Fall in Demand

Workers move from guitar making to banjo making

In (a) where labor demand rises

Short
run
$\left\{\begin{array}{l}\text{Wages rise } w_1 \text{ to } w_2 \\ \text{Employment rises } q_1 \text{ to } q_2\end{array}\right.$

Long
run
$\left\{\begin{array}{l}\text{As more workers enter,} \\ \text{wage falls } w_2 \text{ to } w_3 \text{ to } w_4\end{array}\right.$

In (b) where labor demand falls

Short
run
$\left\{\begin{array}{l}\text{Wages fall } w_1 \text{ to } w_5 \\ \text{Employment falls } q_1 \text{ to } q_5\end{array}\right.$

Long
run
$\left\{\begin{array}{l}\text{As more workers leave,} \\ \text{wage rises } w_5 \text{ to } w_6 \text{ to } w_7\end{array}\right.$

that not many more people are available on short notice at greatly higher wages and not many leave on short notice if wages drop. $S_{Intermediate\ run}$ shows the same thing with a bit longer time for adjustment, say 6 months. $S_{Long\ run}$ is the supply curve with full time for adjustment. This may be a year in a job that requires little training or that is similar to other occupations. It may be 5 or 10 years in an occupation like medicine or college teaching, which requires 4 years of post-graduate training. Through *any point* on a long run supply curve, there is a family of short and intermediate run curves. Only that family at the starting wage-quantity point is relevant for a given problem.

When the demand for banjo makers rises, the wage rises to w_2 initially. Then as more workers enter, it falls gradually until the new equilibrium is reached at w_4, q_4. Meanwhile in guitars, the wage falls to w_5 when demand first drops to D_3. Then as workers leave the occupation, it rises to its new equilibrium at w_7. (This long-run, short-run discussion amplifies why at a given time there may be wage differences for given occupations because of temporary disequilibria.) If banjo making and guitar making are very similar, the long run supply curves in both will be flat (infinitely elastic) and $w_1 = w_4$ in banjos $= w_1 = w_7$ in guitars. The short run rise in banjo wages gives workers incentive to hurry there and the short run drop to w_5 in guitar wages gives incentive to move out of there.

This distinction between short run and long run adjustments applies throughout economics to changes in demand or supply or to the imposition or removal of commodity taxes, tariffs, price supports, or price ceilings. Elsewhere, we have concentrated on the long run equilibrium positions without diagramming the path of movement from one equilibrium to another. And other paths than the one described here are possible, especially if the change in demand itself is gradual and predictable, instead of sudden as assumed here.

Barriers To Occupational Freedom

Most people today would probably agree that freedom of occupational choice is the fairest arrangement for allocating people among occupations. Yet some people frequently support arrangements which impede occupational choice, partly because these arrangements promote other objectives, but also partly because people do not understand how some arrangements affect occupational choice. In this section, we consider two such restrictive arrangements: occupational licensure and collective bargaining.

Occupational licensure. This is a requirement by law that in order to enter some occupation, one must acquire a license from the government.

Licenses are required of the following: doctors, lawyers, barbers, plumbers, real estate salesmen, insurance agents, stock brokers, cab drivers, tree surgeons, potato growers, prizefight promoters, and egg graders, to name a few. Ostensibly set up to protect consumers from incompetent practitioners, occupational licensure is usually used to restrict entry into an occupation, so those in the occupation will receive higher incomes than if there were free entry. Licensing laws, enacted mainly by state and local governments, have these general characteristics: (1) promoted initially by those already in the occupation, not by dissatisfied customers, (2) establish training and/or apprenticeship requirements in excess of those met by many already in the occupation, (3) licensing boards to establish requirements and evaluate applicants are composed of those already in the occupation,[5] and (4) less frequently, requirements which have nothing to do with competence in the occupation, such as non-Communist loyalty oaths or a patriotic attitude.[6]

---

[5] In some states to become a real estate salesman one must not only pass a state exam but to take the exam one must first be employed and sponsored by a licensed broker, and to become a licensed real estate broker, one must be a licensed real estate salesman for several years. Thus, the "ins" can restrict entry.

Another example of delegation of restrictive power to the "ins" is in the admission to America of performing artists—musicians, actors, and dancers. To compel American consumers to patronize American performers, foreigners may receive work visas only if they have "exceptional merit" and qualities not available in the U.S. The evaluation of the merit of pop singers is delegated by the immigration authorities to a union, usually the American Federation of Radio Artists, whose executive secretary decided in 1965, for example, that American consumers should not watch live performances of the Zombies and the Mindbenders, then two of the top recording groups in Britain and America. (*New York Times*, April 25, 1965.) Whether this argues for or against such restrictions we leave to the reader.

In the early 1970's, many states have enacted laws to license new-car dealers. Touted as protection for dealers from aggressive sales pressure by manufacturers and as protection for consumers' warranty rights (which separate laws could accomplish), these laws have restricted competition and freedom. In Texas, for example, the newly created commission has six members, four of them dealers. They denied two people permission to open Dallas dealerships (one Toyota, another Volkswagen) when the existing dealers of these cars protested that there was no public need for more dealers (even though the manufacturers and prospective dealers obviously thought otherwise). The burden of proving a public need is on the applicant and manufacturer, according to the GM dealer who heads the commission. (Reported in *Business Week*, Jan. 8, 1972.)

[6] Such irrelevancy is standard practice in boxing. Ernie Terrell was denied permission to box by the New York State Athletic Commission because he had associated with someone who in turn had associated with someone who in turn had associated with a reputed underworld figure. The commissioner intoned that it would be "detrimental to the best interest of

Occupational licensure clearly fits into our reasons for studying economics, discussed in Chapter 1. The group which benefits (those already in the occupation) is highly conscious of how legislators vote on occupational licensing, while the general public (which loses) is unconcerned and/or unaware, and a plausible argument (protecting consumers) is offered to justify the special interest legislation. The other losing group, people who would have entered the occupation under free entry, having sought employment in other occupations, are generally unaware of the reason why they were deterred.

On the whole, without licensure, incompetent people will fail because of employer or consumer rejection, though sometimes consumers may prefer low quality service for a low price. Without licensure, where customer evaluation of competence is difficult, a private association could form and establish stringent admission requirements. Those consumers wanting assurance of competence could patronize only members of the association. This occurs in real estate appraising, where several national associations exist. As long as nonmembers of the private association can legally practice in the occupation, this device cannot effectively restrict entry into the occupation. Also, the government could require practitioners to display their qualifications—diplomas, etc., without restricting the entry of those who lack such qualifications. Or, the government could give a certification test, but allow anyone to practice whether he passes the test or not. This occurs in accounting where one may be an accountant without passing the certified public accountant's exam. The consumer or employer can decide for himself whether he needs a C. P. A. We cannot pursue fully the question whether all licensing should be abolished, but only indicate that occupational licensing is

---

professional boxing" to allow Mr. Terrell to engage in his chosen occupation. The same commission refused Sonny Liston permission to box because of Liston's prior criminal record—again "detrimental to the. . . ." In 1967, Muhammad Ali was prevented from boxing with Floyd Patterson in several cities (the bout eventually cancelled), because of Ali's opposition to the Vietnam War. Even closed circuit television of Ali's 1966 match with George Chuvalo was banned in Boston, Miami Beach, and San Antonio.

Why can't consumers decide whom they want to patronize? If proper patriotism is a reasonable prerequisite for boxing, why not for truck driving, accounting, barbering, and every other occupation? Then what's left of personal freedom, if a government official can arbitrarily pass on one's entitlement to enter an occupation on such grounds? Everyone would have to tailor his conduct to the whims of this official.

Sometimes licensors consider themselves guardians of the community's morals. Housewives of New York may oppose their husbands' long hair styles with the comforting assurance from the Secretary of State of New York that a woman barber may not wear a see-through uniform or serve cocktails. (*New York Times,* July 10, 1969.)

a growing phenomenon which as currently administered threatens freedom of occupational choice.[7]

Collective bargaining and occupational choice. Collective bargaining, through labor unions, is an arrangement whereby those in a particular

---

[7] Two critiques of occupational licensure are W. Gellhorn, *Individual Freedom and Government Restraints,* Louisiana State University Press, 1956 and M. Friedman, *Capitalism and Freedom,* Ch. 9, University of Chicago Press, 1962. Gellhorn favors reforming licensing procedures; Friedman, with extended attention to medical licensure where the case is strongest for licensing, favors abolition of all licensing.

A vast expansion of inexpensive medical services might result from altering laws to permit lesser-trained people to perform many routine functions now done by doctors, thereby conserving M.D.'s for more complex and critical medical problems. For example, eye-care is provided by lesser-trained optometrists as well as by ophthalmologists. On the growing use of "assistant doctors," see lengthy feature articles in the *New York Times* (11/30/69), *Wall Street Journal* (8/4/69 and 4/23/70) and *National Observer* (2/5/72). The last notes that many military medics retire after 20 years of medical experience, preceded by 600 to 2000 hours of training at a cost up to $25,000. Yet they enter such jobs as truck driver or insurance salesman because most state laws prevent them from performing responsible medical work. Where allowed (Washington is a pioneer state), assistant doctors working with regular M.D.'s have been the decisive factor enabling some small towns and rural areas to retain medical service. Twelve states have followed Washington's lead and others seem about to.

The licensing requirements for lawyers are used to suppress competition and to keep lawyers' income up. In 1965, William F. Dacey wrote a book pointing out exorbitant fees charged by lawyers in probating wills and

"Dissolve two aspirins in a pail of water, pour it around
the roots and call me again in the morning."

employment situation (company, occupation, and/or industry) agree not to work for less than a particular wage. They expect that their employer(s), if faced with the sudden withdrawal of all workers in the bargaining unit and especially if unable to recruit replacements, will be induced to pay them a higher wage than if wage agreements were made individually and if the employer were free to hire other workers than those already working for him (or in the union). We shall assume that in fact collective bargaining does raise wages for those in the bargaining unit.

Now what has this to do with occupational choice? Remember that the market forces which determine wage rates simultaneously determine also the quantity employed. As noted already, because of diminishing returns and the possibilities of substituting one type of input for another, the employer's demand for labor is such that the higher is the wage he must pay, the smaller is the quantity of labor he will hire. Therefore, the result of any collusive agreement among workers which pushes the wage above what it would have been under competition is that employers hire fewer workers than they would have without the collusion.

This is illustrated in Fig. 7-3. Part (a) is a unionized occupation, say machinists, in which W_1 is the competitive wage that would exist without the union. Suppose the union forces the wage to W_2. If employers are free to hire as many as they wish as long as they pay the union scale, W_2 – and this is generally the case, they will hire Q_2. A lot more would like to work at W_2. This is shown by the supply curve at W_2, though the quantity is not marked off.

Thus, there will be a chronic labor surplus in the occupation.

---

included sample legal forms so readers could avoid such expenses. In both New York and Connecticut, he was convicted of criminal contempt for practising law without a license and his book was banned (after sales of 750,000). The convictions were later overturned, but the efforts to prosecute initiated by the bar associations revealed their anti-competitive views. In 1969, two New York lawyers received court threats of disbarment (loss of license to practice) for unethical conduct for putting signs in their windows in large gold letters announcing their availability as lawyers and stating "Tax Returns Prepared. Notary Public." The court ruled: "Indubitably a lawyer has the right to place his name on the entrance to his office and to state that he is an attorney. The purpose is, however, to let those know who are seeking him where he is located, rather than to advise persons seeking a lawyer that one can be found within." Thus, only name and profession are permitted. Anything else is "unethical solicitation." Posting low fees to attract customers would be unthinkable. (*New York Times*, April 19, 1969.)

The legal profession is also resisting suggestions that lesser-trained people called "paralawyers" be allowed to practice narrow specialties like real property or family advocacy after a one year course. Many housewives and moonlighters could have such part-time practices, thereby greatly increasing the supply and reducing the prices of legal services. Such restrictions impair the freedom of both consumers and those who would serve them.

FIGURE 7-3 The Effects of Labor Unions on Wages and Employment

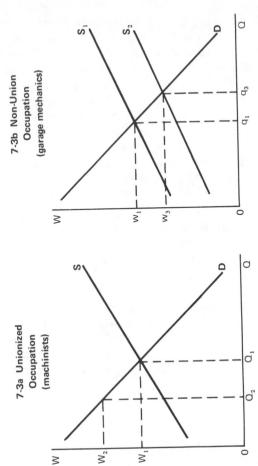

7-3a Unionized
Occupation
(machinists)

7-3b Non-Union
Occupation
(garage mechanics)

The competitive wage is::
W_1 in (a) and w_1 in (b)

In (a), the union causes:
A higher wage, W_1 to W_2
Reduced employment, Q_1 to Q_2
Chronic labor surplus
Non-price job rationing

In (b), because of the higher wage
and reduced employment in (a),
Labor supply rises, S_1 to S_2,
as workers shift from (a) to (b)
Wage falls w_1 to w_3
Employment rises, q_1 to q_3
Freedom of occupational choice is
curtailed for potential machinists

Eventually, most of these surplus workers will seek employment elsewhere. Since there are far more non-union than union occupations, we cannot say which occupations they will move to. And actually most won't "move" to any. If the union has existed for many years and kept wages above the competitive level all this time, this difference, Q_1 to Q_2, will never have been hired in the first place. Nevertheless, this difference, who would have been employed in the union occupation if not for the above-competitive wage, will seek employment elsewhere.

Now turn to Fig. 7-3b. S_1 shows what the labor supply would be if the wages in the unionized occupation(s) were at the competitive level. S_2 shows the increased supply which results from the influx of workers, Q_1 to Q_2 of Fig. 7-3a, who seek work in non-unionized employment, such as garage mechanics. Whether workers *move from* machinist to garage mechanic is irrelevant. The supply in (b) is greater than it otherwise would be because of the reduced employment in (a), in turn, because of the higher wage in (a). (We have not drawn a reduction in supply in Fig. 7-3a, even though employment is less, because the willingness to work there at various wages, which by definition *is* the supply, has not changed.) Clearly, with S_2 in the non-union occupation, the equilibrium wage is reduced in (b) from w_1 to w_3. (It is not necessary that (Q_1-Q_2) in (a) equals (q_3-q_1) in (b), since garage mechanics is one of many occupations that would-be machinists would enter.)

Union leaders often claim that wage increases won by them lead to higher wages for all labor and also to increased purchasing power which aids the economy. Well, it just isn't so. Both economic reasoning and available evidence suggests that (except for employers trying to stave off unionization) union wages cause reduced employment in the unionized industry or occupation, leading to greater labor supply in other occupations and lower wages there. The rise in general living conditions in America, both before and after unions became powerful, has resulted from the rising productivity of labor, caused in turn by education, technological change, and increased capital per worker.[8] Purchasing power or total spending can be maintained only through the government's monetary-fiscal policy (discussed in Chapter 9) and is not affected significantly by private wage settlements.

As a result of the higher wage level of machinists, the freedom of occupational choice of would-be machinists has been impaired. So has the freedom of employers who would like to hire more at lower wages. And indirectly consumer freedom is also reduced. For example, consumer preference for more housing at lower prices is thwarted by the higher housing

---

[8] As shown in Ch. 12, fn 26, the main growth of unions in America occurred after the enactment of legislation in the 1930's requiring employers to bargain with unions. Union membership is currently slightly under one-fourth of the civilian labor force.

prices which follow from above-competitive union wages in the construction industry, where unions are very strong. These are the consequences of collusive arrangements among workers which raise wages above the competitive levels. A labor union is a monopoly collusion among sellers of labor services. Compare Fig. 7-3a with the monopoly diagram, Fig. 2-10 in Chapter 2. The only difference is W for wage here and P for price there.

Unions and value contributed. When a union raises the wage above the competitive level, do the employed workers receive more than their value contributed to production, if the competitive wage equaled value contributed? No. Not as long as employers are free to vary the quantity employed and remain on (not above) their demand curves. When the wage rises from W_1 to W_2 in Fig. 7-3a, then to an *individual firm,* the *wage line* of Fig. 6-1 rises from the competitive level, W_1, to the union level, W_2. The firm hires a smaller quantity, determined by where the higher wage line intersects its VMP. But *at* this intersection, those still employed have a VMP equal to this higher wage.

Wage increases and unemployment. Unions do frequently gain wage increases without there immediately following a cutback in employment. How is this compatible with the effects shown in Fig. 7-3? First, most wage increases occur because the demand for labor rose (from rises in VMP's) and would have occurred with or without the unions. Second, a substantial reduction in employment can occur through attrition—by just not replacing people who retire or quit for other personal reasons or by not expanding the work force as the output expands while introducing different technology. Third, the unemployment which results is often delayed, because of the time required to introduce labor-saving technology. In effect, this means there may be a short run demand curve for labor which goes through the starting wage-quantity point but which is steeper than the long run demand of Fig. 7-3a. Eventually, the long run forces will determine the effect of the wage increase.

Minimum wage laws. A minimum wage law prohibits employers from paying less than the legal minimum. Starting at 25c an hour in the 1930's, there is now pressure to set it around $2 an hour (which means $4000 a year for one who works a 40-hour week, 50 weeks a year). Mercifully, there is no need for another diagram, for the minimum wage law has the same effects as a labor union. Refer again to Fig. 7-3a. Suppose W_1 is $1.55 and W_2 is the legal minimum at $2. The lucky ones still at work will benefit from the minimum wage. But what about those, Q_1 to Q_2, who lose their jobs because of the law? They either have no jobs or are forced into occupations not covered by the minimum wage where supply rises and wages are pushed down further. The minimum wage law harms the very people it is intended to help. Evidence is overwhelming that minimum wages cause unemployment and depressed wages in uncovered occupations for those at the lowest end of the wage scale.[9] What else could be expected? Wages reflect worker productivity. Congressional wage ukase does nothing to productivity. Some states have their own minimum wage statutes set at levels above the Federal level. Among the strongest proponents of Federal minimum wages are labor union leaders, who want to force out of business low-wage companies, especially in the relatively non-union South, and thereby eliminate competitors of the unionized companies elsewhere.

Among those most adversely affected by minimum wages are many teenage school dropouts with low skills, no work experience, and poor work motivation and discipline, whose productivity is just not worth the level set by the government. So they are unemployed, instead of working for a low wage, developing experience, skills, and work habits that would raise their productivity.[10]

Non-price job rationing: race discrimination. When a wage is above the competitive level, as when a union has raised wages, more people would like to work in the occupation than employers would like to hire (the supply of workers exceeds the demand). Who will be the lucky ones to get the jobs? Here again, we encounter non-price rationing. Typically, if wages are significantly above the equilibrium, and the union is a skilled occupation like plumbers, linotype operators, train engineers, or electricians, the union performs the rationing process by deciding who will be admitted to the union. Friends and relatives of those already in the occupation and union get the first preference. The rationing process is often simplified by blanket exclusions of such groups as women, Negroes, Jews, etc. For many years, one furriers' local in New York City admitted only persons of Greek ancestry, until ordered to change after a civil rights suit. Over most of this century Negroes were excluded by all skilled unions.

But if freedom of occupational choice is the objective, then the solution to this discrimination is not merely the admission of some Negroes

---

[9] See J. Peterson and C. Stewart, Jr., *Employment Effects of Minimum Wage Rates,* American Enterprise Institute, 1969. Numerous studies are cited therein.

[10] See "The Effect of Statutory Minimum Wage Increases on Teen-age Employment," by Yale Brozen, *Journal of Law and Economics,* April, 1969. (This is the same issue recommended for the article on airport congestion. It also contains two articles on Soviet economic planning.) Some Congressmen have suggested a separate minimum wage for teenagers. But why any minimum at all? Since 1958, the unemployment rate of persons age 16-19 has been triple that of all other workers.

into the union, for if the wage remains above the competitive level as before, this only rations jobs differently, but still excludes just as many people from the occupation. Free occupational choice will prevail only if employers, without boycotts, picketing, or violence, are free to hire anyone able and willing to do a given job *at any wage acceptable to both parties* whether below the union rate or not. This freedom would open to Negroes vast employment opportunities in skilled occupations virtually closed to them throughout American history. Any real move in this direction would be strenuously resisted by union officials and would require a major revision of the nation's basic labor law, the Wagner Act, passed in 1935.

It is for each person to judge whether those in a given occupation should have a right and even government assistance, in order to get higher incomes for themselves, to prevent others from entering their occupation. For that is the primary effect of most occupational licensure and collective bargaining.[11]

Monopsony

One of the prime arguments in support of labor unions is that they counteract employer monopoly power in hiring workers. Monopoly power in *buying* (rather than selling) is called *monopsony*. Employers are buyers of labor services. Here, we shall describe the consequences of monopsony and how labor unions may eliminate it. In Chapter 12, we discuss whether monopsony power exists.

Monopsony power can exist if one or a few employers hire nearly all the workers in an area or if all the employers collude and agree on lower than competitive wages for given occupations. We shall concentrate on monopsony collusion, first because few employers do hire a large portion of their labor markets, second because the effects of monopsony are the same whether it is from collusion or sheer absence of competitors, and third collusion is a bit simpler to diagram than single-firm monopsony.

The effects of monopsony collusion are shown in Fig. 7-4. The competitive outcome would be E, wage w_1 and q_1 employed. If employers

---

[11] The government assistance is two-fold: (1) laws requiring employers to bargain with unions if the employees want the union, and (2) lax enforcement of laws against violence, thereby rendering it unfeasible for most employers to operate with non-union workers when a strike is called (though such operation is entirely legal). This discussion does not constitute a full treatment of labor unions by any means. For an excellent readable presentation, generally sympathetic to unions, see Albert Rees, *The Economics of Trade Unions*, University of Chicago Press, 1962, available in paperback.

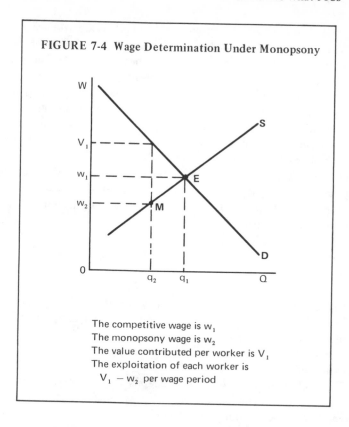

FIGURE 7-4 Wage Determination Under Monopsony

The competitive wage is w_1
The monopsony wage is w_2
The value contributed per worker is V_1
The exploitation of each worker is
$V_1 - w_2$ per wage period

agreed not to compete for workers (a violation of anti-trust laws), they would bring about a lower wage such as w_2 and employ fewer workers.[12] At M, the workers are "exploited." They are paid w_1 but their value contributed (VMP) is V_1 on the demand curve. Enter a labor union. The union may force the wage up to V_1 or somewhere between w_2 and V_1. The outcome compatible with employer and worker freedom (without collusion) is still E. It can be

---

[12] We shall not prove that M would be more profitable for employers than E, though it would be. (It is not obvious from the diagram.) However, at M, each employer is hiring fewer workers than he would prefer, given the wage, so each would have an interest in cheating on the agreement by paying a little more than w_2 and attracting workers from other employers, hoping the others don't do the same. If all try to hire more, the collusion collapses and E is established. With thousands of employers in any metropolitan area, such collusion is not feasible (or legal) in most occupations.

Incidentally monopsony and product monopoly are not related. A small firm in large city could have a monopoly selling some gadget but still compete for workers. An isolated coal mining company might have some monopsony power, but still sell his coal competitively.

shown that at any wage between w_2 and w_1 workers are paid less than value contributed, while at w_1 or higher wage equals VMP. But at wages above w_1, freedom of occupational choice is restricted because the labor surplus is not allowed to push the wage down to E. It can also be shown that at any union wage between w_2 and V_1 employment will actually be greater than at w_2, being the greatest at w_1, where it will be q_1. Thus, the union can bring about the competitive outcome, E, by setting the wage at w_1. But it has no incentive to do so, since wages above w_1 are possible without any loss of jobs from q_2 (unless the union wage goes above V_1) and these higher wages would naturally be preferred by the unionized workers. In conclusion, under monopsony, a union is likely to improve the situation by reducing or eliminating the exploitation of the workers, but it is not likely to bring about the competitive outcome.

Summary

Under competitive private enterprise, who does what jobs is determined simultaneously with who gets what: demand and supply determine both the wage and the quantity employed.

Historically, freedom of occupational choice has been denied to much of mankind and still is.

Wage differentials between occupations or areas may reflect worker preferences. Forcible elimination of such wage differences impairs worker preferences about occupation or residence.

Supply and demand will bring about wages which induce people into unpleasant jobs. Wage relationships between pleasant and unpleasant jobs adjust to compensate for the unpleasantness.

The lump of labor fallacy that there are just so many jobs to go around fails to recognize that the quantity hired is greater the lower is the wage rate.

When consumer tastes change, changes in relative prices, profits, and wages give people incentive to shift employment and output in accordance with these new tastes—the invisible hand at work again.

In the short run, workers do not shift as readily as with longer time for adjustment. Because of this, wages (and product prices) may change more in the short run than in the long run in response to sudden shifts in demand.

Freedom of occupational choice is threatened by spreading licensing requirements, where licensure is a device to restrict entry and to enhance the incomes of those in the occupation.

Alternatives to occupational licensure which still protect consumers from incompetence and fraud are: strengthened laws and more efficient courts, occupational registration, and occupational certification, as with accountants.

Freedom of occupational choice is also limited when wages are pushed above the competitive level through labor unions.

Union wage gains cause reduced employment in the unionized occupation and greater employment at lower wages elsewhere as workers who would have been employed where wages are pushed up seek employment elsewhere.

A labor union is a monopoly in the sale of labor services with effects similar to a product monopoly.

As long as employers can regulate the quantity employed, unions do not cause workers to be paid more than their value contributed.

Most wage increases are not followed by unemployment, because they resulted from increases in labor demand, not from above equilibrium wages.

Minimum wages tend to cause unemployment among the least skilled workers.

When wages are above equilibrium, there is non-price job rationing to determine which persons will get the limited jobs available.

This has often taken the form of race and sex exclusion from some occupations, especially high-skill unionized occupations.

It is for each reader to judge whether it is fair for those inside an occupation to prevent outsiders from entering or to hold wages above competitive levels so employers will not hire as many, in order to benefit themselves.

Monopsony exists when one or a few employers hire most of the workers in an occupation and area.

Under monopsony, wages are less than the competitive level, fewer people are hired, and workers receive less than the value they contribute to production.

Unions can eliminate monopsony power and cause both wages and employment to rise among the monopsonistic employers. However, unions are unlikely to bring about the "ideal" outcome which avoids both labor exploitation and labor surplus.

Study Questions Chapter 7

1. With diagrams, show a wage differential based on worker preferences.

2. Explain why artificial elimination of this differential would infringe on worker freedom.

3. Explain why the unpleasant jobs get done when no one is forced into them.

4. Explain the lump of labor fallacy.

5. What recommendations regarding compulsory education, retirement, and women's work are made by those who believe the fallacy?

6. Explain how changes in prices (including wages), following a change in consumer tastes, lead to reallocation of inputs based on consumer choice.

7. Explain this adjustment with directional arrows, using ratios of prices, wages, investment returns, employment, output, and input demand.

8. Explain, using diagrams, how wages and quantity adjust after a sudden rise or fall in labor demand, distinguishing short run and long run.

9. Which have demand and supply curves used up to now been, short run or long run?*

10. What is the rule for drawing short and intermediate run curves?*

11. What is the alleged justification for occupational licensure?

12. What is its frequent objective and result?

13. What government policies to protect consumers could replace occupational licensure?

14. Using two diagrams, show the effects of a union which raises wages in an occupation: the unionized occupation, nonunion occupations.

15. Union leaders claim that the more wage gains they get for their members, the higher will be wages for non-union workers also. Comment.

16. How does a labor union compare with a product monopoly? Show with diagrams of each.

17. How does collective bargaining relate to freedom of occupational choice?

18. Explain, with reference to Fig. 6-1, the effects of a union within a competitive firm.

19. Explain why, both before and after a union wage increase, wage can equal value contributed to production.

20. Does one always observe reductions in employment after unions raise wages? Why not?

21. What is a minimum wage law? Its objective?

22. With a diagram, show the effects of minimum wage laws.

23. Who are most adversely affected by minimum wages?

24. What is non-price job rationing?

25. What brings it about?

26. Explain why racial discrimination is a likely consequence of union wage determination.

27. Why would opening more unionized occupations to Negroes not eliminate the non-price job rationing?*

28. Define monopsony.

29. Show with a diagram the effects of employer monopsony.

30. What does "exploitation" mean, applied to wages and labor?

31. What is a measure of the degree of exploitation under monopsony? Show on diagram.*

32. Explain the effect of a union under monopsony: its effect on (a) the wage, (b) the quantity employed, (c) monopsony profits, (d) worker freedom of occupational choice.

33. What wage is most consistent with fairness and freedom?

34. Will a union likely bring about this ideal? Why or why not?*

Answers to starred questions.

9. Long run. However, most demand and supply curves, both product and labor, are probably much more elastic than in the diagrams used.

10. They should all pivot through the initial price-quantity of the problem.

27. If the wage is still as far above equilibrium as before admitting more Negroes, the same number of people will still be excluded, just different individuals.

31. At the quantity hired, q_2 in Fig. 7-4, it is the vertical distance between the wage paid (on the supply curve, w_2 in 7-4) and the demand curve (which indicates the value contributed, V_1 in the diagram).

33. The competitive wage where demand and supply intersect. At wages below this, workers receive less than value contributed and at wages above this there is surplus labor in the occupation.

34. No. It could and would likely get a higher wage, at which there would be labor surplus.

"I'm inoculating the females for a scientific reason ... I'm not discriminating."

8

Specialization And The Gains From Trade

The Meaning of Specialization

Specialization occurs when an individual or group produces a narrow range of goods and services in comparison with what the individual or group consumes. For example, a doctor specializes in providing medical services, but consumes a wide variety of goods and services. Similarly specialized are the opera singer, janitor, lathe operator, waitress, or insurance salesman. In fact, it is difficult to think of any worker today who is not highly specialized.

Self-Sufficiency: The Opposite of Specialization

The antithesis of specialization is self-sufficiency, where an individual or group produces everything it consumes. Self-sufficiency for a family would mean the family grows, hunts, or fishes for all its food, makes its own clothes, and builds its own home, providing its own power supply and tools for all these activities. Clearly, such a family, even if it had all the knowledge of modern farming and manufacturing technology and even if its land were unusually abundant in natural resources, would still live little better than the caveman. The family would probably face long hours of drudgery to have only the most rudimentary food, clothes, and shelter. This is not to say that family self-sufficiency is unknown in modern history. It was often approached among American pioneer families and still is among many rural, nomadic, and tribal groups today.[1]

All the products of a modern standard of living—books, electricity, and cars, not to mention rock records and martinis—require a high degree of

---

[1] However, most contemporary youth communes are not nearly self-sufficient, since they purchase, among other things, tools, utensils, appliances, medical services, clothes, and gasoline or electricity.

specialization. The benefits of specialization apply to *regions* as well as to families. And the disadvantages of regional self-sufficiency, though not as great or obvious, act in the same direction as an attempt at family self-sufficiency—to lower total output and the standard of living.

The state of Iowa specializes in growing corn. If the people there decided to become self-sufficient (or if they had to because contact with the outside were cut off), what would happen to the goods and services available in Iowa? True, they could grow oranges in hot-houses and they could probably manufacture clothes, but in both cases at a much greater expense in productive resources than presently required by growing corn and trading it for oranges and clothes. How many cars, refrigerators, and central heating systems could they build and operate with existing metal and petroleum resources—how many in comparison with the quantity they can acquire by specialization and trade? Clearly the goods and services per person would drop greatly if Iowa tried to be self-sufficient. The decline would probably be greater if Northwestern Iowa decided to become self-sufficient and less if the Midwestern states made such a decision. The economic gains from specialization and trade become less obvious as the region being considered is enlarged and includes more diversified natural resources and climate. Nevertheless, any deliberate attempt at self-sufficiency will tend to reduce living standards of the area from that possible through specialization and trade. And this is no less true when the region considered is a nation.

The Correct Degree Of Specialization

Although specialization produces undeniable benefits, one should not conclude that every productive process should be specialized as much as possible. It is still efficient to have general practitioners as well as heart and skin specialists. There is still a demand for truckers who specialize in particular products and for others who carry a wide variety of goods. Some companies gain profits by diversifying: witness the corner drugstore or Olin Mathieson Chemical Company's entry into the aluminum industry. That specialization is appropriate which minimizes production costs and maximizes profits. Thus, the price system provides signals for this aspect of economic organization.

Economic Interdependence: A Consequence Of Specialization

Are there any social disadvantages of specialization? Possibly one is a high degree of economic interdependence. The people of New York City, for example, are vitally dependent on the continued flow of food into the city stores—a flow which depends upon the services of many specialists. Additionally, New Yorkers are dependent upon the services of gas, water, and electric companies, subways, police, garbage collection, carpenters, plumbers, and many others. Yet under normal circumstances there is no anxiety that the flow of these goods and services will discontinue. If some truckers or farmers or subway employees retire, the profits to be made by providing the services will induce others into these businesses and occupations.

The major threats to the continued flow of vital goods and services come from labor strikes, sabotage, and war. The answer to these threats however lies more in the prevention of the events than in a reduction of specialization and economic interdependence.

Routine Jobs: A Consequence Of Specialization?

A second possible disadvantage of specialization is that it has transformed work which was once creative and purposeful into routine, tedious movements which give little sense of accomplishment. One thinks of the contrast between an Eighteenth Century shoemaker admiring the products he has fabricated and the modern assembly-line worker who continuously performs some rote operation on a part of the shoe. Such a criticism of modern production methods, even if partly valid, seems mostly the product of romantic nostalgia. First, there are many occupations today for those with creative abilities and inclinations. With the wide variety of occupations from which to choose, it may be presumed that those who engage in these routine jobs are probably those who mind them the least. Nor is it correct to say that *somebody* has to work on the assembly-lines. The more onerous a job relative to alternatives, the fewer people who will want it at given wages and the higher the price employers will have to pay to get them. At some cost, other production methods would be used.

Furthermore, anyone is at liberty to set up a small shoe shop and perform most of the operations by more manual methods. He would probably find, however, that the loss in leisure and income would not compensate for the gain in enjoyment of work. Indeed, the assembly-line worker today has far more leisure and income to pursue uplifting interests than did the shoemaker of 1750. That he may prefer "I Love Lucy" to an adult class in Shakespeare (or economics) is another problem, but hardly an argument against specialization.

Specialization is thus an indispensible element of a modern economy. And in a free society where no one is forced into or barred from a particular occupation, it can confidently be said that the advantages of specialization are judged by most people far to outweigh its disadvantages. Specialization, of course, prevails in any modern economy, whether private enterprise or not.

Comparative Advantage: The Basis Of Gains From Trade

The result of nearly every voluntary economic transaction is mutual gain—each party values what he receives more than what he gives up, whether it is a boys' swap of a rusty penknife for a captured frog or the sale for $X of an option to purchase shares of stock. Florida has more oranges than it can use, while Iowa has more corn that Iowans want—so they trade with each other. But why did Florida happen to have so many extra oranges and Iowa so much corn? This was no accident.

The fundamental reason areas benefit from trading with each other is that there are *differences among regions in the ratios of costs of producing various goods and services.* We shall illustrate this with a hypothetical example, then comment generally.

An illustrative example of gains from specialization and trade. Suppose the world consists of only two areas, A and B, and that people are interested in consuming only two commodities, corn and wool. To avoid questions about the value of one currency in terms of another, we express production costs in days of labor (and, for simplicity, assume there are no other costs, though, of course, land and capital would also be used). Panel I shows that the corn/wool cost ratios are different in the two regions: 1/2 in A and 4/3 in B. Therefore, we may say Country A has a *comparative advantage* over Country B in the production of corn with respect to the production of wool, because the ratio of the cost of producing corn to the cost of producing wool in A, 1/2, is less than this ratio in B, 4/3. It follows that B has a comparative advantage over A in the production of wool because its *wool to corn* cost ratio, 3/4, is lower than that in A, 2/1. Areas will gain by trading with each other when they specialize where they have a comparative advantage.

Let us suppose each country has a productive capacity of 600 days' labor (per month or some other unit of time). How this would be allocated between corn and wool in each country would depend on consumer tastes. We shall arbitrarily assume that, before trade opens between A and B, the productive capacity in each country is equally divided between corn and wool (Panel II). With the assumed costs (Panel I) and allocation (II), output would be as shown in Panel III. (You should check to see that this is true.)

Now trade opens up between A and B. We can't tell exactly what the new allocation of production would be, but we know each will produce relatively more of what it has a comparative advantage in—A in corn and B in wool. Suppose the new allocation of labor is that shown in Panel IV. Then output, with the costs of I, will be that shown in V. (Check it.) Now comparing III and V, look what has happened to output for A and B combined. With the same productive capacity and level of employment, they are producing 75 more bushels of corn and 25 more pounds of wool!

	Com-	Country	Country	A&B	
Panel	modity	A	B	Combined	Description
I	corn	1 d.l.*	4 d.l.		Costs of production (per bu. of corn
	wool	2 d.l.	3 d.l.		and per lb. of wool)
II	corn	300 d.l.	300 d.l.		A possible initial allocation of labor
	wool	300 d.l.	300 d.l.		before trade. (Productive capacity is 600 d.l. in A and in B.)
III	corn	300 bu.	75 bu.	375 bu.	Initial production before trade.
	wool	150 lbs.	100 lbs.	250 lbs.	(Derived from I and II.)
IV	corn	450 d.l.	0 d.l.		A possible new allocation of labor
	wool	150 d.l.	600 d.l.		after specialization and trade.
V	corn	450 bu.	0 bu.	450 bu.	Output after specialization. (Derived
	wool	75 lbs.	200 lbs.	275 lbs.	from I and IV.)
VI	corn	100 bu. from A to B			A possible trade
	wool	85 lbs. from B to A			
VII	corn	350 bu.	100 bu.		Goods available after trade. (Derived
	wool	160 lbs.	115 lbs.		from V and VI.)
VIII	corn	50 bu.	25 bu.	75 bu.	Net gain from specialization and trade (not counting transportation
	wool	10 lbs.	15 lbs.	25 lbs.	costs). (Derived from VII and III.)
IX	corn	$1/bu.	4s/bu.		Assumed prices, before trade. (For
	wool	2/lb.	3s/lb.		later discussion.)

Illustration of the Gains From Specialization and Trade

* days' labor.

Next suppose they trade as in VI–A gives B 100 bushels of corn in return for 85 pounds of wool. After this trade, with the production of V, the amounts available for consumption are higher in both areas for both commodities: compare VII with III. Both gained by specialization based on comparative advantage and trade; q.e.d.

A skeptical reader, and that should mean every reader, may wonder whether the fact that a gain was shown depended crucially on the particular numbers used. The answer is no, and you are encouraged to experiment with different numbers. The gains from trade will be larger (a) the larger is the difference in cost ratios and (b) the greater is the output shift toward specialization based on comparative advantage. Similarly, if inputs shift away from the direction of comparative advantage, output will decline, as it would if two regions trading with each other decided to restrict trade and aim toward self-sufficiency. An advanced text on international trade would prove that these principles can be extended to more than two areas and two commodities, but, without mathematics, the verbal discussion becomes very involved.

Absolute cost differences are not relevant. Observe that A gained from trading with B, even though A could produce *both* commodities more cheaply than could B. Thus, the cause of benefit is not that one area produces something at a lower absolute cost than another, but that one produces a good or service at a lower cost *in terms of another good* than does another area, which means that the *ratio* of costs is lower in the one area than in the other. But, as we have seen, if the cost ratios are inverted, the other area has a lower relative cost in the other good. So it is nonsense to say that one area (Japan) with low costs can undersell all others, and that while other areas will purchase from it, it has no incentive to buy elsewhere. If an incentive exists in one direction, it must exist in the other, because differences in cost ratios are the basis of gain.

Cost ratios further considered

In A the wool/corn cost ratio is 2/1.

Now let us concentrate on Mr. Jones in A who wants 12 lbs. of wool. How much would this cost him in A? Answer: 24 bu. of corn, because the same resources required to produce 12 lbs. of wool (24 days' labor) can also produce 24 bu. of corn, given the cost ratio. Therefore, Jones will gain if in

"That's impossible!"

trading corn for wool he can acquire 12 lbs. of wool for *anything less than* 24 bu. of corn.

In B the wool/corn cost ratio is 3/4.

Now consider Mr. Smith in B. He has 12 lbs. of wool. How much corn is that worth in B? Answer: 9 bu., because the 36 days' labor which can produce 12 lbs. of wool can produce only 9 bu. of corn. Therefore, Smith would gain if in trading he could receive *any more than* 9 bu. of corn for 12 lbs. of wool.

Clearly, Jones and Smith stand to gain by trading. Jones will gain if he yields anything up to 24 bu. of corn to get 12 lbs. of wool and Smith gains if he receives any more than 9 bu. of corn for 12 lbs. of wool.

Note that the limits within which trade is beneficial are precisely determined by the cost ratios. Without additional information, we cannot tell what the exact terms of trade will be, other than that Jones will give less than 24 but more than 9 bu. of corn for 12 lbs. of wool from Smith. In Panel VI, the exchange ratio was arbitrarily set at 14.1 bu. of corn for each 12 lbs. of wool.

If the respective cost of producing corn and wool in A were changed from 1 and 2 (days' labor) to, say, 3144 and 6288 or to .013 and .026, leaving those in B at 4 and 3, the potential terms of trade would be exactly as just described: the cost *ratios* would still be 1/2 in A and 4/3 in B. Thus, again, it is the difference in cost ratios that provides the gains from trade.

This reasoning means, for example, that if Guatemala has a comparative advantage over other nations in producing bananas relative to producing steel, then if she took resources away from bananas to develop steel production, her increase in annual steel production would be less than the steel she could acquire annually in trade with the quantity of bananas she stopped producing.[2] (It is irrelevant—as well as false—to say she can't acquire steel for bananas anyway because Americans take banana profits out of Guatemala. In this case, she couldn't attract resources out of bananas either.) If someone gave her dollars, and she wanted to increase annual steel consumption, she'd get more steel by investing in banana production in order to increase exports to purchase more steel abroad than to develop a domestic steel industry, given assumed cost ratios. Some of the government-sponsored industrialization of underdeveloped countries is probably more akin to pyramid building for the glorification of nation and rulers than it is to investment which most effectively raises material living conditions. This is to say that areas of investment should be determined by the price system, by relative profitabil-

---

[2] We assume the price of bananas relative to steel does not change when banana production rises.

ity, and not patterned after areas of investment pursued in advanced countries with vastly different input and output cost ratios.

The Invisible Hand Again

Will private incentive automatically bring about trade where it will be advantageous? Yes. Suppose A uses dollars and B shillings. For simplicity, assume a "day of labor" is the same input in corn and wool, that workers can shift freely between corn and wool, that there are no nonmonetary job differences which might affect worker choice between the industries, and, again that no other inputs are used. Also, for this example let us ignore transportation costs which are often small compared to product price anyway. Prices of the goods will be proportional to their labor requirements. They might be:

Prices reflecting input costs

	A	B
corn (per bu.)	$1	4s
wool (per lb.)	2	3

A person in A who wanted, say, 2 lbs. of wool would have two possibilities:

(1) Buy 2 lbs. of wool in A for $4.
or (2) Buy 1½ bu. of corn in A for $1.50;
   Send this corn to B and sell it for 6s;
   Buy the 2 lbs. of wool in B for 6s and send it back to A.

Thus, by trading he would acquire the 2 lbs. of wool for $1.50 instead of $4. Similarly, someone in B who wanted 4 bu. of corn could:

(1) Buy 4 bu. of corn in B for 16s.
or (2) Buy 2 lbs. of wool in B for 6s;
   Send the wool to A and sell it for $4;
   Purchase 4 bu. of corn in A for the $4.

By trading, he could acquire 4 bu. of corn for 6 shillings instead of 16. Thus, there would be ample incentive for people to trade in the direction indicated by comparative advantage. Of course, middlemen, dealing with larger quantities, would indirectly perform the acts just described.

A sharp reader might ask, why would *anyone* buy wool made in A or corn made in B? Wouldn't each country specialize completely? The way this example is constructed, one or both *would* specialize entirely. Yet many nations do produce *and* import the same goods—especially in North America and Europe. The answer to the problem is this. In our hypothetical example, we assumed the cost of producing (days' labor) stayed the same no matter how much a given industry produced. In fact, however, because some inputs are better at producing some goods than others, when one industry (X) expands at the expense of another (Y), inputs less suited to X are shifted into X and out of Y, leaving in Y those best suited to Y. Thus the marginal cost of production rises in the expanding industry, X, and falls in the contracting industry, Y. (Remember the upward slope of the cost and supply curves.)

Now consider the corn/wool cost ratios we started with: 1/2 in A and 4/3 in B. As the comparative advantage product expands in each area, its cost rises and the other's falls. What happens then to the two ratios in A and B? The 1:2 becomes larger, such as 2:3, then 3:4. The 4:3 becomes smaller, such as 3:3, then 3:4. Lo and behold, the ratios are the same! (And the price ratios, Panel IX, would also move to equality.) At this point, there is no gain from expanding trade any further. Trade doesn't stop though. It just continues at the same rate per year until a change in tastes or technology or input availability causes production costs or prices to change.

At the equilibrium, where the two ratios are the same, there may be some production in both countries of both commodities; yet there will be trade also. Now one may ask, but once the cost ratios are the same, why trade anymore? The answer is that, given the technology and tastes, if trade fell off just a little, the cost ratios would immediately differ, providing incentive to expand the trade again. Thus, private incentive, guided by prices of outputs and inputs, brings about this neat balance where trade occurs just to the point where it maximizes the total output between the two countries taken together. And all this applies to any two regions within a country.[3]

Summary

People are specialized if they produce a narrow range of goods and services and trade these for the wider variety they consume.

Self-sufficiency would greatly reduce the standard of living.

---

[3] In all of this discussion of gains from trade, "cost" has meant "marginal cost," the cost of producing an additional unit. If, as assumed initially, marginal cost stays the same as output changes, then marginal cost will be the same as average cost or cost per unit.

The equilibrium described here is an optimum under competitive conditions. However, one nation might benefit at others' expense by restricting trade to get a monopoly price (if it has a monopoly of something it exports). But if the other nations retaliated, they'd all probably end up worse off than under free trade. (Not so though for monopolistic practices by nations producing coffee and some other products, where, to bolster their incomes, the United States Government encourages and promotes monopolistic collusion among countries selling to America, knowing that thereby American consumers will have to pay more for these products.)

Specialization and trade lead to economic interdependence, which is a threat only if a disruption of trade is likely.

Some specialized jobs are tedious, but the leisure and higher income made possible by specialization provide greater variety to life than possible under self-sufficiency.

Areas benefit from specialization and trade when there are differences between the areas in the ratios of costs of production. Such differences imply differences between the areas in the amount of one good that has to be given up to get another.

When specialization occurs in the direction of this comparative advantage, output in the combined areas expands.

If one nation has a comparative advantage over another, the other must also have a comparative advantage over the first, since comparative advantage relates to cost ratios, not to absolute cost levels.

Private incentive tends to bring about the appropriate rate of trade, and to such level, if costs rise as industry expands and conversely, that marginal cost ratios become equal in various nations (or until there is complete specialization by some areas in some commodities). On the basis of this reasoning, economists have almost unanimously opposed import tariffs, import quotas, and most other restriction of international trade (as well as similar interferences within a country).[4]

Study Questions Chapter 8

1. Define specialization.

2. Describe the consequences of attempted self-sufficiency—by a single family, by an area (Guatemala or New England), by a large nation (U.S. or U.S.S.R.).

3. "The more specialization, the better." Comment.

4. "Dependence on others is a reason for avoiding specialization." Comment.

5. "Specialization results in tedious jobs and less dignity and pride of worker accomplishment." Comment.

6. Why do nations benefit from specialization and trade?*

7. "If a country can undersell all other nations, it cannot gain from trade." Comment.*

8. If the ratio of cost of producing sofas to cost of producing TV's in A is

---

[4] A clear, brilliant, and devastating analysis of all the arguments—crude and sophisticated—advanced by special interests to secure tariff protection through Congress is given in *Trade Policy and the Price System*, by L. Yeager and D. Teurck, International Textbook Co., Scranton, Pa. 1966.

$300 to $500 and in B it is £100 to £200, in which product does A have a comparative advantage? B?*

9. Explain why a person in B could get a TV cheaper from A than from B.

10. With a hypothetical example, explain why differences in cost ratios lead to beneficial trade.

11. Make sure you can derive panels III, V, VII, and VIII from the others in the illustration of gains from specialization and trade.

12. What does this example show?*

13. What is the major indication of a comparative advantage?*

14. Given a comparative advantage, why might a country simultaneously produce and import a commodity?*

15. Why do cost ratios in two countries move toward equality when nations expand production of their comparative advantage products?*

16. Why do countries continue trading if cost ratios are equal at equilibrium?*

Answers to starred questions.

6. The benefits from trade derive from comparative advantage: differences in production cost ratios.

7. Comparative advantage must exist in both directions, if it exists at all.

8. $\left(\dfrac{S}{T}\right)_A = \dfrac{3}{5} \cdot \left(\dfrac{S}{T}\right)_B = \dfrac{1}{2}; \dfrac{1}{2} < \dfrac{3}{5}.$ Therefore, B has a comparative advantage in S. But $(5/3) < (2/1)$, so A has a comparative advantage in T.

12. That if nations specialize where they have comparative advantage, their combined output will be higher and trade will be mutually beneficial.

13. A difference in cost ratios.

14. At equilibrium, cost ratios will be the same.

15. The cost ratios change as relative output changes. This is because Supply or Marginal Cost slopes upward, so the greater the output, the higher the MC and where output is curtailed, MC is less.

16. If they stopped or curtailed trading, relative outputs would change and so therefore would relative costs (because of sloping cost curves), creating incentive to resume trade at the higher level.

9

Money, The Price Level, And Relative Prices

What is money? Why is it important to society? If all the money in society suddenly disappeared, would not society still have the same quantity of goods and services, the same human and nonhuman productive capacity, and the same technological knowledge? Then why would not society be just as rich or poor, just as well off, without money as with money?

The Functions Of Money

In an economy without money, exchanges of goods and services would take the form of direct trades, or *barter* of goods and services for other goods and services. Let us consider how this would work. Without money, what would an assembly-line worker in an auto factory receive as wages? One or two whole cars per year? Or fenders, nuts and bolts, and assorted parts each month? In either case, with these wages, how would he find anyone who wanted his car or parts and who would give him the food, clothes, shelter, etc. which he would want? Or if we assume the auto company pays him in food, clothes, and other goods, we then ask, how the auto company could acquire these without money and how the worker could receive the variety of things he wants at convenient times?

The inevitable conclusion is that if the worker could not receive money wages and if the company could not acquire its materials for money and sell its output for money, the cars simply would not be produced. Or consider a lawyer in an economy without money. When he wants a tube of toothpaste, he would have to trade legal services for toothpaste. When paid in money, however, the auto worker or the lawyer can conveniently buy a wide variety of goods and services, although from society's standpoint, it is still true (leaving savings aside) that the auto worker and the lawyer indirectly trade their labor services for the variety of goods and services they buy.

These examples illustrate the main function of money—to facilitate the trading or exchange of goods and services. The necessity of money in a modern economy is brought out logically by the following propositions, which were illustrated above:

1. For a modern standard of living, there must be specialization, rather than self-sufficiency.
2. For specialization, there must be a multitude of trades or exchanges.
3. For these exchanges to occur, there must be money, since barter would be unworkable.
4. Therefore, for a modern standard of living, there must be money, its association with the root of all evil notwithstanding.

The function of money just described is that of *medium of exchange,* a generally accepted unit of purchasing power which is given and received for all goods and services. Besides facilitating trades, as a medium of exchange, money serves three related functions. First, it is a standard of value—a unit in terms of which values of goods and services are expressed and compared. If one cow is worth $600 and one grand piano $4200, then a piano is worth seven cows. Consider the impossibility of conducting a large business without a unit of account. The assets would consist of a list of commodities owned and the liabilities another list of things owed: how would one know whether assets exceeded liabilities. The income statement would be another pair of lists of goods and services received and spent. Unless these were expressed in terms of a common unit, it would be impossible to make sensible decisions about what or how to produce, impossible to determine what activity is more or less profitable.

Next, money is a standard of deferred payment—a unit in terms of which debts are expressed. Without money for this purpose, debts would be stated as so many units of a particular good or service. In general, there is greater uncertainty about the future value of a given good or service than about the future value of money. Thus, transactions involving credit, which play an important role in the economy, are made more convenient with money, providing it is fairly stable in value. Finally, money serves as a store of value, a unit in terms of which purchasing power can be accumulated for future use. With money, as compared to physical commodities, there is less uncertainty about future value, smaller (if any) costs of storage, and less risk of loss or physical deterioration.

What Is Money?

Money is anything that performs the above functions, particularly that of medium of exchange. Throughout history, many commodities have served as money—beads, cows, metals, tobacco, even wives. Most frequently used have been gold and silver. (In the example about the auto worker above, if you thought of paying him in gold or wheat, as a medium of exchange, you were introducing money, which was assumed absent.) In many nations today, money is simply paper or a legal claim to paper money, with little or no commodity (gold) backing.

Why Demand Deposits Are Counted As Money

In America today, the money supply consists of currency—coins and dollar bills—and checking accounts or demand deposits. Demand deposits are appropriately counted as money because payments are made with them and without the use of currency. Most people receive their wages in check form, deposit the check, pay bills by check, which are deposited by their recipients and spent again by check. In each case, the checking account of one person decreases and that of another increases, but no currency need be used, though, of course, some checks are "cashed" and the currency withdrawn. To avoid double-counting of the same money, currency in banks' reserves is not counted as part of the money supply. Demand deposits are over 75% of the money supply in America.

Although everyone will not always accept payment by check, demand deposits are generally more convenient than currency for holding, transporting, and paying out money. When a checkbook is carried about or a check sent by mail, there is no risk to the depositor from loss or theft comparable to the risk from carrying or mailing currency. The person or bank who honors a forged check or forged endorsement stands to lose, rather than the person whose name was forged or who legally made out the check. Another advantage of demand deposits over currency is that when payment is made by check, the payee automatically receives a signed receipt in the form of the endorsed check after it is returned to his bank.

There are other financial entities which could reasonably be included in a definition of money, particularly savings accounts and savings and loan shares, although payments are not generally made with these unless they are first converted into currency or demand deposits.

Money And The Output Of Society

A highly specialized economy cannot operate effectively *without a* monetary system, including divisible monetary units with which both small and large payments can be made. *But printing money does not create goods and services.* Nor does it create productive capacity. A monetary system is one of several conditions which enables an economy to utilize effectively its productive capacity. However, *the standard of living and prosperity of an economy are limited by its productive capacity*—its capital equipment, natural resources, population, level of education, and technology.

If the government gave every family more money, people would have more money to buy things with and would spend more. However, if the economy were operating at near full employment, these attempts by consumers to buy more and by businesses to acquire more inputs with which to expand production would only result in higher prices and higher input costs (including wages), but *no increase in output*. Now don't make the mistake of saying everyone would be impoverished by the higher prices. Prices would rise only as high as consumers bid them, namely, to the market-clearing levels where existing output could just be sold. If more money and more spending were all that were needed to raise output, the poor nations of the world could solve their poverty overnight by adding more zeros to their currency and dropping bundles throughout the countryside.

Some people think more money would mean more output if the additional money were saved and invested. But the investment would bid resources out of consumer production, leaving output of the immediate year the same. More to the point though, as prices rose people would have to spend more to maintain the same consumption. So real investment would not expand unless the *proportion* of income saved rose. And there is nothing about a rise in money and subsequent rise in prices that would raise the fraction of income saved.

The Equation Of Exchange: MV = PT

The role of money in the economy can be explained with the following relationship, called the equation of exchange:

$$MV = PT.$$

M is the money supply, currency plus demand deposits.

V is the velocity of circulation of money, the average number of times per year the money supply is spent. Thus, if M = $200-billion and V = 4, MV is $800-billion for the year.

P is the price level, the *average price* of goods produced, where the price of each good or service is weighted by the quantity of that item produced in the year.

T (for transactions) is a measure of the output of the economy for the year.

P times T. Now what is the product P times T, PT? Since P is the average price of a year's production and T is the amount of this production,

PT is the money value of the production, more familiarly known as the gross national product.

Note that PT is less than *total* spending in the economy during the period. Much of the spending in any period is payments for the sale of goods like used cars and houses produced in an earlier period and payments for the sales of financial claims, such as stocks, bonds, mortgages, etc. These "transfer payments" do not count as part of PT, which is spending for the *current* production of goods and services. However, the commissions or profits of middlemen like stockbrokers or used-car salesmen would be counted, since they represent payments for services which *are* part of the output of the period. So defined, PT equals the money value of a period's output, the GNP of the period, or, if the year's depreciation of productive capacity is subtracted, the year's net national product (NNP).

M times V. Next, what is the product M times V, MV? Obviously, if it equals PT, it must also be the GNP. But let us see why. The money supply times its velocity of circulation per year is the total volume of payments in the year. But we just explained that PT is less than total spending, since transfer payments are excluded. For MV to equal only spending on actual production of the period, V, like T, must not cover all payments made with M. Of course, it is not possible to calculate the velocity of circulation of money by tracing every unit of money and separating transactions for current production from transfer payments. Therefore, V is calculated by dividing M into the total value of the period's output (derived from other data); that is, V = (GNP)/M, which means that MV also equals GNP, and hence by definition of the terms, MV = PT.

An Outline Of Cause And Effect

For clear thinking on economics, it is necessary to understand the direction of causality and interaction among these variables. The left page of the accompanying outline lists the events, forces, and institutions which cause changes in M, V, P, and T, while the right page lists the effects of changes in these variables. In reading over this outline, remember that any change on one side of the equation, MV = PT, must be balanced by a change on the other side. There is no possibility that even temporarily there will be an imbalance between the sides. At this point, read carefully the outline, first including the footnotes and then skipping the footnotes. A thorough understanding of all the points raised is not expected.

M V = P T OUTLINE

The Causes of Changes in M, V, P, and T

M   What causes the money supply to change?

Government monetary-fiscal policy.[1]
Banks' lending and reserve policies.[2]
Public attempts to change the ratio of currency to demand
deposits: a shift between the two types of money.[3]

V   What makes the rate of circulation of money change?

Changes in the preferences of people as to their desired ratio of
money holdings to other (non-money) wealth. For example, if the
desire to hold money decreases relative to the desire for other
assets, people try to convert money into other assets (by spending
M): this means V rises. [4]

T   What makes the output of the economy change?

A rise in T is caused by
A rise in productive capacity, which in turn would have resulted
from investment, education, research (causing technological
change), and population growth.

A recovery from a period of unemployment.

A fall in T is caused by
A rise in unemployment, a movement into a recession or
depression, caused in turn by a decrease in spending, MV,
together with inflexibility in P; if, when MV declines, P fails to
decline as much, then T falls.[5]

P   What causes the price level to change?

Changes in MV relative to T; i.e., changes in spending relative to
output. Large and sudden changes in P are always caused by
changes in M.[6] Thus, while M, V, and T have separate determinants, P is simply determined by the level of the other variables:
P = (MV)/T.

---

[1] Monetary policy is the regulation of M, which in America is done
largely by the Federal Reserve authorities. Fiscal policy refers to the
relationship between government expenditures and tax receipts. When the
government spends more than it collects in taxes, it runs a "deficit." Where
does the government get the money to spend, if not from taxes? It may
borrow from the public by selling bonds. This has no effect on M. It may

M V = P T OUTLINE

The Effects of Changes in M, V, P, and T

M   Changes in M have the following effects (assuming V constant)

A rise in M at a faster rate than T is rising causes a rise in P, or, if unemployment is widespread, causes a rise in T.[7]

A rise in M at the same rate as T is rising has no effect on the other variables.[8]

A fall in M or a rise in M at a slower rate than T is rising causes a fall in T and/or in P.[5]

A substantial and sudden change in M, because of its effect on P and T, will generally lead to a change in V of the same direction (up or down) as the change in M.[9]

V   Changes in V have these effects

They cause P and/or T to change in the same direction as the change in V, except that if there is already full employment, T cannot rise further simply from a rise in V (or in M either).

T   Changes in T

A change in T does not directly affect M or V. Therefore, P will move in the opposite direction from T, unless the government regulates MV to move proportionately with T.

P   Changes in P

The main direction of causation is from MV/T to P, not from P to the other variables. However, changes in P, if they inspire speculation that P will continue to move in the same direction, will make V move in the same direction as P—but the change in P would have been initiated by a change in M.

---

simply print more M. Or, the government may borrow from the banking system, either from the central bank, in which case it is borrowing from itself, or from private banks. In general, when the government finances a deficit by borrowing from banks rather than from the general public, M rises just as if the government printed new money.

When a government collects more in taxes than it spends, runs a "budget surplus," M will decrease, unless the government pays off debts with its surplus revenue.

[2] M is decreased when banks reduce loans and try to increase the ratio of their reserves to their demand deposits. Conversely, M rises from a

Footnotes continued from p. 203.

reduction in this ratio of reserves to deposits. How bank lending affects M is not explained in this book.

[3] M is decreased if the public converts demand deposits into currency outside banks, and conversely. We shall not explain here *why* a change in this ratio, demand deposits to currency, or in the ratio, reserves to demand deposits, of footnote 2, does affect M. It relates to the fact that banks' reserves behind demand deposits are below 100%, currently about 15%. Changes in either ratio may cause M to change by as much as 1/.15 or 6.67 times the dollar amount of change in banks' reserves (in the case of a change in demand deposits/currency) or in excess reserves (in the case of a change in reserves/demand deposits).

[4] A change in the preference for money relative to other wealth may occur because of expected or actual changes in incomes, or in the price level, or in interest rates. When people try to raise the ratio of M to other wealth, M itself does not change: V declines.

[5] If prices, including wages, were not somewhat inflexible, that is, if prices did decline proportionately as MV declined, then T would never fall and serious recessions and depressions would never occur. An indispensible causative factor in the beginning of every depression has been a decline in M, and every time M did decline for over a year, and most of the time when its rate of growth slowed, unemployment followed. A brief synopsis of this history is in *Capitalism and Freedom,* Chapter 3, by Milton Friedman, University of Chicago Press, 1962. The research itself is in *A Monetary History of the U.S., 1867-1960,* by Milton Friedman and Anna Schwartz, Princeton University Press, 1963.

A fall or rise in T could also occur from a change in the inclination to work. Overall, however, this inclination has been quite steady, with a dramatic rise in women's participation in the labor force being offset by an increased proportion of people over 14 in school and retired. A decline of average hours worked per week has held the growth of T down from what it otherwise would have been.

[6] In principle, P could rise simply because labor and management priced themselves out of their markets. This would be a rise in P, causing a fall in T, with MV relatively unchanged. In fact, there is no convincing evidence that any major rise in P or fall in T has occurred from such a cause, though it may have happened in the coal industry since World War II and some economists feel that the excess unemployment of 1959-1965 and 1970-72 resulted from wage and price increases by unions and large companies.

[7] As the level of unemployment becomes smaller and smaller, the effect of a rise in M gradually shifts from increasing T (employment) to increasing P, the rise in M having both effects until, at about 4% unemployment, its effect is entirely on P.

[8] Thus, if T rises 40% per decade, which is not unusual, M must rise this much, plus or minus a trend change in V, in order for the value of the dollar, P, to remain the same.

[9] An inflationary rise in M leads to expectations that P and interest rates will rise further, thus increasing V; a drop in M produces expectations that P and T (and incomes and interest rates) will fall, which expectations lead to a lower V.

The Price Level And The Value Of Money

The value of a dollar is the amount of goods and services one can buy with a dollar. When prices have risen, that is, when there is *inflation,* you can buy fewer goods and services with a dollar and the value of the dollar has fallen. And when there has been a decline in prices, a *deflation,* the value of a unit of money has risen.

So, does the value of money depend on the price level? *No.* Does your weight depend upon the scales? Presumably not. The price level *measures* the value of money and changes in it. The value of money *depends upon* the determinants of P:

$$P = \frac{MV}{T}.$$

Thus, the value of the dollar depends on total spending (MV) relative to output (T). If spending (on currently produced goods and services) rises faster than output rises, then P rises: there is inflation, and conversely. The main reason spending rises too fast, when it does, is that M has risen more than output rose, and this in turn is the fault of the government which regulates the money supply.[1]

What's Wrong With Inflation?

It is generally agreed that a stable price level is desirable.[2] Why? Inflation harms people with fixed incomes, especially retired or disabled people living on pensions or insurance, because with unchanging annual incomes, they are able to purchase fewer goods and services as prices rise. For most wage earners, however, the same force which drives up prices will also pull up wages; so employed people are not harmed much by inflation. Inflation also injures lenders whose fixed interest income and return of principal lent will decline in real value as prices rise. Included among lenders are owners of bonds and people whose insurance or pension contributions are invested in bonds.

Since society's total output is not generally affected by inflation, the relative losses of lenders and fixed income recipients are balanced by gains to

---

[1] Note that one cannot find the determinants of any other variable in the equation by solving for the variable as we did for P. The arithmetic of the equation tells nothing about causality. It is correct economics to say that increases in P result from increases in M. It is not correct to say that increases in M generally result from rises in P, though from the arithmetic of the equation either could be right or wrong.

[2] Some economists feel that a gradual, moderate inflation (under 2% per year) might reduce unemployment and increase economic growth. We shall assume not.

borrowers and those whose incomes rise faster than prices. Thus, inflation redistributes the ability to acquire goods and services. This redistribution, however, is arbitrary, and most people would agree, unfair. Deflation has opposite redistributive effects, favoring lenders and pensioners, also arbitrarily. If the rate of inflation or deflation were moderate and predictable (as suggested in the preceding footnote), some of these adverse redistributive effects would be avoided, because lenders would consider the rate of inflation before agreeing to an interest rate. But the fairest outcome is a predictably stable price level.[3]

On a few occasions governments have gone almost berserk in printing money. The result is *hyperinflation,* in which prices rise by astronomical proportions. A few years after World War I in Germany, the cost of mailing a letter rose to billions of marks, though before the war a mark had been worth 20¢. In Hungary within one year, 1945-1946, the price level rose by a multiple of 10^{27} (not 1027, but 1 followed by 27 zeros). In these cases, money depreciates in value so rapidly that people don't want to accept money, causing a reversion to barter and a decline in economic activity. The values of life savings or pension payments are wiped out, of course. The

---

[3] Improvements in product quality over time are estimated to account for a rise in stated consumer prices of ½% to 1% per year. This much recorded inflation then should not be counted as a decline in the value of what consumers can buy for the dollar. A "moderate" inflation of only 3% per year means prices rise 34% in 10 years and 81% in 20 years. This is calculated from $(1.03)^{10} = 1.34$ and $(1.03)^{20} = 1.81$.

"What eats me is the 70 grand I hid in '39
ain't worth half of that now!"

disaster of hyperinflation, approximated in America during the Revolutionary War, does not occur in a mild inflation of say 2% or even 20% per year. The latter causes little, if any, reduction in output, but is still undesirable for its redistributive effects. And inflation also makes sensible economic decisions more difficult because of the need to predict the changing value of money, along with the usual predictions of changes in tastes and technology.

Many people think inflation has been the usual experience throughout American history. But this is not so. In 1900 the wholesale price index was at the same level as in 1750 and only half as high as it had been in 1800. America had three severe inflations up to 1900, all of them associated with wars: the Revolutionary War when wholesale prices tripled, the War of 1812 with a 50% rise, and the Civil War with a doubling. Aside from wartime, deflation was the normal experience of the 19th Century.

In the 20th Century, with rising gold supply there was gradual inflation up to World War I, then a doubling of prices during the war, followed by a sharp drop, stable prices during the 1920's, deflation between 1929 and 1933, a gradual rise until America entered World War II, then another doubling. The Post-World War II period is the only instance in our history when wartime inflation was not reversed. But since 1950 the rate of inflation has been under 2% per year except during the Korean and Vietnam Wars, when it rose to 5% to 6% per year. Thus, based on past experience, nearly stable prices can reasonably be expected during peacetime.

Why is inflation associated with wars? Because during the war, the government acquires an increased portion of the economy's output. And instead of raising taxes sufficiently to pay for this war materiel and manpower, it creates and spends new money. (In the 20th Century, this has been accomplished by the Treasury's selling government bonds to the Federal Reserve and to private banks which purchase with reserves provided by the Federal Reserve.) Thus, even wartime inflation could have been avoided had the government paid for guns and soldiers with tax receipts and money borrowed from private citizens, instead of partly with newly created money. This is especially true of the Korean and Vietnam Wars which drew on only a small portion of the nation's productive capacity.

Relative Prices Contrasted With The Price Level

The *price level* measures the average of prices. The term *relative prices* refers to how the prices of different goods and services compare with each other. For example, suppose there are only three commodities: oranges, apples, and popcorn, with the following prices. Between years 1 and 2, although the price *average* or price level doubled from 10¢ to 20¢, there was no change in *relative* prices, because the price ratios, 1:2:3, for oranges,

	Year 1	Year 2	Year 3	Year 4
Oranges	5¢	10¢	9¢	6¢
Apples	10¢	20¢	8¢	13¢
Popcorn	15¢	30¢	13¢	14¢
Average	10¢	20¢	10¢	11¢

apples, and popcorn respectively did not change. Now compare year 1 and year 3. The price of apples in year 3 is no longer twice the price of oranges as it was in year 1, nor one-third the price of popcorn. Thus, relative prices changed between year 1 and 3. But the price average is still 10¢, so the price level did not change.[4] And finally between years 1 and 4, both relative prices *and* the price level changed.

One may also think of relative wages, relative profits, and relative interest rates. These refer respectively to comparisons of wages in various occupations, to ratios of investment returns in various fields, and to comparisons of interest rates on various types of debts (such as short term, long term, low risk, or high risk bonds).

Real Economic Forces Contrasted With Monetary Forces

Relative prices (and the other "relative" concepts) are determined by the "real" forces in the economy: consumer, worker, and investor *tastes* for various goods and services, for kinds of work, for work versus leisure, for consumption versus saving, and for risk bearing, *technological knowledge, input availability,* and *institutional arrangements* (such as government by law, laws of contract, extent of monopoly). These real forces which determine relative prices are contrasted with the money or monetary forces which determine the absolute level of prices, wages, and profits, but which have little influence on relative prices, wages, or profits. That is, a change in M, as long as it does not cause expectations of future changes, calls for or determines a new price level, but does not likely affect relative prices, wages, profits, or interest rates. On the other hand, changes in the "real" forces—tastes, etc.—cause changes in the relative variables, but have little if any effect on the price level.[5] For example, a change in consumer tastes does

---

[4] For simplicity, we disregard here the fact that price averages are generally calculated by weighting the prices by quantities of production.

[5] This last point—the neutrality of changes in M on relative prices and wages—has to be qualified because of the inflexibility or rigidity of some prices and wages. M does not affect the relative variables when the price system is working properly. For more on price inflexibility, see footnote 10.

not affect MV, need not affect T, and therefore does not affect P. But as we have explained in the preceding chapters, the change in tastes would affect relative prices, wages, and profits and thereby redirect output without changing the total magnitude of output.

An Important Goal: A Stable Price Level Along With Changing Relative Prices

For reasons explained above, it is desirable to avoid changes in the price level. But it is not desirable to regulate or prevent changes in relative prices. As described under what, how, for whom, and by whom to produce, it is changes in relative prices (and wages and profits) which provide the signals and incentives to adjust production in accordance with changing consumer preferences and changing technology. Suppose, to prevent inflation, Congress rules that no price or wage may change. Or suppose the President restricts price or wage changes through "pursuasion," exhortation, and the announcement of price and wage "guidelines." Then changes in consumer tastes and in other "real" economic forces cannot bring about the changes in relative prices, wages, profits, and interest rates which direct production. The consequent distortion in relative prices and input costs will result in outputs and production methods which fail to meet consumer choice as much as would available alternatives guided by unregulated, competitively determined relative prices, wages, profits, and interest rates. Such regulations interfere with the freedom of consumers to direct production in accordance with their preferences and interfere with the freedom of input sellers and organizers to respond to these dollar votes.

How To Achieve Price Level Stability Along With Flexible Relative Prices

How can the government regulate the price level to prevent inflation and deflation without interfering with relative prices, allowing all private individuals freedom to charge and/or pay any price or wage mutually agreeable? The answer, as should be obvious by now, is to regulate M. Since inflation is caused by "too many dollars chasing too few goods," inflation is prevented simply from preventing M from rising too much. With an appropriate limitation of M, people will not have enough spending power to bid up the average level of prices, no matter what their tastes may be. And since deflation is caused by deficiencies in total spending, deflation is prevented by preventing M from falling or by making sure that M rises as much as output rises. Thus price level stability can be achieved by appropriate regulation of the money supply, at the same time leaving people free to spend and set prices and wages without government interference, without any regulation of relative prices, wages, profits, or interest rates.

How can the government bring total spending, MV, to the appropriate level at which P will be stable? By regulating M through the tools of monetary policy (mainly by regulating the volume of banks' lending through the Federal Reserve's control of banks' reserves and reserve requirements) and by fiscal policy (changing the relationship between government expenditures and tax collections). There are admittedly difficulties in determining how much to do and when. Perhaps the government may have to lower taxes by $1.15 to raise private spending by $1; perhaps private spending, through V, will change independently of M. Nevertheless, the government can, by regulating M and thereby total spending, maintain stable prices without interfering with individual price decisions, that is, without interfering with relative prices.

The appropriate regulation of M does not mean an unchanging money supply. Since output (T) rises about 3½% per year (which is 41% per decade), the government must increase M by about this percent to avoid gradual deflation. You should appreciate that such a rise in M to match the rise in T would not cause inflation. Nor would it cause the rise in output, which results, independently of M, from population growth, technological advance, education, and capital investment. For example, in the years 1864-1892 during which total output tripled, wholesale prices declined about 60%, because M rose more slowly than T.

In regulating spending, MV, the government must concentrate on M, which it can regulate, rather than V, regulation of which would interfere with private choices between spending and saving. In regulating M through monetary-fiscal policy, the government need not concern itself with what use people make of their money. Nor need government, in regulating M, have any effect on relative incomes. The techniques of regulating M affect the total spending power of the economy without affecting the distribution of income, which may be determined by the economic forces described under who gets what is produced and modified by welfare programs (which are also independent of the money supply).

The Wage-Price Controls of 1971

In August 1971 President Nixon ordered frozen for 90 days nearly all wages, prices, and rents. These controls were later extended, with numerous qualifications and exceptions. Their objective was to curtail both inflation and unemployment. According to the reasoning of this chapter and Chapter 2, particularly under price ceilings, such controls are unnecessary, ineffective, and harmful. Let us list the arguments against them and then consider why they were adopted anyway.

Against controls. 1. Inflation is always caused by monetary expansion and can be ended by curbing this expansion. In fact, following the excess monetary growth in 1967 and 1968, the annual rate of inflation (which lags more than a year behind changes in M) *had* receded from over 6% to under 4% for the first seven months of 1971, though the outlook was clouded by renewed inflationary growth in M during 1971.

2. If monetary expansion is not ended, then the controls will only suppress the bidding up of prices caused by too much M; however, for reasons listed below, this suppression will be worse than the inflation.

3. Whenever controls are ended, inflation will resume with a burst, again assuming monetary expansion has not been curbed. Professor Milton Friedman likens price and wage controls to placing a brick on the lid of a kettle of boiling water. If the flame (monetary expansion) is not extinguished, the pressure will eventually overcome the restraint and if it is extinguished, there will be no upward pressure and hence no purpose in the restraint.[6]

4. Price and wage controls interfere with and distort relative prices and wages, thereby misdirecting labor and output away from consumer choice.

5. Controls interfere with freedom of contract, preventing people from buying, selling, renting, and hiring on mutually agreeable terms.

6. Controls declare as illegal much conduct which people feel to be their inherent right, leading to widespread violations and general disrespect for law.

7. Controls are inequitable because: (a) many people violate them with impunity, others are caught, and others are pressured into obeying; (b) they are unenforceable without a huge policing apparatus (which President Nixon said would not be created, voluntary compliance being naively relied upon); and (c) requests for wage and price changes above the legal guidelines are judged by political rather then economic considerations, with special interests getting favored treatment. For example, the Pay Board consists of five people each from labor, business, and the public. All five labor members are heads of large unions. The workers who do not belong to unions, over three-fourths of the labor force, are totally unrepresented. And, predictably, non-union wage increases have been restricted by Pay Board guidelines which have not been applied to major union contracts.

8. Such controls, so vague, sweeping, and suddenly imposed, create great uncertainty and confusion among businesses as to what is and is not

---

[6] *Newsweek*, Dec. 18, 1971. On the same subject, see Friedman's *Newsweek* articles of Sept. 27 and Nov. 8, 1971 and Jan. 10, 1972 and in the *New York Times*, Oct. 28 and 29, 1972. Two more excellent readings on this are *Incomes Policies and Inflation*, by Gottfried Haberler and *Wage-Price Controls in World War II, United States and Germany*, edited by Colin Campbell, both published by the American Enterprise Institute, 1971.

legal, as to whether and when prices can be raised to cover increased costs, and as to interpretations of various rulings. As a result, economic activity, especially capital spending, is curtailed thereby adding to unemployment.

9. Since the economy is always in the process of adjustment to past and expected changes in tastes, technology, and input availability, with an infinite variety of lags and anticipations in price, wage, and other contract terms, a sudden freeze of prices and wages as of some date causes severe inequity to many parties. Here are some reported examples, representative of millions. (1) In 1970, a Baltimore doctor, leasing office space, agreed to pay all costs of remodeling on condition that he would pay no rent for the first year. The year ended during the freeze. The government ruled that the landlord must continue to charge zero rent, regardless of the contract the doctor had signed. (*Baltimore Sun*, Oct. 26, 1971.) (2) A Texas barber was denied permission to raise haircut prices from $1.25 to $1.50, even though the freeze administrator admitted shock that anyone still charged as little as $1.25. (3) School-bus operators were not allowed to institute scheduled fare increases, even if last year's fees would cause huge losses, wages and other costs having risen. (4) Because of poor business, a small company postponed its traditional July 1 wage increase until September 1, but the unexpected August freeze eliminated the 5% raise entirely. (The last three from the *Wall Street Journal*, Oct. 7, 1971.)

10. Extreme measures interfering with private decisions may be appropriate in a dire national emergency, but inflation of about 4% and unemployment around 6%, the levels of summer 1971, though undesirable, constitute no such emergency and are not even exceptionally high by historical standards (such as 1959-61).

11. The particular controls of 1971 were not enacted in any specific form by Congress, but were proclaimed by the President on a very broad Congressional grant of authority and administered by boards appointed by the President without Congressional approval or specific guidelines, thereby substituting government by men (with its attendant threat to freedom) for government under laws.[7]

In short, the controls were unnecessary (by points 1 and 10), ineffective (by 2, 3, 8), injurious to personal freedom (4, 5, 11), destructive of social cohesion (6, 7a), and inequitable (7b, 7c, 9).

For controls. In view of this formidable indictment, why were they supported by the general public, most politicians, and many economists? The fundamental explanation is that most people have no conception of how the economic system functions and how disruptive such controls are. But this

---

[7] See Chapter 10 for the importance to private enterprise of government by law and for other examples of government by men in economic affairs.

cannot be said of economists. Here support came from two groups. First, a few economists, such as Professor John K. Galbraith of Harvard, feel that the economy is dominated by monopolistic rather than competitive forces. They have for years favored price and wage controls as a permanent arrangement.[8]

Second, other economists felt that only dramatic governmental action would reduce the *inflationary assumptions* underlying price and wage decisions of large companies and labor unions. Their reasoning went something like this:

1. During 1971, both unions and business assumed that significant inflation would continue for the foreseeable future.
2. Therefore, unions requested and employers granted larger wage increases than employers could pay if prices were going to remain stable (on the average).
3. Now if the inflationary expansion of M were held down by the government, employers would be unable to raise prices as expected and the wage increases they had granted would result in considerable unemployment (as wage and quantity employed move up along the demand curve for labor, instead of there being a rise in the labor demand curve from a rise in M).
4. Therefore, to be in a position to prevent inflation with the appropriate monetary-fiscal restraints *and* at the same time avoid this unemployment, government had to convince business and labor that inflation really would end. And for a while government should prevent wage settlements predicated on expected future inflation.
5. This is the role of temporary wage-price controls. Once inflationary expectations are reduced unions will, by this reasoning, settle for smaller wage increases, and the regulation of M that will prevent inflation will not be accompanied by so much unemployment. Then the controls can be removed.

This explains the reluctant support of temporary controls by Nixon's economists. For example, Professor Arnold Weber, then in charge of the 90-day freeze (called Phase I), stated: "This is too much power for any group of men. We sit around passing judgment on people's lives. It's not right. The sooner we can return to a free-market economy the better." (*TV Guide,* Oct. 30, 1971.) And on the problem of labor unions and unemployment, Professor Paul McCracken, then Chairman of the Council of Economic Advisors, stated that the "relentless" rise of wages faster than productivity gains "is the single

---

[8] See Galbraith's *The New Industrial State,* Houghton Mifflin, 1967. Also his interview in *Business Week,* Oct. 16, 1971. The extent of monopoly is discussed briefly below in Chapter 12, but it is beyond the scope of this book to deal thoroughly with Galbraith's thesis.

greatest reason for excessive rates of unemployment in many industrial nations today." Opponents of the wage-price controls would argue that the way to curb unemployment caused by labor unions (and minimum wage laws) is to revise labor laws, not to weaken further such freedom and competition as exists by controls, especially when the controls are administered under vague guidelines by the very groups they are supposed to curb.

During all of the 1960's there was a continuing controversy over whether the government should announce "wage-price guidelines" to help curtail inflation and business and labor monopoly. An example of such a guideline would be that wages should rise only 3% per year and prices not at all. Such guidelines have essentially the same defects as price-wage controls, though to a lesser extent because, lacking the force of law, they are largely ignored.[9]

In conclusion, money may be likened to the lubricating oil of a machine. Without lubrication, the machine won't work, but proper lubrication does not run a machine nor make a poor machine a good one. Inappropriate and erratic changes in M have been the major causes of

---

[9] An excellent discussion of the pros and cons of guidelines is in *Guidelines: Informal Controls and the Market Place,* edited by G. Shultz and R. Aliber, University of Chicago Press, 1966, particularly selections by Robert Solow and Milton Friedman. The term "incomes policy" is also applied to guidelines and other government action to maintain economic stability by influencing specific prices and wages rather than simply by regulating total spending through M.

This discussion has ignored several parts of the economic program begun in August 1971, such as the 10% import surcharge, since removed (which nearly all economists opposed for reasons covered in Chapter 8), devaluing the dollar relative to foreign currencies (generally approved by economists), and changes in taxes and government spending.

"As I understand it, the goal is to have voluntary
controls, strictly enforced."

inflations and depressions. But a properly regulated money supply does not ensure economic abundance. It "merely" permits the real economic forces to operate without the disrupting effects of gross economic instability.

Summary

The main function of money is as a medium of exchange. Money is whatever serves this function. Demand deposits constitute most of the money supply.

Without money, a modern specialized economy could not function. However, money itself does not create productive capacity.

The equation of exchange, MV = PT, can be used to explain the causes and effects of changes in money and in the price level.

Inflation is rising prices. Falling P is deflation. Changes in P are caused mainly by changes in M. Changes in M affect mainly P, not relative prices.[10]

The government, by regulating M, can maintain price stability without regulating or interfering with the determination of relative prices.

Relative prices (and the other relative concepts) are determined by the "real" forces in the economy—the preferences of people for goods, work, leisure, and risk, together with the available technology, input supplies, and social institutions.

The freedom of individuals to act as they choose is reduced if relative prices (and relative wages, profits, and interest rates) are not determined by competitive market forces.

Our discussion of the basic economic decisions, what, how, for whom, and by whom to produce, pertains primarily to the determination of relative

---

[10] Inflation and deflation, besides causing inequitable redistributions of purchasing power, may also lead to distortions of relative prices. For example, suppose there were a large, sudden rise in M. P would rise. But, because of price and wage rigidities, some prices and wages would not rise as readily in response to changes in demand and supply as they should, given the rise in M (which itself should not have occurred). These rigidities, greater in some areas than in others, lead to changes in relative prices and profits and give producers signals to invest in and produce goods and services which are not actually demanded. Producers cannot distinguish those changes in relative prices which are caused by changes in consumer tastes from those caused by price and wage rigidity. Eventually, after the inflationary rise in M subsides, the inflexible prices and wages do change and relative prices move toward the relationships indicated by the "real" forces. But by then, mistakened production decisions may have led to accumulated inventories and pockets of unemployment.

A decline in M, because prices and wages are much more inflexible downward than upward, leads to even worse distortions of relative prices and to serious unemployment.

prices, wages, and profits. An extended treatment of monetary-fiscal policy and the maintenance of economic stability is not appropriate here. We have admittedly glossed over some controversial issues in this brief excursion into macro-economics.

Study Questions Chapter 9

1. Explain the difficulties of carrying on economic activity by barter, without money.

2. What is the main function of money?

3. Describe three other functions of money.

4. What is money?

5. What are demand deposits counted as money?

6. In what ways are demand deposits more convenient than money? Less?

7. What other entities could reasonably be counted as part of money?

8. Does more money mean more output? Does the answer depend on whether people spend the additional money? Explain.

9. Define the variables in the equation of exchange: $MV = PT$.

10. Explain the meaning of the products: MV and PT.

11. Why is PT less than total spending? What is omitted?

12. What measurement of economic activity do MV and PT equal?

13. How is V defined so that MV does equal PT?

14. Is the equality of MV with PT the result of a process or must it always be true by definition?

15. What are the main causes of changes in M, V, T, and P?

16. What is monetary-fiscal policy?

17. What is a government deficit?

18. If the public wants to add to its money holdings, what changes?*

19. If people expect prices to rise, what changes?*

20. A fall in T is another way of saying what has occurred?*

21. Why does T rise over time?*

22. Does growth in M contribute to a rise in T?*

23. What is meant by price and wage rigidity or inflexibility?*

24. What is the major consequence of price and wage rigidity?*

25. What are the main consequences of changes in M, V, T, and P?

26. Will a rise in M of about 40% per decade cause inflation?*

27. When is a government deficit inflationary? When not?*

28. What has been the major cause of depressions? Explain with the equation of exchange.*

29. What is meant by the value of money?*

30. How is the value of money measured?*

31. What determines the value of money?*

32. What's wrong with this: $T = \dfrac{MV}{P}$, or this: $V = \dfrac{PT}{M}$?*

33. Who gains and who loses from inflation?

34. How is society's output affected by inflation?

35. "If anyone gains from inflation, someone else must lose (and conversely)." What does this imply?*

36. How would correct anticipation of the rate of inflation affect inflation's impact?*

37. Historically, when has inflation been greatest.

38. "Inflation is the norm throughout American history." Comment.

39. What is exceptional about price trends since World War II?*

40. Why has inflation occurred during wars?*

41. Explain the distinction between relative prices and the price level.*

42. Make an example showing (a) changes in relative prices without a change in the price level, (b) a change in the price level without a change in relative prices, and (c) changes in both.

43. What is meant by relative wages, relative interest rates, relative profits?

44. What causes changes in relative prices? The price level?*

45. How can stable prices be achieved without interfering with relative prices?*

46. Why should this be done?

47. Why is it argued that the price-wage controls of 1971 were unnecessary and ineffective?*

48. Explain how placing a brick atop a kettle of boiling water is analogous to price-wage controls.

49. Explain how controls (a) interfere with personal freedom, (b) unfairly harm some people, (c) lead to disrespect for law, and (d) constitute government by men rather than under laws.

50. Why were controls favored by some economists, such as Professor Galbraith?

51. Explain why temporary controls were reluctantly supported by other economists.

52. In the explanation of #51, what implicitly is the existing inappropriate social arrangement leading to these controls and which the controls do not eliminate?*

53. Explain why and how inflation and deflation may lead to distortions of relative prices.

Answers to starred questions.

18. Not M which is government-determined largely, but V. Attempts to hold more M, given the level of M, cause V to fall.

19. V rises. People spend M at a faster rate to get things before prices rise.

20. A rise in unemployment.

21. Because of growing productive capacity—population rise, technological advance, capital investment, and education.

22. Except for a recovery from a depression or severe recession, no, as explained in answering #8.

23. Failure of prices or wages to change as demand and supply change, especially failure of these to fall when money demand falls.

24. Unemployment. When MV declines and P does not, T falls.

26. Not if output rises this much, as it normally does.

27. Inflationary when financed by printing new money (which occurs when government sells bonds to banks). Not inflationary when government bonds are sold to the non-bank public and private spending is reduced to buy the bonds as it would have been to pay higher taxes (if the government had not incurred the deficit).

28. Declines in M and therefore in MV, accompanied by a failure of P to fall proportionately.

29. How much a unit of money, a dollar, will buy.

30. With the price index.

31. Total spending relative to output, (MV)/T.

32. Nothing wrong mathematically. But both imply incorrect causation, that T depends on spending relative to prices or V depends on the price level, output and money supply. Only P is determined by the level of the other variables. The other variables have independent determinants, though to some extent they do depend on one another.

35. That total output (the pie to be divided) is the same whether there is inflation or not.

36. Inequity would be reduced as people take inflation into account in lending, holding M, signing contracts, etc.

39. The only period following a major war when deflation did not reverse the war-induced inflation.

40. Government prints money instead of raising taxes to finance the war.

41. Relative prices: price ratios or comparisons amongst various goods and services; price level: the average level of prices.

44. Relative prices: the real forces—tastes, technology, input availability, and institutions. The price level. monetary forces—MV and their determinants.

45. Regulate MV by regulating M through monetary-fiscal policy.

47. Inflation can be prevented by regulating M, and without this regulation inflationary pressure will continue despite controls.

52. The monopoly power of labor unions to raise wages for selected groups, even though this causes reduced employment for these groups.

"Play money or not, Wilkins, I told you to cut that out!"

10

Institutional Features Of A Private Enterprise System

This chapter takes up six conditions of society which must prevail if private enterprise is to function satisfactorily. Although some are desirable under any economic system, we shall emphasize why they contribute to the performance of private enterprise. In the order discussed, the six conditions are:

1. competition
2. individual freedom
3. knowledge of alternatives
4. laws of contract
5. stable government by law
6. private property rights

About each one, you should ask: (1) What is its meaning? (2) What would be the consequences of its absence? (3) Can and should society strengthen this feature, and how? (4) Does the feature have any disadvantages which counteract in part its economic contribution?

Competition

Competition in the market for a good or service includes the following: (1) many buyers and sellers for each type of product; (2) no collusion among sellers or among buyers to set common prices, total output, or to divide the market; and (3) no barriers to the entry of outsiders either as sellers or as buyers.

The absence of competition. Chapter 2 already discussed the effects of monopoly in product sales and Chapter 7 covered monopoly in the sale of labor services. The results in both cases are a higher price for what is being sold, a lower quantity sold, restricted freedom of entry into the industry or occupation, and a misallocation of production away from what consumers would prefer.

An absence or weakness of competition among *buyers* has analogous results. Product price will be below the market-clearing level, less produced, non-price rationing occur, and the freedom of some consumers to buy as they prefer (by offering to pay more) will probably be impeded. Noncompetitive hiring of labor (called monopsony) results in wages below the market-clearing level and below value contributed. Monopsony power and profits can be maintained generally only if entry by (potentially) competing employers is restricted.

Forms of competition. Some of the ways competition is manifested are: (1) price reductions, which may be publicly announced or given quietly (below list price) to avoid immediate retaliation by rivals or which may be given obliquely through free credit, free delivery, or a reduced price on a related product; (2) improvements in quality and service without price reduction; (3) introduction of new products substitutable for a competitor's product (especially where the competitor's product cannot be duplicated because of patent laws); (4) advertising; (5) entry of new firms (which includes the expansion of established firms into different industries).

Even industries where a few firms produce most of the output—such as aluminum—face competition from varied sources. For example, high profits in aluminum led Olin Mathieson, one of the largest chemical companies, to enter the aluminum industry. Aluminum faces stiff competition from steel and tin in the market for beer and soft-drink cans, and in both of these from plastic, glass, and paper containers. Likewise, in furniture manufacture, interindustry competition exists among aluminum, steel, wood, and plastics, as well as from the supply of used furniture. Materials from numerous industries compete for use in construction and appliances. In clothing, every year or two sees a new synthetic competitor of natural fibers. In shoe manufacturing, Dupont's synthetic leather, Corfam, introduced in 1965 after $100-million in research, inspired so many competing products, particularly cheaper, lower-quality synthetics, that in Spring 1971 Dupont abandoned the production of Corfam shoes.

Competition and rivalry. Competition is often identified with rivalry and greed and with success at the expense of others. However, in one of the most competitive fields, agriculture, no feeling of rivalry in this context exists among competing farmers, because no single farmer's output has an observable effect on price and any given farmer can sell all he produces at the market price. And in fields where rivalry is explicit, success could just as well be viewed as the outcome of serving consumers better, rather than as the result of taking business from a competitor.

In a competitive sport, a major objective in playing is to win over one's opponent. The winner's success is inevitably at the expense of the loser. In economic competition, victory over someone is not necessarily or even generally a prime consideration. The objective of competitors is higher income for themselves, often without any conscious intention of outdoing or injuring a competitor. Moreover, from the standpoint of society as a whole, one's gains from economic competition are not at the expense of others. Whereas in competitive sport there is a fixed pie (the victory) to be divided one way or another, in economic competition the successful competitor, getting paid only what he has contributed, adds to the total pie to be "won;" his gain does not come from a fixed pie which would have been distributed differently had he not been successful.

In the short run, competition does not always work out this way. The superior company or product or employee does win at the expense of others. But the others can regain their reduced income or lost opportunity by producing better or shifting to other products or occupations or employments. That is, they can still prosper by producing saleable values.

It is perhaps unfortunate that the word competition has been used to describe economic behavior. All competition amounts to is an exercise of one's freedom to pursue his own objectives, providing he does not monopolize. Any barriers to competition inevitably impede the freedom of some people to sell or buy on mutually agreeable terms. Thus, there is considerable overlap between "competition" and "economic freedom."

Despite the general approbation accorded competition in America, including antitrust laws to preserve it, there are numerous examples of government policy which have the effect of preventing competition and creating monopolistic results. Some of these are: tariffs, import and production quotas on oil, regulation of rates and entry into interstate trucking, the farm support program and the encouragement of agricultural marketing associations, numerous state and local licensing requirements restricting entry into occupations and businesses, ceilings on interest rates banks can pay their depositors, resale price maintenance laws by which manufacturers may prohibit price competition among retailers, and laws encouraging labor unions.[1] These policies lend support to the generalization

---

[1] Prohibitions of one kind of competition aften lead to another kind. Since laws prevent banks from attracting checking accounts by offering interest on the deposits, banks use other means of attracting business (surely of less value to depositors). In Waterbury, Connecticut, one bank, to attract people in to cash their pay checks during lunch hour, had a Cream Cheese Lady passing out date-nut bread sandwiches to those waiting in line. In their radio skit advertisement called "Great Loans in History," a skeptical banker, rejecting Alexander Graham Bell's request for financing a new invention, said, "Don't call us. We'll call you." (*Wall Street Journal,* June 26, 1968.) A Dallas

that sellers of most goods and services favor competition in all fields but their own, where they prefer "stability," "fair prices," "fair profits," and "orderly market conditions"—all euphemisms for less competition. As Treasury Secretary Connally stated in justifying a 10% tax on all imports, "We believe in fair trade as well as free trade." (News conference, Aug. 16, 1971.)

Individual Freedom

Individual freedom is one of the primary goals or values of our society. It is desired independently of whether it contributes to the operation of private enterprise. This discussion, therefore, touches on only part of the significance of freedom.

The basic economic freedom is freedom of contract, the freedom to make agreements, except those involving monopolistic collusion, fraud, violence, and contract violation. This means the freedom to buy and sell, hire and rent, borrow and lend, enter and leave an occupation, and engage in or leave a field of production. Freedom to make agreements means individuals are not compelled by other individuals (or government) to enter into agreements on terms set by others, nor are they restrained from entering agreements on terms acceptable to the agreeing parties. One can think of numerous cases where such freedom does not exist in America (see the last paragraph on competition). The most important recent attenuation of economic freedom has been laws against racial discrimination in economic transactions. But on the whole, economic freedom does exist in America and the exceptions could be eliminated if the public so desired.

Consumer freedom. For consumers, economic freedom means their freedom to choose among alternative goods and services offered for sale, to choose among alternative sellers, and to compete with other consumers in bidding for available goods and services. Without these freedoms consumers would derive less satisfaction from their incomes (unless the coercing agent was a better judge of consumers' interests), would pay monopoly prices or

---

banker in December 1971 attracted funds by giving a $265 shotgun as advance interest on any 30-month deposit of $1800. In effect, he exceeded the legal interest he could pay. After national TV exposure, he received deposits from all over the country.

In the pricing of prescription drugs, 28 states prohibit advertising or competitive price promotion and the Am. Pharmaceutical Assn. considers price competition "unethical." However, in 1971 the Asco Drug chain defied both the laws and the "ethics" in 17 states, with some encouragement from Federal antitrust authorities. Typically, the state laws are enforced by boards of pharmacists. State efforts to close Asco stores for posting prescription prices were being resisted in the courts.

would be faced with arbitrary non-price rationing. And, of course, the process by which prices and profits direct production would not operate to consumers' benefit.

Worker and employer freedom. Individual freedom regarding the terms of employment is a requirement for freedom of occupational choice, for adoption of technological change, for equality of wage with value contributed to production, and for an absence of non-price allocation of workers among occupations. Such freedom is also necessary if input prices are to guide job-seeking workers and input organizers to efficient use of inputs.

Entrepreneurial freedom. The freedom of individuals to invest in fields of their choice, to select methods of production, and to reduce investment where desired is also an essential part of economic freedom. Without this freedom, monopoly would prevail, prices and profits would not direct production in accordance with consumer choice, and methods of production would not minimize real costs.[2]

---

[2] Here are several bizarre impediments to economic freedom, the first one a threat which did not materialize: (1) In 1965, the Senate Judiciary Committee (but not the whole Senate) voted to bar professional sports teams from signing college athletes, even those who dropped out of school. Whose interest do you suppose this was intended to serve? (2) The Federal Government prohibited Millard Cohen from making five gallons of strawberry wine a year for his own use. Seems only heads of families may make tax-free wine at home. Mr. Cohen, a bachelor and 29, did not qualify. To set up as a commercial winery would be more costly in red tape than the red wine was

"Hey kid -- I want to talk to you."

Knowledge Of Alternatives

If economic freedom is to result in an efficiently functioning private enterprise system, individuals must have knowledge of alternatives. Consumers must be aware of available goods and services, including prices and qualities. Sellers must be aware of consumer choices—the prices consumers will pay for various goods and services. Workers must be aware of alternative job possibilities, including wages and other terms of employment, costs of training and movement, and an understanding of their own aptitudes and capabilities. And investors should be aware of rates of return in alternative areas of production, and of alternative production techniques, including the technology and the cost of various inputs.

Since nearly everyone is a consumer, potential employee, and investor, the acquisition of all the knowledge implied above may seem an overwhelming obstacle to a satisfactory economic organization under private enterprise. Indeed, lack of adequate knowledge, together with impediments to freedom, does contribute to many economic problems, especially to unemployment, depressed areas, and low incomes. Nevertheless, as we shall see, a little knowledge goes a long way: the results of perfect knowledge can be approximated even if most people are unaware of most alternatives, as is certainly the case. To appreciate the economic importance of freedom and knowledge of alternatives, you should visualize not simply why *your* having freedom and knowledge would benefit *you*, but why you benefit from the knowledge *others* have, why the economic system functions better for everyone when some people are aware of some alternatives.

Consumer knowledge of alternatives. To obtain the maximum benefit from their incomes consumers should be aware of a wide range of goods and services. For any given person, however, there are many goods and services about which he need have no knowledge. A shoeshine boy need have no

---

worth. (*Wall Street Journal* June 28, 1968.) Again, who benefits from such restrictions? (3) In Riverhead, N.Y., numerous backyard tree houses were ordered destroyed because they did not conform to the building inspector's specification—four walls at least 42 inches high, floors an inch thick, affixed to hardwood branches at least 5 inches in diameter or 7 inches for softwood, not over 12 feet off the ground, etc., etc. (*Life*, August 14, 1967.) (4) Another licensing absurdity: In February 1972, a Maryland state's attorney launched a police campaign to halt backyard rummage sales by private individuals who do not have a state trader's license. The action was initiated after small businessmen complained about the competition. No doubt each of these businessmen would claim to be a staunch believer in "American free enterprise." Such pandemic hypocrisy, however, argues not for abolishing the system, but for educating the public and abolishing the laws which throttle the system.

knowledge about prices and qualities of yachts, nor need a bachelor to evaluate competing diaper-wash services. But this still leaves much to be known by the typical consumer.

Yet the problem is easily exaggerated. Suppose there are forty clothing retail shops in a given metropolitan area. No single consumer will be aware of prices and qualities in every shop. But if, among each store's customers, a substantial portion are aware of alternatives in a few other stores, then each seller's efforts to keep this portion of buyers may well bring about the same price uniformity among stores for given product quality that would result if each customer had complete knowledge of all forty stores. Thus those habitual shoppers with no knowledge of alternatives benefit from competitive prices, if enough other customers are knowledgeable and mobile and the store owners are in no position to charge habitual customers higher prices than knowledgeable ones.

In this example, as in many others in economics, one should distinguish the short run picture from the longer run. In the short run a seller might charge higher prices than his competitors and gain more from customers who remain (from habit and ignorance) than he loses from those who leave to buy elsewhere. But it is likely that if the price differential persisted, more and more customers would become aware of it and shift, and become similarly attached (out of habit) to different stores. Then the original seller might have to incur considerable cost to regain enough customers for a volume of business that would provide the former profit rate on investment. In general, *in the long run, more resources, human and nonhuman, and more customers will shift in response to a given difference in wages, investment returns, or product prices and qualities than in the short run.* Which is more relevant in most actual situations—the short run or the long run? Of course, it varies.

How large a portion of customers must have this knowledge? How long is the "short run," the "long run?" In general, the better informed are consumers, and the less costly for them to shift from one seller to another, the shorter will be the "long run." And the more rapidly consumers shift because of price and quality differences, the more it behooves the seller to heed the long run results of charging higher prices than competitors for given quality products.

These same considerations apply to durable consumer goods, of which an accurate evaluation of quality would require extensive testing and technical knowledge. The manufacturers and distributors of such goods—refrigerators, air conditioners, autos, oil burners—have a long run incentive to improve quality for a given price in order to retain and attract customers. In the short run, a company with an established favorable reputation could raise its profits by selling inferior merchandise which costs less to produce, but which consumers cannot evaluate. However, the long run effects on profits might be quite damaging if the favorable reputation becomes an unfavorable one, as would occur when customers of different companies compared results. Again, the consumer with almost no knowledge of product quality benefits from the knowledge possessed by others and from the fact that, in the long run, knowledge of persistent price and quality differences would spread.

Worker knowledge of alternatives. From the worker's standpoint, knowledge of alternative employments forces a given employer to match wages elsewhere. From society's standpoint, this knowledge enables the wage system to direct human productive capacity to where it will earn and therefore contribute the most.

In the short run an employer may retain some employees even though he pays them less than available alternatives. But after some time, many of his employees will leave and he will be unable to find replacements. Which is more decisive in determining wages? The short run possibility of higher profits from paying workers less than they could earn elsewhere? Or the long run loss because such underpaid workers would leave? Again, it depends on how much of a wage differential one assumes, how mobile the workers are, and how great is their knowledge of alternatives. Just as with consumer knowledge, it is not necessary that all workers have knowledge of all job alternatives. All workers will benefit, and resources will be allocated efficiently, and the results of perfect knowledge approximated if a "sufficient" portion of the workers have knowledge of a number of alternatives and if the employer is unable to discriminate between knowledgeable, mobile employees and those who are ignorant of alternatives. Generally, the larger employers delegate employment details to a personnel office which would not know who is or is not mobile.

Entrepreneurial knowledge of alternatives. Here the relevant knowledge pertains to methods of production, input prices, and returns to investment in various fields. Only a small minority of the population need have small bits of this knowledge for economic efficiency benefiting everyone to result.

Sources of knowledge of alternatives. For consumers, knowledge comes from advertising and from comments of other consumers. For some expensive purchases, consumers often hire assistance, such as a mechanic to help judge a used car, or an interior decorator for furniture, or an appraiser for a house. Magazines such as *Consumer Reports* provide independent evaluations of various brands and models of many consumer products. Better Business Bureaus (operated privately) and State Bureaus of Consumer Fraud both assist consumers who have been cheated. The former will steer inquiring consumers away from disreputable firms. Finally, there are books and articles with advice on major purchases like a house, insurance, or college education. Just consult a library catalogue or an index of books in print.

Knowledge of alternatives for workers is also provided through employer advertising and through acquaintances. In addition, there are private and government employment exchanges and similar services offered by schools and professional associations. Knowledge of one's abilities and of general opportunities in various occupations is available through books, tests, and school counsellors.

Entrepreneurial knowledge of alternatives comes from financial reports, newspapers, statistics compiled by government and trade associations, investment counsellors, management consulting services, discussions, and by the "pirating" by one company of skilled research and management employees of other companies. In addition, sales efforts by businesses communicate knowledge of new products and techniques.[3]

Both government and private groups are taking steps to improve knowledge. In 1971 the Federal Trade Commission began requiring industries to substantiate their advertising claims concerning safety, performance, efficiency, quality, and comparative price. About the same time, private advertising interests and better business bureaus established a National Advertising Review Board to hear protests about advertising claims.

In 1963, the Bureau of Repair Services was created in California to get after repairmen, mainly radio and TV, who charge for unnecessary or fictitious work. To detect fraud, investigators take sets with known defects to

---

[3] For example, Real Estate Research Corporation is one of many firms which specialize in advising investors, developers, and city governments whether a shopping center ought to be built at a given location, if so, what stores to include, or the feasibility of using the land for other purposes, or estimating the future economic outlook of a community for a decade or two. Firms that have problems with labor turnover, excess inventory costs, marketing of new products, entering new territory, deciding about drastic technological change, relocating, or that just want an independent appraisal of conflicting intra-company viewpoints may turn to management consultants like Booz, Allan and Hamilton, or Arthur D. Little, Inc., or McKinsey, three of the largest in a rapidly growing field. Another specialist in knowledge is the market researcher, of which the largest is the A.C. Nielson Co., of TV rating fame. These companies estimate the reception and appropriate promotion of new products, suggesting how the product can be tailored for the market. And serving small businesses in financial trouble who can't afford professional consultants, the government's Small Business Administration has teams of retired businessmen who volunteer as management consultants.

Then there is Harry S. Samuels of Lawrence, N.Y., "a millionaire whose biggest asset is 70 pocket-size notebooks filled with private telephone numbers." Mr. Samuels makes his living as a middleman finding companies with a mutual advantage in merging, and arranging such deals as the purchase by one company of a division of another. He has plenty of competition in this field. (*Wall Street Journal*, July 31, 1968.)

repair dealers about whom consumers have complained. This was followed in 1972 by a similar agency to police auto repairmen. The state wisely rejected licensing repairmen in favor of registration and policing, recognizing that the consumers' problem was more one of fraud than of incompetency. These California laws are being widely adopted in other states. (*Wall Street Journal*, Jan. 11, 1972.) While effective prosecution of fraud does not add to consumer knowledge, it does reduce the chances that unknowledgeable consumers will be cheated.[4]

In 1969, the "truth-in-lending" law took effect, requiring that true interest rates in percent per year be stated, so consumers would know what interest rates they are paying on loans and credit purchases. For example, suppose you borrow $1200 and pay back $100 per month starting in one month. If you paid $72 interest for this one-year loan, would the interest rate be 6%, since 6% of $1200 is $72? No. It would be about 12%, depending on when the $72 is paid (at the beginning or the end or $6 per month). Actually, you have the use of the full $1200 for only one month; $1100 for two months, $1000 for three months, etc., as the amount due is repaid; so the average amount borrowed for the whole year is $600, not $1200. The truth-in-lending law lets consumers know what rate they are paying. It is not a usury law which forbids consumers from paying any particular rate.

Another private effort to provide knowledge is Forty Plus, a California group which has successfully helped unemployed executives over age 40 to find jobs. It mails profiles of members to over 5000 companies in Southern California each month. (*Wall Street Journal*, Oct. 22, 1969.)

Sometimes government gets overzealous. In 1965, the Commissioner of Markets of New York City ordered every item for sale at retail to be clearly price-tagged. The rule was eventually relaxed after a flood of objections from pet stores, antique and used book shops, milk companies, auctioneers, and jewelers, especially Tiffany's who thought tags would detract from their artistic window displays.

Other times governments contribute to consumer ignorance. Even into the 1960's, many state governments, on religious and moral grounds, barred dissemination of birth control knowledge by private advertising, by counseling through government welfare workers or government hospitals, and even

---

[4] Some reporters in Dallas took a freshly tuned and tested car, in perfect condition except for a defective distributor rotor (99c and five minutes to replace), to twelve garages. Only one fixed it for $1. Some others also replaced the rotor, but having kept it overnight, added miscellaneous charges for unnecessary or fictitious work with bills up to $54.60, revealing varying combinations of dishonesty and incompetence. Honest inspectors, stiffer penalties, and a more efficient court system would help considerably to make honesty the most profitable policy. (Reported in the *Wall Street Journal*, April 20, 1971.)

by private counseling. Following a Federal requirement in 1967, New York State welfare counselors in 1968 began advising welfare women about birth control, without exerting any pressure for the use of the information. At least partly as a result of this (and the legalization of abortion in New York), between 1968 and 1970 there was a dramatic drop in the proportion of welfare women who gave birth—down from 20% in 1968 to 11% in 1970. (*New York Times,* July 5, 1971.)

Again on the anti-knowledge side, New York in 1971 ruled it illegal for agencies to make profits by referring women (many out-of-state) to doctors for abortions. Free referral services are still permitted. But if free services were providing all the information wanted (such as ads in college newspapers all over the country), profit-making agencies would have no business. If abortion itself is legal, why should anyone be prohibited from bringing doctor and patient together for a fee? Indeed, why shouldn't doctors themselves advertise? This would surely reduce fees and the many six-figure incomes made from abortions. (Any doctor who advertised would, like a lawyer, be accused of unethical practice, jeapordizing his license.) See the *Wall Street Journal* article, "Liberal Abortion Law Proves To Be A Bonanza For New York Doctors," June 1, 1971.

Then there's the case of the young New York mother, a Phi Beta Kappa, who was handcuffed and jailed for endangering the morals of a minor. Lacking a babysitter, she had taken her infant daughter (vocabulary of four

"I had a man-to-man talk with my boy about the facts of life, Doctor. I'd like to check on a number of things he told me."

words) to a birth control lecture. The lecturer was also jailed. (*Life,* Aug. 8, 1971.) The charges were eventually dropped.

It should be recognized that the acquisition of knowledge itself costs time and money. Suppose one had the alternative of buying a used car with no outside assistance and no knowledge of auto mechanics or of becoming an automative expert before buying the used car (a choice which no one really faces). The cost of acquiring the automotive knowledge would be greater than the likely gains. Thus it is efficient to proceed with deficient knowledge. One economist has aptly cautioned against an "irrational passion for dispassionate rationality."

In conclusion, knowledge of alternatives, in conjunction with the freedom to act on alternatives—and together with the signals of price, wage, and profit changes—contributes toward an efficient allocation of productive resources under private enterprise, toward the production of those things most consistent with dollar votes and in each case at a minimum real cost in goods foregone.

The Difficulty Of Centralizing Useful Knowledge

This topic, while tangential to knowledge of alternatives, provides some insight to the problem of economic organization. Under competitive private enterprise the basic economic decisions, what, how, and by whom to produce, are not coordinated and decided by a planning agency, such as a National Transportation Board, a National Fuel Board, a National Food Production Board, etc. Instead these overall economic decisions are made unconsciously as the result of millions of individual decisions and if the result is sensible for society as a whole, it is because the "invisible hand," the signals of the price system, direct individual efforts sensibly. Under central planning, even if prices are used somewhat, a more deliberate effort is made to determine the overall allocation of resources. In this case, if the best decisions are to be made, the central planners must have at their disposal the relevant knowledge which under private enterprise is diffused and not known to any unified group.

One of the alleged advantages of "planning" by the invisible hand over central planning is that even the most skillful planners will create inefficiency and impede innovation because in making their production decisions they cannot assemble and utilize all the knowledge of individual circumstances that is relevant and that is used under private enterprise. We cannot demonstrate here whether this allegation is correct.[5] We shall, however, note

---

[5] As noted in Chapter 3, critics of central planning also allege that inefficiency arises under planning because vested producer-labor interests thwart desirable production changes (which might cause loss of job status,

some of the obstacles to centralizing knowledge. This is turn suggests why decentralized decision-making *may* be desirable, and, therefore, why the use of prices and profits may be required. As shown in Chapter 3, even the economies which are ideologically committed to central planning are taking steps to give greater autonomy to individual plants.

The main reason that central, overall planning is (or may be) ineffective is that much of the information needed to decide what a particular plant or company should do concerns circumstances that are *unique to the individual plant or company* and central planners simply cannot learn about and act on these unique circumstances.[6] The following is a very incomplete list of some of the circumstances about which plants and companies—even in the same industry—differ widely, circumstances which must be considered if the best use is to be made of the productive capacity, circumstances which are likely to be ignored in sweeping directives from central planners.

(1) The ability and skills of entrepreneurs and management. In some companies, management is adept at directing a large work force on a rather impersonal basis; in others, management is best suited to operate a small establishment having close personal contact with all workers. Some competent executives are able to delegate authority, others cannot. Thus, the size of firm, upon which many other decisions rest, depends on managerial skills.

Managers and owners have a wide variety of miscellaneous skills and information to draw on: a college minor in chemistry, a relative who manages a construction company, a woodworking hobby, to name a few possibilities. These provide ideas for making profits which would not occur to others. When one combines ten or twenty executives with varied backgrounds the possibilities multiply for some unique combination of knowledge justifying company action which could not be anticipated by central planners.

Some managers are adept at seeking out new ways of making profits, others are followers who adopt the innovations of the leaders. Some are good at technological innovation in production methods, others at developing new

---

interrupt comfortable routine, and involve risk of failure), which changes would be introduced by *someone* under competitive private enterprise even if other established producers resisted them.

[6] Lest this seem a capitalist bias, consider the following from a Soviet publication: "The basic flaw in planning and management was that every detail was supposed to be decided from the center and, since it was impossible to know the circumstances of each enterprise, the center proceeded from average conditions that did not exist in reality in any one enterprise. . . ." Quoted by Abram Bergson in his chapter, "The Current Soviet Planning Reforms," in A. Balinky, *op. cit*, p. 52. Bergson's source was A. Birman, *Current Digest of the Soviet Press*, April 13, 1966, Part II, p. 3.

products. There is room for all these, but the appropriate production policies are not the same for all.[7]

(2) Availability of inputs, human and nonhuman. The particular products a company will develop and the methods of production depend partly on the relative abundance of skilled and unskilled workers, natural resources, transportation facilities, local customs and preferences regarding nightwork, work by married women, supply of temporary summer workers, etc. Moreover, there may be sudden changes in these conditions which warrant changes in production methods, hours of work, or product lines. Perhaps a nearby company has suddenly closed, making available certain materials, workers, or real estate. To take advantage of such availability, important decisions must be made quickly and locally.

(3) Specific needs and demands of customers. To take advantage of profit opportunities and thus best to serve customers, companies must be free to change, drastically at times, their production schedules, product lines, and terms of sale. Long delays for permission from a central government mean loss of profits and inferior service to customers.

(4) Predictable variations in demand. Here we refer to known local variations, such as the way a food store's demand fluctuates at different hours—10AM, 3PM, 6PM, or between Tuesday and Saturday afternoon, or how department store demand varies seasonally—pre-Christmas, January, Easter, summer, pre-school, etc. These variations depend on such factors as climate, average family size, local income level, whether many mothers have jobs, apartment versus single-family residence, transportation facilities, etc. In turn, these predictable, but local, variations in demand affect decisions as to appropriate firm size, how much to rely on part-time employment, how to combine product lines, when and how to promote different products.

---

[7] A *Wall Street Journal* article of May 12, 1971 described several company presidents (and owners) who find that decision-making is best done away from the office. One spends hours sitting in the park or hiking. Another, the head of a conglomerate which has acquired 74 companies in the past 7 years, works in a stable on a farm 400 miles from company headquarters. The owner of an auto supply company near Detroit runs his company from Hawaii. Another just stays home and works. The head of a Philadelphia public relations agency operates five months a year from his yacht in the Chesapeake Bay. These are all active presidents, not simply owners who let someone else run their interests. Such arrangements would be disastrous for some enterprises, but successful for others.

(5) Appropriate adjustments to changes in demand. Suppose demand declines for cotton textiles. Some plants should curtail production, some should close down, some should try to develop other products such as synthetic fibers. The appropriate adjustment depends on local circumstances. Furthermore, even when demand declines overall, it may rise for some firms. A decline in demand is usually gradual and unannounced. It occurs differently in different places and in some places will be temporary, in others permanent. Again the adjustment which is most profitable and best serves consumers differs with different firms.

(6) Condition of plant facilities. The most profitable adjustment to changes in consumer demand or production technology or input costs depends partly on the condition of plant facilities, whether they are new or nearly worn out so that replacement decisions are at hand, whether they are adaptable to other products, whether they can be moved to other locations.

(7) Preferences for risk-taking. There are many ways the risks of business can be allocated among owners, lenders, customers, and employees. Some owners prefer risky ventures where a big loss or profit is possible, others want security of income. When a company is to expand, should it sell more stock, thereby diluting the ownership of existing stockholders, or should it borrow? If it borrows, should it sell long term or short term bonds? Should it make the bonds convertible into stock at some fixed price (thereby

"Why didn't we think of this before -- alternate streets for men and women drivers?"

reducing the interest cost, but giving bondholders a chance to get some of the high profits if the new investment pays off well)? Should it extend credit to its customers or try to get credit from those from whom it buys? Should it enter long term contracts at assured prices, taking the risk that costs may rise or product demand may rise and it could sell at higher than contract prices? Should it buy things on long term contracts? Would the workers be interested in profit-sharing arrangements, which mean lower set hourly rates and make their incomes, like the owners', depend partly on how well the business does? All of these questions relate to who loses or gains first and most from unpredictable changes in the demand or costs facing the firm. Given free choice, people will make many different arrangements to allocate these risks.

To repeat, these and many other local conditions and preferences in varying combinations mean that the most efficient production decisions are made by individual firms rather than by national or regional planning boards. The enthusiasm for a "national transportation policy" or a "national housing policy" coordinating a whole industry or the whole economy often reflects a failure to appreciate the way in which the price and profit system leads to efficient economic decisions.[8]

Laws Of Contract

These are laws stating that agreements must be kept. A large part of economic activity involves promises to pay later for goods and services delivered prior to payment, or promises to buy or sell, on the basis of which promises the parties commit themselves to other agreements. Without laws of contract, including penalties for violation of agreements, many agreements would simply not be made, much economic activity would not take place, and the standard of living would be lower.

Let us contemplate the ubiquity and indispensibility of contractual agreements in four familiar economic relationships: (1) consumer-business; (2) employer-employee; (3) entrepreneurial-lender; and (4) inter-business transactions.

(1) Nearly all families buy some goods and services on credit. If their promises to pay were not enforceable by the government (in court), credit sales would virtually disappear and consumers could acquire only goods and

---

[8] For an excellent discussion of the problem of utilizing knowledge for economic activity, see F.A. Hayek, *The Constitution of Liberty*, University of Chicago Press. 1960, especially Chs. 2-4. Also a famous article by Hayek, "The Use of Knowledge in Society," *American Economic Review*, Sept. 1945, reprinted in *The Invisible Hand*, A. Klaasen, editor, Henry Regnery Co., 1965.

services for which they could pay cash. This would affect most adversely the purchases of houses, which are almost always bought with borrowed money. Imagine how long such purchases would be postponed, and at what inconvenience to growing families, if cash payments of $15,000 or $30,000 had to be made by those who buy houses of these prices. As it is, lenders provide families with money to purchase houses in return for mutually agreeable interest payments, knowing the family income can be expected to cover the payments, and knowing that if the family fails to keep up the payments the house will be sold to someone else—the mortgage foreclosed—and the original loan repaid to the lender from the sales price of the house.

To appreciate the importance of laws of contract, consider the following soap-opera situation. The mother of seven children, three sick, works nights to support her children and ailing husband. She is unable to make the $90 monthly payments on the $17,000 house the family has been living in for ten years. The mortgage holder—a philanderer, millionaire, twice divorced, and once convicted of a hit-run accident— sues to have the family evicted and the house sold at auction as stipulated in the mortgage in the event of default of payments. (Of course the mortgage holder receives no more than the balance of the loan and interest due him. Any further proceeds from the sales go to the owner of the house, minus sales costs.)

Question: should the judge have the authority to abrogate the contract because of his sympathy for the family and/or his dislike of the lender? Are the personalities or personal circumstances of the contracting parties relevant? If you think so, consider the impact of this policy on the willingness of people (or banks or insurance compies) to lend to house buyers in the first place. Couldn't most defaulting debtors, with the right lawyers, come up with a convincing sob-story? Would it really be in society's interest if government officials could set aside contractual obligations because the government official felt one party was "nicer" than the other? (And incidentally, what would be the effect on individual freedom if one's financial or any other important rights rested on the approval or evaluation of one's moral worth by a government official?) One might feel the mortgage lender *ought* to be more sympathetic, or that society as a whole, through established welfare procedures, should assist the family (as it would). But laws of contract must be upheld if this economic activity—buying houses on credit—is to take place.

Even if discretionary contract abrogation by judges did not completely destroy credit buying, the interest rates at which money would be lent would rise greatly, thereby reducing the total quantity of housing purchased and, in effect, infringing on the freedom of lenders and borrowers to make *enforceable* contracts at lower interest rates.

(2) In employer-employee relationships, credit extension with implied contractual obligations is inevitable and occurs continuously. Since it would

be inconvenient to pay workers every hour or every minute, obviously workers have to be paid either before or after a period of labor. Thus, one party will extend credit to the other. In practice, the worker is usually paid after a fortnight or month of labor services. The smoothness with which these relationships are conducted is facilitated by laws of contract, which establish the employer's legal obligation to pay agreed upon wages (even if no written contract exists).

(3) Credit agreements are also widespread and essential between lenders and entrepreneurs. Most of the larger and more successful companies finance a significant portion of their current operations with borrowed money—primarily from banks and from the sale of bonds. Without laws of contract, these loans would not be made and economic growth would be retarded.

(4) Finally, in interbusiness relationships, extension of credit among companies is frequent in the delivery of goods; and alternative noncredit arrangements would often be inconvenient and cumbersome. Also important among businesses are promises to deliver or complete goods and services of a specified quality by a specified time, such as a guarantee that a factory will be completed by a certain date with penalties against the builder for failure to finish on time. Such agreements enable businesses to proceed confidently with other commitments. Again, without these agreements and their enforcement, economic activity would be impaired and the nation's output and living standards would suffer.

Stable Government By Law

This is an indispensible element of any free society whether the economic system is private enterprise or not and hence its benefits are broader than those emphasized here. Let us first describe government by law, then discuss stability and the importance of stable government by law to a private enterprise system.

What it is. "Government by law" encompasses the following principles: (1) On the basis of written laws and court decisions, any individual can ascertain in advance of doing something whether or not that something is legal. This means that those government officials, both executive and judiciary, who administer and interpret the law have a *minimum of discretion* as to what the law is and what it means. (2) There are recognized and accepted limitations on the kinds of laws which the legislature may adopt, especially regarding limitations of personal freedom, and a separate branch of government which may invalidate any legislative act which violates these limitations. Such limitations are found in the American Constitution, especially in the Bill of Rights and in the existence of judicial review.[9] (3) Everyone, including government officials, is equally subject to the provisions of the law. (4) Laws affecting individual action tend to prohibit rather than to compel given acts.

It is difficult to conceive what government by law in its ideal form would be like, because, judging from experience, none of these principles can be followed perfectly. Some uncertainty about the law and some discretion on the part of government officials are inevitable in a changing society. Likewise, it is impossible to articulate for all time what kinds of laws should be invalid. And some laws will be compulsory as well as prohibitive: indeed, all prohibitions involve some compulsion to alternative acts. Equality under the law is probably the most completely attainable of the conditions listed, but it too seems vague, if it is compatible with peacetime compulsory military service applicable only to healthy single males of particular ages.

Government by law should not be confused with democratic or representative government. Logically it would be possible to have government by law in an undemocratic setting, say with an oligarchic or "philiospher king" legislature, providing it complied with the limitations of its power and there were a separate judiciary. Experience suggests, however, that without some form of popular selection, government leaders would not accept these limitations (the familiar maxim that "power corrupts" comes to mind) and their decisions would not be accepted by the population. Of greater significance is the point that a democratic selection of leaders is itself no guarantee of government by law as defined above.

Stability in government means that the laws—the rules of the game—are not frequently and radically changed. Obviously, minor changes must be made continuously, so what constitutes stability will be a matter of judgment.

Government by law is often contrasted with government by men, where the legality of given conduct is not predictable, where government officials decide on the spot—judging each case "on its merits"—what is legal, where government recognizes no limitations on the kinds of laws which may be passed. Under such a system, an individual's freedom and property are subject to the arbitrary whims of government officials, and flattery, bribery, and special privilege are the prerequisites for survival. It is not difficult to think of

---

[9] It should be noted that the Bill of Rights was not intended to exhaust the limitations on the legislative powers of Congress: this is explicitly stated in the Ninth Amendment. Indeed, some of the founders, including Alexander Hamilton, opposed the Bill of Rights, fearing (prophetically) that these amendments would be interpreted as the only limitations of the Federal legislature. For an elaboration of this point and an excellent discussion of government by law see Hayek's *The Constitution of Liberty, op. cit.,* especially Chapters 10 and 14.

aspects of American government, including local bodies, which resemble government by men. On the whole, however, government by law predominates in America. Government by men at its worst is seen in the regimes of Hitler, Stalin, and Mao Tse-Tung. It has also characterised many Latin American governments.

Private enterprise and stable government by law. How does stable government by law relate to the operation of a private enterprise system? Consider these facts: (1) Having the responsibility for national defense, for the maintenance of domestic law and order, for taxation, and for the adjudication of disputes among individuals, government inevitably possesses the physical power to coerce people and to seize property. (2) Because of the great advantage of specialization and exchange over self-sufficiency, economic activity is of great value to many people, and those enterprises which perform this activity receive large sums of money (individually and collectively). Now combine these two facts—government's power to coerce and the money received by business enterprises—with government *by men* and what do you have? (1) The confiscation by government officials of private property for their own enrichment. This is often done by "graft"—payments to government officials for the privilege of doing business, entering business, or remaining in business.[10] (2) Arbitrary and harrassing regulations and orders to business which cause loss of income and investment.[11] (3) Seizures of business property or income to enhance the political prestige of government officials.[12] (4) Theft and property damage by private individuals who are given special privilieges and immunities by government officials.[13]

---

[10] One of many examples pertained to the New York State Liquor Authority in the early 1960's. Huge payments to government officials from SLA Chairman down to inspectors and policemen were standard for receiving a license to sell liquor, for license renewal, and even to avoid fictitious incidents to justify suspension or revocation of the license—such as a SLA inspector's planting a prostitute in a bar, whose planned discovery would cause license suspension if a payoff were not made. After the scandal broke, Governor Rockefeller belatedly commented, "The SLA's basic weakness is that it has too much personal power. Individuals can make decisions based on their own beliefs." Recent indictments and convictions of government officials from Jersey City to Texas to Seattle attest to the widespread continuation of such corruption.

[11] Experience under New York City's rent controls provides many examples of this.

[12] Many leftist politicians in Latin America have built their careers on seizing American investments and in imposing costly requirements to stay in business, after prior governments had encouraged the initial foreign investment.

[13] In the Spring of 1971, government-financed gangs roamed the country-side in Chile seizing private farms, then received government loans to

The consequence of all this is that the property, income, and personal freedom and safety of investors and entrepreneurs are continuously in jeopardy. If potential investors foresee that once an enterprise is developed and earning profits, government officials are apt to seize it or its profits, then many people will not invest. Instead, people will hoard their savings, or invest abroad, or consume instead of saving; and inventive, innovative, and creative efforts to make profits and thereby serve consumers will be discouraged and foregone. In short, private enterprise will not work under such conditions.

Of course, private enterprise does exist where stable government by law is weak. In part this may be because business has, for a price, bought the favor of the government. Also it may be that the returns are sufficient to offset the cost of bribery and the risk of future harrassment or confiscation. That is, projects yielding a 30% per year return may be worth undertaking, because considering the estimated probability of adverse government action in the near future, a net return of say 9% seems quite certain. Yet, in such an environment, many potential ventures yielding 8% to 10% may exist, but will not be undertaken because the risk of adverse government action pushes the probable return, with this action considered, to below the supply price of investment funds. In conlusion, uncertainty about government policy discourages individuals from economic activity which would provide goods and services desired by consumers at prices agreeable to both investors and consumers (and to input suppliers).

The damaging influence to private enterprise of government by men rather than by laws will be illustrated with three current policies: (1) rent controls in New York City; (2) Peru's seizure of property; and (3) oil import quotas. All three are lawful policies carried out by elected governments.[14] But they violate the principles of stable government by law, with consequences not only unfair to the affected property owners but damaging to the long run freedom and living conditions of people generally.

Rent controls in New York City. Throughout American history, and especially in large cities, housing demand has led investors to build and operate apartments. Given free entry, there is no reason why the price and profit system would not lead to competitive returns in this activity. Investors

---

operate the farms, which loans became the responsibilities of the former owners. *New York Times,* May 24, 1971. Also in this category have been the ineffectual prevention of looting and arson in American cities, which has resulted in an exodus of business from the affected areas. In a similar vein, Governor Orville Freeman of Minnesota once called out the National Guard to close down a Wilson meatpacking plant, because striking workers there were creating a disturbance in preventing non-striking workers from (legally) operating the plant (an action later reversed by court order).

[14] Many others could be cited. Another, discussed in Chapter 9, is the wage-price freeze of 1971.

have built to earn returns on the presumption, justified by decades of precedence and custom, that as property owners they could enter into rental contracts on whatever terms were mutually acceptable to both owners and tenants. During World War II, in conjunction with price and wage controls to curb inflation, rent ceilings were enacted. In most of the nation, except New York (where tenants are a larger fraction of the electorate), these were repealed in 1946-7. However, in New York City, with some minor exceptions, rent controls have been kept on all pre-World War II apartments and in 1969 were extended to those constructed after the war.[15] While some rent increases have been permitted in controlled apartments since the war, these have been small in comparison with rises in costs of maintenance, operations, interest rates, and taxes. To a large extent, rent increases have depended on voluntary departures of tenants, so that as time progressed tenants who had not moved since before the war lived in apartments renting for well under half the rent for similar apartments in uncontrolled post-war buildings.

The consequences of these rent controls have been: (1) deprivation of investment returns to property owners, (2) a severe shortage of apartments (since rents are far below market-clearing levels), (3) illegal payments to get into rent controlled apartments, (4) deterioration of buildings which landlords have little incentive to maintain, (5) reluctance of people to move out of controlled buildings, reducing the normal apartment shifting which occurs with changes in family size, jobs, and income, (6) harsh and punitive measures to force owners to make repairs, (7) a huge bureaucracy with much litigation and wrangling over repairs (partly because minor rent increases were allowed when apartments were vacated, so landlords wanted tenants to move, but were not allowed to harass tenants into moving), (8) discouragement of private housing investment in New York City.

The major conflict between this and government by law is the drastic change in the "rules of the game" from freedom of contract before World War II to rent controls so as to cause loss of investment returns. If such prospects faced investors in all economic activity, production, employment and consumption would decline as severely elsewhere as it has in housing in New York City.[16]

---

[15] Indeed, in 1969 landlords were ordered to rescind most rent increases of the preceding inflationary year in their *then* uncontrolled apartments and even to give tenants refunds for part of these increases. Further rent rises were limited to 5% a year in the postwar buildings.

[16] Despite a great demand for apartments as shown by an extremely low vacancy rate (1.2%), the city's apartment construction the past several years has declined to under 20% of the average of the 1950's and early 1960's, (Also contributing to this have been restrictive building codes, high labor costs, and high interest rates.) Indeed, many structurally sound buildings are abandoned by owners, who, under rent controls, cannot cover maintenance costs and taxes and who face fines and imprisonment for failing

Peru vs. IPC. As another example of government policies which discourage private enterprise we cite Peru's treatment of the International Petroleum Co. (IPC), a subsidiary of Standard Oil of New Jersey. In 1889, two Britons purchased an oil field called La Brea y Parinas from a Peruvian.

---

to maintain their buildings as required by law. Once a building is abandoned, maintenance ceases, utility bills are unpaid, tenants begin to move out, and vacant apartments are vandalized, looted of fixtures, and occupied by junkies and other criminals, accelerating the physical deterioration of the building and rendering it uninhabitable. "The abandonment of buildings has climbed precipitously in recent years. In 1961 there were 1000 abandoned buildings on record: in 1968 there were 7000." *New York Times,* June 5, 1969. By the end of 1970, abandonments reached a rate of 1000 housing units a week.

One woman paying $55 a month in 1970 said she could not afford a 15% rent increase because she had to pay $45 a month to park her car in an open lot near the Hudson River. The landlord, who maintains the building largely for sentimental reasons, has offered without success to sell it to his tenants for $1. *New York Times,* Sept. 13, 1970.

Or consider the disheartening experience of George Frank, 69, who immigrated from Hungary as a skilled cabinetmaker. In the early 1950's he purchased a small factory building in Harlem where he and 10 to 12 others worked. With improvements, this cost him $65,000. Several years later he bought the adjoining building, a four-family house for $12,500. Since the mid-1960's, heat, taxes, and minimal maintenance on this house have exceeded income by about 25%. He was fined four times for not making repairs required by the building code. In desperation, he offered without success to give the house free to several churches or to the four tenant families. Finally, because he did not like being summoned to criminal court "when my only crime is that I dared to own a building in New York," he sold his factory with the house thrown in for $50,000 less than their cost over 15 years ago. He says he will badly miss his shop where he spent 49 happy years, but "I am no longer a slumlord!" (*New York Times,* Jan. 30, 1972.) The law forced him to provide shelter and heat to the four families for less than his cost.

For a picture of the housing chaos in New York City, see these *New York Times* articles and those already cited: "Housing Woes Dim Hopes of City," 1/1/70; "Housing Supply in City Eroding Amid Construction Standstill," 2/8/70; "Private Sector Paralyzed in Housing Slump Here," 2/15/70; "Cost Rise Found Outracing Rents," 3/29/70; and "Case History: A Queens Property Fights For Survival," 4/12/70. See also from *Barrons* "Rent Control Blight," 12/1/69 and from the *Wall Street Journal,* "Shortage of Housing in New York City Gets Worse Every Day," 12/2/70.

This is a depressing lesson in the consequences of political harassment of private enterprise. Besides the gross unfairness to property owners, the hardships imposed on the city's residents far exceed their benefits from rent controls. And there is every reason to predict housing in Fun City will continue to worsen. The city government's reaction to the mess is to berate the failures of private enterprise and call for billions of dollars of Federal housing grants.

In 1971, much to the outrage of city officials, the New York State legislature voted to decontrol apartments as they become vacant (which is

After Peru raised the tax on La Brea some 4000-fold in 1911, protests by the British owners and the British government led to a settlement by international arbitration and a treaty in 1922 which specified a $1-million tax payment and fixed tax rates through 1972. IPC purchased the property in 1924. To appease continued resentment of this settlement, IPC, in 1959, offered to view its oil rights as concessions on government-owned land, in effect giving the land to the government, providing the concessions were taxed at the same rates applied to other private mining concessions. The Peruvian government rejected this proposal.

In 1963, the Peruvian Congress voided the 1922 settlement. IPC offered the goverment 65% of its annual profits, but the government insisted on 90% or more and finally in 1967 authorized confiscation, without payment, of the land and some $200-million of company equipment. In retroactively voiding the 1922 tax agreement (reached before IPC purchased the property), the government assessed retroactive taxes and penalties of $690-million, which the seized land and equipment only partly cover. This leaves Peru owing nothing for the property, a matter still under appeal by IPC.[17]

Such experience has occurred repeatedly in recent years in Latin America. In 1952, the Bolivian government seized British-owned tin mines, with disastrous results for production and profits. Again, after encouraging Gulf Oil since 1955 to invest $150-million to explore and develop fields near Santa Cruz and to build a costly pipeline over the Andes to a Chilean port, in December 1969, shortly after completion of the line, Bolivia confiscated the entire property amid denunciations of "large profits" and "international blackmail." Chile has recently seized the vast copper operations of American companies, Peru the sugar operations of W.R. Grace, and Fidel Castro confiscated billions of dollars of American investment. And more of the same seems certain in much of Latin America and parts of Africa. Is it any wonder that private investment has not responded to the vast development potential of Latin America, why the investment envisioned by President Kennedy's

---

quite slowly under rent controls). Deploring this move, a *New York Times* editorial said: "The threat of withholding rent increases or reducing current rent levels could no longer be used to pursuade landlords to meet the minimum code requirements and make essential repairs." (July 1, 1971) This threat would be unnecessary if rents were at market-clearing levels, because tenants could move elsewhere if maintenance were not to their liking. Ironically, shortly after this minimum decontrol took effect after a quarter century of controls, rents were again placed under Federal control by President Nixon.

[17] While Peru's oil production and exploration were steadily dwindling and all other oil fields (which are government-owned) were losing money, IPC was the largest single taxpayer in Peru. See "Tiger in the Tank of Peruvian Fields," *Wall Street Journal,* March 20, 1968 and "Peru Seizes All International Petroleum Holdings," *New York Times,* February 2, 1969.

Alliance for Progress failed to materialize, and why this area remains one of dismal poverty instead of dynamic growth?

Oil import quotas. The development in the 1940's of oil reserves in the Middle East and Venezuela led to a vast increase in American oil imports and downward pressure on oil prices. American oil producers sought protection from this competition. On the alleged grounds that American dependence on overseas oil shipments would constitute a national defense threat (imports were about a sixth of domestic production), President Eisenhower in 1957 instituted voluntary restrictions on oil imports. The total to be imported was set by the government and the privilege of importing this total was allocated by the government to individual companies.

For what follows, it is critical to understand the economic consequences of import quotas. The restriction of imports, coupled with the restriction by state governments of domestic production meant that the U.S. price of oil was well above the world price. Therefore, the privilege of importing oil at the lower world price was worth about the difference between the U.S. price and the world price. In 1969, this privilege was worth about $1.25 per barrel of crude oil. Given the imports allowed, the government has had import privileges worth over half a billion dollars a year to distribute.

One obvious method of distribution would be to sell the import allotments to the highest bidders. Then the proceeds would accrue to the government (or to society as a whole), while the domestic producers would still have the protection of higher prices and profits resulting from restricted imports and domestic production. However, much more to the liking of the industry, the government chose to give away these import privileges, which is where government by men inevitably entered. Who would be allowed to import how much? At first, import rights were allocated on the basis of recent import volume. But this created inequities to companies which had experienced temporary reductions in imports and blocked out newcomers.[18]

The *voluntary* import quotas proved unworkable because (a) companies exceeded their quotas, even though the government said it would not buy from noncompliers, (b) many companies which had not formerly imported began doing so because of the disparity between world price and domestic

---

[18] For example, Tidewater Oil Co. had closed a refinery in Bayonne, N.J. in 1954 and built another for $200-million at Delaware City, Del. designed for the imported grade of oil but unsuited for domestic, with a planned operation of 84,000 barrels per day in 1957. But because of their low imports of 1954-6, their allotment was only 34,000 barrels per day. (This is typical of the kind of inequities which occur from price and wage controls such as imposed by President Nixon in the summer of 1971.)

price, and (c) importation of oil *products* jumped dramatically, since only crude (unrefined) oil was covered by the quotas.

So in 1959, import quotas were made mandatory, covering crude and refined oil and oil products, limited to 9%, later 12%, of domestic "demand" which was interpreted several ways. Special consideration was initially given to long-time importers, but during the 1960's the basis of allocation was gradually shifted to a percentage of refiner's output, the percentage being smaller the larger the refinery. This formula led some large refiners to contract out their capacity to nominally separate companies so as to qualify for larger quotas.

Initially, oil imports from an *overland* route (meaning from Canada or Mexico) were exempted from the quota, since such imports did not have the same wartime vulnerability as overseas imports (pipeline sabotage being more easily prevented than ship sinking presumably). However, imports from Canada rose 400% during the 1960's, leading first to voluntary then to mandatory quotas on Canadian oil. Again, import privileges were based on prior experience. But this meant those who had complied with voluntary restriction in 1967-9 were penalized for having complied. This and Canadian objections led to numerous complicated decisions and exceptions, all affecting the profitability of various pipelines, refiners, public utilities, and domestic producers in the upper Mid-West. For example, the U.S. and Canada made a secret agreement that oil would not be transmitted before 1970 through a newly constructed pipeline built specifically to bring oil from Canada to the Chicago area. The agreement became known when a Chicago refiner sued the pipeline for defaulting on its common carrier responsibilities.

Since there is no pipeline from Mexico to the U.S., Mexican oil could not be imported under the regulation that *overland* shipments were exempt from the quota. But for political reasons, partly to induce Mexico not to sell oil to Cuba, the government wanted to allow Mexican oil imports the same status as Canadian. On the other hand, it did not want to abolish the "overland" criterion for exemption, since this would weaken the national defense justification for the quotas. Therefore, to qualify as an "overland" shipment, oil from Mexican Gulfports was shipped to Brownsville, Texas, unloaded, carried by truck into Mexico, back into the U.S., becoming an "overland shipment," then reloaded on the tanker and shipped to the East Coast. The first entry, being "on bond," didn't count. After nine years of this, the government finally decided to admit Mexican oil without this procedure, but the changeover was delayed because it would cause unemployment at the loading facility in Brownsville. (This illustrates how one vested interest after another gets created in government programs that interfere with market forces.) If Mexican oil shipped to New York qualifies as "safe," why not shipments from the much larger oil fields in Venezuela, since the boat trip to New York is 700 miles shorter from Venezuela than from Mexico? This leads one to wonder whether national defense was more an excuse than a reason for restricting oil importation. Besides, if more domestic production is desired, why continue the state restrictions of oil production? In addition, untapped reserves of shale oil, mostly on Federal lands in the Rocky Mountains, are estimated sufficient to meet America's oil requirements for over 150 years.

Several lucky companies, particularly Phillips Petroleum, Sun Oil, and Hess, built new refineries in Puerto Rico and the Virgin Islands to which they are allowed to import oil for resale as oil products in the U.S. In return the companies contributed to island "conservation funds." The value of the Phillips import privilege is estimated at $15-million a year. There is no general principle by which these companies were favored and not others. Note that the abolition of the quota program, eliminating the disparity between American and world oil prices, would destroy the profit basis of these island refineries, which have cost several hundred million dollars. Thus, the program has created strong built-in pressures for its retention.

Another group which came in for special consideration is American petrochemical companies—those who make products with oil. Clearly, these companies are at a competitive disadvantage on the world market when they pay more for oil than do chemical companies in Europe, Japan, and elsewhere. So, beginning in 1966, some of these companies were given import allotments. Here, too, the distribution was quite complicated and arbitrary, because some petrochemical companies are also refiners, they buy different types of refined oil or use different portions of crude oil and sell the rest, and their finished products consist of varying percentages of oil products.

This entire program, lasting through four presidents, two of each party,

"Hold your signature on that merger, Mr. Selmeyer.
The Justice Department's changed its mind again."

has been conducted without explicit Congressional authorization or guidelines, but by Presidential proclamation and myriad subordinates' directives, all based on national defense exceptions to trade acts which purportedly promote free trade. While the oil import program has not had quite the damaging effect on an industry's output as the other two examples of government by men—rent controls and seizure of foreign investment—it does nevertheless illustrate the disadvantages of discretionary authority—inequity, favoritism, price and output inconsistent with freedom, growth of vested interests in retaining the program, growing complexity and coverage as unanticipated effects unfold, and policies unresponsive to either political ballot or dollar votes. Indeed, the brief sketch given here obscures the *ad hoc* nature of the program, wherein what is permissible and who gets what favors are unpredictable and depend on decisions of government officials who themselves have virtually no guidelines to go by. Fortunately, the government's role in the oil industry (or in agriculture) is not typical—yet.[19]

Property Rights

By definition, private enterprise means private ownership of the nonhuman means of production. If this arrangement is to serve society, it is essential that these private owners have incentive to use their property productively, including the use of property to develop more and better productive capacity. Otherwise, it might be preferrable that this property be owned and managed by the government. Two important property rights are freedom of choice in the use of property and the right to buy and sell property. These are included in the concept of individual freedom, discussed earlier. The third property right and that which provides the major incentive to socially advantageous use is the right of the owner to receive income from the property. Since property like labor receives income in proportion to the money value of its contribution to production, this income provides incentive to use property in the most productive manner and also incentive to develop new property and new methods of using property.

Special taxes on the income and ownership of property reduce the incentive to develop new property. Most notable in America is the Federal corporation profits tax of about 50%, which tax is in addition to the taxation of dividends as personal income. These taxes are generally supported by those who regard property income as "unearned" and therefore less deserved than

---

[19] This discussion has been based on the excellent 60-page article, "Implementation of Import Quotas: The Case of Oil," by Kenneth Dam, *Journal of Law and Economics.* April, 1971.

wage and salary income. Others favor higher taxes on property than labor income as a means of taxing the rich. However, since much property is jointly owned by both high and low income recipients, this objective, whatever its merits, could more efficiently be achieved through the personal income tax—the taxation of property income only when it is turned over to the owner (in the form of dividends).[20]

The removal or substantial reduction of corporate income taxes might be a short run boon to stockholders, but would undoubtedly result in lower prices, as well as increased investment, as corporations and investors competed for the higher after-tax profits. This in turn would reduce pre-tax rates of return on investment, though not necessarily to present after-tax levels. Some of the gains to stockholders would be taxed when increased dividends were paid to them. Any windfall would also be reduced if the removal of corporation income taxes were accompanied by raising the tax on capital gains (the profit from the sale of stock or other assets) to that on current personal income. Then, any profits realized because stock prices rose in response to lower profits taxes would also be taxed as personal income.

One might still feel that property income should be taxed more than labor income, despite the investment disincentive.[21] The point here is that an acceptance of the principle that property incomes should go to the owners of the property is a necessary part of a private enterprise system. Otherwise, this property will not be used as productively as it could be, and new nonhuman productive capacity will not be developed to the same extent.

Summary

The decisions of economic organization—what, how, for whom, and by whom to produce—will be made more efficiently under private enterprise if

---

[20] Another possibility is to abolish both the corporate income tax and the tax on dividend income, but to tax each corporate owner for his pro rata share of the corporation's income, regardless of whether this share is paid out as dividends: in effect, tax corporations as partnerships are now taxed. Thus if you own ten of the ten million shares of a corporation's stock, you would be taxed on one one-millionth of the corporation's income, even if you received no dividends, and the corporation itself would pay no income tax. Aside from increasing incentives to invest and eliminating double taxation of investment income, this would have an additional advantage of removing an artificial tax incentive to reinvest profits within the corporation where they were earned even if somewhat higher profits could be earned elsewhere. This tax change would thus improve the allocation of funds to where profits are greatest and at the same time would reduce tax incentives for company mergers and increase the supply of investment funds to newly formed companies, thereby strengthening the competitiveness of the economy.

[21] This discussion does not pertain to property taxes which finance services received from the government, such as fire and police protection.

the conditions discussed in this chapter prevail. These conditions are ingredients of a free society where individuals may pursue their own economic as well as other interests without coercive impediments from other individuals or from government, but subject to prohibitions against violence, fraud, monopolistic collusion, or contract violation.

Economic efficiency requires knowledge of alternatives as well as freedom, but the diffused and overlapping knowledge of a minority of consumers, workers, employers, and investors who are prepared to take advantage of better alternatives may produce results approximating those of complete knowledge.

When the basic economic decisions are made by central planners, economic efficiency is apt to be impaired because of the difficulty of assembling and using the relevant but diffused knowledge of local conditions. And without market-determined prices, wages, and profits, central planners must also have knowledge about consumer preferences and input contribution which would otherwise have been indicated by such prices, wages, and profits.

The voluntary development and operation of profitable and efficient enterprises will not occur unless contracts are enforceable, unless people and property are safe from arbitrary regulations and harassment by government officials, and unless owners of property have the freedom not only to employ their property where it is most profitable but also to receive the income from that employment. The absence or weakness of these conditions will mean that some economic activities which would otherwise have been undertaken will not be done, even though the benefiting consumers are willing to pay the costs.

Study Questions Chapter 10

1. What are the three ingredients of economic competition?

2. What are the four main consequences of monopoly?

3. What forms may competition take?

4. What is interindustry competition? Give an example.

5. Contrast economic competition with athletic competition.

6. What is economic freedom?

7. Describe economic freedom for consumers, workers, and entrepreneurs.

8. What are the consequences to each group and to society as a whole if economic freedom is restricted?

9. Explain how knowledge of alternatives benefits consumers, workers, businessmen, and investors.

10. Explain also how this knowledge benefits society generally as well as those who have this knowledge.

11. Explain how the absence of knowledge of alternatives harms not only those without the knowledge but also harms society generally.

12. Specifically, explain how all consumers, including those without knowledge of alternatives, benefit if a few shoppers are knowledgeable of a few alternatives in a metropolitan area where stores have overlapping clientel and sellers cannot tell who is and is not knowledgeable.

13. Explain the same situation with reference to workers and job opportunities: some knowledgeable and mobile, others not, but how all benefit.

14. Explain how consumers benefit if some investors are knowledgeable about investment returns and about technology.

15. Explain why businesses may not find it advantageous to take advantage of consumer or worker ignorance of alternatives, distinguishing short and long run consequences of business action to capitalize on this ignorance.

16. Explain how the problem of centralizing knowledge relates to the efficacy of national planning.

17. What are the key elements about knowledge calling for decentralized decision-making?*

18. Why is enforcement of laws of contract important? Illustrate with a hypothetical example. Consider consumer-business relationships, employer-employee, entrepreneur-lender, and inter-business relationships.

19. What is government by law: four components?

20. Contrast government by law with democratic government. Does one imply the other? Explain.

21. Describe government by men.

22. Explain how stable government by law contributes to the operation of a private enterprise system.

23. What two conditions about government and economic activity make government by men and private enterprise (at least free, competitive private enterprise) incompatible?*

24. Explain how New York City's rent control policy is inconsistent with government by law as defined.

25. Explain the consequences if such policies were applied to business generally.

26. Do the same (24 & 25) with Peru's policies toward IPC.

27. The same for oil import quotas.

28. What are three basic property rights?*

29. Why are they necessary if private enterprise is to operate effectively?

30. What would happen to profits, prices, and investment if corporate profit taxes were eliminated?

31. Explain how corporate income might be taxed without taxing the corporation.

32. What would be some advantages of this method of taxing corporate income?

Answers to starred questions.

17. (1) Knowledge about conditions unique to individual enterprises cannot be centralized and used effectively. (2) The benefits of mass production technology do not require centralized production or planning.

23. (1) government's coercive powers, and (2) the large benefits and money generated by specialization and exchange.

28. Use, transfer, receive income.

11

Present Versus Future Consumption: The Determinants Of Economic Growth

We now turn to the fifth and last of the basic decisions of economic organization: present versus future consumption, the decision whether to produce output for current consumption or to produce more productive capacity. It is this decision which determines how rapidly the output and standard of living of a people will rise. You are advised at this point to reread the introduction to this topic in Chapter 1.

What Causes Economic Growth?

Four general events raise productive capacity and output: (1) population increase, (2) capital accumulation, (3) technological change, and (4) education.

We shall have little to say about population increase as a cause of economic growth. While population growth raises total output, it reduces output per capita because of diminishing returns from increased labor relative to other inputs. (This is true only if, as seems the case, the rates of improvement of the other growth forces are not themselves significantly raised by population growth.) Indeed, in many nations, a *reduction* in the growth of population is a major requirement for improving per capita output.

Capital accumulation means the creation of more nonhuman productive capacity—more factories, buildings, desks, tractors, etc. Technological change is the development of new methods of producing by which more can be produced with a given amount of inputs. And education, in this context, means any training which increases the productive capacity of people. Some economic events may involve more than one of these growth forces. For example, the development and installation of an atomic generator involves both technological change *and* capital accumulation. Still, to study how the "present versus future consumption" decision is made, it is useful to discuss separately the determinants of each of these forces. After that, we shall ask how and whether the government should raise the economy's growth rate above that which the sum of individual choices brings about.

Capital Accumulation: The Creation Of Nonhuman Productive Capacity

It is the rate of return on investment in capital that induces people to create and employ nonhuman productive capacity. Basically, private individuals undertake capital accumulation for the same reason they go to work, namely, in order to receive income with which to purchase more goods and services for themselves and their families, including their heirs. And for some people the higher income may be a source of satisfaction even though nothing is bought with it, as it provides security or status or makes possible charitable donations which please the donor. The income from capital accumulation may also enable the recipient to enjoy more leisure and retire at an earlier age, since he need not depend as much on his labor income.

We wish to answer the question: how is the rate of capital accumulation (or capital investment) determined under private enterprise? Then we'll consider the criteria for government investment. First, however, we should clarify several points—what investment is and is not, the role of saving in getting investment done, gross and net investment, more about the return to investment, and diminishing returns to investment.

What is investment? When an individual buys stocks or bonds or when he contributes to a pension fund or an annuity for his retirement, as far as he is concerned, he is investing. From society's standpoint, however, no investment occurs from these activities. Unless the stock is just being issued by the company, the purchase of stock merely represents a change in ownership of part of an existing company from one person to another. This does not change the productive capacity of the company which issued the stock. Even the purchase of newly issued stock merely gives the issuing company more money. Increased productive capacity does not occur until and unless this money is actually used to pay for an expansion in plant and equipment. Similarly with bonds. When they change hands and even when they are originally sold, no investment occurs, except when the issuing company pays for additional productive capacity. Hereafter, "investment" or capital accumulation will mean the actual creation of additional productive capacity.[1]

Saving and investment. As explained in Chapter 1, any rise in investment must be accompanied by a decrease in consumption (or in government spending), which means a rise in saving, in order that inputs may shift from consumption to investment.[2] Thus, while most individuals do not "invest" as we use the term, they do play an important role in making investment possible—by saving.

There cannot be investment without saving; but can there be saving without investment? Let's see. Suppose people decide they don't want to consume as much as last year, but at the same time nobody wants to invest additionally either. If production stays the same, as consumption decreases, then inventories will rise; hence investment does occur (see footnote 1). But if no one wants to hold additional inventories *or* to invest additionally by the amount consumption decreased, then income itself (gross national product) will fall as saving rises. The fall in income will reduce the amount people want to save so that the actual amount saved will equal investment. When income falls either (a) output and employment will decline, or (b) prices and wages will decline so that previous output can be sold with less spending, or (c) some combination of (a) and (b), reduced output *and* deflation, will occur.

Therefore, saving is a necessary condition for investment. Without saving, no investment. And, given the variability of income (GNP) which makes saving equal investment, saving is also a sufficient condition for investment.[3]

_____

[1] There are two exceptions. Investment also includes (1) change in inventories, and (2) any difference between exports and imports. If inventories rose during a year, society produced more than it consumed from previous stocks of goods. The amount of inventory rise represents production during the period that is available for future consumption; hence inventory rise is investment. Similarly, a decline in inventories is disinvestment, because society used up in consumption, not only this year's production, but something from earlier years too.

When exports exceed imports, the nation acquires a claim against foreigners for the excess, which claim can later be used to buy goods for consumption. Therefore, investment includes any positive difference between exports and imports, and conversely. These are minor exceptions to the generalization that investment means the creation of productive capacity.

[2] Saving may be done by individuals, corporations, or government.

[3] An elaboration of the equality between saving and investment is given in the chapter on determination of national income in any principles of economics text.

Could there be investment without saving if the government printed new money and spent this on investment? No. The ensuing inflation of prices would cause real consumption (that is, consumption adjusted for price

The rate of return on investment. This is the income per year received from an investment as a percent of the original cost of the investment, after allowance has been made for the wearing out of the capital. We illustrate with a $10,000 machine:

Original cost of the machine	$10,000
Gross income from the machine per year	1,500
Depreciation: wearing out of the machine in the first year	1,000
Net income from the machine in the first year	500
Rate of return on investment: net income as a percent of original cost	5%

Suppose the above figures refer to the first year's operations. What would be the gross and net income the next year, if the return on investment is to remain 5%? This depends on whether the first year's depreciation was reinvested in the machine. If so, the figures remain exactly the same and could do so indefinitely (providing, of course, the machine's output could be sold at the same price). With depreciation reinvested, the level of investment continues to be $10,000, falling $1000 each year because of depreciation and rising $1000 each year because of reinvested depreciation.[4] The investment return is still 5% per year, even if it continues 100 years and the accumulated net income is $50,000. On the other hand, if that part of gross income which equals depreciation is not reinvested (is spent on consumption), then the amount invested declines each year by the amount of depreciation, to $9000 the second year, $8000 the third year, etc. A 5% yield then would mean that for the second year net income would be $450, and in the third year would be $400, etc. Thus, the return on investment is the net income (after depreciation) and the rate of return is this net income as a percent of the outstanding investment.

Gross and net investment. Now let us distinguish gross investment from net investment. Both are dollar amounts per year (or per other time period).

---

changes) to decline, while the increase in money supply would count as government saving. The added money bids resources out of consumer uses. This reduction of real consumption is called "forced saving" because it occurs without a voluntary reduction in consumption by private individuals.

[4] You might alternatively view these figures as representing ten $1000 machines, one wearing out each year, and the $1000 yearly depreciation ($100 for each machine) being used to purchase one new $1000 machine, keeping investment as ten $1000 machines: $10,000.

They do not measure the total value of capital equipment in society, but only *the amount created in a year.* The total expenditures for investment in a year are gross investment. Net investment is gross investment less depreciation. Should gross investment equal depreciation (and net investment be zero), then the total dollar value of society's capital equipment stayed the same during the year: the decline from depreciation equalled the gain from the year's investment. If net investment is positive, then nonhuman productive capacity rose; if net investment is negative, nonhuman productive capacity decreased and we say there was disinvestment. There is no automatic tendency for net investment to be any particular value, no force which guarantees that investment will at least equal depreciation. All investment, whether there is any net investment or not, is motivated by the expected returns. Moreover, you cannot look at any given investment expenditure and classify it as part of gross but not net investment according to whether it represents replaced or additional capital equipment. Net investment is simply the dollar amount of gross investment in excess of the dollar amount of depreciation.[5]

Diminishing returns to investment. The principle of diminishing returns predicts that as capital equipment rises relative to the labor force, as it has dramatically in America over the past century, the marginal physical product of additional capital equipment should decline and so, therefore, should the return on investment, which return is derived from the productivity of capital. In fact, however, there has not been a decline in the return to investment over the long run. Why not? Because advances in technology—better capital equipment—have raised the productivity of capital (moved to the right in Table 5-2) faster than diminishing returns have reduced this productivity.

There is no inherent force, however, which assures that diminishing returns to capital will not occur in the future, although if there is a minimum return to investment below which most people will not save and invest (say 8%), then, when investment returns fell below this level, the quantity of investment per year would decline until rising population and advancing technology brought a rise in capital's productivity. Such a tendency would result in the fairly stable return on investment which has prevailed over the long run (interrupted by sharp swings during business depressions and recovery therefrom).

In the short run, however, that is, within any given several years, diminishing returns to investment is to be expected. At any given time, there will be a few investment opportunities which will yield returns of 20% or

---

[5] One should relate this discussion to that about inter-industry shifts of nonhuman inputs, footnote 10, Chapter 3.

more, because of recent unanticipated changes in consumer tastes and the introduction of new products and technology. Imagine, if you will, a list of all possible investment opportunities for a given time, arranged from those giving the highest yields to those yielding 2% returns and suppose beside each is stated the dollars which could be invested to give this return. (Some opportunities may earn 15% for the first million dollars invested, 10% for the second million, 5% for the third, etc.) If such a listing were available, investors, seeking maximum returns, would select opportunities from the top and work downward until the return from the last dollar invested was just enough to induce saving the last dollar saved. Now if the government decided to raise the economy's growth rate by expanding investment beyond the level so determined, the additional money invested would go into lower yield projects further down the list. And the greater the expansion in investment in a given year, the lower would be the return to the additional investment. Furthermore, the government would have to compel people (probably by taxation) to reduce consumption in order to release inputs to undertake this additional investment.

Of course, there is no such central list of investment opportunities. But, as discussed under knowledge of alternatives, investment decisions may be virtually the same as if there were such a list, as long as the knowledge of each opportunity is spread among sufficient competitors and as long as there is freedom to act on this knowledge. Still, there are undoubtedly many opportunities giving high returns that are not taken up because no one knows about them or because those who are knowledgeable cannot convince savers to provide the funds—there being considerable uncertainty and difference of opinion about almost any investment opportunity. But there is little reason for expecting a government agency to be any more informed about such opportunities than private investors. So again, an involuntary expansion of investment will involve lower-yield projects. On the other hand, there may be projects with high yields which only the government can or should undertake (roads, missles, biological research, more jails, court buildings), but this likelihood does not refute the proposition that at any given time, a substantial expansion of investment from what would be done voluntarily would require investment in lower-yield opportunities; i.e., that in the short run there are diminishing returns to investment.

The basis of investment returns (or profits). Who pays the investment returns and for what? We considered a $10,000 machine which added $1500 to production while wearing out by $1000, so that its net contribution was $500.The $1500 is the value of the goods (or services) which the machine produced. Thus, the returns from investment, gross or net, depend upon (1) the physical productivity of the capital and (2) the price of this output. These determinants may be expressed as follows, recalling that, under competitive conditions, capital as well as labor receives the value of its contribution to production:

				Product
VMP	=	MPP	X	Price
the return to investment	depends on	the physical productivity of the capital, which in turn depends on technology and the quantity of other inputs with which the capital is combined	and	consumer preferences for the output produced by the capital

The return to investment is thus determined by the same forces—technology and consumer preference—which determine wages. Indeed, the return on investment is in effect the wage of capital. To answer the question which opened this section: the return on investment is paid by consumers for the output produced by the capital equipment.

The rate of capital accumulation. Under private enterprise, the amount of capital investment per year, like the number of cars, razors, or whistles produced, results from millions of individual decisions, decisions which depend upon (1) the willingness of people—workers and owners of companies—to consume less than they could and to provide and spend these savings on capital investment, (2) the anticipated consumer demand for the output produced by these investments, and (3) the physical productivity of the additional capital. These forces determine both the total amount and the specific areas of investment. Profits go to those who reduce consumption and provide the funds for investment.

The total investment so determined does not result in any predetermined rate of growth of capital equipment or of the economy—this growth may be high or low. Any suppression of investment below the amount determined by voluntary saving and investment decisions would mean people are willing to provide funds in response to available returns based on anticipated consumer desires, but are deterred from doing so. Any forced investment above this amount would mean people are required to reduce consumption (and/or leisure) and provide investment funds, even though they would prefer the consumption (or leisure). Thus, only one rate of capital accumulation is compatible with the freedom of people to choose between consumption and saving and between work and leisure. And it is this rate which tends to occur under private enterprise.

The criteria for government investment expenditures. Considerable capital investment is done by governments—for roads, hospitals, dams, parks, airports, flood control, water supply, harbors, national defense, etc. By what criteria should such investments be made? As explained in Chapter 3, if the government's objective is to serve consumers as their preferences are expressed by dollar spending, then the government should undertake investments only when the potential returns are as good as or better than what capital earns under private enterprise.

In many cases, the government earns little or no return on its investment, because it doesn't charge fees for the investment's output. There are various reasons for not charging fees. Sometimes, the *costs of collecting* user fees would be inefficiently expensive. For example, think how costly it would be to have toll collectors at each street corner to charge for road services. (However, gasoline and other user taxes may approximate such fees.) Sometimes, as with police protection, it is not feasible to ascertain how much a given consumer benefits and it is not possible to provide the service to some people who would voluntarily pay without providing it to others who wouldn't. There, direct fees are not appropriate. Also, government may want to subsidize some people; i.e., to charge some people (by taxation) to pay for investments which benefit others. Finally, government may want to provide services (museums and libraries?) which dollar votes may not justify but which government feels people should have even if they would not voluntarily pay the costs.

For all of these reasons governments often do not charge fees and earn returns on their investments. Nevertheless, sensible investment decisions by government should still be made on some *estimate* of consumer demand. Consider, for example, a proposed state or national park. Government should estimate the market-clearing price and resulting revenue which could be collected if fees were to be charged. Then calculate the capital and operating costs and the potential return on investment. Also, compare the return which could be earned from alternative uses of the same land—for lumber, water-power, homes, ski resorts, steel mills, etc. The use with the highest potential return is that preferred by consumers (as preferences are expressed by spending decisions).[6]

Frequently, such comparisons of potential returns are not made. In the political discussions preceding the establishment of a national park at the sand dunes on the Indiana shore of Lake Michigan near Chicago, the choice was presented as (a) the well-being of hard-working middle and low-income

---

[6]This is not to say the government should actually charge fees for roads, parks, museums, and other investment services. But whether fees are charged or not, consumer demand should be estimated from what people would pay for the service *if* fees *were* charged. Of course, if fees aren't charged, taxpayers must pay the cost.

people in the greater Chicago area versus the profits of the rich powerful steel companies who owned the land. However, the relevant choice was (b) consumers of recreation services versus consumers of steel products. Why shouldn't dollar votes (relative potential profitability) have determined the use of this land, which besides having sand dunes is ideally located for industrial use?[7]

Technological Change

Technological change, the second of the three major forces of economic growth, is any development which enables producers to turn out more or better output with a given amount of inputs. It includes both new and cheaper processes of making existing goods as well as the invention of new products which, for a given price, satisfy consumers more than old products.

Two steps in technological change are (1) the research which results in the discovery of new ideas and (2) the implementation of these ideas into production. This implementation generally involves capital investment, which, as just described, is inspired by expected profits. We shall therefore, concentrate on the decision to do research.

But is there really a great difference in the motivation behind research and behind capital accumulation? The discovery of new ideas is not something that happens entirely by chance. Rather, it is the result of deliberate efforts—efforts which require expenditures of money to divert people and nonhuman resources from alternative uses into research. Of course, one cannot predict precisely the outcome from scientific research,

---

[7]Maybe recreation would have won out anyway after a correct estimate of consumer choice. But one doubts it. For, if so, the steel companies would have found it profitable to develop parks themselves and charge admission (or to sell the land to a park developer whose purchase price would reflect the greater profitability in recreation than in steel production). But, one may ask, don't the elected politicians reflect consumer preference for recreation over steel mills? Hardly. What conscious political votes did steel consumers throughout the nation register on this decision? See Chapter 3 on the relative efficacy of political ballot voting and market dollar voting to register consumer choices.

Similar issues arise whenever the government stops using land, such as the former receiving point for immigrants, Ellis Island in New York Harbor, or the Brooklyn Navy Yard, or Alcatraz Prison in San Fransisco Bay. Selling the land to the highest bidder for the most profitable use is rejected out of hand. Only non-profit uses like a college, United Nations memorial, or culture center are considered. Likewise, see the article opposing the California ski resort built by Disney, "The Battle of Mineral King," *New York Times Magazine*, Aug. 17, 1969.

especially basic research as done by an Einstein or a Darwin. But why do companies like Dupont or RCA undertake research? Basically, because it pays. How do they decide how much to spend and for what? Again, on the basis of anticipated returns. While they cannot predict the returns from a specific scientist or project, some general idea of probable returns, allowing for failures and successes, disappointments and surprises, must lie behind their choices about research expenditures.

Granted that private companies undertake research for expected gains, do such considerations underlie research done in universities and government laboratories? Probably not explicitly. But the rationale, if sensible, is quite similar. There are expected social benefits from basic research, even though these benefits are difficult to estimate and cannot and/or will not be sold. Those who support this research have limited funds and must choose among alternative individuals and areas. How can a sensible choice be made among mathematician A, geneticist B, atomic reactor C, etc. without evaluating expected costs and benefits in terms of some common denominator—dollars? And from such a comparison should not the funds go where the expected returns to society will be the greatest?[8]

What is the "correct" amount of expenditure on research and technological change? It is that amount up to where the assessed money value of the benefits in relation to costs is the same as in alternative areas of investment. This is the payment for which people are willing to give up current consumption for future consumption. Will this amount automatically be done under private enterprise? In the area of applied technology, where the investors who incur the costs do receive the immediate benefits in the form of profits, the price system may well give the proper signals for investment in technological change. But not so regarding basic research. A basic research project may benefit society far more relative to costs than the competitive return on investment, yet no private individual has incentive to undertake it, because he cannot sell the benefits. That in turn is generally because once the new idea is published, it is free, however valuable it may be in raising output. Such worthwhile research may go undone unless private philanthropy or government finances it. The invisible hand, guided by prices

---

[8] Often only a hazy range of estimates is possible. Say, the benefits in longevity and disease prevention from knowing why cells deteriorate with age would be at least $100,000,000 and maybe billions. The probability of finding out (or of making significant progress thereto) from a grant of $100,000 to Professor X is somewhere between .01 and .1, of $2,000,000 to Professor X is .02 to .2, etc. Such calculations may be made only implicitly by weighing the general importance of the project, the reputation of the researcher, the conviction that useful results will follow, and the costs. The point is that without some weighing of returns and costs, those with funds to allocate are not likely to make the best use of these funds.

and profits, does not work in the allocation of resources to basic research. Private choice errs in underinvestment in basic research.[9]

In the short run at least, the principle of diminishing returns applies to research. The number of qualified scholars and scientists is limited as are projects which can yield given returns. As additional dollars are spent on additional research, they probably go to successively less capable individuals for successively less important projects—hence diminishing returns. But since, basic research, outside of the defense program, accounts for under 1% of the GNP, a large percentage expansion of this research would cost relatively little.

The beneficiaries of technological change. It is sometimes asserted that unless someone—government or unions—regulates prices, wages, and perhaps profits, the benefits of technological advance all go to stockholders, not to laborers or consumers. However, if competition is brisk enough, companies will receive only competitive returns to investment in research and technological change. But successful projects must earn more than competitive returns to offset losses from projects that fail, if the net return on research is to be competitive. Even successful projects will not yield these high returns for long with sufficient competition.

High returns to research are sometimes prolonged by patents. A patent is a deliberate government grant of monopoly, generally for 17 years. This grant is made to encourage inventive activity, on the ground that, without patents, new processes and products could immediately be copied after their introduction, thereby so reducing the returns to the developer that beneficial inventive activity would be greatly discouraged. (The same reasoning lies behind copyrights.) Profitable patents frequently inspire developments of related products and processes which can be patented separately and compete

---

[9]Whether the present tax structure is a fair way of allocating the burdens of paying for subsidized research is another question. It certainly does not allocate the costs proportionately to those who benefit as is the case of private investment, which is ultimately financed by the consumers of the increased production.

For an interesting and easily understood discussion of whether government may or may not need to supplement private research efforts, see "Information and Efficiency: Another Viewpoint," by Harold Demsetz, *Journal of Law and Economics*, April, 1969.

This discussion pertains only to research which advances technology, not to research where the results themselves are a consumer good to some people. For example, devotees of Shakespeare may enjoy knowing more about the details of Shakespeare's life. Suppose, however, the sale of these findings would not cover the research and publication costs. Nothing in this discussion suggests that such research should not be done if some private individual or group volunteers to finance it. However, government financing of such research would involve forcing one group (the taxpayers) to subsidize the tastes of others (Shakespeare fans).

with the original idea. Examples of this are the numerous synthetic fibers which followed Dupont's introduction of Nylon and the synthetic wrapping materials which followed cellophane.

The spread of benefits from technological advance occurs in the following steps:

1. technological advance in Co. A_1 in Industry A leads to
2. decreased costs of production in Co. A_1, which leads to
3. increased profits (P/I) in Co. A_1 which, as knowledge of the higher profits and new technology spreads, leads to
4. adoption of the new technology by others in Industry A, which leads to
5. increased output in Industry A, which leads to
6. decreased prices in Industry A, until P/I in A equals P/I elsewhere.

Occurring throughout all industries,

Technological advance→ ↓costs of production→ ↑profits→ ↑investment→ ↑output→ ↓prices→ ↓returns to investment (P/I), until P/I is at competitive levels.

If, through the government's monetary policy, the money supply rises as society's output rises, the deflation caused by rising output need not occur. Money incomes then will rise more than had M not risen, but real incomes will rise the same whether or not M increases, because, the real income rise reflects the greater productivity of labor and capital resulting from the technological advance and accompanying capital investment.

If technological advance did not raise the productivity (the MPP) of labor but only that of capital—a trend which has yet to occur and, therefore, seems unlikely if past experience is any guide—then the adoption of new technology would gradually reduce the fraction of national income going to labor. Carried to extreme, capital would do all the producing and everyone could retire. But this is fanciful. Technological advance has historically raised the productivity of labor and has not reduced labor's share of national income (indeed, this is higher in the more advanced countries) and there is little reason to forecast such a development within the next century.[10]

This diffusion of benefits from researcher and inventor (and their backers) to entrepreneur, to investor, to consumer does not require any benevolence or generosity on anyone's part. Rather, it is a natural consequence of the freedom of people to pursue their own interests—to

---

[10] After that, who can tell? When you consider the remarkable changes in technology and living conditions of the past 100 years and some of the exciting prospects for the next—deliberate control of hereditary characteristics, including intelligence, arrest of aging processes, harnessing of nuclear and solar power, etc.—prediction of social conditions past 100 years becomes almost pointless, except that, if population growth doesn't slow down, serious problems will eventually arise, as is evident in much of the world right now.

develop and introduce new ideas and products when it serves their interests, to invest and produce where profitable, to reduce prices below competitor's, and, as consumers, to spend as they choose: it is the invisible hand once again. But the initiating of basic research may require some subsidy from private donations or government, because the benefits of such research cannot be appropiated by those who finance it.

Education

The third major effort by which society raises the output of goods and services per person is education—used here to include all training which makes laborers more productive, not only vocational and on-the-job training, but also the basic knowledge of reading, writing, and arithmetic. How are expenditures on education determined? What are the roles of individual versus collective choice? Do prices and profits play a role? Should they?

Benefits. The benefits of education may be divided into three groups: (1) Private-monetary, which raise the income of the student. In this sense, education is investment in human capital. (2) Private-nonmonetary: any satisfaction from learning per se or because education improves the esthetic quality of life independently of raising income. In this sense, education is a consumer good to the student.[11] (3) Neighborhood benefits, which accrue to others than to the student and which may be monetary or nonmonetary. Among the neighborhood benefits of education are the following: (a) an educated electorate makes better decisions and preserves democratic processes from totalitarian demagogues; (b) the greater productivity of educated laborers enchances the productivity of other inputs, labor and nonhuman; (c) the quality of life for any given person is improved if others than himself are educated, because others' behavior and consumer tastes will be more esthetic and less offensive to him,[12] and (d) insofar as the income gains from education are taxed for collective use, others benefit from part of the added productivity of the educated person.

---

[11] A Carnegie Commission report found that college graduates are happier than others both in their jobs and in family relationships. It also noted the neighborhood benefits of education. (*New York Times*, Oct. 6, 1971.)

[12] This, of course, involves value judgments which some might deem rather presumptuous. For example, it suggests that after taking a course in music appreciation, present owners of ear-shattering transistor radios regurgitating acid rock all over mankind would instead be at home with their stereos rapt ecstatically in Beethoven's Archduke Trio or Waldstein Sonata. Rather presumptuous. And optimistic.

In terms of specific courses, engineering and typing are largely investment courses which raise income; literature and music appreciation are mainly consumption courses which provide nomonetary satisfaction; and introductory economics, while not without these aspects, if it substantially improves one's competence as a voter, may have greater neighborhood than private benefits (which, if true, explains why economics should be a *required* course for all students!)

Most of the benefits from education are probably private: they accrue to the student. But the existence of nieghborhood benefits, which the purchaser has no incentive to consider, may mean that, under individual decision-making, there will be too few resources devoted to education, especially in certain subjects. Moreover, as we shall see, the existing decision-making process is so inefficient that many people probably do not purchase education services even when the private benefits alone would warrant.

The costs of education. As with other economic activities, the real cost of education is the alternative goods and services which could be produced with the resources devoted to education. Besides expenses for teachers, administrators, books and buildings, over half the cost of education (for persons over 14) is the foregone production or income students would have earned if they weren't in school.

The return to investment. The percentage return to investment in education (ignoring nonmonetary and neighborhood benefits) is the addi-

"The gold record? It was awarded to me by my
teen-age daughter, for having to listen to
one million rock and roll records."

tional annual income stream resulting from education, as a percentage of the cost of education.[13] There is no question that educated people earn considerably more money than those less educated. But estimates of how much education per se contributes to income are obscured by the fact that, on the average, those with higher education have more ability and motivation and would probably have earned more than the less educated even if they had not gone further in school. A major study of the return to investment in education, which attempted to adjust for these ability differences, concluded that the rate of return from educational expenditures for men is somewhat higher than the return from capital investment.[14] Since these calculations omitted any neighborhood or nonmonetary benefits, it is a reasonable conclusion that there is underinvestment in education, that considering the returns people receive from nonhuman capital investment, both individuals and society have incentive to spend more on education.

Then why isn't more spent? The reasons lie in the unusual arrangements by which educational spending decisions are made, arrangements which suppress individual incentive to calculate costs and benefits and to spend more where it would benefit them.

The ideal. If educational services were being ideally provided and investment in education ideally made, the following would be true: (1) expenditures for each student would be carried to where the total return—monetary, nonmonetary, and neighborhood—on the last dollar equalled the competitive return to nonhuman investment of a similar risk (subject to the freedom of adult students not to invest in their own education despite favorable returns), (2) educational services would reflect "consumer"

---

[13]The return to nonhuman capital investment, being net of depreciation, is a potentially perpetual income stream. But "depreciation" of humans is not calculated and the differential income from education terminates with retirement or death. Therefore, for comparison with the rate of return on nonhuman capital, a conversion of this nature must be made to the income gain: an income gain (from education) of, say, $1000 a year for, say, 40 years is equivalent in value to what perpetual income? Formulas for this are covered in mathematics of finance. For example, $1000 a year for 40 years has the same value as a perpetuity of $954, if an interest rate of 8% is assumed. This equivalent income, divided by the full cost of whatever years' education are considered, gives the rate of return to education. The appropriate interest rate is the return earned on capital investment of similar risk. The cost of education, which is actually spread over several years, must be figured, with appropriate formulas, as of the date when the income gain starts. And other calculations must take into account that the income gain is not a constant annual amount.

[14]Gary S. Becker, *Human Capital*, Columbia University Press, 1964. Returns to education for women are less because women spend fewer years in the labor force than men.

choice, the consumers being (a) the taxpayers who are purchasing the neighborhood benefits, (b) the parents whose preferences presumably reflect their children's interests (a debatable point we cannot pursue), and (c) the students, whose preferences would have increasing weight as they approach "adulthood," or, perhaps, as they pay for their own education, and (3) a given quality of educational services would be provided at minimum cost.

This ideal cannot be uniquely determined without specifying the weights given to various components of consumer choice and the extent to which these preferences should reflect ability to pay (as do dollar votes for most other things). Furthermore, the ideal is practically unattainable because the neighborhood benefits from education cannot be measured at all accurately and because the monetary benefits, while they can be measured, cannot be predicted accurately. Nevertheless, this ideal could be approached more closely than it is.

The decision-making process. There are (at least) four aspects of decision-making in education which impede approaching the above ideal:[15]

(1) Decisions are made largely through political ballot.

(2) Payment for education is not geared to benefits (insofar as education is financed through taxation).

   (a) Those who receive education do not pay *for receiving.*

   (b) Those who pay do not receive *for paying.*

(3) To receive tax-financed services, the student must attend a government-operated school.

(4) Institutions have not developed for direct equity investments in individuals.

Though there are probably more, we shall list five ways that these facets of educational decision-making lead to "incorrect" results.

(1) For all the reasons discussed in Chapter 3, consumer preferences are not effectively registered through political ballots. This is especially true when important educational decisions are made by several levels of government—Federal, state, and local, and by various officials—state legislators and governors, Boards of Education, state and local, superintendents of schools, state and local, etc. There is no single place to put the blame for poor service, to direct requests for change, or to reward good service.

(2) Those taxpayers who do not have children in public schools have considerable incentive to vote against education expenditures, especially when given a chance to do so specifically, as in school bond issues. Not only do single people and childless couples have this incentive, but so do parents whose children attend private (including parochial) schools, who may understandably resent being taxed to educate others' children while paying

---

[15] The following discussion draws heavily on Chapter 6 of Friedman's *Capitalism and Freedom, op. cit.*

separately for their own children's schooling. And many more have little incentive to support tax funds for college finance, because their children are not attending state colleges.

(3) Now consider parents who do want to invest heavily in their children's education. For example, assume the state's services (including prorated capital expenditures) cost $1000 per pupil per year and a given couple would be willing to buy an additional $500 worth of education. They cannot do this by sending their child to a private school, because they would immediately lose $1000 worth of public school services. That is it would cost them $1500 to buy $500 more of education. They cannot presently buy additional services from the public school. They are stymied. The best they can do is buy private dance and music lessons, summer camp, weekend tutors, etc. But these are poor substitutes for the better basic education which can be acquired for $1500. The most feasible option is for the parents to move to a neighborhood with higher per pupil expenditures. But this generally also means higher housing and commuting costs, which the parents may not be able or willing to purchase along with better schooling.[16] Considering the wide variations in parents and children, it seems certain that this inability of parents to supplement conveniently the government's education subsidy reduces considerably the total investment in education.

(4) Now consider parents who are dissatisfied with public schools but are not able or willing to spend more on education than the government's (presumed) $1000 per pupil. Perhaps they want from schools certain services not provided: religious instruction, more patriotism, less, a different emphasis on racial problems, more stress on science and math, different teaching techniques, more parental voice in school policies, or less, different disciplinary procedures, different hours, such as programs which keep children at school until five in the afternoon, etc., or perhaps they just feel the public schools are not satisfactory and want to try some alternative. By and large, without losing the $1000 subsidy, they must accept public schools as they are, or possibly move to a different neighborhood, where, for the same per pupil cost, they're likely to get about the same school services. Thus, educational services are not geared to consumer preferences, as are most other products. In fact, under political ballots, these preferences are never registered.

(5) The absence of arrangements for direct equity investment in another's education probably means that many people are deterred from

---

[16] It is assumed there that more money buys more education, either in quantity or quality. This might mean better qualified teachers, a longer school day with more courses, use of expensive teaching machines, smaller classes, specialized classes for gifted, retarded, emotionally disturbed children, etc.

college—especially from the more expensive programs, such as law, medicine, and graduate school.

Some suggested reforms. There are three reforms that would virtually eliminate these impediments to ideal decision-making in education. The first listed is by far the most important:

(1) Private school aid: the voucher program. To any parents who send their children to private schools and colleges, the government should pay an amount equal to the per pupil subsidy of educating the children in a public school.

(2) Subsidies based on need. Public schools should charge tuition fees based on family income, but not to exceed the full per pupil cost.

(3) Laws should be enacted facilitating equity investment in another's education and/or providing government participation in such investment.

We shall explain the implications of these proposals and consider some objections to them. In discussing (1), private school aid, we shall assume (2) is not in effect, that is, taxes are collected to finance schools as at present. But in considering public school tuition, we'll assume it is added to the voucher program.

The voucher program to finance private school attendance.[17] This is a program wherein the government pays toward *private* school tuition as much as it would have spent had the student attended a public school. Consider the Jones family with two children attending public schools. Suppose they are dissatisfied with public schools but cannot afford private schools. Under this program, if the government's cost per pupil is $1000 per year, the Jones' could be given a voucher, useable only for tuition at approved private schools. The Joneses give this voucher as tuition payment (or part payment) to the private school of their choice. Then the school is reimbursed by the government for the vouchers it receives. (The voucher is like welfare food stamps which the government redeems when the grocer turns them in.) The government in turn would collect the money to pay for these vouchers from the same taxpayers who now pay for the public schools. Parents of children who remain at public schools would, naturally, not receive the vouchers. Private schools, as is now the case, would be inspected by government officials to ascertain that they meet prescribed educational standards.

---

[17] In 1971, voucher plans, similar to that described here, were being adopted by several state governments, to be financed experimentally by the Federal Government. (*New York Times,* June 2, 1971.) Since the funding is temporary and the private school's tuition may not exceed the amount of the voucher, these experiments are not a fair test of the voucher proposal. In Texas and Georgia, tuition equalization grants similar to the voucher plan are a potential savior for financially troubled private colleges unable to compete with low-tuition state education.

The per pupil cost of public schools (which the voucher payment would equal) should be calculated to include not only operating expenses (salaries, equipment, utilities, etc.), but also the prorated cost of land and capital equipment and a competitive return on this capital investment. These are the true costs of public school education. (See Chapter 3 on why profits should be included in the prices of government services.) With vouchers set at such levels, profit-seeking investors, as well as non-profit religious and other groups, could offer standard educational services without charging tuition significantly above the voucher level, which means parents of *all* income levels could afford to choose private schools if they wished. Private schools could competitively charge more than the vouchers only if offering some advantage over the public schools.

Let us now consider four arguments that have been advanced against this program: (1) it undermines the public school system and creates divisiveness; (2) private schools are too expensive for any but the rich to benefit from the program; (3) schools should not be run for profit; and (4) it conflicts with the separation of church and state.

(1) Is the public school system an end in itself or merely one means of getting children educated? Public schools may have been a useful unifying force during large waves of non-English-speaking immigration. But perhaps today the danger, inherent in government-operated schools, of enforced conformity and indoctrination of government-favored social and political views outweighs any danger of undue divisiveness associated with private schools. A full consideration of this cannot be made here.

(2) If private school costs are much above public schools, then, true, not many low-income people will seek their services. But why should this be? Are public schools more efficient because they are large or because their administration covers many schools? There is no evidence to substantiate this and some reason to suspect that the large public school bureaucracy impedes efficiency, innovation, and responsiveness to consumer choice. In pre-auto times when the nation was largely rural, many public schools probably were "natural monopolies," like water and electric companies today, where more than one school in an area could not operate without raising costs per pupil. Now, greater population density and improved transportation have eliminated this. Competing schools *can* serve the same group of parents without raising costs. Therefore, if the voucher covers the full costs of public schools, it could cover the costs of private schools too, though presumably, many parents would still prefer public schools.

(3) Assertions that schools (or hospitals or housing or food stores) should not be operated for profit generally reflect a failure to understand that profits pay for capital's contribution to production, and often presuppose ignorant consumers and monopolistic sellers. However, given assurance through state inspectors or private accrediting agencies that adequate

academic standards are maintained, there is no reason why higher profits shouldn't reflect efficiency and better service, leading to emulation by competing schools. With standardized tests of academic achievement, as well as tests of social, cultural, and emotional traits, and with books available which rate private schools, it would not be difficult for parents to determine the job schools are doing.[18]

(4) The proposed voucher plan involves no greater conflict with church-state separation than does the Federal assistance to veterans' education, the "GI Bill," under which veterans have been aided since World War II whether they attended church-affiliated colleges or not. Finally, the voucher program could cover only a fraction (say 70% of public school costs if some fraction of private school tuition (say 30%) went for religious instruction.

The important consequences of this voucher program are (1) parents have genuine freedom of choice between public and private schools; (2) parents may buy more and/or better schooling by adding to the state's subsidy and sending their children to more expensive private schools. In particular, low-income parents can buy more education without having to move to higher-income neighborhoods; (3) public schools might improve because of competition from private schools; (4) educational services would be more responsive to consumer choice, as parents select schools with particularly desired features (which it will be profitable to develop); and (5) the present inclination of private-school parents to vote against educational tax funds would be eliminated, thereby increasing total investment in education.

---

[18] Education for profit is being tried in some public schools too. In Gary, Indiana one public school is operated by a private company for a fee equal to the government's cost per pupil. From the fee, the company rents the school building from the school district and pays all salaries and other expenses. It also guarantees to refund the government its $800 per pupil fee for each student who scores below the national average in reading and math, a level not attained by most Gary pupils. With programmed textbooks, fewer teachers are used, but those employed are offered overtime for helping students after class hours. (*Wall Street Journal*, June 2, 1971.) After the first year, the portion of the school's children (all black) meeting or exceeding national norms in math and reading rose from 25% to 73%. Both the faculty and parents overwhelmingly endorsed continuation of the program. The per pupil cost was about 10% under Gary's average and the operating firm, Behavioral Research Laboratories, made a good profit. (*Newsweek*, Oct. 11, 1971.)

In several Federally financed contract programs, results have been less satisfactory. But who knows the potential for valuable innovations under the voucher plan, with its greater freedom and incentive for profitable change? The fact that most teacher groups, particularly the teachers' union, "have adamantly opposed performance contracting," according to Fred Hechinger of the *New York Times* (Feb. 6, 1972), argues further for the greater freedom of choice afforded under the voucher program.

Graduated public school tuition. In tax-supported education, we may distinguish three ways in which subsidies operate: (1) from high to low-income people, (2) from one group to another within the same income class, and (3) from low to high-income people.[19] Tuition fees based on family income would largely eliminate (2) and (3) without much affecting (1). Here is one possible set of tuition charges:

Proposed public school tuition charges per year
if public school costs are $1000 per pupil

family income	tuition	family income	tuition
under $4000	none	$ 9000-10,000	$300
$4000-5000	$ 50	10,000-11,000	350
5000-6000	100	11,000-12,000	400
6000-7000	150	12,000-13,000	500
7000-8000	200	13,000-14,000	600
8000-9000	250	over 14,000	700

The maximum tuition is 70% of the cost on the vague guess that neighborhood benefits are 30% of total educational benefits. These benefits should be charged to the general taxpayer, not to parents specifically. These tuition charges are virtual taxes, since parents would not have an option of withholding their children from school to avoid paying. Parents who choose private schools (under the voucher plan) would receive vouchers equal only to the subsidy they would have received from public schools, i.e., the state's per pupil cost ($1000 in this example) minus their public school tuition charge. A family earning over $14,000 would receive a voucher for $300 per year for each child attending a private school.

In terms of the impediments to optimum educational investment, this would improve educational decision making by (1) making parents, who are consciously paying tuition, more concerned whether they are getting their money's worth, and (2) making non-parents less resistant to tax funds for education, since these taxes would be reduced considerably. However, the primary question about this proposal—for or against—is whether, after subtracting out the value of neighborhood benefits—parents should bear the costs (including education) of rearing their own children, or whether others, with the same income but with smaller families, should, through taxation, pay part of these costs. We leave this value judgment to the reader.

---

[19] In state colleges, the average income of students' families is well above that of the average taxpayer, so tax-financing rather than tuition-financing of these colleges is a case of the poor subsidizing the rich (to exaggerate slightly).

Equity investment in others' education. In professional boxing, investors support and train boxers in return for a stated percentage of their furture earnings in boxing. Why not similar arrangements for prospective doctors, lawyers, and others? Were this done, investors (including insurance companies) could seek out promising students who could not afford professional training, make mutually beneficial deals, and substantially raise investment in "human capital" without imposing costs on others. One reason this is not done is the difficulty the investor might incur in preventing cheating by the investee, but this could be surmounted by contracts for investor audit of investee's records, for investor signing of investee's income tax return, and for required lie detector tests. No illegal slavery would be involved, as the investee would be free to change jobs or professions, to work part-time, or to loaf, these being risks of the investment.[20]

These proposed changes—the voucher plan for private school attendance (applied from nursery school through college), public school tuition based on family income, and arrangements for private investment in human capital—would all provide the price and profit signals and incentives to direct educational expenditures to the students and for the services which yield the best returns and which reflect the preferences of parents and older students. In view of the high returns to education, it is reasonable to predict these reforms would raise investment in education and raise somewhat the economy's growth rate, but the fundamental argument for them is that they give people incentive and freedom to create and take advantage of more favorable alternatives than are now available.

Another looming impediment to efficient education decision-making is the proposal to equalize per pupil expenditures on education in all school districts (within each state). In effect, this says to a higher-income area: you may spend your greater incomes on vacations, yachts, and tennis courts, but

---

[20] In February 1971, Yale University and the Ford Foundation announced a plan whereby students would repay tuition "loans" from banks (guaranteed by the Foundation) by paying back *a fixed percentage of future income* over an extended period after leaving school. A similar proposal was made in 1967 by a Presidential panel. (*New York Times,* Feb. 6, 1971.) Duke University initiated a similar plan a month later. In March, 1971, Governor Gilligan of Ohio proposed deferred tuition for the state's colleges, the payments to range from $50 a year out of a $7000 income to $1000 from an income of $100,000 or more. A dubious state legislator commented. "If this is good policy, for example, should we then ask high-school students to pay back the costs of their education and welfare recipients to return state funds after they get jobs?" (*Newsweek,* April 12, 1971.)

In a similar vein, several students at the Wayne State University Medical School in Detroit have offered to indenture themselves: in return for loans during medical training and the provision of an office, the student agrees to set up practice in a small town which needs a doctor. Proposed in 1971, the response from small towns was brisk.

if you spend any more on your children's education than is spent in the poorest area, then you must contribute an equal amount per pupil to the education of all other children (in the state). If effectively enforced, this would lower education expenditures in affluent areas, depriving residents there of important freedom and depriving society of substantial neighborhood benefits, without improving the quality of education elsewhere. And this applies as well to moderate-income communities with greater than average preferences for spending on their children's education. Granted that certain educational opportunities should be available to all children, doesn't it almost elevate spite and envy to official policy to effectively prohibit some people from spending their own money on their children's education?

Education Subsidy For Future Tax Revenue?

We should not leave the subject of education subsidy without considering a familiar but largely fallacious argument for such subsidies. It runs like this: (1) Education subsidies add to the later taxable income of the students; (2) The higher taxes more than pay for the cost of the subsidies; (3) Therefore, education subsidies are self-financing and cost nothing to society and are desirable without further justification. For convenience, we'll call this the "later-taxable-income argument" for education subsidies.

The truth of (1) and (2) depends on the abilities of the students and their fields of study, which means (3) may argue for subsidizing the education

"I understand you've been calling our
safety patrols 'piglets'."

of only selected students and fields of study. But even where (1) and (2) *are* true, (3) does not necessarily follow.

There are two reasons why people incorrectly accept (3) from (1) and (2) (aside from an uncritical self-interest of some students and parents who prefer that others pay their way through life): (1) a failure to consider alternative uses of the funds, and (2) a failure to consider individual equity, as opposed to collective welfare.

To consider the merits of this later-taxable-income argument, we must assume that other possible justifications of education subsidy are absent or are irrelevant. Therefore, we assume that education investment is carried to the point where the private pre-tax return (monetary and non-monetary) equals the competitive pre-tax return on investment elsewhere and that, except for future tax revenue, there are no neighborhood benefits from education. One may immediately react—but is this assumption correct? Perhaps not, but, independently of the later-taxable-income argument, we could approximate this result, as nearly as uncertainty allows, by revising education finance and administration (already discussed) and with a level of *partial* tuition subsidy based *only* on the neighborhood benefits of education. If this were done, would the later-taxable-income argument be a further basis for additional subsidy? That is our question.

Consider individual A, age 20. He (or someone in his behalf) says to society (or government): "Take money from taxpayer B. Give it to me. I'll invest it in (a) my education, or (b) a new business, or (c) the stock market." [There is no reason in advance to expect that any one of these will yield any more than another, and if the later-taxable-income argument justifies subsidizing A's investment in his education, why not A's investment elsewhere?] "Then you (the government) can tax the investment income and we'll both be better off—I'll have a higher income and your tax receipts will be higher." But taxpayer B can retort: "No. Let me keep my money for two reasons: (1) I earned it and am more entitled to it than is A; and (2) I'll invest it and you (government) will have the same tax revenue as had you given it to A."

Thus, the later-taxable-income argument, if it has any merit, justifies any transfer of money from individual B to A, regardless of B's or A's age, schooling, or income level, as long as A guarantees to invest it and will pay taxes on the returns. And the argument collapses if B agrees to invest the money and if there is any presumption that B is more entitled to his income or wealth than is non-B. The later-taxable-income argument is, therefore, not a sound basis for subsidizing education.

Furthermore, one may well feel that B is entitled to spend his money on consumption if he likes and does not have to guarantee to invest it (to raise the government's tax revenue) to justify keeping it. And, on this note, if there *is* some reason for redistributing income from B to A, why shouldn't A also be free to spend it on consumption or investment as he chooses?[21]

Should Government Increase The Economy's Growth Rate?

The economy's growth rate was a much discussed issue in the 1960 presidential campaign between John F. Kennedy and Richard Nixon. Democrats claimed the government should take steps to raise the economy's growth from the 3.3% rate of the 1950's to about 5%. We shall consider three questions which relate to such a proposal: (1) How much does a one or two percentage-point change in growth matter to society over the long run? (2) What would be the cost of raising the growth rate by such amounts? Then we can better answer (3) Should the government so raise the growth rate?[22]

The significance of a given rise in economic growth. Some examples will show that over a century a one or two percentage-point difference in economic growth makes a tremendous difference in the standard of living. First, the arithmetic of growth. In these examples, assume for simplicity that the price level remains constant, so that changes in GNP mean changes in output. If GNP were $1000-billion in 1970 and grew at 3%, what would it be in 1971? Answer (in $ billions): $1000 + .03 \times 1000 = 1000 (1.03) = 1030$. Suppose it grows another year at 3%. What would it be in 1972? Answer: $1030 (1.03)$, which is $1000 (1.03) (1.03)$ or $1000 (1.03)^2$. In general, if any magnitude, X, grows at i% per year for n years, then it will be $X (1+i)^n$.

The following table, based on this formula, shows the fantastic differences which seemingly small differences in growth make.

---

[21] Nor can this argument be ressurected by reasoning that the taxpayers are merely supporting education subsidies which they themselves already received, so that it evens out for everyone. Some people, for reasons of ability and interests, do not go to college or even complete high school, while others go on to graduate work. If a genuine attempt were made to "even out" by taxing people (for education finance) in proportion to education subsidies they received, including proper interest rate calculations to equate subsidies at one date with tax payments at a later date, the subsidy would disappear, having been converted into a loan or an equity investment by the government (depending on how the tax were determined). But without this attempt, there is no "evening-out" and the ressurection fails.

[22] During the 1960's, the growth rate did rise to 4.2%, but it is doubtful that deliberate government policy caused this.

Multiple By Which The Economy's Output Grows Each 10,
20, 40, And 100 Years At An Annual Growth Rate Of "i"

Years: exponent of (1+i)

1+i	10	20	40	100
1.01	1.10	1.22	1.49	2.70
1.02	1.22	1.49	2.21	7.24
1.03	1.34	1.81	3.26	19.22
1.035	1.41	1.99	3.96	31.19
1.04	1.48	2.19	4.80	50.50
1.05	1.63	2.65	7.04	131.50

Consider the row of numbers starting with 1.02. The table shows that $(1.02)^{10}=1.22$. This means that at a growth rate of 2% per year, the economy's output would rise 22% in ten years. In 20 years, at 2% per year, output would have risen 49%, and in a century it would be 7.24 times as large. But at 3½% per year, in a decade output would be 41% higher, would nearly double in one generation, would quadruple in 40 years, the average work-life of an adult, and would increase 31-fold in a century.

To convert the *total* growth rate (of an economy's output) into *per capita* growth rate, simply substract from (1+i) the annual rise in population. Thus, if population rises at 1½% per year, and if the total growth rate were 3½% per year, then per capita growth would be at the rate of 2% (these being approximate past rates); or with a total growth rate of 5%, the per capita rate would be 3½% (this being the target suggested during the 1960 campaign).[23]

Now consider living conditions in the future with these growth rates. Applying these multiples to America's 1970 income per family—nearly $10,000— we have the following:

Future Real Income Per Family For Various Annual
Growth Rates, Starting From $10,000 In 1970
(thousands of dollars)

Annual Growth Rate, %	1980	1990	2010	2070
1	$11	$12	$15	$ 27
2	12	15	22	72
3	13	18	33	192
3½	14	20	40	312
4	15	22	48	505
5	16	27	70	1315

[23] More precisely, if the total output and population growth rates are respectively 3½% and 1½%, then the per capita growth rate of output is $\frac{1.035}{1.015}$ − 1=.0197 or 1.97%, slightly smaller than 3½% less 1½%.

In America, the long run growth rate in per capita output—going back into the early 19th Century—has been about 2%.[24] There is no convincing evidence that this 2% per capita growth could be raised and kept as high as 3½%, but there is little reason for predicting it will fall either. Suppose then growth continues as in the past. Then, going across the 2% row, we see that in 20 years the average family income will be about $15,000 and in 100 years it will be over $72,000.

But suppose prices double over the next century. How would this change the prediction? The *real* forces causing the growth in output would still operate the same. But the *monetary* forces would have doubled money incomes from what would have occurred had prices not risen, though they would not affect the real rise. So, if prices double and output rises 2% per year, the average family income in 100 years would be around $144,000, though in terms of 1970 prices it would still be $72,000. By the same token, should prices have dropped 50% on the average, the money income predicted would be only $36,000, representing the same standard of living as $144,000 if prices doubled. Indeed, the price level did drop 50% during the 30 years following the Civil War, a period of substantial rise in output.

Just as future incomes can be predicted from this formula, we can look back 100 years by taking the current average income and *dividing* it by $(1.02)^{100}$ to find roughly the average family income 100 years ago based on current prices, $1380. (Since prices are higher now, their average money incomes were well below $1380.) You will note this is dire poverty by today's standards. And, as always, many families had income far below the average.

Poverty and growth. Some writers, using today's standards, describe past wages and living conditions with horror, pointing an accusing finger at capitalists. But incomes were low 100 years ago because productivity was much lower and they have risen because of the forces of economic growth—capital investment, education, and technological advance. No short-run redistribution of income or revision of the economic system could have significantly raised living conditions 100 years ago. Take any poor nation in the world today or any nation, rich or poor, over 100 years ago, divide that

---

[24] A better measure of the *productivity* rise is output per manhour, which has grown 2.3% per year during this century. Per capita output grows less than this, as people work fewer hours per year. In transferring from per capita to per family output, we assume hours worked per family will change the same as per person. However, apparent hours worked per family may rise as more married women take jobs. But since GNP counts only output traded for money, a rise in GNP because more married women get jobs overstates the actual gain in output, assuming, of course, that women at home are producing services for the family.

nation's total income by its population. The resulting per capita income is grinding poverty for everyone. True, there are some very wealthy people in India and Latin America and their wealth, divided up, would help some people, but poverty would be virtually untouched by wealth or income redistribution, because per capita income is so low. In America, poverty is disappearing because of the basic forces of economic growth. The real danger of trying to eliminate poverty by vast income or wealth redistribution is that the incentives to undertake growth-oriented activities will be so dulled that the growth rate will be retarded and everyone, poor as well as rich, will be worse off after a few years than had the short-run anti-poverty measures not been taken. Compare the results of 1% growth with 2% growth.

Throughout most of human history, life has been a fierce struggle for the barest essentials—food and protection from cold. Even today, for two thirds of the world's population, mostly in Asia, Africa, and parts of Latin America, long hours of drudgery yield only meager food, clothes, and shelter. And this was true in the Western World for 90% of the population up into the 19th Century. Only in the 20th Century have personal comforts and enjoyable leisure been attainable on a mass basis. Thus, the only successful "war on poverty" has been the combination of forces which have brought the gradual growth in per capita output. And, so far, these forces have worked to give the highest living conditions where individuals have been free to seek to better their own lives, without being tied to particular occupations, social classes, or localities, where economic freedom and political stability have prevailed, and where the much-maligned "invisible hand" has guided self-seeking individuals to unconsciously serve others in serving themselves. These comments do not imply that nothing should be done about current proverty. Today's poor middle-aged adult is not going to benefit much from these long-run forces of growth, though his children will. But solutions to immediate problems should be proposed with the longer run in mind. One fact to remember from the growth numbers is that, at 2% per capita, real income rises about 50% in just 20 years. And the average worker's income, especially if he has 12 or more years of education, rises even more than this, because, with work experience, his productivity rises relative to the economy.

Lest the recent highly publicized explosion of welfare rolls give the wrong impression, the dramatic decline in poverty in America should be high-lighted. In 1929, nearly 60% of American families received less than today's "poverty" level, $3600 per year (in 1969 prices). This percentage, after rising during the depression, fell to 35% in 1947, to 26% in 1959, and to 13% in 1969. And it will surely dwindle further as the elderly poor are replaced by more affluent retirees, as the movement off small farms continues, as the average education of Negroes rises (in 1960, 36% of Negro men aged 25-29 had finished high-school, in 1969, 60% had), as knowledge about and availability of birth control techniques spreads (including liberalized abortion laws), and, of course, as product per manhour grows.[25]

The cost of raising the growth rate. From the two tables, one might have either of two opposite reactions to whether our growth rate should be increased by government action. On the one hand, the tremendous results of a higher rate may suggest that the government should indeed raise it if at all possible. On the other hand, the substantial rise in output forthcoming (but not inevitable) at the past 2% rate of growth might lead one to wonder why the present generation should make the necessary sacrifices of present consumption and personal freedom, when the future looks so rosy for the coming generations anyway—average family income of $72,000 in 100 years. The critical question is: what is the cost of raising the growth rate?

Here is a crude estimate of the cost of raising the economy's growth rate by one percentage point:

1. What fraction of GNP has historically been devoted to growth-related activities? Answer:26%.
2. What is the proposed percentage increase in the growth rate? Answer: 50%.
3. Therefore, it would cost 13% (50% of 26%) of GNP to raise the economy's growth rate by one percentage point. Since consumption is roughly 65% of GNP, current consumption would have to be reduced 20% (13%/65%) or one fifth to bring this about.

---

[25]These income figures overstate existing poverty. First, in any given year, many families have temporarily low incomes because of illness, migration, work layoffs and strikes, or because they recently left school and are just starting in the labor force. Their "poverty" lasts only a short while. Second, careful analysis of the government's estimates of "poverty" in 1962 when $3000 was the dividing line, shows that, by the government's nutritive standards, the dividing line for a family of four should have been $2200 and the percent in poverty 10%, not 20% as reported, which suggests the 1969 poverty is 7%, rather than 13%. (See *Poverty, Definition and Perspective*, by Rose Friedman, American Enterprise Institute, 1965.) Of course, even 7% of 200 million is a lot of people. We cannot discuss thoroughly what to do about current poverty. President Nixon's proposed revision of welfare programs follows closely the negative income tax proposed by Milton Friedman in *Capitalism and Freedom, op. cit.*, Chapter 12.

It is not only whites' incomes that are rising. Between 1957 and 1968, the portion of Negro families earning $8000 or more (in 1968 dollars) rose from 10% to 32% and was 43% in the North and West. For an excellent discussion of poverty and urban problems by a political scientist with considerable understanding of economics and sociology, see E. F. Banfield, *The Unheavenly City*, Little Brown, 1968.

Let us elaborate on the answers given.

1. The percentage of GNP devoted to growth activities:

	A		B	
a	gross investment	15%	net investment	6%
b	education	6	education	4
c	research	2	research	1
d	health	3	health	2
	total	26		13

2. The proposed percentage rise in growth rate:

> per capita, from 2% to 3%: 50%
> total output, from 3½% to 4½%: 29%.

Two estimates are given of the portion of GNP devoted to growth. The "B" estimate, which totals 13%, would reduce to 6½% of GNP or 10% of current consumption the cost of raising per capita growth 50%. For reasons explained below, the "A" estimate seems more reasonable and in fact may understate this cost considerably.

1a. The choice between using gross or net investment revolves around this question: did the reinvestment of past depreciation funds contribute to economic growth? In principle, this reinvestment merely kept productive capacity from declining and only net investment, above depreciation, contributed to growth. But no one accepts this. Much of the contribution of research is embodied in the replacement of depreciating capital with technologically superior capital. Therefore, perhaps replacement of depreciating capital did contribute to growth and in order to expand the growth rate by X%, it is gross investment, not merely net investment, which must expand X%. This suggests A is the correct assumption. But one might argue that all that is needed to increase the contribution of the depreciation part of gross investment is more expenditures on research, that if research rises X%, its benefits are spread over all investment without any rise in investment. This would indicate that B is correct. The right answer is simply unknown.

One consideration which definitely points to A is short run diminishing returns to investment. A large rise in annual investment will surely include lower return projects. This means an X% rise in investment spending is going to raise the contribution of investment to economic growth by less than X%.

1b. During much of American history, the fraction of GNP devoted to education was under 3%, though it has risen to over 6% recently. But this ignores the cost of foregone production because students are withdrawn from employment and also neglects the considerable cost of on-the-job training, which was probably larger when less was spent on formal education. Therefore two estimates are given.

1c. Since the 1950's, expenditures on research and development have been over 2% of GNP, recently exceeding 3%. Much of this has been military research which probably contributes less to economic growth than research motivated by expected profits from consumption. Data on research in earlier years are sketchy, but apparently research has risen relative to GNP since World War II, which explains the low estimate in B.

1d. Medical expenditures could be viewed as an investment in human capital, though certainly such expenditures are motivated not simply to make people more productive but also to make them feel better. From a level of 3.6% of GNP in the late 1920's, they have risen to nearly 7% in 1969. The numbers in A and B reflect arbitrary assumptions that some but not all such expenditures contribute to economic growth.

2. A one percentage point rise in economic growth is a 50% rise in per capita growth and a 29% rise in total economic growth. The choice of 50% as the revelant measure is based on the following reasoning:

  i. The items listed under A and B are the forces which caused per capita economic growth.
  ii. These items plus population growth cause total economic growth.
  iii. Assume the total growth rate equals the per capita growth plus the rate of population growth. (Footnote 18 qualifies this.)
  iv. If total growth is to be raised without raising population—and no proposal to raise the economic growth rate suggests population growth should be raised—then, by point iii, a one percentage point raise in total growth must be achieved by raising per capita growth one percentage point also.
  v. Therefore, by i, to raise per capita growth by one percentage point, the items in A or B, must be raised by at least whatever percent one percentage point is of the per capita growth rate, 2%.[26]

So far, the truth would seem to lie between estimates based on A and B. But with population growth unchanged, drastic diminishing returns must be expected from a 50% rise in these items, which means it would take more than a 50% rise in them to raise per capita growth by 50%. For example, with nearly all children in school already and given that many simply would not benefit much from college or longer school days, a 50% expansion of education expenditures, while it would do some good, would certainly not raise education's contribution to growth by 50%.

---

[26]The "at least" could be deleted only if there were no diminishing returns to more of the items in A or B and if we were certain that these items covered everything that caused per capita growth. In fact, population increase itself may have contributed to per capita growth, especially a century ago, because greater density made low-cost large-scale production techniques profitable.

If the per capita growth rate is to be kept at 3%, instead of 2%, this estimated cost, 13% of GNP, must be met every year. The spectacular results of higher growth rates over long periods assume the higher rates are maintained. A one year rise in growth followed by a return to the former level would not have these significant results. Even if the crude estimate, 13% of GNP, is too high, it seems clear from the underlying reasoning that it would cost a lot to raise the per capita growth rate by one percentage point.[27] This conclusion accords with the pioneering and far more sophisticated analysis by E.F. Denison, although Denison did not give a cost estimate for raising economic growth by a percentage point.[28]

Research: a short-cut to greater growth? Some economists have asserted that technological advance accounts for a large portion of past economic growth. If this is true, the social returns to the small portion of output devoted to research have been fantastic and far greater than the private returns to investors. Could it be that a large percentage rise in research, which would cost relatively little compared to raising other growth expenditures, would significantly raise the growth rate? (The improved technology could be incorporated in the capital investment occuring anyway.) It is conceivable, but one must be skeptical. First, part of technological advance comes from on-the-job, trial and error, experience, which deliberate research is not going to accelerate much. Second, there is little reason to expect that applied research is not being carried out close to where social returns equal the competitive level, because most of the returns are appropriable by those who finance the research. Third, some of the large gains ascribed to technological advance have come from the spread of ideas originating outside America. Therefore, since a given percentage rise in American research does not raise worldwide research by that percent, the gains from research will not rise in proportion to the rise in American research. Notwithstanding these doubts and considering the small cost, it may still be a reasonably good bet to invest substantially more in non-defense basic research and see what happens.[29]

---

[27]The 5% total growth rate, proposed during the 1960 campaign, would be even more costly. From the 3.3% total growth rate of the 1950's, this is a 1.7 percentage point rise, which means an 85% increase in the 2% per capita growth rate. Ecomonic growth rates are highly erratic. Per capita growth rates of 4% or 5% do occur (as do zero and negative rates). But such rates for decades seem unattainable.

[28]E.F. Denison, *The Sources of Economic Growth and the Alternatives Before Us*, Committee for Economic Development, New York, 1962.

[29]Basic research, as opposed to all research and development, costs under ½% of GNP and, therefore, could be expanded tremendously at little cost. This means more government and private research funds for such fields as biochemistry, molecular biology, mathematics, oceanography, meteorology, physics, physiology, and genetics, most of which research is done in the major graduate universities and a few private companies.

Unfortunately, this is one of the first areas to be cut on those rare occasions when the Federal budget is pruned.

Here's another view of the cost of raising economic growth. Suppose consumption is $C and 20% of C must be sacrificed to raise per capita economic growth from 2% to 3%. (This 20% is in addition to whatever saving and investment is required to get the 2% growth.) How long would it take for the reduced C, growing at 3%, to catch up with the higher C, growing at 2%? This can be answered as follows:

$C_1 = C(1.02)^n$. C_1 is how high C will be after n years growing at 2%.

$C_2 = .8C(1.03)^n$. C_2 is how high C will be after n years, with .8C growing at 3%.

The above question is: when will C_2 equal C_1? This is found by setting them equal and solving for n. $C(1.02)^n = .8C (1.03)^n$. n = 23 years. Thus, if society sacrifices 20% of current consumption for 23 years, thereafter they could consume as much as had they not sacrificed and still maintain the higher growth rate. But note, it would still take considerable government compulsion all the subsequent years continuously to hold down consumption below what people would prefer with the available productive capacity. Some might view this as an unwarranted exploitation of one generation for another.

How government might raise the growth rate. If we waive the unlikely possibility of spectacular returns from more basic research, to raise economic growth by a percentage point or more, government must somehow reduce private consumption by about 20% and divert this forced saving into investment, education, and research, and into projects whose returns are not sufficient to inspire voluntary saving and investment. Moreover, this reduced consumption may seriously impair the profitability of many of the private investment plans which would have occurred anyway. Thus, to increase growth activities by $1, the government may have to forcibly expand these activities by more than $1, to offset the extent to which reduced consumption discourages private investment.

The government could reduce private consumption by raising income taxes or by taxing consumer spending. To expand investment, the government could either undertake investment itself or give or lend (at subsidized interest rates) the money to private industry. Almost certainly, on the magnitude envisioned, prices and profits would not determine the direction of much investment, but government decisions based on estimated "public needs" would dominate the determination of what, how, and for whom to produce. Thus, a radical change in the economic system might be necessary to expand growth activities enough to raise per capita growth by one percentage point.

Another approach to raising economic growth would be the removal of arrangements which discourage growth-oriented activities: elimination of government sponsored monopoly and inefficiency, repeal of tax laws which heavily penalize property income and risk-taking and which create artificial incentives to reinvest within given companies even if better returns are available elsewhere, and changes in educational decision-making. It is doubtful though that these steps would raise the growth rate by anywhere close to one percentage point (which is not to say these steps shouldn't be taken on grounds of personal freedom and fairness).

Should the government raise the growth rate? The preceding discussion by itself does not answer this question, but hopefully it provides a background for a more intelligent value judgment. We list the usual arguments for and against this proposal, leaving the reader to his own conclusions.

For
(1) The higher growth rate makes possible a much higher standard of living in the future.
(2) To maintain our relative advantage over the Soviet Union's standard of living, we must grow at least as fast as they do.
(3) To convince the uncommitted nations of the superiority of our way of life and to keep them from Communism, we must compare favorably in growth rate with the Soviet Union.
(4) The higher growth rate helps eliminate poverty.
(5) We must grow faster to be better able to afford an expensive military program and expanded foreign aid to underdeveloped countries.

Against
(1) Compared with the present, future generations will live in luxury anyway, without a forced sacrifice of current consumption for a higher growth rate. Such compulsion would constitute an exploitation of the present generation for the future akin to policies followed by the USSR and China.
(2) Why should America have to maintain its relative superiority in living conditions over other nations? Currently America's per capita income is about three times the USSR's and they cannot possibly overtake us in this century. One general humanitarian grounds, as well as in the interests of world stability, shouldn't we welcome a relative rise in others' living conditions?
(3) The superiority of America's economic system lies as much in individual freedom as in greater material prosperity. In fact, it is

through the institutions of freedom that our prosperity developed. The most pressing need in underdeveloped nations is the creation of such institutions—government by law, respect for property rights, and the elimination of restrictions on personal mobility and of barriers to private investment. It is by encouraging these changes that we can both stimulate their economic growth and steer them away from Communism.

(4) A higher growth rate, because it cuts down on current consumption, does not help current poverty.

(5) In order to raise the per capita growth rate by 50% or more, the government would have to direct such a large segment of resources, on top of the 25% of GNP already collected by government, that the freedom and initiative that bring about the 2% growth would be impaired.

Those who feel the private enterprise system determines satisfactorily the basic decisions of economic organization generally feel that, with any impediments to investment removed, investment should occur only if people will voluntarily undertake it for prospective returns. With this level of investment and with appropriate subsidy of research and education, and with public works carried out to give competitive returns, the resulting growth rate is viewed as "correct" whether it is 1%, 2%, 3% or any other figure. Those who disagree feel there are social or community needs for a growth rate different from that brought about by private choice and that individual choice should be subordinated to these collective needs. You decide.[30]

Summary

Growth in per capita output results from capital investment, technological change, and education.

Capital investment occurs when some people save (consume less than their incomes) and they or others invest this saving. Investment is undertaken to acquire the returns from investment, which returns depend on the physical

---

[30] Recently, there have been suggestions that government should actually *suppress* the economy's growth rate to reduce pollution, on the presumption that greater per capita output means greater per capita pollution. However, with proper taxes or regulations on polluting activities (discussed in the next chapter), this presumption would be invalid and so would this argument for suppressing economic growth. This does not negate another proposal, which we shall not pursue here, namely that government suppress population growth. For a provocative attack on growth per se (which one writer has called "the ideology of the cancer cell"), see *Technology and Growth: The Price We Pay*, by E. J. Mishan, Praeger, 1971.

productivity of the new capital and consumer desires for the output produced by the capital.

Net investment is gross or total investment less depreciation. The percentage return on investment is the investment's net income (gross income less depreciation) divided by the depreciated value of the capital.

In the short run, there are diminishing returns to additional investment expenditures.

There is only one rate of capital accumulation which reflects individuals' freedom to choose between consumption and saving, and between work and leisure, and their willingness to bear uncertainty. If government investments are to be consistent with these preferences, then such investments should be made only if the potential returns are as high as could be earned on private investments of similar risk.

Technological change results from expenditures on research and development, which expenditures are motivated by expected returns, just as are expenditures on capital investment.

Private interest may lead to underinvestment in basic research, because the fruits of basic research, new ideas, cannot be sold. Therefore, government or private philanthropy should subsidize basic research to the point where expected social returns equal the competitive return on investment.

Under competitive private enterprise, the benefits of technological advance are widely diffused in the form of more and better products and lower prices. Real wages also rise because technological advance raises the productivity of labor as well as of capital.

The benefits of education are both monetary (income-raising) and nonmonetary and both private (accruing to the student) and neighborhood. A major cost of education is the foregone production of unemployed students. Returns to investment in education seem somewhat better than returns to capital investment.

Underinvestment in education occurs because, under present political-ballot decision-making, consumer preferences are neither registered nor followed. Education decision-making would better reflect consumer choice if (a) consumers were allowed more effective freedom of choice between public and private schools, through tuition vouchers to parents who prefer private schools, and (b) school subsidies were based on need, and (c) equity investment in others' education were facilitated.

A one percentage point rise in per capita growth (a 50% increase) would substantially raise living conditions in the distant future, increasing average family income in 100 years to about $192,000 instead of the $72,000 which the past growth rate will achieve. However, this increase could be realized only by a forced reduction in current consumption of about 20%, unless a substantial but relatively inexpensive rise in basic research had surprising results. This vast compulsory redirection of productive capacity would likely make the government the main determinant of what to produce.

Study Questions Chapter 11

1. What four events cause economic growth? Explain the meaning of each.

2. Which of these does not raise per capita growth? Why not?*

3. What motivates people toward capital accumulation?*

4. What acts may constitute investment from an individual's standpoint, but not from society's? Why not?*

5. What *is* investment from society's standpoint?*

6. What are two exceptions to this?*

7. Why cannot there be investment without saving?*

8. Explain why there cannot be saving without investment. What happens if people try to save more than society collectively tries to invest?*

9. Explain how saving occurs if the government prints money and spends it for investment purposes.*

10. What is the "rate of return on investment?"*

11. Show its calculation with an example.

12. How could the investment's return continue forever?*

13. Distinguish gross and net investment.*

14. What amount is net investment if gross investment equals depreciation?*

15. What happens to society's nonhuman productive capacity if net investment = 0?*

16. What assures that net investment will be positive?*

17. How can one distinguish investment expenditures which are part of gross investment but not part of net investment?*

18. Why have there historically not been diminishing returns from investment?*

19. Considering an array of investment opportunities, explain why a rise in the annual rate of investment would result in short run diminishing returns to investment.*

20. Even without such an array, why might investment expenditures be patterned as if there were one? Why not?*

21. What three conditions or forces underlie the returns to investment?*

22. Who pays the return on investment and for what?*

23. What three forces determine the rate of capital accumulation?*

24. Explain how individual freedom is reduced if investment is at a different level (greater or lower) than that determined by these forces.*

25. "To say that the government should invest only if a potential competitive

return could be earned is not to say that the government should actually receive this return." Explain.

26. Why might government not wish to earn the potential return from its investment?

27. In arguments about the use of Indiana's dunes, the issue was inappropriately presented as between what two parties, when in fact it should have been viewed as between what other two parties?*

28. What is technological change?

29. What motivates people to bring about technological change?*

30. Why does private choice fail to bring about the appropriate level of basic research spending;*

31. What useful role is played by patents?

32. Explain how technological change benefits consumers.

33. How does an expansion of the money supply affect or relate to the benefits of technological change?*

34. How does technological change affect the distribution of income between workers and capitalists?*

35. What motivation causes consumers to benefit from technological change?*

36. What are three benefits from education?*

37. Give examples of the neighborhood benefits of education.

38. What is the largest part of the cost of college education?*

39. Roughly (without specifying formulas), how is the rate of return to investment in education measured?*

40. How does the return to investment in education compare with that on capital equipment?*

41. What conclusion follows if the returns from educational investment are significantly higher than those on capital investment?*

42. What are the conditions for the ideal rate of investment in education?*

43. What four aspects of education decision-making impede ideal investment in education?

44. Explain generally why ballot decision-making is defective and how this relates to education.

45. Explain why some voters have little incentive to vote for education expenditures.

46. Parents or students who want more education per year cannot conveniently acquire it. Explain.*

47. Explain how the voucher program might lead to increased educational

investment by some parents and might give parents (and older students) greater freedom of choice than at present.

48. To determine the vocher amount, how should the government's educational subsidy be calculated?*

49. Consider these arguments against the vocher plan: (1) divisiveness, (2) benefits rich only, (3) schools should not be run for profit, (4) church-state separation.

50. Explain three directions in which educational subsidies operate under present school finance.*

51. How would graduated tuition to public schools affect these subsidies and educational decision-making?*

52. How would equity investment in others' education improve education decision-making?*

53. Evaluate the contention that educational subsidies are justified if the recipient will eventually repay the subsidy out of taxes on the income gain resulting from his education.

54. If per capita growth is 2% per year, roughly how much higher will per capita income be after 20 years, after 100 years?*

55. How would a rise in prices (say a doubling) affect the money value and the real value of per capita income 100 years from now?*

56. Roughly how has the percent of families with real income below $3600 (in 1969 prices) changed since 1929?*

57. Explain roughly how it was estimated that the cost of raising the economic growth rate by one percentage point would be about 20% of current consumption expenditures?*

58. How is this estimate affected by diminishing returns to additional expenditures on growth-related activities?

59. What would be the cost of raising basic research by 50%?*

60. How might the government raise the growth rate?

61. Should the government try to raise the economy's growth rate? Why or why not?

Answers to starred questions.

2. Population growth. The more people, the lower the output per capita, by diminishing returns, assuming population growth itself does not spur per capita investment or technological change.

3. Desire for income.

4. Purchases of stocks and bonds. These transfer ownership of existing property.

5. Creation of more nonhuman productive capacity.

6. Inventory rise and net exports.

7. Without saving, all income is spent on consumption and all productive capacity is used to produce consumer goods, none devoted to producing more nonhuman inputs.

8. Income will fall causing saving to fall too, until it declines to where saving equals investment.

9. Ensuing inflation reduces real consumption, government having bid resources out of consumption with money created and spent for investment.

10. Net income earned (gross income less depreciation) as a percent of investment or net worth.

12. Because the reinvestment of depreciation funds keeps investment at a constant level indefinitely.

13. Gross investment = net investment + depreciation.

14. Zero.

15. Stays the same in principle. Actually it may rise because new equipment embodies improved technology.

16. Nothing.

17. Can't. No particular investment expenditure corresponds to gross but not net investment.

18. Technological change has raised capital's productivity (as it has labor's) by as much as increased capital per worker has decreased it. And there may be a return below which people will not save and invest.

19. The highest return projects get first priority with investors; the more investment per year, the further down the list society goes, assuming knowledgeability of investment returns.

20. If some people know of each opportunity and are free, the top ones will be undertaken. Those who know cannot convince those with money of the merits of the better projects.

21. Consumer preference, technology, quantity of labor and other inputs with which capital is combined.

22. Consumers pay for the productivity (MPP) of capital.

23. Willingness to save and invest, anticipated consumer tastes, productivity of capital.

24. If investment is greater than free choice would indicate, people are forced to reduce consumption, though the returns are not worth the reduced consumption. If investment is less than the free choice level, people are prevented from investing, though profits and consumer choice make them willing to save and invest.

27. Steel companies and local recreation consumers; consumers of steel products and consumers of recreation services.

29. Income earned from applying the change (except for basic research which may lack profitable direct application).

30. The benefits are diffuse and free once published, so they cannot be sold by those who develop them. Therefore, private incentive does not inspire investment in basic research, even if social and private benefits exceed competitive returns.

33. No "real" effect. The rise in money supply prevents a deflation which would otherwise result from the rise in output caused by the technological change.

34. Can't tell—it depends on whether the productivity of capital or of labor is raised more.

35. The pursuit of self-interest by producers to imitate any profitable innovation.

36. Private monetary, private nonmonetary, and neighborhood (monetary and nonmonetary).

38. Income (and output) students could have produced if they weren't in school.

39. Find the interest rate which equates the cost of education with the present value of the differential income stream from the education.

40. At least as high, without counting nonmonetary benefits.

41. There is underinvestment in education.

42. (1) Rate of return equals the competitive return on investment; (2) educational services reflect consumer choice; (3) educational services are produced at minimum money and real cost.

46. To buy "more" they have to forego that provided by the government. This assumes more money buys more (or better) education.

"Merry Christmas, staff!"

48. To include capital costs and a competitive return on the capital, as well as obvious operating expenses.

50. Rich to poor, within the same income class, poor to rich.

51. Eliminates two, leaving rich to poor.

52. Increase chances that socially desirable investments would not be foregone for lack of funds.

54. 49%, 624%.

55. Double the money value; not affect the real value.

56. From 60% to 13%.

57. Find the % of GNP devoted to growth-related activities, say X%. Find the percent change in per capita growth rate that one percentage point represents, say Y%. Assume that to raise economic growth Y%, Y% of X% must be devoted to economic growth, above that necessary to achieve the current growth.

59. Under ¼% of GNP.

12

An Evaluation Of Private Enterprise

The preceeding chapters have described how a private enterprise economy works, primarily under competitive conditions, bringing out the roles of prices and profits, the operation of the "invisible hand," and the institutions necessary for its successful operation. In this chapter, we summarize briefly the results of competitive private enterprise and then turn to the major criticisms that have been directed against private enterprise.

The Results Of Competitive Private Enterprise

1. **What is produced.** Those goods and services are produced that are most desired by consumers, as their desires are expressed by dollar votes.
   a. Any shift of resources away from competitive equilibrium would result in a less desirable use of these resources – the goods given up by the shift would be more desirable than those gained.
   b. Whenever individual preferences for goods and services change, then, through incentives of self-interest and signals provided by prices and profits, inputs automatically shift in accordance with these new preferences.
2. **How things are produced.** Goods and services are produced at the least possible cost, both in money terms and in real terms; that is, the production of any good, A, is done with a minimum sacrifice of the other goods, non-A, which could have been produced with the inputs used to produce A.
   a. Any change in technology or in the availability of various inputs will automatically bring about changes in the prices of inputs and shifts in production methods so that real cost will still be minimized.
3. **Who gets what is produced.** Income is distributed in accordance with the money value of contribution to production by human and non-human inputs.
   a. Everyone has incentive to use the inputs he owns (including his laborpower) in the most beneficial manner in order to acquire more income and, thereby, more goods and service—"most beneficial" in terms of values expressed by dollar votes.

b. There is no surplus value—the total income of each enterprise is exactly exhausted by payments to inputs, hired and owned, equal to value contributed.

4. **Who produces.** Everyone is free to seek employment or invest his nonhuman inputs in the occupation, industry, and locality of his choice, subject to the freedom of others to deal or not to deal with him.

5. **The invisible hand.** Production in accordance with consumer choice, at minimum real cost, and payment equal to value contributed all occur without central direction, without anyone consciously trying to serve society, but with each individual serving his own interest as he sees it.

6. Everyone is free to spend his income as he wishes.

7. **Economic growth.** There is incentive and opportunity for innovation, economic growth, and the improvement of one's own economic well-being.

   a. The annual growth of productive capacity reflects the willingness of people to forego current consumption and devote resources to investment, education, and research, in response to anticipated returns, which returns are based on anticipated consumer desires.

8. **Necessary institutions.** Individual action will bring about these results only if the following prevail:

   a. People have knowledge of alternatives as consumers, workers, employers, and investors.
   b. There is stable government by law, so that individuals are willing to create productive capacity without fear that government will unexpectedly change the profitability of given conduct.
   c. Contracts are enforced and property rights clearly defined and protected.
   d. Government preserves the freedom of people to engage in voluntary transactions at the same time preventing fraud, violence, and monopolistic practices.
   e. Government regulates the money supply so that changes in money do not cause wide changes in the price level, which in turn impede the attainment of equilibrium prices, wages, outputs and employment.

These results are better viewed as what *tends* to happen under competitive private enterprise rather than what actually occurs. There are continual changes in the economy—changes in consumer tastes, technology, worker job preferences, and in the availability of non-human inputs. Before the economy adjusts to the changes of the last month or year, other changes occur, so that, at any given time, input shifts are in process or are being planned and the economy will not be at the equilibrium implied by the attainment of these results. However, even a tendency toward them would be extremely difficult if not impossible to direct from above, because much of the relevant knowledge, relating to unique local circumstances, cannot be centralized.

Objections To Private Enterprise

Private enterprise has been widely criticised ever since the factory system emerged from feudalism and handicraft production. In the Twentieth Century, many nations, both old and new, have rejected private enterprise in favor of socialism or have modified it with considerable central planning. Most prominent has been the opposition by China and the Soviet Union. But even in the United States many politicians are elected primarily on promises to modify substantially the outcome of individualistic private enterprise. Why? From the preceeding description, private enterprise seems to be a beneficient, indeed marvelous, arrangement for making the basic economic decisions. Doubtless, every reader has thought of some objections or qualifications and, indeed, some have been pointed out.

The following list covers, to our knowledge, all the prominent objections made against private enterprise, both by socialists and communists who would abolish capitalism altogether and by others who want a "mixed" system of private enterprise and government planning. Most of these objections are quite independent of each other. That is, one may be correct and another entirely wrong. Further, some may apply to only part of the economy. Conceivably, any one of these objections, all others invalid, could justify rejecting private enterprise. Conceivably, too, all the objections could have some merit, but private enterprise might still be the best arrangement if the alternatives have even greater shortcomings, utopia being unattainable. We shall outline the objections, then comment about each.

1. The "right" goods and services are not produced because people don't want the "right" things.

   a. People don't have enough knowledge to make decisions that are really in their interest.

   For example, people can't judge the quality or technical characteristics of goods or the competence of services they buy, they can't evaluate their own abilities for selecting an occupation, they don't know about alternative job opportunities or what work conditions are like elsewhere, and they don't know the profitability of alternative investments.

   b. Even with all the knowledge, people simply don't have sense enough to know what is good for themselves.

   Witness the substantial dollar votes for narcotics, liquor, tobacco, trashy books and magazines, the TV wasteland, conspicuous consumption, the excessive influence of advertisers, and the generally vulgar tastes of the common man.

   c. Individual interests, even if sensibly assessed from the individual's standpoint, should be subordinated to higher social community interests.

   Some such goals are better education, better housing (even if people would rather spend on something else), a higher growth rate, conservation of wildlife and natural beauty, the pursuit of knowledge for itself, the grandeur of the nation, and the worship of God.

For all these reasons, objectors say, dollar votes are not necessarily appropriate guides for production and government should take a hand in deciding what to produce.

2. The "right" goods and serivces are not produced because the distribution of wealth or income is improper and unjust.

   a. The inequality that occurs under private enterprise is unfair and immoral, even if payments *are* equal to value contributed.
   b. Income payments based on "value contributed" have no validity because the values themselves reflect the crass and foolish tastes of unfairly distributed incomes to start with.
   c. Nonhuman inputs were made by past labor, so payment for the contribution of nonhuman inputs should go to labor, not to private owners.
   d. Those who contribute high amounts, both labor and property owners, should receive some *fraction* of their additional contributions, to give incentive and reward for greater productivity, but they need not and should not receive their full contributions.

3. Neighborhood effects, public goods, and high private transactions costs—under individualistic private enterprise, the wrong production decisions will be made under these three conditions.

   a. Neighborhood effects arise where there are significant disparaties between social and private production costs or between social and private consumption benefits.

      For example, a smoke nuisance or stream pollution in the production of a product imposes social costs not borne by the consumers. Purchases which provide neighborhood benefits beyond those received by the buyer include safe tires, treatment for a contagious disease, lawn fertilizer, and some education.

   b. Public goods exist where the output must be consumed collectively, if at all, and especially where it is not feasible to exclude non-payers from comsumption and where consumption by additional people does not reduce the quantity available to others.

      Standard examples are lighthouses (which, if provided for some ships, are available to all), national defense, some flood control, some police protection, and TV programs (under present broadcast arrangements).

   c. Where private transactions costs are considerably higher than coercive arrangements through government.

      For example, the costs of collecting individually from consumers of local streets and city parks are much greater than the costs of financing streets and parks through taxation.

4. Monopoly and monopsony. Competition might work well, but monopoly and monopsony predominate both for technological reasons and because collusion is so profitable.

5. Waste and inefficiency of competition. Competition results in an inefficient duplication of efforts, excess capacity, a proliferation of small, inefficient firms, and a huge, wasteful expenditure on advertising.

6. Economic instability. All too much of the time a private enterprise economy is in the throes of widespread unemployment or rampant inflation, boom and bust. Such instability is inherent in private enterprise or can be avoided only with considerable government regulation of the economy.

7. Private enterprise, because of its incessant stress on self-interest, has a damaging effect on peoples' personalities and on the general quality of life.

These are the basic objections to private enterprise and a rather formidable list it is. We shall comment briefly on each point.

(1a) Lack of knowledge. As we have already noted, lack of knowledge does indeed prevent people from making the best economic decisions. One may doubt though that an alternative economic system would remedy this. Anyway, if people recognize their lack of knowledge and its effects, the profit system provides incentives for remedies—books, magazines, shopping services, professional appraisers, etc. Quite possibly, since knowledge is a public good (see below), government should play a role by furnishing some knowledge, by requiring certain information on containers, by improving the courts so that disputes are settled more efficiently, by strengthening and clarifying producer liability for faulty product performance, and by inspecting service shops (such as TV and auto repair) to protect consumers from dishonest practices.

(1b) Poor judgment. One may readily agree with the contention that people (sometimes) don't know their own interests, but at the same time dispute (a) that government knows better and (b) that government should coerce people into acting in their own interest as government sees it. The loss of personal freedom may be worse than the errors prevented. Current policy regarding cigarettes, marijuana, heroin, gambling, prostitution, homosexuality, sale of contraceptives, pornography, radio and TV programming, and subsidy of museums and other cultural activities all presume that government should prevent adults from being naughty, frivolous, and vulgar, as government sees it.[1] In none of these areas is government preventing

---

[1] In the spring of 1971, outdoorsman Representative Morris Udall of Arizona introduced a bill (not passed) to prohibit telecasting football, baseball, and basketball games outside of their regular seasons, because he feels people spend too much time watching TV sports. Said Udall: "The jokes about the endless football-watching-weekends of the American male are not funny any more." Quoted in the Wall Street Journal, April 22, 1971. Others may feel the Congressman's zeal for regulating how people live is not funny either. Similar comments pertain to proposed laws that cars with motors running have annoying buzzers which will not stop unless passengers are secured by seat belts.

Lest Udall's proposal seem too far-fetched to take seriously, in 1961

people from harming *others,* only from presumably harming themselves. We leave to the reader to judge to what extent this is a proper function of government—whether a majority of the population should impose its esthetic, religious, and moral preferences on the rest.[2]

(1c) **Collective goals.** Regarding collective goals, again, personal value judgments are paramount. For example, libertarians (or, by an older name, individualists, or, by an even older name with a different meaning today, liberals) would abolish military conscription and rely on a volunteer army—note that one man's "mercenary" is another's "patriotic volunteer"—on the grounds that involuntary servitude, however noble the cause, is unacceptable in a free society. On the other hand, collectivists want to expand conscription to cover *all* young people, putting them to work on "social" projects like teaching assistance, cleaning slums (whatever this means), conservation projects, babysitting for working mothers, etc. The

---

Congress banned the telecast of any pro-football contest on a Friday or Saturday in any locality within 75 miles of a high school or college game, thereby denying consumers an opportunity to choose. By this law, in mid-December 1971, the Philadelphia area was blacked-out of a critical Baltimore-Miami game because of the small-college Boardwalk Bowl in Atlantic City. And the scheduling of two playoffs on Christmas Day 1971 has inspired further demands to prohibit by law what consumers could freely reject if they wished.

[2] It is one thing for a person to refuse to asociate with, say, prostitutes or with those who patronize prostitutes. But it is another thing to support laws prohibiting prostitution or gambling or narcotics, and other non-victim moral offenses. Majority disapproval does not necessarily justify prohibition.

"This is your two-minute warning—to get to the dinner table."

basic issue regarding (1c) is whether individuals exist to serve society at the collective will regardless of their own preferences. They do in Communist China. There is also the question whether the price and profit market system effectively guides individuals, serving personal interests, to serve others. (For example, are all young people really qualified for these social projects and who for which?). Many who opt for collective and coercive programs clearly do not understand the market system. But some who understand it still don't like it.

(2) **Income distribution.** The ethical issues regarding income distribution have been discussed in Chapter 6. Note again that payment according to contribution has two important benefits on efficiency grounds which are likely to be lost with any alternative payments system.

As to (2c), that capital is embodied labor, frequently cited by Marxists, those workers who (along with nonhuman inputs) helped create a given nonhuman input, a machine, were paid the value of their contribution when they worked, a value which depended on the price of the machine, which price in turn depended on the expected productivity of the machine. Its purchaser provided the money to pay the "embodied labor" when he bought the machine and, therefore, is not taking labor's contribution when he receives the subsequent earnings of the machine.

Objection (2d) and objection (2) in general are based on the contention that poverty can and should be eliminated by income redistribution. This was discussed in Chapter 11, with the warning that vast income redistribution might impair the economic growth which has been the most effective long-run force for reducing poverty.

(3) Neighborhood effects, public goods, and prohibitive private transaction costs, together, are probably the most valid basis for rejecting the economic decisions, especially "what" and "how," determined under private enterprise.

Neighborhood effects. These abound, and to an increasing extent as population rises.[3] When most people lived on farms and most city-dwellers in single-family houses, what one family did at home seldom bothered anyone else. Now with most people in thin-walled apartments (Bedlam arms, as the *New York Times* once put it), or in homes with mini-yards, with a radio and TV for each member of the family, and worse yet with portable radios and

---

[3] In fact, begetting and rearing children probably have greater neighborhood effects than any other conduct. May not society someday face a choice between (a) regulating family size and allowing greater freedom for other conduct or (b) regulating most other conduct because of the neighborhood consequences of excessive population growth and incompetent parents?

TV's, one can hardly escape the din of others' noise. But what solution is feasible? To outlaw transistor radios? Tax them heavily? Require earphones for outdoor use? More stringent laws against disturbing others? Of course, the ideal solution would be more considerate people. But until that utopian day arrives, other remedies are needed.[4]

It is not always true (as sometimes inplied) that neighborhood costs should necessarily be eliminated. One must balance the value of the associated production (rubber from a smelly factory) against the money value of the neighborhood cost (which means the compensation the aggrieved parties would accept to be as well off as without the neighborhood costs). Conceivably, society is better off producing the rubber and the smell than having neither.

Whether those who object should be compensated is a separate issue. For example, if a community grew from scratch after rubber factories located in a relatively isolated area, presumably those who voluntarily moved there and stay feel the advantages (jobs in the factory or in serving factory workers) outweigh the disadvantage (the smell). Then too, the cost of adopting a less odiferous technology should be weighed against the discomfort of the smell. If a different technology would cost $5-million (more than the present), but the reduced odor is worth only $2-million, it is better to stink.

But suppose the odorless technology would cost an additional $2-million and the residents would value the fresher air at $3-million. Clearly, it is socially desirable to institute the new technology. Will the companies install it then? Not likely, because the fresh air is not going to benefit the company owners by $2-million.

---

[4] One objection to noise was registered near a busy truck terminal in Patterson, N.J. Under a large billboard sign: "This is a Trucking Company That Never Sleeps," someone wrote: "And Neither do its Neighbors." (*Reader's Digest*, December 1970, p. 208.)

"This set has a feature you'll really enjoy -- it interferes with your neighbor's power tools."

This is where the government may be useful. True, the residents could get together voluntarily to collect and pay the companies $2-million to adopt the new technology. But this is not likely for two reasons: (1) individual residents may "free-ride," decline to contribute on the possibly insincere grounds that they don't mind the odor or on the more likely grounds that if others contribute enough, any given person needn't contribute anything, and (2) the cost of organizing residents may be prohibitive. Thus, in this example, we encounter a combination of neighborhood effects, public good, and transaction cost problems. The odor is the neighborhood cost of producing rubber. The fresh air is a public good. If acquired for some, it is available for all in the area. And it is expensive for the resident-purchasers of the fresh air to negotiate with the "seller," the rubber factories.

There are several possible roles for the government to take. The most fundamental and minimum role is to establish liability for the odor nuisance. If a court states the factories are not liable, then consumers, acting voluntarily or through government, have greater incentive to pay the factories to reduce the smell. If the factories are liable, they have incentive to correct the smell (or to compensate the residents should the correction be more costly, though identifying and compensating people is probably not feasible without government determination). In general, where neighborhood costs are involved, if we ignore transactions costs, the same adjustment of production will occur by voluntary private initiative once the liability for the nuisance is established, whether the liability is placed on one party (the factories) or the other (the residents).[5] Government may have to do more than determine liability if the companies cannot feasibly compensate the residents nor the residents feasibly agree to pay the company. Government might tax the residents to pay for the odorless technology or tax the company to compensate the residents or compel the company to change technology. In any case, its decision (to the extent possible) should be based on estimates of the value of the product, the negative value of the nuisance, and the cost of different technologies which reduce or eliminate the nuisance, as well as the question of liability.

To illustrate further the deficiency of the invisible hand here, neighborhood costs and benefits may be analyzed with the following diagrams, which are modifications of Figure 2-3.[6] MPC is the marginal private cost and demand measures the market-clearing price. Consider first Figure 12-1a. Point

---

[5] See R.H. Coase, "The Problem of Social Cost," *Journal of Law an Economics*, Vol. III, October, 1960. Coase's example was damage from cattle straying onto a neighboring corn farm, where the damage was less than the cost of fencing. With only two parties (as contrasted with a whole community), it is easy for them to get together, once liability is established.

[6] One may get the general idea without following precisely this more difficult discussion.

FIGURE 12-1 Neighborhood Costs and Benefits

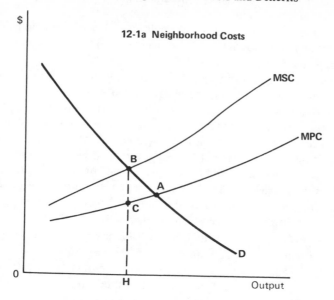

12-1a Neighborhood Costs

A designates the output and price which would prevail under competitive private enterprise, where the market-clearing price equals the (private) cost of producing another unit. Private firms have no incentive to consider the neighborhood costs in setting price or output. The *vertical distance* between MPC and MSC (marginal *social* cost) measures the neighborhood cost associated with a given output of the good or service. For example, at output OH, the neighborhood cost is $CB.[7] The "correct" output, based on consumer preferences, is OH, where the market-clearing price is HB and the value of foregone goods, HC, plus neighborhood costs, CB, is also HB.

The government could bring about this outcome by imposing a tax of CB per unit. This would raise MPC to the producers by the distance CB, so that MPC would cut D at point B. (Recall the effects of a commodity tax on supply and on output.) Then private initiative would lead to outcome B rather than A. The government could then use the tax preceeds to compensate those who bear the neighborhood costs and could offer to reduce the tax if a

---

[7] If MSC remains equidistant or diverges from MPC as output expands, this vertical distance is the *marginal* neighborhood cost. But if as output expands, the marginal neighborhood cost becomes smaller, perhaps even reaching zero after some output, then the vertical distance should be the neighborhood cost *per unit* of output rather than the, in this case, smaller marginal neighborhood cost.

different technology reduced the neighborhood costs, moving MSC down toward the before-tax MPC.

The possibly insurmountable difficulty in achieving this simple solution is that it requires knowledge of the diagram. Under competitive private enterprise, outcome A is brought about by the invisible hand, by self-seeking people, without any knowledge of these curves. But to correct to outcome B, the government must know (a) the dollar value of the neighborhood costs at various outputs, (b) what the market-clearing price would be at various outputs, and (c) the MPC at various outputs.[8] Since only vague estimates of this information can be obtained, and this at considerable expense, and since special interest pressures are apt to lead government regulators even further from B than A, and since additional government interference with private activities is itself a neighborhood cost, one may venture to suggest that only in compelling and obvious cases should the government attempt to do anything about neighborhood costs, beyond establishing liability.

Some local governments do levy "effluent charges" on industries which cause water pollution. An attempt in 1969 by Senator Proxmire of Wisconsin to introduce Federal taxes on pollution was rebuffed, apparently on the grounds that pollution must be stopped without regard to cost-benefit comparisons.[9] In March, 1971, the Treasury proposed taxing sulphur emissions of plants at 1¢ per pound, rising by 1975 to 10¢ a pound. If emissions were not reduced, as they surely would be, the tax would cost $4-billion in 1975. Again, this tax was scorned as a "license to pollute." *Business Week's* editorial (Mar. 10, 1971) said "the nation's air is not for sale at any price."

A similar proposal is to tax the lead in gasoline to eliminate the lower price of leaded than lead-free gas, leaving consumers whose engines would be damaged by lead-free gas free to pay the higher price. So far, consumers (some of whom demand immediate expensive clean-ups by big business) have been unwilling to pay the added 2¢ to 4¢ a gallon for unleaded gas.

A failure to weigh costs and benefits resulted in numerous laws against phosphate detergents in areas where phosphates cause no harm (eutrophication of streams).[10] Many of these were repealed after the Federal government determined that alternative detergents were more harmful than those with phosphates. The need for cost-benefit comparisons rather than sweeping prohibitions of all pollution was also shown by a study of 129 major polluters

---

[8] In the unlikely coincidence that the vertical distance between MPC and MSC were the same for all outputs, only knowledge of (a) would be needed; for a tax of that distance per unit, coupled with the invisible hand, would bring about the "correct" outcome without knowledge of the other curves.

[9] See "Objections to a Tax on Pollution," *New York Times,* Dec. 19, 1969.

[10] Barrons, "What Price Ecology," May 3, 1971.

in Kansas City.[11] If all 129 cut emissions as much as technologically possible, emissions would drop over 50% to 85 micrograms per cubic meter of air at a cost of $24.6-million. However, if abatement requirements are varied according to emmision reductions per dollar, the study concluded that for $7.5-million emissions could be cut to 86 micrograms.

In addition to a failure to employ the price system to give producers (and consumers) incentive to weigh neighborhood costs, government has also failed for decades to enforce statutes such as the Refuse Act of 1899 which prohibits pollution of navigable waters. These problems are worldwide,[12] but seem of increasing urgency because of years of neglect, rising per capita consumption, and rising population relative to a fixed supply of air, land, and water. Still, according to Eugene Cuccione, senior editor of the *Engineering and Mining Journal*, particulates per cubic foot in American cities have decreased from 510 micrograms in 1931-2 to 120 in 1957 and 92 in 1969.[13]

---

[11] *Wall street Journal*, Dec. 16, 1971.

[12] *New York Times*, "The Seven Wonders of the Polluted World," Sept. 20, 1971.

[13] *New York Times* editorial article, Aug. 28, 1971. While the cities covered by these three surveys were not identical (the coverage rising on successive dates), Mr. Cuccione is certain that "our air is far cleaner today" than in the past. For a lively book on neighborhood costs by two economists, see *Environmental Economics*, by T.D. Crocker and A.J. Rogers III, The Dryden Press, 1971.

"Have you considered that cutting the lawn
may upset the ecology?"

With the proper use of taxes on neighborhood costs, as recommended by economists for decades, today's pollution crisis would never have arisen. Even at this point, a gradual change in technology, inspired by taxes, can greatly reduce pollution, though not overnight (without prohibitive costs on society). McGraw-Hill estimates pollution control expenditures by 26 major industries in 1971 of $3.6-billion, up 46% from 1970.[14]

FIGURE 12-1 Continued

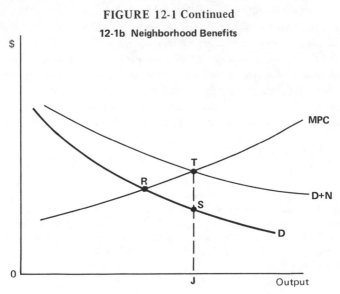

12-1b Neighborhood Benefits

In Fig. 12-1b, D+N measures the private plus neighborhood benefit, the vertical distance between the curves being the marginal neighborhood benefits at given quantities. The private enterprise outcome, R, can be improved upon by a subsidy to producers or consumers (it doesn't matter which) of ST per unit to bring about outcome T at which private plus public benefits equal the value of foregone goods to get the last unit.[15] The same difficulties of estimating the diagrams, private pressure groups, and disadvantage of further government interference again caution against trying to correct for small differences between private and social benefits.

Public goods. Now let us consider why the invisible hand does not operate satisfactorily in the case of public goods. We may distinguish two

[14] *Business Week,* May 15, 1971. For a case study, see "A Corporate Polluter Learns the Hard Way," the story of Union Carbide's stubborn resistance and eventual acquiescence to pollution control in Marietta, Ohio, *Business Week,* Feb. 6, 1971.

[15] For brevity, we omit a proof that the subsidy, ST, either to consumers or to producers will bring about outcome T and that either subsidy will have the same effects on both consumers and producers.

types of public goods. There are those, like national defense or traffic lights, where if quantity X_1 is available to anyone, it is available to all, because one person's consumption does not reduce the amount available to others and because it is not feasible to exclude people from consuming the good.

Suppose the cost of producing a given quantity, X_1, of such a public good is $100. And suppose each of 1000 people in the area values X_1 as worth $10 to himself, so the total value of X_1, $10,000, far exceeds its production cost, $100. Would private dollar votes bring about the production of X_1? If X_1 were, say, theater performances, an entrepreneur could sell tickets to recover his costs. But by our definition of public good, non-payers cannot be excluded, so once X_1 is produced, no one has incentive, except out of charity, to pay for it. And since no one person will pay the $100 cost, it may not be produced. Possibly, where the total value so far exceeds production cost, voluntary contributions might still get X_1 produced. But then the burden of paying would probably be born unfairly since any one person has incentive to be a free-rider. And when we consider the question of how much X to produce, X_1 or X_2 or X_3, clearly there is no automatic tendency to produce additional quantities as long as the production cost is less than the collective value.

In principle, the government can bring about the "correct" production of such goods. Since free-riders cannot be excluded, the usual arrangement is to charge nothing for the good or service, but to finance it from taxes (where payment is involuntary). But without market-clearing prices and with cumbersome political processes replacing dollar votes, it is close to impossible to determine that quantity where the value to consumers equals the value of alternative goods foregone.

One reason inefficient decisions are made in government provision of public goods and services is that little or no attempt is made to relate payment to benefits received. Consider a lighthouse near a reef at the entrance to a harbor. It is a public good. If the light shines for one ship, others can see it too. Who should pay its costs? Most public goods are financed from general tax revenues on the vague premises that (1) if a given taxpayer doesn't benefit from one government good, he benefits from others, and (2) the distribution of income wasn't just anyway, so financing by progressive taxation tends to reduce income inequality by having goods that are available to all paid for disproportionately by high-income people.

Even if these two premises as stated are correct (which we do not concede), both the provision of public goods and income redistribution are inefficiently achieved by not making beneficiaries of public goods pay for them in proportion to their benefits. First, while everyone may benefit from one or another government-provided good or service, all will not benefit equally. Nor will all benefit equally within any given income class, because some consumers will have a high preference for things provided by the government and others a low preference (relative to saving or buying other things). So there is no equity in saying that since everyone uses highways (or buys goods carried by trucks), general tax revenues should finance highways. (The alternative is gasoline and deisel fuel taxes and other user charges.)

Secondly, if low-income people were given *money* (taken from high-income people), they would probably prefer some other goods than the public good. This means that a given dollar redistibution would benefit low income people more in the form of money than as free access to some public goods (assuming, of course, low-income people are the best judges of their interests).

Thirdly, when public goods are priced below production costs (as when offered free) so that each taxpayer does not feel that by consuming more of public good X *his* taxes will rise proportionately to the production cost, then people will tend to vote through political ballots for "too much" of the good, to where the value of the additional units is less than the value of the foregone production (past point A in Figure 3-1a.)

Therefore, even if the public good cannot feasibly be sold for a specific price, the government should try to tax that segment of the population (boat owners for lighthouses) which will benefit and let that segment decide whether it wants to raise its taxes and have the good. While it is impossible to relate taxation and benefits perfectly, this could be done far more than it is. Modern technology makes possible considerable use of referenda by selected voters on selected subjects. Without such efforts, it is unlikely that public goods will be produced at rates consistent with consumers' preferences among various public and private goods.

A second category of public goods covers situations where additional consumers can be served at little or no additional cost once a give quantity is produced, but where it *is* possible and feasible to exclude non-payers and charge direct fees.[16] Again, it is quite difficult to determine ideal production and pricing policy. A good example is television broadcasting. Under present arrangements, a program is a non-excludable public good. If a program is being transmitted at all, it costs almost nothing for additional consumers to watch it (ignoring depreciation of the TV set and the cost of electricity to operate the set). On the other hand it *is* possible to transmit the program as a scrambled picture for a given TV set.

It would seem that such pay TV would surely reduce total social welfare, because excluded non-payers *could* be allowed to watch without any additional expenditures of resources, as they could be watching under present broadcasting arrangements. But with pay TV, consumer dollar votes could

---

[16] For the jargon-minded, the first type might be called "non-excludable" and the second "excludable" public goods.

pay for many programs not worth producing under present arrangements. For example, a program which one million people would pay $1 to watch might be highly profitable, yet if only two million would watch it free, it might not pay a sponsor to provide it free. Thus, pay TV might be socially beneficial in directing resources to programs that would not have been profitable otherwise; but it may be harmful in reducing the audience to many existing programs (especially professional football, if we may inject a private foreboding). Possible alternatives include government subsidy of programs appealing to small groups (but who should pay the costs and what programs should be produced?) or some combination of pay and "free" TV, with legal limitations on the profits earned from pay TV.

Also in this second category of public goods are the services of toll roads and bridges. Except for rush hours when the facility is used to capacity, additional cars can be admitted at little or no cost. Therefore, if the toll discourages some non-rush-hour traffic, it reduces the total satisfaction possible from available resources. But if tolls are abolished, who will pay for the roads and bridges? Why anyone other than the users? Similar considerations apply to sports events, movies, and plays, at times other than a full house and to buses, trains, and airplanes with empty seats. The cost of admitting more spectators or passengers in near zero, so shouldn't they be admitted for nothing? Some alternative policies for these situations are discussed below under "natural monopoly."

There are two other categories of goods and services which should be noted with public goods, though they are discussed elsewhere. First, some goods with neighborhood benefits—education and research—are largely private goods (in that more for one person means less for someone else from the same use of resources and the benefits go mainly to those who acquire the good), but their neighborhood benefits are public goods. Second, some goods, like electric power, produced under "natural monopoly" conditions (explained below) have a public good quality in that more consumers can be served at little additional cost, even though they are otherwise private goods.

In conclusion, the tendency of self-seeking individuals guided by prices of outputs and inputs, to bring about a "correct" determination of what and how to produce does not apply where goods and services have neighborhood costs or benefits, or for public goods, or where private transactions costs are substantially higher than coercive government policy. In theory government can improve on private action, and while we have cited several reasons for doubting that government will do so if it nominally tries, there is no question that in many obvious cases—limitation of air and stream pollution, prevention of contagious disease, subsidy of basic research, local zoning of land utilization, to name a few—government can greatly improve on the operation of individualistic private enterprise.

(4) **Monopoly and monopsony.**[17] The misallocative consequences of these were discussed earlier. Space limitations preclude a thorough examination of whether the American economy is competitive enough so that the foregoing chapters, which largely described *competitive* private enterprise, do depict economic organization in America. The following then only suggests superficially why competition rather than monopoly seems to characterize the American economy.

First, consider the three main sources of monopoly: (1) private collusion, (2) technology, and (3) government. There is no doubt, as anti-trust convictions attest, that private collusion to fix prices, restrict output, and bar the entry of competitors does exist. Indeed the same Adam Smith who originated the "invisible hand" metaphor, also wrote in 1776: "People of the same trade seldom meet together, even for merriment and diversion, but the conversation ends in a conspiracy against the public, or in some contrivance to raise prices."[18] Smith doubted this could be prevented by law, but American experience with anti-trust laws since 1890 suggests that the worst forms of monopolistic behavior can be prevented.

Collusion is often ineffective because each participant has a strong incentive to cheat by slightly undercutting the agreed price or raising output beyond his agreed share, hoping others abide by the agreement. Collusive arrangements are also vulnerable to changes in tastes and technology and to new products, because these changes render obsolete (i.e., relatively unprofitable) old price and output agreements, giving firms further incentive to deviate unless a new agreement is reached. But each new agreement, especially when market conditions are changing rapidly, must overcome difficult bargaining about the best price, or about who should have what share of the market, or how outsiders can be restricted, all without being caught and convicted of violating anti-trust laws which clearly prohibit such conduct. Finally, without government assistance, it is difficult to exclude outsiders (including foreign competition) from a highly profitable industry. In the past decade, several concerted efforts by cattlemen (not covered by anti-trust laws) to withhold beef in order to raise prices failed, as non-compliers took immediate advantage of any rise in price. Likewise, the post-war years have seen the collapse of numerous multi-national government

---

[17] Part of what is included here in "monopoly" is sometimes called "oligopoly." An oligopoly is an industry where a few producers account for most of the output, such as autos, aluminum, liquor, cigarettes, and typwriters, to name a few. Whether the outcome under oligopoly will resemble monopoly or whether it will be closer to competition depends on the number of firms, the extent of foreign competition, the ease with which small firms can enter and compete, the extent of inter-industry competition, as among metals or among railroads, trucks, barges, and airlines, and whether the government promotes or suppresses competition.

[18] Adam Smith, *The Wealth of Nations*, Book I, Ch. 10, Pt. II.

efforts (America leading the way) to raise world prices of wheat, coffee, sugar, cocoa, and other products by restricting output.

Technical conditions: natural monopoly. In some economic activities, such as providing electricity or water to a locality, the technology of production in relation to consumer demand is such that the entire market can be served by one firm (or a very few) more cheaply than by several firms. This is called "natural monopoly" or "technical monopoly." Here, there is no satisfactory alternative to monopoly. What to do about this is discussed below.

Many people grossly exaggerate the extent of natural monopoly. They think that in most economic activities, the larger is the size of the firm, the lower will be the unit cost of production: one large steel company could produce steel more efficiently than many companies, one large food chain could market food more cheaply than many, one large farm, one large airline, . . . etc. This notion is a total misconception. In fact, there is evidence that in many industries (steel is one) firms that are less than a quarter as large as the largest firm produce just as efficiently, or more so, as the largest, or stated differently, if the largest firms were broken into several smaller firms, costs per unit would not rise.[19] Thus, not only is it incorrect to assume that *one* company per industry is most efficient, but in most industries well over a dozen can operate efficiently, not counting as many more from foreign competition.

Another reason people exaggerate monopoly from technological considerations is that they incorrectly assume all *large* companies have monopoly power. For example, the Sharon Steel Co., with sales over $100-million and 7000 employees, is a large company, but it is small relative to the steel industry (1%) and for this reason has no monopoly power.[20] Similarly, many "conglomerate" firms, with subsidiaries in several unrelated industries, though large in absolute size, have no monopoly power if their share of each industry is small. Monopoly power comes from being large *relative to* an industry (or local market where outside competition is not feasible), not from being large per se.

Another technology-related exaggeration of monopoly runs like this:

---

[19] Such a division of firms is not without precedent. In 1911, both the American Tobacco Co. and the Standard Oil Company were so dissolved, the latter into over 30 companies, many of which are now large competing companies. Again in 1945, the Aluminum Company of America was ordered to sell its Canadian subsidiary, Aluminium Ltd., now a competing company.

[20] An article, "Thinking Small: More Steel Users Cut Costs By Purchasing From Tiny New Mills," tells of the recent growth of "minimills," giving quick, convenient, specialized service in many localities. New technology has lowered production costs in small relative to large steel plants. Happily, these minimills are avid consumers of rusting auto hulks and other junk. (*Wall Street Journal*, Oct. 26, 1970.)

(1) Economic theory (more advanced than studied here) shows that the precise equality of price with marginal cost necessarily occurs only when the number of competing firms in an industry is quite large and no one firm produces a significant portion of the industry's output; (2) In many industries, these conditions do not prevail; (3) Therefore, monopoly exists in many industries. While it is true that many industries do not conform to the theoretical ideal for perfect competition, it is not reasonable to consider every departure from this abstraction as significantly monopolistic. Indeed, monopoly profits do not show up with any regularity in industries where the four largest firms together account for less than 50% of the industry output. Yet, outside of regulated public utilities, this degree of concentration is exceeded in a small fraction of industries, the most prominent being automobiles, which produces 2% of GNP or 6% of all manufacturing.

The third and most significant source of monopoly is government. As cited in earlier chapters, government suppresses competition by restricting entry into some industries and occupations, by encouraging collusive price fixing in some (for example, trucking, and citrus fruits and with resale price maintenance laws), by restricting output (oil and some farm products), by impeding technological advance (railroad full-crew laws, some building codes), by subsidizing inefficient operations (shipping, shipbuilding), through farm subsidies, by tariffs and import quotas, by tax laws which impede the shifting of investment funds from one company to another, and most importantly by strong support of labor unions.[21] Additionally, state and local governments encourage monopoly by failing to enact and/or enforce anti-trust laws relating to *intra*-state commerce (Federal laws apply only to *inter*-state commerce).

Remedies for monopoly. The remedies for monopoly are quite obvious once the sources are recognized. Basically, they are an end to government promotion of monopoly and vigorous anti-trust enforcement by all levels of government. This will never occur until there is a wide popular appreciation of and desire for economic freedom and an insistence that the government not interfere with competitive market forces. This in turn requires an economic sophistication which only a small minority now possesses. Until then, special-interest logrolling with dominate government policy.

Notwithstanding this foreboding, competitive forces do and shall likely continue to predominate because in most economic activities, outsiders *can* enter if profits are attractive, successful collusion is *not* feasible, substantial inter-industry and inter-product competition severely limits such monopoly power as exists, and government, while inconsistently promoting some

---

[21] Patents and copyrights also deserve mention, though here at least government's provision of monopoly rights seems necessary for promoting innovation and creative effort.

monopoly, effectively inhibits monopoly elsewhere. As long as aggressive and brilliant inventors and business organizers are free to develop new products, and to attract or "pirate" one another's key executives and scientists, monopoly will be short-lived. Eastman Kodak's dominance of the camera industry, abetted by tariffs, did not prevent Edwin H. Land from developing the Polaroid camera. The monopoly power of a few typewriter companies, also aided by tariffs, has been reduced by Chester Carlson's invention of Xerography. And today William P. Lear, Sr. of Lear Jet fame is investing millions to develop a steam or gas turbine engine to replace the internal combustion engine.

Crude attempts to estimate total monopoly profits in America (including any monopsony profits, but excluding monopoly wages) come up with figures of under 2% of GNP and quite possibly well under 1%, a substantial portion of which seems to be received by GM and Ford. Other crude estimates of the value consumers would gain if monopoly were eliminated (again excluding labor monopoly) have come to well under ½% of GNP.[22] Such estimates, however, place no money value on the loss in personal freedom entailed in some monopoly, or on any neighborhood costs associated with government policy which caters to special interests in promoting monopoly (such costs as lack of integrity of officials, lack of respect for government, other undesirable legislation as a price for monopoly favors), or to any income inequity inherent in monopoly profits.

In conclusion, while monopoly could be a sound basis for rejecting private enterprise, it is neither inherent nor dominant in the American economy (or in any foreign nation which allows free international competition) and much that exists could be reduced by government policy in a way that would enhance personal freedom and competitive private enterprise.

Regulating natural monopoly.[23] Society's main alternatives in dealing with natural monopoly are (1) government ownership and operation, (2) public utility regulation of privately owned companies, and (3) unregulated private monopoly. None is satisfactory. In principle, either (1) or (2) could bring about the ideal price and output, but in practice, government ownership stifles technological advance in order to preserve jobs for government employees (witness the postal service) and sets prices and output without relation to consumer choice (again, the postal service, as well as most government-owned transit companies, water supply, toll bridges, and the TVA). Regulated private enterprise fares better technologically (compare

---

[22] Several articles on the welfare loss of monopoly are in a book of readings on price theory edited by D. S. Watson, *Price Theory in Action,* 2nd edition, Houghton Mifflin, New York, 1969.

[23] This more difficult section can be omitted without loss of continuity.

telephone and postal service) and more heed is paid to dollar votes in setting prices, but inappropriate politics are still influential (as in railroad commuter service, Blue Cross rates, local bus fares and regulated interest rates). Finally, unregulated monopoly involves excessive prices and profits and generally less output than appropriate. Which of the three alternatives departs least from consumer choice defies generalization, though where neighborhood and public goods considerations are slight and where the monopolized product faces significant inter-industry competition (as do railroads), unregulated monopoly may serve better than public utility regulation. However, where competition is lacking (as with water), unregulated monopoly is virtually unthinkable.

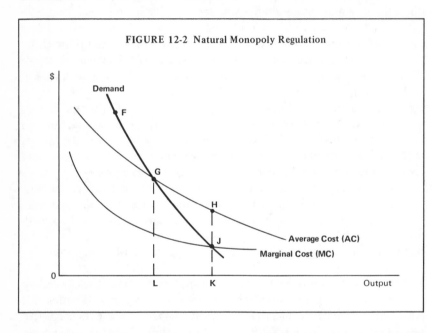

FIGURE 12-2 Natural Monopoly Regulation

The difficulties of natural monopoly regulation are illustrated in Figure 12-2, which refers to *one* firm (while prior demand and supply diagrams represented an industry of many firms). The demand curve shows the market-clearing price at various outputs and marginal cost is the cost of producing another unit. The new curve is average cost, the cost per unit of output (which mathematically must lie *above* MC wherever AC is declining with output). AC is presumed to include, as a "cost," the competitive return on investment, so that if price equals AC, the firm is just earning the competitive return. Point F designates the price and output which would be most profitable for the unregulated monopoly. Monopoly profits per unit are the vertical difference between F (on the demand curve) and the AC curve.

At point G, the market-clearing price equals the cost per unit, with competitive returns earned. But price is above marginal cost at G. Therefore, by our earlier reasoning in Chapter 2, additional units of this product would be worth more than the goods sacrificed: more should apparently be produced.

At point J, price equals MC, which we reasoned in Chapter 2 is the ideal output. But with AC above price, the firm loses money (or earns less than a competitive return on investment), which means if the output were zero and the company had never been formed, more valuable goods could be produced with the released resources. Many economists favor output-price J, with a government subsidy of JH per unit, so the company will be willing to produce J. But who pays the subsidy? If there is no reason for redistributing income in favor of consumers of *this* product, then the funds for the subsidy should come from the product's buyers, that is, from a tax of JH per unit. However, such a tax simply makes the effective price to consumers KH rather than KJ. Yet at price KH, consumers won't voluntarily buy as much as quantity K, as the demand curve shows, which again moves us back of the quantity where price equals MC.

What is the ideal solution? One possibility is "multi-pricing." Charge LG for quantity L, and at the same time charge lesser prices for additional quantities beyond L. In this way, the competitive return can be earned, while in a sense price can equal MC. But it is very difficult and sometimes impossible to operate a scheme of multiple pricing. This leaves price-quantity G as probably the most acceptable solution even though price exceeds MC. It can be shown that if AC is quite flat instead of steep where D cuts it, then the difference between price and MC at point G will be very small.

Monopsony.[24] A presumption of employer monopsony power is (implicitly) a prime basis for encouraging labor unions (which are monopolies, not monopsonies). The need for labor unions is generally expressed as stemming from a "bargaining power advantage" of employers over unorganized workers. But such bargaining power advantage exists only under employer monopsony, not with competitive wage determination (which was described in Chapter 6 under who gets what is produced).

Consider the plight (if you like) of one ncn-union accountant working for U.S. Steel in Chicago. The bargaining power theory goes like this. The worker needs the job to acquire food, housing, and other basic needs. The company needs the worker to produce steel and make profits for the owners. But the worker's need is more urgent. In a contest to see who can hold out the longer without the other, the worker must give in and accept the employer's terms before the company gives in and accepts the worker's since the company can continue operating without the one worker, but the worker can't eat without his income. The union, it is said, "equalizes" the worker's

---

[24] A review of this topic in Ch. 7 might be advisable at this point.

bargaining disadvantage in setting wages and other work conditions by forcing the company to shut down if it doesn't pay the *collective* wage demand.[25]

Notice how this reasoning presumes monopsony power. If the worker has alternative employments, then how long he can hold out without working *at U.S. Steel* is irrelevant. U.S. Steel must pay the market wage or the worker goes elsewhere. (And, as we saw in Chapter 6, U.S. Steel will hire that quantity, at the competitive wage, where the wage equals the worker's VMP.) Thus under competitive wage determination, there is no bargaining disadvantage.[26]

Of course, if all the employers of accountants colluded, then monopsony power would arise. But such collusion is illegal and unfeasible because in any large metropolitan area there are thousands of companies which hire accountants. If labor monopoly exists in America, it is only for highly specialized skills or in extremely isolated areas (where there are no unions anyway) or where employer collusion is legal, as in some professional sports.

The competitiveness of the labor market has undoubtedly increased in recent decades as people have become more mobile, better educated, and more in touch with conditions outside of their immediate locality. Recall

---

[25] This bargaining disadvantage assumption occurs in the Norris-La Guardia Act of 1932 which curbed employers' use of court injunctions to thwart unions: "...the individual worker is commonly helpless to exercise actual liberty of contract...," and in the Wagner Act of 1935 which compelled employers to bargain with unions: "Experience has proved that protection by law of the right of employees to...bargain collectively... promotes the flow of commerce...by restoring equality of bargaining power between employers and employees," and in Chief Justice Hughes' 1937 decision sustaining the Wagner Act: "Long ago we stated the reason for labor organizations...that a single employee was helpless in dealing with an employer, that he was dependent ordinarily on his daily wage...that if the employer refused to pay him the wages he thought fair, he was nevertheless unable to leave...the union was essential to give laborers opportunity to deal on an equality with their employers" (National Labor Relations Board *vs.* Jones and Laughlin Steel Company). Perhaps it bespeaks some effrontery to question so hallowed a tenet, but a search for truth cannot be cowed by Sacred Cows.

[26] For clarification, consider an analogous discussion of *monopolistic* bargaining advantage. Does the A&P have any bargaining advantage over its customers? If any one customer had no alternative but to buy at A&P or starve, then, yes, A&P could hold out longer and, therefore, could set food prices to extract virtually the customer's entire income for food. In fact, however, the customer has numerous alternatives to buying at A&P, so A&P must charge competitive prices or lose customers. Therefore, their relative ability to "hold out" is irrelevant and there is no bargaining advantage between the rich A&P (or Huntington Hartford, its rich major stockholder) and its poorest customer. Thus, either monopoly power or monopsony power implies absence of alternatives (or collusion among all the alternatives).

from the discussion of knowledge of alternatives that the results of perfect knowledge are approximated if only a few workers are knowledgeable and mobile and if the employer cannot discrimminate between the knowledgeable and the ignorant. Add to this the fact that over 15% of the workers in a typical company voluntarily quit their jobs every year, so that most companies, to avoid loss of workers, must always be recruiting new workers and offering terms as good as alternatives, and it seems a reasonable conclusion that, except for monopoly on the selling side (labor unions and licensing requirements), on the hiring side, the labor market is quite competitive in America, and that the competitive theory of Chapters 6 and 7 does describe fairly well the determination of wages and allocation of labor among employments.[27]

(5) Waste and inefficiency of competition. Alleged manifestations of competitive waste and inefficiency are: (1) a proliferation of small firms, (2) excess capacity, (3) advertising, and (4) the disposal of useful materials.

The allegation that competition results in many small inefficient

---

[27] As a percent of the civilian labor force, union membership in America was 6% in 1903 and was again 6% in 1933, having risen sharply during World War I when Federal law, to ensure labor peace, encouraged unions, and having fallen during employers' anti-union drives in the 1920's. Following the Wagner Act, membership grew rapidly, reaching 15% in 1940, 23% by the end of the Second World War and peaking at 27% in 1953, from which it has gradually declined to 24%, as non-unionized industries have grown faster than unionized.

It is clear that union strength derives in large part from Federal laws and court decisions, along with sympathetic local enforcement (or non-enforcement) of laws against violence. While some unions are far more effective than others, it is estimated that, as of the late 1950's, union members' wages were about 7% to 11% higher than they would have been without unions and, because higher union wages mean fewer employed in unionized industries and more people seeking employment elsewhere, non-union wages were about 3% to 4% lower than were there no unions. (Estimates are from H. G. Lewis, *Unionism and Relative Wages*, University of Chicago Press, 1963.) These measures far exceed the estimated effects of product monopoly and they omit the social costs of prolonged strikes and of union barriers to technological advance (which are most damaging in the construction industry).

But isn't the unorganized worker at a bargaining disadvantage during mass unemployment in depressions when there are few alternative jobs (which is when the basic labor laws were passed)? First, these abnormal periods can be prevented, or if not prevented, cured, by appropriate monetary-fiscal policy, so they hardly justify labor monopoly during normal prosperity. Second, if we assume a depression and a failure of government to apply monetary-fiscal policy, then the only route to more jobs *is* through wage and price reductions. That is, given the too-low level of MV, T (employment) will rise if P falls.

firms generally presumes that natural monopoly is the rule rather than the exception. Yet one does observe many small firms, with owners and family working long hours and earning far less than they could if working as diligently for someone else. These firms abound in retail trade, in consumer services, and in farming. For most of this century, the returns, both to labor and capital, in agriculture have been well under half their levels in the rest of the economy, the lowest going to those on small farms.

This situation reflects two attitudes. First, many people with little competence to manage a business have a strong desire to be their own bosses and are willing to accept smaller monetary returns in return for this independence. Is this wasteful? Not unless the pursuit of non-monetary returns is regarded as inferior to the pursuit of monetary rewards. Small struggling firms are an inherent part of a free society.[28] Strangely, those who criticize competition as wasteful are among those who denigrate the emphasis on monetary rewards. The second explanation of the abundance of small firms is the eternal hope that the family store will grow and prosper into a Macy's or Gimbel's or the one-man carry-out will expand to a Howard Johnson's chain. There are thousands of failures for each such success, but without the freedom to try, none of the successes would occur either.

The excess capacity complaint may be another version of the small firm criticism just considered—too many resources devoted to inefficient firms. Alternatively, apparent excess capacity may simply reflect irregular consumer buying habits. A supermarket on a Tuesday evening around dinnertime seems larger than necessary. But the same store on Friday evening or midday Saturday seems too small. Or notice the "excess capacity" of a department store some morning in mid-January, then come again in mid-December. Similarly, automobile dealers, libraries, toll bridges, roller-coasters, and cement manufacturers—nearly all businesses have to be "too large" for their slack periods, and "not large enough" for peak demand. As long as consumer freedom is accepted, including the freedom to pay higher prices in December than January and to buy heavily in December and lightly in January, then it is efficient to organize production to meet this demand, even if a more regular rate of consumer purchase could be accommodated with fewer resources.[29] Other sources of excess capacity are general downturns in

---

[28] An acceptance of such firms as a consequence of free choice in no way implies that they should be subsidized by government, for such subsidy infringes on the taxpayers' freedom to spend their own money and, in effect, places some peoples' pursuit of non-monetary economic independence *above* others' tastes.

[29] Perhaps the world record for seasonality occurs in the delivery of New Year's Day postcards in Japan. Huge stacks of the cards accumulate in post offices during the preceding weeks, then *on* New Year's Day, all of them, 12% of the whole year's mail, are delivered. It is inefficient to accommodate this custom?

business (see point 6 below), some monopolistic collusion, and declines in the demand for particular products (which no economic system can avoid, given consumer freedom).

Advertising is said to be wasteful because (1) it adds to the cost of products advertised without adding to their usefulness, (2) it creates artificial wants consumers would have been just as happy without, and (3) it is misleading and/or irrelevant, leading consumers to make purchases which are less satisfying than what they would have bought without advertising. No doubt there is some truth to all of these points. But surely not enough to indict either advertising per se or private enterprise. First, advertising does not raise costs much on the average, because total advertising expenditures amount to only 2% of GNP or 1% of corporate sales. Furthermore, a significant portion or advertising does provide useful information: radio and TV advertising (at which most criticism is directed) account for only 23% of advertising expenditures. Also, much of the advertising—informative or not—pays to support services which consumers would buy anyway if there were no advertising, namely, radio and TV programs, newspapers, and magazines. So the amount which is "waste" must be well under ½% of GNP.

Laws against misleading and false advertising exist. But laws to prevent "irrelevant" advertising or "artificial creation of wants" would greatly infringe on freedom of speech. If, because of advertising, a man feels more virile by smoking a Marlboro, who's to say this isn't genuine satisfaction? Anyway, advertising didn't create the desire for this feeling. Is the average politician any more candid, relevant, sincere, informative, or correct than the average advertisement? Censor them too? One hopes that truth, beauty, and decency will prevail in the long run, but an attempt by government to force on society a particular version of these is a virtual guarantee that they won't. Advertising is one of the many ways that people endeavor to pursuade others to act differently. The fact that these efforts may displease some (as do efforts by some political and religious leaders) or may be mutually cancelling is hardly a basis for suppressing them in a free society.[30]

---

[30] Advertising is also criticized as a source of monopoly (think of cigarettes here) on the presumption that for some products large scale advertising is more effective and cheaper per unit and that, therefore, only large firms can survive and large costs are required for entry, whereas without advertising, costs of entering the industry would be less and small firms could compete. In refutation of these claims, are the facts that the ratio, advertising to sales, is no larger for large than for small firms, that the advertising to sales ratio is not significantly larger in industries where a few companies produce most of the output than where many do, and that consumer attachment to particular brands seems no stronger for heavily advertised than for lightly advertised products. See articles by G. Stigler, *Journal of Law and Economics*, 1958 and G. Telser, *Journal of Political Economy*, December, 1964. Still, in some instances advertising may well raise the costs of entering an industry and thereby curtail competition. However, a recent study also

Another source of alleged waste is the huge volume of materials, especially paper and containers, that are thrown away. In response, there is much pressure to recycle metal, glass, and paper for reuse. But if the costs of recycling—the biggest cost being the collection and separation of dispersed bottles, cans, and newspapers—are greater than the value of the material recycled, then it is wasteful to recycle. The resources devoted to recycling could produce greater value otherwise employed. The same is true regarding appliance repairs. If a prospective high repair bill leads you to throw away a faulty toaster (or give it to Goodwill Industries), this indicates the repairman's skills are better employed elsewhere than in fixing your toaster.

When it's a case of exhaustion of depletable resources, then as known reserves diminish, scrap values will rise and recycling will pay. As to pollution by discarded cans or bottles, taxes or penalties against littering would redirect incentives appropriately. But to throw away an item at location X (your home) when the item at location Y would be useable but the cost of getting it from X to Y is greater than its value at Y—this is not waste. The same goes for discarding as garbage in an American home what would be welcome food in India or Pakistan or China.

In 1964, Victor Brown formed a company to build processing plants to separate municipal trash into paper, metals, glass, and other items. In 1970, processing 25% of Houston's waste, he was losing $2 a ton for lack of buyers. He could sell only 200 of 1200 tons of paper a week. About half the copper, lead, and iron used in America is recycled, 30% of aluminum, 20% of zinc and paper (the largest trash item), and under 10% of textiles, rubber, and glass. (*Wall Street Journal*, June 23, 1970.)

(6) Economic instability. Until the last decade or so, even the supporters of private enterprise generally conceded that periods of inflation followed by widespread unemployment were an inherent part of private enterprise, for such had occurred in all industrial nations since the Industrial Revolution. But economic theory and experience since World War II, along with study of past instability, have changed this prognosis. Today nearly all economists agree that if the government maintains total spending properly, as it can through monetary-fiscal policy, both rapid inflation and severe recession or depression can be avoided. And this can be done with little interference in the private determination of what, how, for whom and by whom to produce. Thus, what has historically been one of the most severe criticisms of private enterprise has almost disappeared.

(7) Private enterprise and personality defects. People who are free to live their lives as they wish without interfering with the rights of others, faced with the economic problem (not having as much as they would like), will seek

---

shows that prices of eye-glasses and eye examinations are lower in those states where the advertising of them is permitted.

their advantage—better incomes, lower prices for what they buy, higher profits for what they sell, etc. This seeking to make the best of one's limited opportunities need not make people inconsiderate of others or prone to defraud, cheat, misrepresent or injure. We all know plenty of decent people who have made a success in private enterprise.

Yet this does not fully answer the objection. It may be true that private enterprise does not *necessarily* create personality defects and does not *always* do so and still it may do so to a significant extent. Indeed, there are too many people who are dishonest, vulgar, excessively selfish, and inconsiderate. But did the economic system make them that way? Would any different economic system have a different effect on personalities? If we concede that people could be better, what are the most fruitful avenues for achieving improvement? One way to make people less aggressively self-seeking is to destroy their freedom to seek their own interest, as in a strict caste society and in Communist China, or to condition people *a la* Huxley's *Brave New World* to be satisfied with what they have.

Under socialism, if people are free and don't have all they want and can get more somehow, will not those who would have sought to profit at others' expense under private enterprise still do so if there are opportunities? And if the socialist government pays higher officials more than lower officials, if some officals have power to allocate money, jobs, and goods and services, as must be the case, won't there be ample opportunity for dishonesty and corruption? We can't prove one way or another, but we find no reason to think the proportion of personality defects would be less under a government-regulated economy than under private enterprise.

Suppose then it be true that regardless of the economic system there will be in society many people who have one or both of these inclinations: (1) willing to promote their own material welfare in a way which harms others and which is illegal and in a deceitful, unscrupulous manner, and (2) an interest in acquiring financial wealth and/or power of direction over other people for neurotic reasons. Under competitive private enterprise, these people have less chance to harm others than under monopoly or socialism or regulated private enterprise. In any of these alternatives, the principle positions of power are not checked by the possible loss of abusers' gains to those who provide better goods and services at cheaper prices or who treat subordinates better. Under competitive private enterprise, where those who might be harmed by neurotics have alternatives from which to buy or for which to work, the potential harm of the neurotic is lessened. But where the neurotic has monopoly power or where he is a government official with powers of coercion or operates a government business which does not face competition or which can make up losses from tax receipts, personality quirks are less subject to check.

Moreover, if consumers and workers are reasonably informed of alternatives, then under competitive private enterprise, the only route to power and wealth (aside from marriage and inheritance), however neurotic the motive for it, is through providing better products or producting at lower cost than others. Thus, potentially anti-social drives are directed into socially beneficial activity. The solution to neurotic personalities, if one is to be found, lies in happier family life, the teaching of mature and esthetic values, an expansion of psychological counselling, and possibly in developments in electrical and chemical personality control, all of which become more feasible as average income rises and people have more left after meeting other "needs."

There are those who argue that private enterprise would collapse if business weren't successful in stimulating and creating artifical wants. This is nonsense. Basically, if people don't want to consume, they won't want to work either. As real income has risen, many people *have* opted for less work through shorter hours, longer vacations, more holidays, and a longer fraction of life spent before entering and after retiring from the labor force. Many others, with different tastes, have chosen to moonlight—to hold two jobs—and to have both husband and wife work. There is nothing about the system that requires or compels everyone or anyone to "keep up with the Joneses" or to enter the "corporate rat race." Those who share the views of Mr. Tinguely of the philosophical machines are perfectly free to join the bucolic youth communes or to buy a small farm and live a rugged pioneer life, though it must be admitted that compulsory education laws infringe somewhat on this freedom. If ever most people work just for the fun of it but not to consume, then real wages and output prices will fall until this strange preference can be accommodated profitably. But this will occur only when the basic economic problem has disappeared.

The quality of life pursued by many free people may be distasteful to some. Still, one may doubt that a long run genuine improvement in popular tastes and conduct is more likely to be achieved by a collective imposition of "superior" tastes than through the gradual process of trial and error and private pursuasion and exhortation, where people are free to take or leave the advice given and to go their diverse ways, as long as they do not interfere with the rights of others.

We have come to the end of our story about how the basic economic decisions—what, how, for whom, and by whom to produce—are determined under competitive private enterprise. Whether you like the system or not, we hope you understand it better, especially the roles of prices, profits, and the search for personal gain, checked by competition, which means checked by the freedom of people to seek and create alternatives. The basic reason for approving of private enterprise and of the outcome of each basic decision is that the system allows and the outcome conforms with the freedom of people to make their own decisions. Indeed, private enterprise is *the* arrangement which naturally evolves from the freedom of people to deal on a voluntary basis with one another. Neither private enterprise, nor freedom generally, guarantees individual happiness, prosperity, progress, dignity, or morality. Nor does any alternative economic system. But its supporters are convinced that competitive private enterprise, because it is most compatible with personal freedom, is also most conducive to the individual fulfillment of these goals.

Study Questions Chapter 12

1. What are the consequences of competitive private enterprise? Answer re: (a) what to produce, (b) how to produce, (c) who gets what is produced, (d) who produces, and (e) economic growth.

2. What institutional conditions are critical for achieving the above?

3. Why, even under competitive conditions, are these results never achieved?*

4. Regarding objections to private enterprise, if only one has any merit, does that mean private enterprise is the best system?*

5. If all objections have some merit, does that mean an alternative system is better?*

6. Give six reasons why some might claim that the "right" goods and services are not produced under private enterprise.

7. Evaluate the following objections to private enterprise: (a) lack of knowledge, (b) poor judgment of self-interest, (c) collective goals, (d) fairness of income distribution, (e) profits should go to labor because capital is embodied labor.

8. Consider alternative policies regarding smoke nuisance.

9. What is the most basic role of government regarding neighborhood costs like smoke pollution?*

10. How may "transactions costs" justify a government role in pollution problems?*

11. How does exaggeration and free-riding impede voluntary arrangements?*

12. With a diagram, show how neighborhood costs lead to incorrect output and show how a tax could correct this.

13. What practical difficulties make this correction unlikely, if tried?*

14. Show with a diagram how government might improve "what to produce" where neighborhood benefits occur.

15. What is a "public good?" Explain two types.*

16. Explain why private choice does not lead to the correct production of public goods.

17. What difficulties does the government encounter in determining how much of a public good to produce and at whose expense? What effort should government make in order to produce what consumers perfer?*

18. Explain how pay TV (instead of the present arrangement) might improve consumer welfare, and how it might reduce it.

19. Should tolls be charged on roads? Why and why not?

20. Explain the three sources of monopoly.*

21. Define oligopoly. Does it imply monopoly?

22. Large size per se does not necessarily mean monopoly power. Explain.*

23. Why do many people tend to exaggerate the extent of monopoly?*

24. Roughly what percent of GNP is estimated to be monopoly profits?*

25. Define natural monopoly.*

26. What are three possible policies toward natural monopoly?

27. With a diagram, explain arguments for and against various price-quantity outcomes under natural monopoly.

28. In Fig. 7-2, what does point F represent?*

29. What does point G represent?*

30. What does J represent?*

31. What possible policy eliminates the loss at J and keeps output there?*

32. What is wrong with this solution?*

33. What is another solution to avoid subsidy and have output at the "ideal" quantity where market-clearing price equals marginal cost?*

34. What is a substantial problem with this?*

35. Define monopsony. What is labor monopsony?

36. Under what conditions does an employer have a bargaining advantage over his workers? Explain how this relates to monopsony.*

37. Does A & P have a bargaining advantage over one of its customers? Why? Why not?*

38. Roughly what percent of America's civilian labor force belongs to unions?*

39. What two forces account for union strength?*

40. Roughly what was the average gain of unions for their members in the late 1950's? How did this affect non-union workers?*

41. In a recession or a depression, are workers at a bargaining disadvantage? Comment.*

42. "The existence of many small firms which earn poor returns is an indication of wasteful private enterprise." Comment.*

43. "Idle capacity indicates competitive waste." Comment.*

44. "Advertising indicates competitive waste." Comment.

45. Under what conditions is recycling efficient? Wasteful?*

46. Discuss the contention that competitive private enterprise adversely affects personalities.

Answers to starred questions.

3. Changes in real economic forces occur before equilibrium is achieved.

4. No. Any one of those listed could justify rejecting the system.

5. No. The next best alternative might have even greater faults.

9. Defining liability and property rights.

10. It is too costly for voluntary arrangements to bring together the polluter, those harmed, and those benefited from the polluting activity.

11. If the polluter is liable, those harmed tend to exaggerate their losses. If those harmed must pay for the improvement, some individuals may claim not to be harmed to avoid contributing, leaving the burden to others.

13. Government does not have knowledge of the diagram.

15. The amount consumed by any one person does not reduce the quantity available to others. (1) nonexcludable: if available to anyone, it must be available to all; (2) excludable: consumption can be restricted to those who pay. National defense and "free" TV are (1); toll roads and pay TV are (2).

17. Problems of determining consumer choice without dollar votes. Political pressures to subsidize consumers of the good. To balance costs and benefits, and acquire some idea of consumer demand, government must try to make the beneficiaries pay through taxes or direct fees.

20. Collusion and merger, technology, and government.

22. Monopoly power comes from being large *relative to* an industry.

23. Incorrectly assume size per se means monopoly; assume large size always means lower costs per unit; view as monopoly every firm which produces a noticeable portion of industry output.

24. Under 2%, possibly under 1%.

25. An industry where technology is such that one firm can produce the entire output for a lower cost per unit than any two or more firms.

28. Price and quantity of an unregulated monopoly.

29. Price and quantity where market-clearing price equals cost per unit; no monopoly profits.

30. Price and quantity where market-clearing price equals marginal cost, but where the company loses JH per unit.

31. A subsidy of JH per unit.

32. Who pays the subsidy? If consumers of the product in proportion to the quantity bought, then the price is KH, not KJ, and consumers will no longer purchase quantity OK. If not consumers, why anyone else?

33. Mulitple pricing. Charge price LG for quantity L, then reduce price for each additional unit, moving down the demand curve.

34. Deciding who gets the lower-priced units. Deciding how to lower price, since the demand curve is not known.

36. When workers do not have alternative places to work. This implies the employer is the only or nearly the only one for the worker's skill.

37. Not if there are competing stores from which people may buy food.

38. 24%

39. (1) Laws requiring employers to bargan with unions, and (2) a tacit freedom of workers to engage in violence, by intimidating a struck company's workers, and its customers and sources of delivery.

40. 10% to 15% above what would have been wages in the absence of unions. About 4% less.

41. No. Wages are above equilibrium if there is unemployment. Wage reductions will help reduce unemployment, though monetary-fiscal policy should also be used to raise total spending to reduce the need for wage reductions.

42. Not necessarily. In order to be their own bosses, some people may be willing to earn less than they could if working or investing elsewhere.

43. Not necessarily. It may also reflect seasonal and other demand variations, a declining industry, and mistakened predictions of consumer demand.

45. When it pays. If it doesn't pay, the resources required to recycle could be employed more productively elsewhere.

APPENDIX A   ELEMENTS OF ACCOUNTING

This appendix is designed to help you understand economics, not to teach accounting. The meanings of investment, profits, return on investment, shift of nonhuman resources, growth in nonhuman productive capacity and other concepts will be clarified by some familiarity with the two main financial statements, the balance sheet and the income statement, the connection between them, and the significance in each of "depreciation."

The Balance Sheet

The balance sheet lists, as of some date, what a company *owns* (its assets), what it *owes* (its liabilities), and the difference between these, the *owners' equity* in the business (its net worth). Consider the balance sheet of the XYZ Corporation. First the assets. Cash is usually small compared with other items. Since cash earns no income, companies will reduce bank loans or lend out their cash rather than hold a large balance. Accounts receivable refers to money owed to the company by its customers. Inventory is the materials, semi-finished and finished products on hand as of 12/31/72.

Plant and equipment includes all the physical assets except the inventory. When an item of plant or equipment is purchased, it is listed on the balance sheet at its pruchase price. The company then estimates how long this asset will last. Say 20 years. Then one-twentieth of the purchase price is subtracted each year. If the asset is still being used after its value on the books is down to zero, then no further depreciation is recorded. If the asset wears out or is sold before it is fully depreciated, then the company records a loss for that year equal to the depreciated value of the asset less the sales or scrap price. Should the asset be sold for more than its depreciated value, a profit is recorded, but such a profit or loss is not listed on the balance sheet. Of course, it is impossible to predict accurately how long every asset will last, but some such prediction must be made, for without any depreciation the recorded asset values would far overstate the value of old and worn out assets.

Liabilities are what the company owes. Bank loan is self-explanatory. Accounts payable are money owed to businesses from which the company purchased things on credit. Bonds represent money the company borrowed and now owes from its issuance and sale of bonds. Each bond is a paper stating the XYZ Corporation will pay the bearer (whoever owns the bond) $1000 at a specified date and meantime will pay a specified rate of interest. Generally, companies sell bonds to raise money for plant and equipment and they borrow from banks for short term needs such as to pay for labor and materials.

327

Balance Sheet of the XYZ Corporation		
December 31, 1972 ($ millions)		

Assets			Liabilities	
Cash		1	Bank loan	6
Accounts receivable		10	Accounts payable	4
Inventory		9	Bonds	20
			Total liabilities	30
Plant and equipment				
At cost	85		Net Worth	
Accumulated			Common stock	5
depreciation	25			
			Retained earnings	45
Net value		60	Total net worth	50
Total assets		80	Total liabilities	80
			and net worth	

The net worth is the owners' equity. In principle it is what would be left if the assets were sold for their book values and the liabilities paid off. In fact, for a long established company with huge facilities, some recent, some quite old, it is extremely unlikely that the assets would sell for precisely their book (i.e., balance sheet) values. Whether sold piece by piece or in large operating units which could be operated as complete companies, their prices would depend on their expected earnings, not on their original production costs, less depreciation. While the original prices too reflected anticipated earnings, consumer tastes may have changed, the rate of depreciation and obsolescence may have been different from the depreciation formula adopted, tax rates may have changed—all of this could cause actual earnings to differ from those originally expected. Thus, a company's liquidation value is not apt to equal assets minus liabilities, even though net worth equals that.

New worth may be viewed as the accumulated investment by owners in the company. The item, common stock, measures the money (or value of other assets) received when the company originally issued the stock. Once the stock is issued, changes in its price (on the stock market) are not reflected on the company's balance sheet (or its income statement either). So "common stock" represents money (or other assets) contributed by the stockholders. The next item, retained earnings, measures earnings reinvested in the business over the life of the company. On some balance sheets, "retained earnings" is called "surplus." However, it does not represent a hoard of cash. In fact, no particular item on one side of the balance sheet corresponds to any particular item on the other side. The money received from past earnings as well as that received from the issuance of bonds would likely have been used to purchase plant and equipment, which form the bulk of the company's assets.

Note there is nothing on the balance sheet which tells how profitable the company was in 1972 or any other year. The fact that the balance sheet balances signifies nothing about profits. Whether the company loses or gains, it will always balance if the accounting department avoids mistakes. Again, the balance sheet describes the company's financial position at a date.

The Income Statement

Now to the income or profit and loss statement. This describes the operations of the company *over a period*, such as a year. It shows the money which comes into the company (sales revenue in this example) and that which goes out (expenses and taxes) and how much is left as profits.

Expenses for labor, materials (including utility bills), and local taxes need no explanation. Interest includes that paid on the bank loan and the current year's interest on the bonds.

Income Statement of the XYZ Corporation	
for the year 1972 ($ millions)	
Sales	100
Expenses	
Labor	64
Materials and fuel	12
Depreciation	10
Interest	2
Local taxes	2
Total expenses	90
Profit before taxes	10
Federal income tax	5
Profit after taxes	5
Dividends	2
Retained earnings	3

Depreciation is the amount *in 1972* by which the assets were written down. Of course, this is much less than the accumulated depreciation of the balance sheet for all the years since the assets' acquisition. Depreciation is not any actual money spent in the year. Suppose the company purchased a building for $1 million in 1972. Since that building will last for many years, it would be inappropriate to view this $1-million as an expense of producing 1972's output. This purchase of the building would not be listed at all on the income statement. Instead, the $1-million expense is prorated over the expected life of the building and shows up each year in the expense, depreciation. Thus, on the income statement, depreciation may be viewed simultaneously as (1) the proration of past capital expenditures, reflecting the capital equipment used in producing that year's output, and (2) the amount by which the capital equipment is estimated to have worn out during the period. It is a proration of money actually paid for assets in an earlier period but not then counted as a production expense.

Sales revenue less the sum of expenses is profit before Federal income taxes.[1] During most of the years since World War II, the Federal income tax on corporate income has been about 50% on profits above $100,000. After subtracting these taxes, we have profits after taxes. The owners may pay this to themselves if they wish, but generally some will be kept for investment back into the company. Payments to owners are in the form of "dividends"—so much per share of stock.[2] Here we assume the company pays out $2-million in dividends and keeps $3-million for reinvestment—a decision usually made by the "directors" of the company, who are elected by the stockholders, one vote per share, not one-man-one-vote.

The Connection Between The Balance Sheet And The Income Statement

There are two important connections between the two financial statements: (1) Accumulated depreciation on the *balance sheet* in 1972 is $10-million higher than in the 1971 balance sheet because of the $10-million depreciation of the 1972 *income statement*; and (2) retained earnings on the 1972 *balance sheet* are $3-million higher than on the 1971 balance sheet from

---

[1] In this abbreviated version, we are omitting many complications, such as the treatment of a change in the size of the inventory, prepaid and deferred expenses, insurance, sinking funds, contingent liabilities, and preferred stock—all of which are covered in an accounting text.

[2] Note that even though the corporation has paid a 50% Federal tax (plus state and local taxes), when the stockholders receive dividend income, they must pay a tax on this along with their wage income tax. This is sometimes referred to as "double taxation" of corporate income.

the profits after taxes and dividends on the 1972 *income statement.* Over the years, retained earnings on the balance sheet rise as profits are reinvested or fall if there are losses.

P/S, P/I, and I/S

For 1972, the profit as a percent of sales is 5/100 or 5%. And the return to investment is the $5-million profit divided by the net worth (the owner's accumulated investment): 5/50, which is 10%. Finally, investment per dollar of sales is net worth/sales, which is 50/100 or 50¢.

Productive Capacity With Zero Retained Earnings

Suppose reinvested earnings had been zero in 1972's income statement. The owners' investment could still remain at $50-million and could do so indefinitely with zero retained earnings year after year. How? The company could reinvest each year the amount equal to depreciation. If this much is spent on new equipment, then the decline in equipment from wearing out is just matched by new equipment, leaving plant and equipment constant. Likewise, owners could, if they wished, declare dividends in excess of profits after taxes and thereby cause a reduction in net worth. In effect, this would mean depreciation is not matched with equipment replacement, so the productive capacity of the firm would decline.

"The final straw was when I learned he has me on his expense account under miscellaneous!"

Returns To Assets

The return on investment, P/I, as discussed in Chapter 2 is (profits after taxes)/(net worth). Another way of measuring investment returns is: (profits after taxes + interest expense)/(assets), which for the XYZ Corporation in 1972 would be 7/80 or 8.75%. This is the return on the total assets received by those (owners *and* lenders) who provided the funds to acquire the assets. This return to assets will generally be lower than the return on investment, (after-tax profits)/(net worth). Since lenders receive their interest before stockholders are paid any dividends and are guaranteed the repayment of their loans while stockholders are entitled to no repayment of the price of the stock, interest rates on debt are usually lower than the riskier return on equity investment. However, in companies with poor earnings or losses, this is not true.

Stock Price

The market price of a company's stock may change daily. This has no effect on the company's balance sheet or income statement. In general, stock prices reflect expected company earnings. Any event apt to raise a company's earnings (including the reinvestment of earnings) will usually raise the price of the company's stock, and conversely.

Government And Depreciation Rates

For tax reasons, the Federal government regulates depreciation rates. Suppose a company made exceptionally large profits in 1972. If free to do so, it would have incentive to record a large amount of depreciation. Since this expense is recorded before computing profits and therefore taxes, the larger the amount of depreciation recorded, the lower the stated profits and taxes. Firms with profits would, therefore, record high depreciation rates for buildings and other long-life assets (writing them off in 5 or 10 years), just to raise depreciation and lower taxes. Of course, in later years, with these assets fully depreciated on their books, annual depreciation expense would be lowered, causing recorded profits and taxes to be higher. But companies would have postponed some tax payments for several years. And that would save them some expense of borrowing. To prevent this, the government has pages and pages of depreciation rates (X years for a lathe, Y years for a warehouse, Z years for a desk, etc., etc.) and also specifies several formulas, such as constant amount or constant percent, for calculating depreciation.

Inflation And Depreciation

If capital expenditures in a company equal depreciation, the nonhuman productive capacity of the company should remain constant, replacement offsetting wearing out. This assumes that the actual wearing out does equal depreciation. While this is unlikely for any given asset, differences in one direction may offset differences in the other, so that for society as a whole, any investment expenditure above total depreciation for all companies does suggest growth in nonhuman productive capacity, because new equipment exceeds wearing out.

Such is not true, however, if inflation occurs. Suppose a company owns ten $5000 trucks, each depreciating at $500 per year. And suppose the trucks do in fact wear out by 10% per year. Total depreciation on all ten would be $5000 per year, just enough to buy one new truck per year. So the company could always have ten trucks if it spent its truck depreciation on trucks.

Now introduce inflation, say truck prices rise 10% per year. Immediately, an expenditure of the $5000 depreciation will not suffice to replace the one truck which wore out that year. And this will continue to be the case as long as inflation lasts and for some time after prices stabilize, until recorded depreciation for all trucks is at 10% of the current (inflated) truck price. Thus, since government regulates depreciation rates to prevent firms from manipulating recorded depreciation to postpone taxes, there is a strong case for the government's reducing the recorded life of assets (thereby raising recorded depreciation) during inflation or permitting automatic cost-of-living adjustments to all depreciation expenses, in order that depreciation would reflect the rising cost of replacing assets.

Study Questions Appendix A
(All questions are answered briefly below)

1. What is a balance sheet?

2. In equation form, what are its three main components?

3. What does depreciation on a balance sheet represent?

4. Which represents better the value of an asset—its cost price or its depreciated value? Why?

5. What would be wrong with not recording any depreciation?

6. Explain two ways of defining net worth.

7. On the balance sheet, what determines the value entered for common stock?

8. How is the balance sheet affected if the price a the company's stock changes? Why?

9. If a company liquidated, why would the owners probably not have left an amount equal to the net worth?

10. What does a balance sheet tell about a company's profits for the year preceding the balance sheet date?

11. As to dates and time, what is the critical difference between a balance sheet and an income statement?

12. What is an income statement?

13. What does depreciation on the income statement measure? Give two views.

14. Does this indicate money actually spent in the given year? If not, to what actual expenditure does it refer?

15. What has been the approximate Federal corporate income tax for the past 25 years?

16. In what way do a company's owners receive payments from company profits?

17. Who determines the payments to be made?

18. What is meant by "double taxation" of corporate earnings?

19. What are two connections between the income statement and the balance sheet, re (1) depreciation and (2) retained earnings?

20. Are retained earnings on a balance sheet a sum of cash on hand? If not, what asset are they?

21. How could a company's capital investment remain constant if assets do wear out and if no additional funds are invested in the company?

22. (a) May owners pay dividends in excess of profits? (b) If done, how does this affect the balance sheet? (c) What would it indicate about the company's productive capacity? (d) Where does the money come from?

23. Regarding the equation of Chapter 2, $\frac{P}{S} = \frac{I}{S} \times \frac{P}{I}$, what balance sheet or income statement items are P,S, and I?

24. What is a second way of measuring returns to investment?

25. Why is this second way lower than the more usual way?

26. Which direction does causality primarily run: Company's stock price affects company's earnings, or company's earnings affect its stock price?

27. What does government say about depreciation rates?

28. What would happen if government did not regulate depreciation rates? Why?

29. How does inflation affect the significance of depreciation?

30. If capital equipment expenditure equals depreciation, what happens to a company's nonhuman productive capacity under (a) stable prices, (b) inflation, (c) deflation? Explain why. (Assume no rental of assets.)

31. To prevent this, what might government do?

Answers to study questions on accounting.

1. Financial statement at a point in time.

2. Assets = Liabilities + Net Worth.

3. Reduction in asset value because of wear.

4. Depreciated value: this reflects the decline from wear.

5. Assets would be overvalued, giving an exaggerated picture of financial worth. Also the full cost of an asset would be recorded as an expense in the year the asset was purchased, making profits appear unreasonably low in that year.

6. Owners' equity; accumulated investment by owners.

7. Usually, original sales price of the stock.

8. Not at all. The company receives or loses no money simply because partial ownership in the company is sold from one person to another.

9. Depreciation formulas are not perfect estimates of decline in asset value, so book value does not necessarily equal liquidation value. If complete operating units are sold, their value depends on expected income, not piece by piece price. These differ because customer relationships have value, called goodwill, not listed on companies' books.

10. Nothing.

11. Balance sheet: financial picture at a date; Income statement: financial operations over a period.

12. Record of income and expenses over a period.

13. (1) Estimated wear of assets in the given period; (2) prorated purchase price of assets attributable to the given year's production.

14. No. When the asset was actually purchased or built.

15. 50%.

16. As dividends.

17. A company's board of directors, elected by the stockholders.

18. Taxation of corporation income, then taxation of dividend income when corporate income after taxes is distributed to owners. (An alternative method of taxing corporate income is suggested in Chapter 10 under "property rights.")

19. (1) Change in depreciation on the balance sheet from the preceding year equals depreciation of the income statement for that year (except for assets sold or scrapped). (2) Change in net worth on the balance sheet from the preceding year equals the income statement's entry for retained earnings, which is profits (or loss) after taxes and dividends.

20. No. Not any particular one.

21. An amount equal to depreciation is spent for capital equipment.

22. (a) Yes, (b) Net worth will decrease (and so will assets or liabilities will rise). (c) Decline in assets will indicate a drop in nonhuman productive capacity. (d) Company's cash inflow, which may be from product sales, new borrowing, asset sales, or sale of new stock.

23. P: profits after taxes (income statement); S: sales revenue (income statement); I: net worth (balance sheet).

24. (profits + interest expense)/(assets). Return to assets.

25. Because the interest rate at which the company borrows is usually lower than the return on investment.

26. Earnings to stock price.

27. Fixes expected life of assets and establishes formula for calculating depreciation.

28. Companies could postpone taxes by recording excess depreciation expense in the early life of their assets.

29. If capital prices are rising, the recorded depreciation expense is not enough to replace depreciating plant and equipment.

30. (a) stays the same, (b) declines, (c) rises.

31. Allow additional depreciation during and after inflation, possibly through a cost-of-living adjustment to depreciation expense.

APPENDIX B DEMAND AND SUPPLY

Everyone knows that "demand" and "supply" are basic concepts in economics, just as is Einstein's theory of relativity in nuclear physics. Unfortunately, "everyone" understands demand and supply about as well as relativity. And economics about as well as physics. These concepts are used throughout the main text, especially in Chapters 2, 3, 6, 7, and 12. Our objective here is to explain demand and supply clearly and painlessly. In the privacy and quiet of an appendix, we shall try to dissipate the Freudian blocks against anything mathematical that for decades have made diagrams the bête noire of economics. But analysis requires the patient's patience. So, forbear.

Suppose Table B-1 represents the demand for sirloin steak by the Adam Smith family. At $4 a pound, they eat steak one a month, with small servings and no seconds. At $3, twice a month. And so on down the table. At $1, they have steak twice a week. And at 20¢/lb. even Fido has steak for dinner.

Now look at the diagram. It conveys all the information in the table. Prices of steak are on the vertical axis and quantities per month on the horizontal axis. Any point in the space bounded by the axes, if it refers to demand, designates that at the price directly to the left of it, the quantity directly underneath is demanded. For example, what does point C mean? At a price of $2, the quantity demanded is 10. Point E? At price 50¢, the

Table B-1. Demand Schedule
For Sirloin Steak

Point on Demand Curve	Price Per Pound	Quantity Demanded Per Month (pounds)
A	$4	2
B	3	4
C	2	10
D	1	20
E	.50	30
F	.20	50

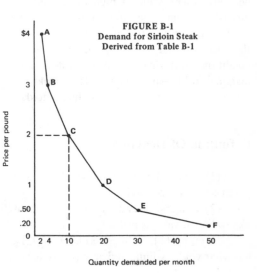

FIGURE B-1
Demand for Sirloin Steak
Derived from Table B-1

337

quantity demanded is 30 per month. See? Nothing to it. Connect all these points and we have a demand curve.

The demand curve for a whole country is the horizontal sum of each individual's demand curve. Take P = $4. Add up the quantity demanded by the Smith's, by the Joneses, etc., and get the quantity demanded by everyone at $4. Do the same for the other prices and you have the demand for steak by everyone.

The Law Of Demand

Both the table and the curve conform to the (unlegislated) law of demand: the lower is the price, the more people will want to buy. Can you think of anything people would buy more of if its price rose? Prestige items like mink coats or diamond rings? Not likely. Mink coats do look and feel nice and do keep people warm. So if they were $100 instead of $1000, a lot more would be bought by ordinary people, even if fewer showed up at opening night of the Metropolitan Opera (when it's usually too warm for mink anyway). By the law of demand, demand curves slope downward. This is what you'd expect and what empirical studies show.

The reasons why the law holds almost universally are less important than that it does hold. Nevertheless these reasons are: (1) The greater the quantity consumed per unit of time, the smaller the additional satisfaction gained from additional units and therefore the smaller the price one will pay to get another unit. Economists call this "diminishing marginal utility." (2) Differing incomes—as price declines, more people can afford any item. (3) Differing tastes—as price declines, people with less urgent desires for the good will buy some, while at high prices, only those with a real craving will still buy (if they have the money). (4) Differing uses—if water is $5 a quart, you drink, but don't bathe often; at 1¢ per 100 gallons, you drink, bathe, wash the car, water the lawn, and don't fix leaky faucets. These conditions—differing incomes, tastes, and uses, along with diminishing marginal utility—are why people demand more at lower prices than at higher prices; that is, why the law of demand holds.

Definition Of Demand

(1) Demand is the willingness and ability of an individual or group to purchase a good or service.

(2) Demand shows the quantities that the individual or group would like to buy at various prices.

Note, by (1), willingness *and* ability. Demand isn't just what you'd like, but what you're willing and able to pay for. By this definition, a pauper dying of thirst in the desert has no demand for water (unless he could buy on credit), which points to a qualification frequently noted in the main text—the acceptability of outcomes based on demand and supply depends partly on whether buying power is fairly distributed. In (2), the s's are italicized to emphasize that "demand" is not just how much people would like at one price, but is the whole set of price-quantity relationships, the whole curve.

The Determinants Of Demand

The quantity of steak demanded depends on (1) the price of steak, (2) consumer tastes for steak and for other things, (3) income (or wealth), and (4) prices of related goods—substitutes and complements. This can be written with symbols as:

$$Q_d = f(P_{stk}, T, I, P_s, P_c),$$

where Q_d stands for the quantity of steak demanded, P_{stk} is the price of steak, T is tastes, I is income, P_s is the prices of substitutes, P_c is the prices of complements, and f simply means "depends on."

The general notation, $y = f(x, z, w)$ means that y depends on x and z and w, without specifying how y is related to x and z and w. A specific relationship might be:

$$y = 4 - 2x + 3z + 6w.$$

Now suppose we want to plot the relationship between y and x on a two-dimensional, x,y diagram which does not have axes for z and w. This can be done only if some values are assumed for z and w. Let's say z = 1 and w = 2. Then substituting these values into the above equation, we get y = 4 − 2x + 3 + 12 = 19 − 2x. This is shown in Fig. B-2 by D_1. If we assume a different value for z and/or w, say z = 4, with w = 2 still, we get y = 28 − 2x or D_2, another relationship between y and x. Thus, a specific x,y line is "determined by" the assumed values of z and w (as well as by the parameters, 4, −2, 3 and 6).

So it is with demand. The quantity demanded depends not only on price, but also upon tastes, income, and prices of related goods. A demand curve showing only price and quantity demanded must assume given values of the other variables (usually the prevailing values, whatever they are). Any change in these other forces causes a shift in the curve, just as D_1 shifted to D_2 when z changed from 1 to 4.

In elementary economics, it is not necessary to specify particular demand equations or particular values for the other determinants of demand. All you need understand is: (1) what a demand curve shows, (2) what its downward slope indicates, (3) what forces other than price determine quantity demanded, and (4) in what direction demand will shift from

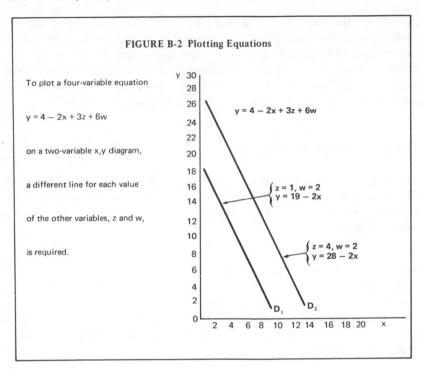

FIGURE B-2 Plotting Equations

To plot a four-variable equation

$y = 4 - 2x + 3z + 6w$

on a two-variable x,y diagram,

a different line for each value

of the other variables, z and w,

is required.

increases or decreases in these other determinants. (We've already covered the first three.)

A rise in steak demand, such as D_1 to D_2, will result from:

1. A rise consumer preferences for steak (a change in tastes).
2. A rise in consumers' incomes.
3. A rise in the price of a substitute (such as chicken, pork chops or fish).
4. A decline in the price of a complement (such as steak sauce, onions, mushrooms, charcoal burners, or anything else usually consumed with steak).

Similarly, a decline in demand, such as D_2 to D_1, would result from opposite changes: a decrease in consumer preferences, a fall in consumer incomes, a fall in the price of a substitute, and a rise in the price of a complement. The direction of these shifts is obvious. Sometimes the affects are asymmetrical in magnitude. A large rise in the price of steak will cause a substantial decline in the demand for steaksauce (which isn't used for anything else), while a large rise in the price of steaksauce will only budge the demand for steak, since many people don't use steaksauce with steak anyway. A rise in income may decrease the demand for a few products like potatoes or lard, which are

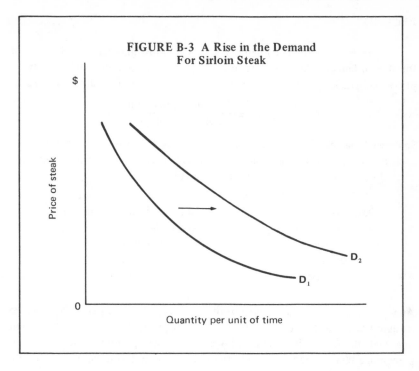

FIGURE B-3 A Rise in the Demand
For Sirloin Steak

consumed more by low-income people, but generally as income rises so does
the willingness and ability to buy most goods and services.

A Semantic Distinction

The word "demand" means the whole curve. So a *change in demand*
means a *shift in the whole curve,* and it results from a change in tastes,
income, or prices of related goods. A movement *along a curve,* such as from A
to E in Fig. B-1, is *not* a change in demand. It is described as a *change in
quantity demanded.* Such a movement along a demand curve is generally
caused by a shift in supply (meaning, of course, a movement of the whole
supply curve).

While this distinction may seem arbitrary, it aids in clear thinking.
Anyway it won't hurt to humor this whim of economists. There are more
important things to rebel over. So remember, if you say demand increased,
mean the whole curve shifted to the right. Don't say a decline in price will
increase demand: it will only raise the quantity demanded. OK?[1]

---

[1] For simplicity, we have omitted other determinants of demand, such
as expectations about future prices, the overall price level, the distribution of
income, income taxes, knowledgeability of consumers, and costs of making
and enforcing agreements between buyers and sellers.

Elasticity

Here is where the Freudian barricades are most impregnable. So prepare for the onslaught. Elasticity has to do with the stretchability of quantity as price changes. It refers to movements along a curve, not to shifts of a curve.

$$\text{Elasticity is } \frac{\text{Percent change in quantity}}{\text{Percent change in price}}.$$

Since each percent is a number, elasticity, being the ratio of two numbers, is itself a number. All the possible values of elasticity from zero to infinity are divided into three "degrees" of elasticity as follows:

Degree of elasticity	Numerical value of elasticity
elastic	greater than one
unitary	one
inelastic	less than one

As you can see from the definition of elasticity, when the percentage change in quantity exceeds the percentage change in price, the ratio is greater than one and the curve is elastic (between the two points). When the two percentage changes are equal, elasticity is unity, and you can work out the statement for inelastic.

So that elasticity will be the same between two points whether we move up or down the curve (from A to B or B to A), the percentage changes are calculated differently from what you learned in the third or fourth grade:

$$\text{Percent change in quantity is } \frac{\text{change in quantity}}{\text{average quantity}}.$$

The same for price. So armed, let's calculate the elasticity between each pair of successive points in Fig. B-1.

$$\text{Between A and B, elasticity} = \frac{\%\text{ change in Q}}{\%\text{ change in P}} = \frac{\dfrac{\text{change in Q}}{\text{average Q}}}{\dfrac{\text{change in P}}{\text{average P}}} = \frac{\dfrac{2}{3}}{\dfrac{1}{7/2}} = 2\frac{1}{3}.$$

So the curve is elastic between A and B, since $2\frac{1}{3} > 1$. The percentage change in quantity is $2\frac{1}{3}$ times as large as the percentage change in price.

Between B and C, elasticity works out to $\dfrac{6/7}{\dfrac{1}{2\frac{1}{2}}} = 2\frac{1}{7}$. In ten minutes you can work out the rest. Here they are:

Between	Numerical value	Degree of elasticity
A & B	2	elastic
B & C	2	elastic
C & D	1	unitary
D & E	$3/5$	inelastic
E & F	$7/12$	inelastic

It is of interest to note how consumer expenditures on a good are affected by elasticity of demand. We define consumer expenditures as price times quantity demanded. At point A, the Smith's buy 2 lbs. at $4 per lb., so P × Q is $8. At point C, they buy 10 lbs. at $2 and PQ is $20. The relationship between PQ and elasticity is as follows:

When a demand curve is	From a decrease in price, consumer expenditures, PQ, will
elastic	rise
unitary	stay the same
inelastic	fall

And if price rises, the opposite holds—PQ falls when a curve is elastic and rises when it is inelastic. Of course! If PQ rises going from A to B, it must fall going from B to A. The data in Table B-1 are repeated to show how this applies:

Points on demand	P	Q	PQ	Change in PQ from decrease in price	Degree of elasticity
A	$4	2	$ 8	rise	elastic, $2^1/3$
B	3	5	15	rise	elastic, $2^1/7$
C	2	10	20	same	unitary, 1
D	1	20	20	fall	inelastic, $3/5$
E	.5	30	15	fall	inelastic, $7/12$
F	.2	50	10		

Some final comments about elasticity: (1) Elasticity is not the slope of the curve. (2) You cannot look at the curve and tell its elasticity, except for the extremes of elasticity, zero and infinite. (3) However, other things equal, the flatter is a curve, the more elastic it is and conversely. (4) The numerical

values of elasticity of demand are really negative, not positive numbers. (5)
The extremes of elasticity look like this:

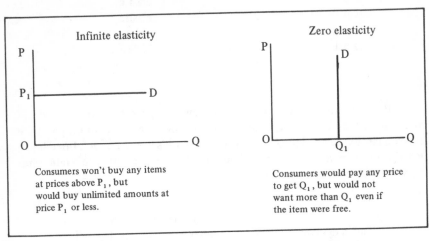

Infinite elasticity

Consumers won't buy any items
at prices above P_1, but
would buy unlimited amounts at
price P_1 or less.

Zero elasticity

Consumers would pay any price
to get Q_1, but would not
want more than Q_1 even if
the item were free.

(6) Goods and services which have close substitutes (like white shirts,
wrought iron chairs, butter, and sirloin steak) have more elastic demand—
larger percent changes in quantity from given price changes—than do goods
with poor substitutes (like eyeglasses, auto tires, kidney dialysis machines,
and heroin for the addicted). (7) Similarly, the elasticity of demand for
generic goods like cigarettes or soap may be low because substitutes are poor,
but the elasticity of demand for any one brand—Ivory or Winstons—may be
high since the other brands are good substitutes. (8) For most goods, the
elasticity follows the pattern shown in Table B-1—it is high at high prices and
gets lower at lower prices. (9) Finally, a monopolist or group of colluding
companies would never operate on an inelastic portion of the demand curve.
By raising price and cutting back output, they would *raise* their total revenue
(PQ rises moving *up* an inelastic curve) and save the expense of producing
some output, so profits would rise. Nor would they operate where demand is
unitary elastic because, by raising price and reducing quantity, they save the
expense of producing some output while taking in the same revenue. Thus, a
monopolistic collusion would always raise price in order to be on an elastic
portion of the demand curve.

Supply

Table B-2 shows a supply schedule, which is plotted in Fig. B-4.
Connecting these point for prices inbetween those in the schedule, we have a
supply curve, or supply. Point J says that at price $3 per pound producers will
offer to sell 2500 lbs. per month. But at 50c/lb., sellers would only offer to sell

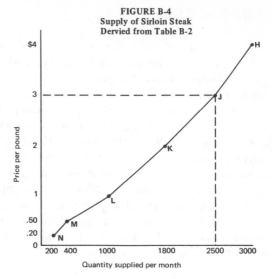

FIGURE B-4
Supply of Sirloin Steak
Dervied from Table B-2

Table B-2. Supply Schedule
Of Sirloin Steak

Point on Supply Curve	Price Per Pound	Quantity Supplied Per Month (pounds)
H	$4	3000
J	3	2500
K	2	1800
L	1	1000
M	.50	400
N	.20	200

400 lbs. Note "offer to sell," not "sell." Supply tells what sellers would like to sell—it says nothing about anyone's willingness to buy. Analogously, demand describes *buyers'* preferences irrespective of what anyone would be willing to sell at various prices. For $1000, you might "demand" a furnished villa on Lake Geneva or a 100-foot yacht, but for that price you'll have no suppliers beating at your bank account.

"C'mon, Dad -- just because of a little hair?"

Definition Of Supply

1. Supply is the willingness and ability of those in an industry, including potential entrants, to sell a good or service.

2. Supply shows the quantities offered for sale per unit of time at various prices.

A supply curve tells what a whole industry will offer, not just one firm. (That's why we put larger numbers in the supply schedule than in the Smith's demand schedule.) What one firm would sell at various prices (its supply curve) is based on its marginal cost curve. The theory of price, quantity, costs, and profits within a firm is not covered in this book—see any text in price theory. With some qualifications, a supply curve is a horizontal summation of the upward sloping portions of firms' marginal cost curves. And marginal cost curves slope upward, showing marginal cost is higher the greater is output, because of diminishing returns and the bureaucratic difficulties of managing large firms.

A Law Of Supply?

The upward slope of supply shows that the higher is the price, the more will be offered for sale. Just as with demand, it is not critical that one understand why supply slopes as it does. Because of what economists call "external economies," it is possible for the industry supply curve to slope downward even though all firms' marginal cost curves slope upward. This occurs if the expansion of the size of the industry causes firms' cost curves to shift downward. (It will still be true that industry S is a sum of firms' MC's at each given price.)[2] Because of this, there is no "law of supply" which says supply always slopes upward, though we shall draw supply curves that are upward sloping.

The Determinants of Supply

The quantity supplied depends on the price and two other forces: input price (or, better, input supply curves) and technology. Thus, we could write a supply equation for steak as:

$$Q_s = f(P_{stk}, P_i, K),$$

where P_i is the prices of inputs and K designates the state of the arts or technological knowledge relevant to producing and marketing steak. Any

---

[2] The best explanation of the transition from firms' cost curves to industry supply is Chapter 5 of *Price Theory*, by Milton Friedman, Aldine, 1962.

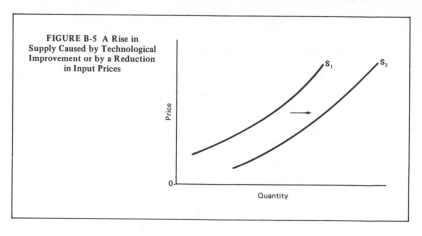

FIGURE B-5 A Rise in
Supply Caused by Technological
Improvement or by a Reduction
in Input Prices

two-dimensional supply relating quantity supplied to price implies given or constant values of P_i and K. Therefore, changes in input prices or technology cause shifts in the supply curve, as shown in Fig. B-5, which shows an increase in supply. A decrease in supply, such as from S_2 to S_1 would result from a rise in input costs, but in the absence of a nuclear holocaust or a universal drug binge, technological knowledge does not decline and cause supply to decrease.[3]

As with demand, the word "supply" refers to the whole curve. A shift in supply means a movement of the whole curve and is caused by a change in input prices or technology (or one of the items in footnote 3). A movement along a supply curve, such as from M to H in Fig. B-4, is described as a rise in the quantity supplied, not a rise in supply, and would likely have been caused by a rise in demand.

The concept of elasticity also applies to supply: same definition, $\frac{\% \text{ change in Q}}{\% \text{ change in P}}$, same three degrees, same extremes, zero and infinite. The main difference is that PQ rises with a movement out along a supply curve, regardless of its elasticity.

After mastering the following study questions, you should be ready for the "marriage" of demand and supply. Neither curve by itself determines anything, but together, they, or, better, their underlying forces—tastes, incomes, prices of related goods, input prices, and technology—determine price and output. (We shall not press the analogy as to which is male, demand or supply, and which female. There are cynics who would argue either way.)

---

[3] Some other determinants of supply are: (1) investment returns in related areas, if they are not equal everywhere, (2) expectations about future prices, (3) the overall price level, (4) time for adjustment to price changes, (5) costs of acquiring information and of making and policing contracts, and (6) investor tastes regarding the industry.

Study Questions Appendix B

1. From the demand schedule in Table B-1, what does row C denote?*

2. What does point C on the demand curve denote?*

3. If you had such demand curves for every family, how would you combine them to get the demand for steak by everyone?*

4. Does point F show that Smith's will buy 50 lbs. per month at price 20¢/lb.?*

5. What is the law of demand?*

6. What follows from the law of demand about the appearance of demand curves?*

7. Why do demand curves conform to this law?

8. What does diminishing marginal utility mean?*

9. Define demand.

10. What besides willingness to buy does it show?*

11. Besides the price, upon what else does the quantity demanded depend?*

12. What is meant by "the determinants" of demand?*

13. If a determinant changes, how does this affect demand?*

14. Show with a diagram the effects on demand of (a) a rise in incomes, (b) a rise in tastes, (c) a fall in the price of a substitute, and (d) a rise in the price of a complement.*

15. Explain the meaning of "substitute" and "complement." Give examples.*

16. Distinguish (a) shift in demand, from (b) change in quantity demanded.*

17. Define elasticity. Give formula.

18. How is elasticity expressed?*

19. What are the three degrees of elasticity?

20. What is the range of values of each degree?

21. Using the formula, confirm that the values of elasticity given for Table B-1 are correct.

22. How are consumer expenditures measured?*

23. What is the relationship between consumer expenditures and elasticity of demand: (a) if price rises, (b) if price falls?

24. Suppose there is a change in price and a movement along a demand curve. How does the change in what consumers would spend before and after the price change vary with the elasticity of demand?

25. Confirm this with the figures applicable to Table B-1.

26. What are the two extremes of the elasticity of demand?

27. Show each extreme with a diagram.

28. For each extreme, describe verbally what a demand curve says.

29. Is elasticity the slope of the curve?

30. Draw a demand curve with unitary elasticity at all points along the curve. Hint: Set PQ equal to any number, say 64, and plot for various values of P and Q.

31. What does this diagram illustrate about elasticity and the appearance of the curve?*

32. Explain how the elasticity of demand is affected by the closeness of substitutes.

33. Relate this to the elasticity of demand for TV's and for Zenith TV's. Which determinant of demand is relevant here?*

34. How does the elasticity of demand usually change as price falls along a demand curve? Does this follow mathematically from the formula?*

35. Explain why a monopolist would always operate on an elastic part of the demand curve facing him.*

36. Define supply.

37. From what of an individual firm is the supply curve of an industry derived?*

38. What is the law of supply?*

39. Why do supply curves usually slope upward?*

40. What are the determinants of supply?

41. With a diagram, show the effects of changes in these determinants.

42. Distinguish change in supply and movement along a supply curve.

43. What determines each?*

44. How does elasticity apply to supply?

45. Concerning the way P X Q changes with a movement along a curve, what major difference is there between demand and supply?*

46. Answer questions 27 and 28 for supply.

Answers to starred questions on demand and supply.

1. At a price of $2 per pound, the consumer would like to purchase 10 lbs. of steak per month.

2. Same as #1.

3. Add them horizontally.

4. No. What people would *like* to buy, the demand, is not necessarily what they *will* buy. The latter depends upon supply as well as demand.

5. The lower the price is, the more people will want to buy.

6. Demand curves will be downward sloping to the right (or negatively sloped).

8. The greater the rate of consumption, the less satisfaction from the marginal unit.

10. Ability to purchase.

11. Tastes, incomes, prices of substitutes and complements.

12. The forces upon which it depends, answered in #11.

13. The curve shifts.

14. a & b: D will rise, D_1 to D_2 in Fig. B-2; c & d: D will fall, as D_2 to D_1.

15. Substitute: used instead of—margarine and butter; Complement: used with—toothpaste and toothbrush.

16. a: movement of curve, caused by change in its determinants; b: movement along a curve, caused usually by change in supply.

18. As a number.

22. Price times quantity, for a given point on the curve.

31. A curve can look steep or flat and have the same elasticity.

33. Prices of substitutes. TV's in general have poor substitutes (radio, books, going out or to bed); Zenith has close substitutes (other brands).

34. Elasticity declines as price declines from high to low. No.

35. If the curve is inelastic, he can gain in revenue by raising price and reducing output until he gets to an elastic part of the curve.

37. Marginal cost.

38. There is no such law.

39. Diminishing returns, which cause cost curves to slope upward and the limited quantity of some inputs, which cause firms' cost curves to shift upward as an industry's output expands.

43. Change in supply: shift in determinants of supply; movement along a supply curve: usually a shift in demand.

45. PQ rises moving out a supply curve, regardless of the elasticity of supply.

INDEX